INTRODUCTION TO EUROPEAN UNION LAW

Walter Cairns

**Senior Lecturer in Law and Languages,
Manchester Metropolitan University**

Cavendish
Publishing
Limited

London • Sydney

First published in Great Britain 1997 by Cavendish Publishing Limited, The Glass House, Wharton Street, London WC1X 9PX.
Telephone: 0171-278 8000 Facsimile: 0171-278 8080
E-mail: info@cavendishpublishing.com
Visit our Home Page on http://www.cavendishpublishing.com

Cairns, Walter
Introduction to European Union Law
I. Title
341.2422

ISBN 1 85941 205 X

Printed and bound in Great Britain by
Biddles Ltd, Guildford and King's Lynn

Preface

As someone who has invariably taken a lively, if at times highly critical, interest in all aspects of the EU, I welcome this opportunity to publish my own perspective on its legal system. My first words of gratitude must therefore be addressed to Cavendish Publishing and its staff for allowing me to do just that.

This publication appears at a time when Community law has just integrated yet another fundamental instrument in the Amsterdam Treaty – which is the reason why it has appeared somewhat later than originally planned. (That is my story, and I'm sticking to it.) The author is particularly grateful to his sister, Annette Cairns, for her effort in extracting this instrument from the nether regions of the Internet and providing me with a copy.

It would have been very difficult indeed to produce this volume without the constant encouragement and support from those surrounding me both professionally and socially. Mention must be made here in the first place of my colleagues Bob McKeon and Jane Beattie of Manchester Metropolitan University, as well as many of my students whose interest in the progress of the work was not only quite touching, but also very often shamed me into continuing the project!

Finally, I would like to express my sincere gratitude to the Institute for Advanced Legal Studies, for allowing me to use their excellent library facilities at all times of the year.

The law contained in their work is that which applies as at 30 June 1997. Needless to say any omissions and/or errors are exclusively the responsibility of the author.

Walter Cairns

Contents

Preface   v
Table of Cases   ix
Tables of EU Legislation   xxi
Tables of Statutes   xxvii

1   Introduction   1
2   The Community Institutions   19
3   The Community Decision-Making Process   45
4   The Sources of Community Law   61
5   Community Law and National Law   81
6   Judicial Remedies in Community Law:
    Direct Actions   105
7   Community Judicial Remedies: Indirect Actions   125
8   The Free Movement of Goods   137
9   The Free Movement of Persons   163
10 The Free Movement of Capital   185
11 Competition Policy   191
12 Customs Law: External Aspects   227
13 Social Policy   243
14 Discrimination Based on Gender   261
15 Intellectual Property   273
16 The Future   291
17 European Union Law: A Practical Guide 303

Glossary   318
Bibliography   329
Index   335

Table of Cases

ACF Chemiefarma v Commission (Quinine Cartel Case)
(Cases 41, 44, 45/69) (1970) ECR 661. .197, 199

AEG-Telefunken v Commission (Case 107/82) (1983) ECR 3151. .196

AKZO Chemie v Commission (Case 62/86) (1991) ECR I-3359 .206, 209

AM & S Europe v Commission (Case 155/79) (1982) ECR 1575. .216

Adams v Commission (Case 145/83) (1985) ECR 3539 .121

Adoui and Cornouaille v Belgium (Cases 115, 116/81) (1982) ECR 1665 .175

Ahmed Saeed Luftreisen and Silver Line Reisebüro v Zentrale
sur Bekämpfung Unlauterer Wettbewerbs (Case 66/86) (1989) ECR 803. .220

Alcan Aluminium Raeren et al v Commission (Case 69/69) (1970) ECR 385. .111

Algera v Common Assembly of the ECSC (Cases 7/56, 3–7/57)
(1957–1958) ECR 39 .11, 120

Allied Corporation v Commission (Cases 239, 275/82) (1984) ECR 1005. .112

Allue and Coonan v Università degli Studi di Venezia (Case 33/88)
(1989) ECR 1591 .170

Amministrazione delle Finanze dello Stato v Denkavit Italiana
(Case 61/79) (1980) ECR 1205 .134

Amministrazione delle Finanze dello Stato v Simmenthal
(Case 106/77) (1978) ECR 630 .96

Analog Devices v Hauptzollamt München and Hauptzollamt
München-West (Case 122/80) (1981) ECR 2781 .231

Arbeiterswohlfahrt der Stadt Berlin v Bötel (Case C–360/90)
(1992) ECR I-3589 .262, 266

Asia Motor Finance v Commission (Case T-7/92) (1994) 4 CMLR 30 .215

Australian Mining and Smelting Europe Ltd v Commission
(Case 155/79) (1982) ECR 1575 .78

Ayse Süzen v Zehnacker Gebäudereinigung GmbH
Krankenhausservice (Case 13/95) (as yet unpublished) .251

BASFG and Others v Commission (Cases T-79, 84–86, 89, 91–92,
94, 96, 98, 102, 104/89) (1992) ECR II–315 .75

BMW v Belgium (Case 32/78) (1979) ECR 2435 .195

BP v Commission (Case 77/77) (1978) ECR 1513 .210

BRT v SABAM (Case 127/73) (1974) ECR 51 .88, 218, 220

Barber v Guardian Royal Exchange (Case C–262/88) (1990) ECR I-1889 .262, 266

Bauhuis v Netherlands State (Case 46/76) (1977) ECR 5 . . . . 140, 141, 156

Bayerische HNL Vermehrungsbetriebe v Council
(Case 88/76) (1978) ECR 1209 122

Belasco v Commission (Case 246/86) (1989) ECR 2117 197

Benedetti v Murani (Case 52/76) (1977) ECR 166 134

Bettray v Staatsecretaris van Justitie (Case 344/87) (1989) ECR 1622 164

Bilka-Kaufhaus GmbH v Karin Weber von Hartz (Case 170/84)
(1986) ECR 1607 . . . . 262, 265

Blesgen decision (Case 75/81) (1982) ECR 1211 144

Bock v Commission (Case 62/70) (1971) ECR 897 112

Bonsignore v Oberstadtdirektor Köln (Case 67/74) (1975) ECR 297 174

Bordessa and Others (Cases C–358/93, C–416/93) (not yet reported) 187

Borker, Re (Case 130/78) (1980) ECR 1975 126

Bouchoucha (Case C–61/89) (1990) ECR I-3551 178

Bouhelier (Case 53/76) (1977) ECR 197 149

Brasserie de Haecht v Wilkin (Case 23/67) (1967) ECR 407 194

Brasserie du Pêcheur v Germany (Case C–46/93) (unreported) 93

British Telecom OJ 1982 L 360/36 210

Broekmeulen v Committee for Registration of Medical Practitioners
(Case 246/80) (1981) ECR 2311 126

Brother International GmbH v Hauptzollamt Giessen
(Case 26/88) (1990) ECR 707 233

CLIFIT v Ministro della Sanità (Case 283/81) (1982) ECR 3415 . . . . 38, 131–33

CNL-Sucal v Hag (Second Hag decision) (Case C–10/89) (1990) ECR I-377 . . . 278

Calpack v Commission (Cases 789/89, 790/79) (1980) ECR 1949 112

Capolongo v Azienda Agricola Maya (Case 77/72) (1973) ECR 611 138

Capolongo v Maua (Case 77/72) (1973) ECR 611 86

Casati (Case 203/80) (1981) ECR 2595 185

Centrafarm v Sterling Drug (Case 15/74) (1974) ECR 1147 . . . . 274, 275, 279

Centrafarm v Winthrop (Case 16/74) (1974) ECR 1183 . . . . 274, 276, 280

Chanel v Cepeha Handelsmaatschappij (Case 31/68) (1970) ECR 403 . . . . 128, 129

Chevalley v Commission (Case 15/70) (1970) ECR 975 115

Cohn Bendit Case (1980) 1 CMLR 544. 71

Collins v Imtrat Handelsgesellschaft GmbH (Cases C–92, 326/92)
(1993) ECR I-5145. 287

Coloroll Pension Trustees Ltd v Russell (Case C–200/91) (1994) ECR-I 4389 263

Commission v Belgium (Case 77/69) (1970) ECR 237 107

Commission v Belgium (Case 156/77) (1978) ECR 1881 . . . . 113, 118

Commission v Belgium (Case 149/79) (1982) ECR 1845 175

Commission v Belgium and Luxembourg (The Gingerbread case)
(Cases No 2, 3/62) (1962) ECR 425 139

Commission v Belgium and Luxembourg (Cases 90, 91/63) (1964) ECR 625 108

Commission v Council (Re European Road Transport Agreement (ERTA))
(Case 22/70) (1971) ECR 263 . . . . .82, 113, 114

Commission v Council (Staff Salaries decision) (Case 81/72) (1973) ECR 575 76

Commission v Council (Case 45/86) (1987) ECR 1493 46

Commission v Denmark (Case 158/82) (1983) ECR 3572 .157

Commission v France (Case 152/78) (1980) ECR 2299 147

Commission v France (Case 232/78) (1979) ECR 2729 108

Commission v France (Case 90/79) (1981) ECR 283 157

Commission v France (Case 290/83) (1985) ECR 440 221

Commission v France (Case 318/86) (1988) ECR 3559 268

Commission v France (Case C–30/89) (1990) ECR–1 691 75

Commission v Germany (Case 24/62) (1963) ECR 63 115

Commission v Germany (Sekt case) (Case 12/74) (1975) ECR 181 151

Commission v Germany (Case 205/84) (1986) ECR 3755 .179

Commission v Germany (Case 427/85) (1988) ECR 1123 .181

Commission v Greece, Re KYDEP (Case C–35/88) (1991) ECR 1–3123 109

Commission v Ireland (Case 55/79) (1980) ECR 481 154

Commission v Ireland (Case 74/82) (1984) ECR 317 107

Commission v Italy (Case 7/61) (1961) ECR 317 . . . . .107, 142

Commission v Italy (Case 7/68) (1968) ECR 423 139

Commission v Italy (Case 24/68) (1969) ECR 193 141

Commission v Italy (Case 28/69) (1970) ECR 187 154

Commission v Italy (Case 39/72) (1973) ECR 101 . . . . .66, 74

Commission v Italy (Case 173/73) (1974) ECR 709 221

Commission v Italy (Case 51/83) (1984) ECR 2793 106

Commission v Italy (Case 101/84) (1985) ECR 2629 107

Commission v Luxembourg and Belgium (Cases 2, 3/62) (1962) ECR 425 154

Commission v Luxembourg and Belgium (Cases 90, 91/63) (1964) ECR 625 139

Commission v United Kingdom (Tachographs case)
(Case 128/78) (1979) ECR 419 . . . . .89, 107

Commission v United Kingdom (Case 170/78) (1980) ECR 417 156

Commission v United Kingdom (Case 32/79) (1980) ECR 2403 69

Commission v United Kingdom (Case 804/79) (1981) ECR 1045 . . . . .69, 82

Commission v United Kingdom (Case 61/81) (1982) ECR 2601 267

Commission v United Kingdom (Case 40/82) (1982) ECR 2793 152

Commission v United Kingdom (Case 165/82) (1983) ECR 3431 269

Compagnia Italiana Alcool v Commission (Case C–358/90) (1992) ECR 2457 121

Concentration between Aérospatiale SNI and Alenia-Aeritalia e
Selenia and de Havilland, Re (Case IV/M53) (1992) 4 CMLR M2 213

Concentration between Digital Equipment International and
Mannesman Kienzle GmbH, Re (Case IV/M57) (1992) 4 CMLR M99 213

Conegate v Customs and Excise Commissioners
(Case 121/85) (1986) ECR 1007 150

Confédération Nationale des Producteurs de Fruits et Légumes v
Council (Cases 16, 17/62) (962) ECR 471 112

Conradsen v Ministeriet för Skatter og Afgifter
(Case 161/78) (1979) ECR 2221 10

Continental Can Decision (Case 6/72) 205, 208, 211

Costa v ENEL (Case 6/64) (1964) ECR 585 . . . . 81, 87, 95, 130, 131

Council v European Parliament (Case 34/86) (1986) ECR 2155 59

Cristini v SNCF (Case 32/75) (1975) ECR 1085 167

Da Costa en Schaake (Cases 28, 29, 30/62) (1963) ECR 31 132

De Geus en Uitdenborgerd v Bosch en Vin Rijn (Case 13/61)
(1962) ECR 45 . . . . 62, 128, 129

Defrenne v Belgium (Case 80/70) (1971) ECR 445 262

Defrenne v SABENA (No 1) (Case 43/75) (1976) ECR 455 . . . . 88, 261, 263

Defrenne v SABENA (No 3) (Case 149/77) (1979) ECR 1365 264

Dekker v Stichting Vormingscentrum voor Jonge Volwassenen
(Case C–177/88) (1990) ECR I-3941 . . . . 269, 270

Deutsche Grammophon Gesellschaft v Metro-Grossmärkte
(Case 78/70) (1971) ECR 487 274

Di Faelice v Institut National d'Assurances Sociales pour les
Travailleurs Indépendants (Case 128/88) (1989) ECR 923 172

Donckerwolcke v Procureur de la République (Case 41/76)
(1976) ECR 1921 82

Draft Agreement on a European Economic Area, Re (1991) ECR 1-6079 72

Dyestuffs case (Case 48/69) 197, 199

East (t/a) Margetts and Addenbrooke) v Cuddy
(Case 143/86) (1988) ECR 625 187

Eggers v Freie Hansedtadt Bremen (Case 13/78) (1978) ECR 1935 151

Einfuhr-und Vooratstelle für Getreide und Futtermittel v Macksprang
(Case 2/75) (1975) ECR 607 76

Elba v Hauptzollamt Berlin-Packhof (Case 205/80) (1981) ECR 2097 231

Elliniki Radiophonia Tileorassi AE v Dimotiki Etairia Pliroforissis
and Sotirios Kouvelas (Case C–260/89) (1991) ECR I–2963–64 78

Emir Gül v Regierunps-präsident Düsseldorf (Case 131/85) (1986) ECR 1573 168

Eridania v Commission (Case 18/68) (1969) ECR 459 113

Eunomia di Possor v Italian Ministry of Education
(Case 18/71) (1971) ECR 811 138

European Parilament v Council (Case C–65/90) (1992) ECR I–4593 51

Faccini Dori v Recreb Srl (Case C–91/92) (1994) ECR 1–3325 90

Fazenda Publica v Americo (Case C–345/93) (1995) ECR I–479 153

Fink-Frucht v Hauptzollamt München (Case 27/67) (1968) ECR 223 155

Foster v British Gas (Case C–188/89) (1990) ECR I–3313. . . . . 88, 91

France v Commission (Cases 188–90/80) (1982) ECR 2545 219

France v Commission (Case 264/86) (1988) ECR 973. 66

France v Commission (Case C–301/87) (1990) ECR-I 307 222

France v United Kingdom (Case 141/78) (1979) ECR 2923 . . . . .69, 109

Francovich, Andrea and Bonifaci, Daniela v Italian Republic
(Cases C–6/90, C–9/90) (1990) ECR 1–5357 . . . . 92, 312

Fratelli Cucchi v Avez SpA (Case 77/76) (1977) ECR 987 157

Fromageries Le Ski decision (1972) CMLR 330 71

GAEC v Commission (Case 253/84) (1987) ECR 123 222

GVL v Commission (Case 7/82) (1983) ECR 483. 220

Garland v British Rail Engineering Ltd (Case 12/81) (1982) ECR 359 263

General Motors v Commission (Case 26/75) (1975) ECR 1367 210

Generics (UK) Ltd v Smith, Kline and French Laboratories Ltd
(1990) CMLR 416 132

Germany v Commission (Cases 52, 55/65) (1966) ECR 159 140

Gesellschaft für Überseehandel MbH v Handelskammer Hamburg
(Case 49/76) (1977) ECR 41 232

Gilli and Andres (Case 788/79) (1980) ECR 2071 145

Grad v Finanzamt Traunstein (Case 9/70) (1970) ECR 825. 93

Granaria v Produktschap voor Veevoeder (Case 18/72) (1972) ECR 1163 66

Greece v Council (Case 204/86) (1988) ECR 5323 69

Grimaldi v Fonds des maladies professionelles
(Case 322/88) (1989) ECR 4407 68

Groener v Minister for Education (Case 378/87) (1989) ECR 3967. 167

Groenveld v Produktschap voor Vee en Vlees (Case 15/79) (1979) ECR 3409 . . . 148, 149

Haim v Kassenzahnärztliche Vereinigung Nordrhein (Case C–319/92)
(1994) ECR I-425..181

Handels- OG Kontorfunktionaerernes Forbund i Danmark v Dansk
Arbejdsforening, ex p Aldi Marked (Case C–179/88) (1990) ECR I-3979..............270

Handles- OG Kontorfunktionaerernes Forbund i Danmark
v Dansk Arbejdgiverforening, ex p Danfoss (Case 109/88)
(1989) ECR 399..127, 268, 270

Hansen v Hauptzollamt Flensburg (Case 148/77) (1978) ECR 1787..........................64

Harz v Deutsche Tradax (Case 79/83) (1984) ECR 1921...91

Hauptzollamt Mainz v Kupferberg (Case 104/81) (1982) ECR 3644..........................93

Hauts Fourneaux et Aciéries Belges v High Authority
(Case 8/57) (1958) ECR 245..74

Hein (Case 10/71) (1971) ECR 430..220

Heintz van Landewijck v Commission (Cases 209–215/78) (1980) ECR 3125............195

Hessische Knappschaft v Maison Singer (Case 44/65) (1965) ECR 965....................170

Hoffmann-LaRoche v Centrafarm (Case 102/77) (1978) ECR 1139..........................276

Hoffmann-LaRoche v Commission (Case 85/76) (1979) ECR 461......................207, 208

Horvath v Hauptzollamt Hamburg-Jones (Case 50/80) (1981) ECR 385....................236

Humblot v Directeur des Services Fiscaux (Case 112/84) (1985) ECR 1367................154

Hydrotherm v Andreoli (Case 170/83) (1984) ECR 2999..195

ICI v Amministrazione delle Finanze dello Stato (Case 66/80) (1981) ECR 1191.........134

IGAV v ENCC (Case 94/74) (1975) ECR 699...154

IHT Internationale Heiztechnik GmbH v Ideal Standard GmbH
(Case C–93) (1994) ECR I-2789..281

IZA International Belgium (Cases 96-102, 104, 105, 108, 110/82)
(1983) ECR 3369...200

Iannelli v Meroni (Case 74/76) (1977) ECR 557...154

Imperial Chemicals Industries v Commission (ICI Case) (Case 48/68)
(1972) ECR 619...192

Inno v Aftab (Case 13/77) (1977) ECR 2140...143

International Fruit Company v Commission (Cases 41–44/70)
(1965) ECR 411...111, 112

International Fruit Company v Produktschap voor Groenten
en Fruit (Case 21-24/72) (1972) ECR 1219...71

Internationale Handelsgesellschaft (Case 11/70) (1970) ECR 1125.............................77

Interquell Stärke-Chemie v Council and Commission
(Cases 261, 262/78) (1979) ECR 3045...121

Italian Flat Glass Cartel, Re (Cases T-68, 77, 78/89) (1992) ECR II-1403.........199, 207

Jan van de Haar decision (Cases 177, 178/82) (1984) ECR 1797 144

Jenkins v Kingsgate (Clothing Productions) Ltd
   (Case 96/80) (1981) ECR 911 . . . . .264, 265

John Walker v Ministeriet for Skatter (Case 243/86) (1986) ECR 875 155

Joseph Danis (Cases 16-20) (1979) ECR 3327 .145

Kalanke v Freie Hansestadt Bremen (Case C–450/93) (1995) (not yet reported). 270

Kampffmeyer et al v Commission (Cases 5, 7, 13/66) (1967) ECR 245 121

Keck ruling (Cases C–267, C–268/91) (1993) ECR I–6079 146

Kempf v Staatssecretaris voor Justitie (Case 139/85) (1986) ECR 1741 164

Koninklijke Scholten-Honig v Council and Commission
   (Case 83/76) (1979) ECR 3583 122

Kowalski (Case C–33/89) (1990) ECR I–2591 .264

Kramer (Cases 3,4,6/76) (1976) ECR 1279 82

Kupferberg (Case No 104/81) (1982) ECR 3641 .72

Lawrie-Blum v Land Baden-Wurttemburg (Case 66/85) (1986) ECR 2121 164

Laying-Up Fund, Re (1976) ECR 741 72

Leonesio v Ministry of Agriculture (Cases 89, 93/71) (1972) ECR 287 94

Levin (Case 53/81) (1982) ECR 1035 164

Liefting v Directie van het Academisch Ziekenhuis bij de Universiteit
   van Amsterdam (Case 23/83) (1984) ECR 5225 .263

Luisi and Carbone v Ministero del Tesoro (Cases 286/82, 26/83)
   (1984) ECR 377 . . . . .177, 185, 186

Lütticke v Hauptzollamt Saarlouis (Case 57/65) (1966) ECR 327 . . . . .85, 87

Macarthys v Smith [1979] 3 All ER 325 100

Marchandise (Case C–332/89) (1991) ECR I–1027 145

Marleasing SA v La Comercial Internacional de Alimentacion SA
   (Case C–106/89) (1990) ECR 1–4135 92

Marshall v Southampton Area Health Authority
   (Case 152/84) (1986) ECR 723 . . . . .90, 91

Merck v Stephar (Case 187/80) (1981) ECR 2063 275

Merckz and Neuhuys (Joined cases C 171–94, C–172/94) (1996) ECR I–1253 251

Meroni v High Authority (Case 9/56) (1957–58) ECR 133 114

Métropole Television and Others v Commission (Cases T-528/93,
   T–542/93, T-546/93) (not yet reported) 203

Milchwerke Wöhrmann v Commissioner (Cases 31, 33/62) (1962) ECR 501 118

Ministère Public Luxembourg v Müller (Case 10/71) (1971) ECR 723 85

Ministère Public v Auer (Case 136/78) (1979) ECR 437 180

Ministère Public v Deserbais (Case 286/86) (1988) ECR 4907 129

Ministère Public v Mutsch (Case 137/84) (1985) ECR 2660 167

Morson v Netherlands State (Cases 35, 26/82) (1982) ECR 3720 167

Moulijn v Commission (Case 6/74) (1974) ECR 1287 62

Mulder et al v Commission (Cases C–104/89, C–37/90) (1992) ECR 2337 . . 122

Musik-Vertrieb Membrean GmbH v Gesellschaft für Mudikalische
Aufführungs- und Mechanische Vervielfaltungsrechte
(GEMA) (Cases 55, 57/80) (1981) ECR 147 . . . . 277, 281

Musique Diffusion Française v Commission
(Cases 100–03/80) (1983) ECR 1825 78

NTN Toyo Bearing v Council (Case 113/77) (1979) ECR 1185 112

NV1AZ International Belgium v Commission
(Cases 96–102, 104, 105, 108, 110/82) (1983) ECR 3369 197

Napier Brown/British Sugar OJ 1988 L 284 207

National Panasonic (UK) v Commission (Case 136/79) (1980) ECR 2033 . . 78

Neath v Hugh Steeper Ltd (Case C–152/91) (1993) ECR I-6935 263

Nederlands Government v High Authority (Case 6/54) (1954–56) ECR 103 . . 115

Nederlands Spoorwegen v Minister van Verkeer en Waterstaat
(Case 36/73) (1973) ECR 1299 126

Newstead v Department of Transport (Case 192/85) (1987) ECR 4753 . . 263

Nimz v Frei- und Hansestadt Hamburg (Case C–184/89) (1991) ECR 297 . . 265

Nold v Commission (Case 4/73) (1974) ECR 491 78

Nordsee Deutsche Hochseefischerei GmbH v Reederei Mond
(Case 102/81) (1982) ECR 1095 127

Nungesser v Commission (Case 258/78) (1982) ECR 2015 202

Oebel (Case 155/80) (1981) ECR 1993 149

Officer van Justitie v Kramer (Case 3/76) (1976) ECR 1279 71

Openbaar Ministerie v Van Tiggele (Case 82/77) (1978) ECR 25 143

Ozlizlok v Commission (Case 34/77) (1978) ECR 1099 79

P v S and Cornwall County Council (Case C–13/94) (as yet unreported) . . 271

PPW Internationaal v Hoofdproduktschap voor
Akkerbouwprodukten (Case 61/72) (1973) ECR 301 62

PVC Cartel, Re Decision 89/190 OJ 1989, L 74 199

Parke Davis v Probel & Centrafarm (Case 24/67) (1968) ECR 55 273

Paris v Council (Case 130/75) (1976) ECR 1589 78

Parliament v Council (Case 13/83) (1985) ECR 1513 117

Parliament v Council (Case 377/87) (1988) ECR 4017 116

Pfizer Inc v Eurim-Pharm (Case 1/81) (1981) ECR 2913 277

Pharmon BV v Hoechst BV (Case 19/84) (1985) ECR 2281 . . . . 275, 280

Philip Morris Holland v Commission (Case 730/79) (1980) ECR 2671 223

Piraiki-Patraiki v Commission (Case 11/82) (1985) ECR 207 111

Plaumann v Commission (Case 25/62) (1963) ECR 95 . . . . 110, 111

Politi v Ministry of Finance of the Italian Republic
   (Case 43/71) (1971) ECR 1408 130

Polypropylene, Re (OJ 1986 L 230) 195

Poole v Council (Case 49/79) (1980) ECR 569 122

Pretore di Salo v X (Case 14/86) (1987) ECR 2545 126

Procureur de la République v Chatain (Case 65/79) (1980) ECR 1345 236

Procureur de la République v Rivoira (Case 179/78) (1979) ECR 1147 82

Procureur du Roi v Dassonville (Case 8/74) (1974) ECR 837 . . . . 71, 143,
   144, 147, 148

Procureur du Roi v Debauve (Case 52/79) (1980) ECR 833 177

Procureur-Général v Buys (Case 5/79) (1979) ECR 3203 145

Pubblico Ministero v Ratti (Case 148/78) (1979) ECR 1629 89

Queen v Secretary of State for the Home Department, ex p
   Evans Medical and Macfarlane Smith (Case C–324/93)
   (1995) (not yet reported) 152

R v Bouchereau (Case 30/77) (1977) ECR 1845 175

R v Henn and Darby (Case 34/79) (1979) ECR 3795 . . . . 150, 151

R v IAT, ex p Antonissen (Case C–292/89) (1991) ECR I-745 165

R v Intervention Board for Agricultural Produce, ex p Mann
   (Sugar) Ltd (Case 181/84) (1985) ECR 2889 77

R v Kirk (Case 63/83) (1984) ECR 2689 79

R v Pieck (Case 157/79) (1980) ECR 2171 166

R v Secretary of State for Social Security, ex p Smithson
   (Case C 243/90) (1992) ECR I-467 272

R v Secretary of State for Transport, ex p Factortame
   (No 1) (1990) ECR I–243; (1990] 2 AC 85 . . . . 71, 96, 101, 102

R v Secretary of State for Transport, ex p Factortame and others
   (No 2) [1991] 1 AC 603 101

R v Secretary of State for Transport, ex p Factortame
   (No 3) (Case C–48/93) (unreported) 93

R v Tymen (Case 269/80) (1981) ECR 3079 69

Racke v Hauptzollamt Mainz (Case 98/78) (1979) ECR 69 75

Retter v Caisse de pension des employés privés (Case 130/87) (1989) ECR 865 74

Rewe v Bundesmonopolverwaltung für Branntwein
(Cassis de Dijon decision) (Case 120/78) (1979) ECR 649 . . . . . 144–48, 158, 189, 265

Reyners v Belgium (Case 2/74) (1974) ECR 631 . . . . 86, 87, 178

Rheinmühlen v Einfuhr- und Vooratstelle (Case 166/73) (1974) ECR 33 129

Rinner-Kühn v FWW Spezial-Gebäudevereinigung GmbH
(Case 171/88) (1989) ECR 2743 . . . . 262, 265, 266

Robert Bosch v Hauptzollamt Hildesheim (Case 1/77) (1977) ECR 1473 234

Roquette Frères v Council (Case 138/79) (1980) ECR 3333 . . . . 32, 51

Royer (Case 48/75) (1976) ECR 497 173

Rubber Agreement, Re (1979) ECR 2871 72

Rummler v Dato-Druck GmbH (Case 237/85) (1986) ECR 2101 268

Rutili (Case 36/75) (1975) ECR 1219 172

Sabbatini v European Parliament (Case 32/71) (1972) ECR 345 264

Sacchi (Case 155/73) (1974) ECR 409 219

Samenwerkende Electriciteits-Productiebedrijven NV v
Commission (Caser T-39/90) (1992) ECR II-1497 215

Schwarze v Einfuhrstelle für Getreide und Futtermittel
(Case 16/65) (1965) ECR 877 115

Security International v Signalson and Securitel Bulletin
(Case C–194) (1996) (not yet reported) 161

Siemens/Fanuc OJ 1985 L 376 200

Simmenthal v Italian Minister for Finance (Case 35/76) (1976) ECR 1871 140

Sociaal Fonds voor Diamantarbeiders v Brachfeld
(Cases 2, 3/69) (1969) ECR 211 139

Société Les Commissionnaires Réunis v Receveur des Douanes
(Cases 80, 81/77) (1978) ECR 927 141

Société pour l'exportation des sucres v Commission
(Case 88/76) (1977) ECR 709 76

Société Technique Minière v Maschinenbau Ulm (Case 56/65) (1966) ECR 235 198

Sotgiu v Deutsche Bundespost (Case 152/73) (1974) ECR 153 176

Spijkers (Case 24/85) (1986) ECR 119 251

Stanton v INASTI (Case 143/87) (1988) ECR 3877 171

Stauder v Ulm (Case 29/69) (1969) ECR 419 . . . . 38, 78

Steinike und Weinlig v Germany (Case 78/76) (1977) ECR 595 154

Stergios Delimitis v Henninger Bräu (Case C–234/89) (1991) ECR I-935 198

Steymann v Staatssecretaris voor Justitie (Case 196/87) (1988) ECR 6159 164

Südmilch v Ugliogla (Case 15/69) (1969) ECR 363 173

Suiker Unie v Commission (Cases 40–48, 50, 54–56, 111, 113, 114/73)
(1975) ECR 1663 197

Svensson (Case C–484/93) (1995) ECR I-3955 188

TWD Textilwerke Deggendorf GmbH v Germany
(Case C–188/92) (1994) ECR 1–833 113

Tasca decision (Case 65/75) (1976) ECR 291 . . . . 143, 144

Tepea (Case 28/77) (1978) ECR 1391 196

Terrapin v Terranova (Case 119/75) (1976) ECR 1039 279

Tetra Pak II OJ 1992 L 72 210

Thieffry v Conseil de L'Ordre des Avocats à la Cour de Paris
(Case 71/76) (1977) ECR 765 178

Toepfer v Commission (Cases 106, 107/63) (1971) ECR 411 111

Töpfer v Commission (Case 112/77) (1978) ECR 1019 115

Transocean Marine Plant Association v Commission
(Case 17/74) (1974) ECR 1063 79

UDS v Conforama (Case 312/89) (1991) ECR I–997 145

Unectef v Heylens (Case 222/86) (1987) ECR 4112 168

Union nationale des entraineurs et cadres techniques
professionnels du football (UNECTEF) v Heylens
(Case 222/86) (1987) ECR 4097 79

United Brands v Commission (Case 27/76) (1978) ECR 207 . . . . 205, 207, 210

United Kingdom v Council (Case 68/86) (1988) ECR 855 69

Ursaff v Société Hostellerie Le Manoir (Case 27–91) (1991) ECR I-5531 171

VAG France v Etablissements Magne (Case 10/86) (1986) ECR 4071 203

VBVB amd VVVB v Commission (Cases 43, 63/82) (1983) ECR 19 199

Vaasen v Beambtenfonds Mijnenbedrijf (Case 61/65) (1966) ECR 261 126

Van den Bergh en Jurgens BV and Van Dijk Food Products
(Lopik) BV v Commission (Case 265/85) (1987) ECR 1155 76

Van Duyn v Home Office (Case 41/14) (1974) ECR 1337 . . . . 39, 71, 90, 173, 174

Van Gend en Loos v Nederlandse Adminstratie der
Belastingen (1963) ECR 1 . . . . 35, 84, 85,
87, 95, 132, 138

Van Tiggele (Case 82/77) 144

Van Zuylen Frères v Hag AG (First Hag Decision)
(Case 192/73) (1974) ECR 731 278

Vaneetveld (Case C–316/93) (1994) ECR 763 91

Verbond van Nederlandse Ondernemingen v Inspecteur der
    Invoerrechten en Accijnzen (Case 51/76) (1977) ECR 113 90

Vereniging van Cementhandelaren v Commission
    (Case 8/72) (1972) ECR 977 197

Viho Europe v Commission (Case T-102/92) (1992) (unreported) 195

Von Colson and Kamann v Land Nordrhein-Westfalen
    (Case 14/83) (1984) ECR 1891 .... 91, 92

Werhahn Hansamühle v Council (Cases 63–69/72) (1973) ECR 1229 120

Wilhelm and others v Bundeskartellamt (Case 14-68) (1969) ECR 1 194

Wood Pulp, Re (Cases 89, 104, 114, 116, 117, 125/85) (1988) ECR 5193 193

Worringham and Humphries v Lloyds Bank Limited
    (Case 69/88) (1981) ECR 767 262

Zerbone v Amministrazione delle Finanze dello Stato
    (Case 94/77) (1978) ECR 99 94

Zinc Producers Group, Re OJ 1984 L 220 199

Zuckerfabrik Schöppenstedt v Council (Case 5/71) (1971) ECR 975 122

Table of EU Legislation

Act of Accession for the United
Kingdom, Ireland and Denmark—
Art 42 142
Amsterdam Treaty 1997 ....3, 6, 10,
17, 20, 21, 31,
41, 42, 51–55,
60, 62, 78, 184,
252, 261, 271

Belgium Civil Code 119
Budget Treaty 1975 62

Constitution of the Fifth
Republic 1958—
Art 55 108

Directive 64/221 ....172, 174
Art 1 172
Art 2(1) 172
Art 3 175
Art 3(1) 90, 173, 175
Art 3(2), (3), (4) 173
Directive 68/151 (First Company
Law Directive) 92, 182
Directive 68/360 166
Directive 70/50 142
Directive 75/117 (Equal
Pay Directive) 101, 261,
266, 267, 269
Arts 1(1), 2(2) 267, 269
Directive 75/129 251
Directive 76/207 (Equal
Treatment Directive) 269–71, 311
Art 2(1) 271
Art 2(4) 270
Art 235 269
Directive 77/91 182

Directive 77/187 251
Directive 78/546 107
Directive 78/660 182
Directive 78/855 182
Directive 79/7 ....272, 272
Art 2 ....272, 272
Art 3(1) 272
Art 7 272
Directive 80/987 (Insolvency
Directive) 92, 251
Directive 82/891 182
Directive 83/49 182
Directive 83/189 (New technical
standards and regulations) 160
Directive 84/253 182
Directive 85/583 187
Directive 86/378 272
Directive 86/613 272
Directive 88/361 187
Directive 88/627 182
Directive 89/48 (General Systems) ...181
Directive 89/104 282
Art 2 282
Art 3(1) 282
Art 3(2) 283
Art 5(1), (2) 283
Arts 7, 9, 10(1), 11, 12 283
Directive 89/391 249
Arts 2, 16 249
Directive 89/667 182
Directive 91/250 286
Arts 4, 5, 6 286
Directive 92/10 282
Directive 92/51 181
Directive 92/56 251

Directive 92/57 249
  Art 6(1), (2) 250
  Arts 7, 8, 9(1), 10–12, 13(1), (2) 250
  Art 17 249
Directive 92/85 249
  Art 17 249
Directive 92/100 285
  Art 2 285
Directive 93/83 287
Directive 94/45 251

Enlargement Protocol—
  Art 1 22
  Art 2 44

EC Treaty 23, 28, 29, 33, 39, 42, 45, 46, 53, 55, 59, 62, 63, 65, 68, 70, 72, 73, 77, 85, 98, 108, 184, 190, 252
  Art 1 .... 166, 252
  Art 2 .... 4, 166, 208
  Art 2(1) 166, 168, 252
  Art 2(2), (3) 166
  Art 3 .... 4, 64, 166, 208
  Art 3(1) 168
  Art 3b 6, 77, 97
  Art 4 114
  Art 4(1) 252
  Art 4(2), (3), (4), (5) 252
  Art 5 .... 53, 91, 98, 252
  Art 6 .... 32, 53, 74, 163, 167, 219, 252
  Art 7(1), (2) 167
  Art 7a 184
  Art 8e 51
  Art 10 167
  Art 11 168
  Art 12 .... 85, 87, 138, 139, 157
  Art 13(2) 86, 138–40, 142
  Arts 14, 15 139
  Art 16 138
  Art 23 227
  Art 25 229
  Art 28 .... 50, 229

  Arts 30–34 139
  Arts 30–36 25
  Art 30 .... 142–46, 149, 150, 152
  Arts 31–33 139
  Art 31 142
  Art 32(1) 142
  Art 33 142
  Art 33(7) 142
  Art 34 .... 148, 149
  Art 36 .... 139, 149, 150, 152, 172, 274, 276, 277
  Art 37 214
  Art 37(2) 87
  Arts 38–46 64
  Art 40(3) 77, 122
  Art 43 .... 41, 46
  Art 43(2) 24
  Art 43(3) 32
  Art 44б 50
  Arts 48–51 163
  Art 48 .... 38, 164, 167, 169, 170, 178
  Art 48(2) 166
  Art 48(3) 70, 90, 172
  Art 48(3)(d) 24
  Art 48(4) 175
  Art 49 .... 41, 53
  Art 51 .... 24, 169
  Art 52 .... 87, 176, 180
  Art 53 87
  Art 54 .... 41, 179
  Art 54(1) 51
  Art 54(2) 53
  Art 54(3)(g) 181
  Art 55 .... 177, 178
  Art 55(1) 178
  Art 56(1), (2) 172
  Art 57 .... 24, 53, 178, 180
  Art 57(1) 180
  Art 57(2) 180
  Art 57(3) 53, 180
  Arts 59–61 180
  Art 59 117
  Art 60 180
  Art 63 .... 177, 180
  Art 66(7) 176, 177
  Art 66(7) 205
  Arts 67, 69 179
  Arts 67, 69 186

Art 70. 24
Art 73b. 188
Art 73c. 50
Art 73g(2) 32
Art 75. . . . . 24, 41
Art 75(1)(a) 117
Arts 77–81 193
Art 79. 63
Arts 85–93 279
Arts 85–94 . . . . 193, 219
Art 85 . . . . 24, 88, 194–97,
199, 208, 214,
216, 218–20, 224, 225
Art 85(1) 196–98, 203,
205, 214, 218
Art 85(2) 218
Art 85(3) 77, 200, 203, 214, 215
Art 86 . . . . 24, 83,
88, 194–96,
204–11, 214,
216, 218–20, 224
Art 86(1) 205
Art 87 214
Art 90 214
Art 90(1) 219, 220
Art 90(2) 86, 220
Art 90(3) 24, 55
Arts 92–94 221
Art 92 . . . . 77, 214,
220, 222–24
Art 92(1), (2) 222
Art 92(3) 222–24
Art 92(3)(c) 223, 224
Art 93 . . . . 214, 220, 224
Art 93(2) 105, 109
Art 93(3) 106
Arts 95–98 153
Art 95 . . . . 87, 141, 153–57
Art 95(1), (2), (3) 87
Art 96 153
Art 97 63
Art 99 153
Art 100 . . . . 46, 47, 151, 159
Art 100a. 46, 47, 53
Art 100a(1), (2), (3). 47
Art 102a 188
Art 106. 186

Art 106(1) 185
Art 106(6) 32
Arts 109j, 109m. 188
Art 113. 46
Art 113(3). 72
Arts 117–22 243
Art 118. . . . . 246, 249
Art 118(1), (2). 246
Art 118a. 244, 246
Art 118a(1), (2), (3). 246
Art 118b. 68, 244, 246
Art 118b(1). 246
Art 118c. 246
Art 119 . . . . 53, 74, 88,
101, 261, 263,
264, 266, 267, 271
Art 119(1) 261
Art 119(2) 262, 271
Art 119(4) 271
Arts 123–25 243
Art 123 247
Art 124 247
Art 127(4) 53
Art 128. 53
Art 128(5) 68
Art 129 53
Arts 129b–29d 257
Art 129c(1), (3) 258
Art 129d 258
Arts 130a–30e 245, 253
Art 130b 247, 254
Art 130d(1), (2) 55
Arts 130e, 130i 53
Art 130s(1) 53
Art 137. 31
Art 138(2) 30
Art 138(3) 30, 55
Art 138b. 50
Art 138c. 33
Art 140(3) 33
Art 143. 33
Art 144. . . . . 22, 33
Art 145. . . . . 28, 66
Art 146, (2) 26
Art 147. 26
Art 148, (1), (2) 27
Art 149(2) 52

Art 151(1)	29
Art 152	28, 48
Art 155	23, 68, 143
Art 156	25
Art 157(1)	20, 21
Art 158(1)	22
Art 158(2)	21
Art 159(1), (2)	22
Art 160	22
Art 164	70, 73
Art 165(1)	34
Art 165(2)	36
Art 166(1)	34
Art 166(2)	35
Art 167(1), (2), (3)	35
Art 167(6)	34
Art 168	34
Art 168a(1)	34, 35
Art 168a(3)	35
Art 169	23, 67, 96, 101, 105–09, 135, 139, 143, 156, 179
Art 170	106, 109
Art 171	108, 109
Art 173	8, 9, 36, 73, 105, 109, 110, 112–14, 116, 118, 134, 217, 225
Art 173(1)	109
Art 173(2)	35
Art 173(4)	110
Art 175	33, 105, 116, 117, 217
Art 175(3)	35
Art 177	8, 113, 125–28, 133, 134, 139, 169, 301
Art 177(3)	130–32
Art 178	120
Art 184	113, 118
Art 188b(1)–(5)	42
Art 188c(1), (2), (4)	42
Art 189	10, 64–66, 68, 89, 90, 94, 112
Art 189(4)	67
Art 189a(1)	50
Art 189a(2)	24, 50
Art 189b	24, 32, 52, 53, 258, 304
Art 189c	32, 52, 247, 258, 304
Art 190	49, 115
Art 191	304
Art 191(2)	66, 67
Art 191(3)	67, 68
Art 191a	53
Arts 193–98	40
Art 194(2), (3), (4)	41
Art 198c	41
Arts 198d, 198e	43
Art 199	56, 261
Art 201	56
Art 201a	50, 56
Arts 202, 203	57
Art 203(1)	57
Art 203(2)	25
Art 204	59
Arts 205, 205a	25, 60
Art 206(1)	60
Art 209	60
Art 209a	53
Art 211	11
Art 214	121
Art 215	73, 119–21
Art 220	46, 47
Art 222	219, 273, 279
Art 227	63
Art 228	72, 114
Art 228(1)	65
Art 228(3)	55
Art 228(6)	72
Art 232(2)	229
Art 235	46, 47
Art 234	73
Arts 237, 238	32, 55
Art 240	63

Euratom Treaty 1957

Art 208	63

European Coal and Steel Community Treaty 1952 .... 7, 9, 13, 45, 62–65, 229

Arts 71, 72	62–65, 74, 205
Art 208	229

European Convention of Human Rights 1950 .... 1, 3, 77, 78

European Defence Community
Treaty 13

European Social Charter 248
Arts 27, 28 248
Art 29 249

French Civil Code—
Art 1382 121

Luxembourg Agreement 1996 . . . . . . 27, 28
Item (b) I 27

Merger Treaty 1965 . . . . 14, 62
Art 11 21
Art 14 21

Regulation 17/62
(OJ 1962 204) 24, 202, 214
Arts 1, 2 214
Art 3 . . . . 215, 217
Art 4(2) 215
Art 5 215
Art 9(3) 217, 218
Art 10(1), (2) 217
Art 11 217
Art 11(1) 215
Art 13 217
Art 14 215
Art 15 . . . . 214, 216
Art 15(2) 216
Art 15(5) 215
Art 16 . . . . 214, 216
Art 17 . . . . 216, 217

Regulation 27/62 215
Regulation 40/94 283
Regulation 91/533 248
Regulation 99/63 216
Regulation 123/85 204
Regulation 417/85 204
Regulation 418/85 204
Regulation 556/89 204
Regulation 802/68 (Implementing
Regulations) 233

Art 5 233
Art 62 237
Art 142(1)(d) 235
Art 169(1) 236
Art 178 236
Art 179(1) 236
Arts 205, 254, 255 237
Arts 259, 264 238

Regulation 918/83 229
Regulation 950/68 . . . . 227, 230
Regulation 1224/80 233
Regulation 1251/70 168
Regulation 1463/70
(OJ 1970 L 164) 89
Regulation 1408/71 169
Art 2(1) 170
Art 3(1) 170
Art 4(1), (2) 170
Art 12(1) 171
Arts 13, 18, 38, 45, 67 171
Regulation 1612/68 166
Regulation 1969/88 187
Regulation 1983/83 204
Regulation 1984/83 204
Regulation 2052/88 254
Regulation 2144/87
Arts 2, 3 242
Regulation 2349/84 204
Regulation 2367/90 212
Art 2(3) 213
Art 8 213
Regulation 2526/85 215
Regulation 2545/93 228
Regulation 2658/87 228
Regulation 2913/92
(CCC Regulations) . . . 228, 233, 234, 239
Arts 23, 24 232
Art 29(1), (3)(a) 234
Art 30(2)(b), (c), (d) 235
Art 31(2) 234
Arts 32, 33 234
Art 35 236
Arts 36–38 232

Arts 59, 61 237
Art 68 233
Arts 97, 98, 101, 109 239
Arts 114, 117, 130–36, 145–47 240
Arts 154–59, 161, 163 241
Arts 209–11 242
Art 214(1), (2) 242
Art 215(1), (2) 241
Arts 788–98 240
Regulation 2981/93 254
Regulation 3295/94 . . . . 238, 285
Regulation 3491/88 231
Regulation 3842/86 285
Regulation 4064/89
(OJ 1989 L 388) (Mergers
Regulation) 24, 193,
                                211, 212, 311
Arts 1, 3 212
Art 3(1) 211
Art 4 212
Regulation 4078/88 204
Regulation 4253/88 254
Rules of Procedure 36
Title II 36
Art 63 37
Arts 69, 97, 98, 99 38
Single European Act 1986 . . . . . . 5, 8, 16,
                                30, 32, 34, 47,
                                49, 50, 51, 55,
                                60, 62, 67, 77,
                                97, 148, 157, 187–89,
                                243, 244, 291, 292, 296

Arts 8, 9 55
Statute of the Court of Justice—
Arts 15, 16, 36 36
Art 43 120
Treaty of Brussels 1948 12
Treaty of Paris 62
Treaty on European Union
(Maastricht Treaty) 1991 . . . . . 2, 4–8, 10,
                                17, 30, 32,
                                41, 45, 50–53,
                                56, 60, 62, 65,
                                77, 80, 81, 97,
                                108, 116, 183, 186,
                                188, 222, 244, 245,
                                251–53, 257, 292–96, 298
Art A 184
Art B 2, 10, 184
Art B(2) 184
Art C 10
Art D 29
Art F 3
Art F(1) 3
Art F(2) 3, 78
Art Fa 3, 77
Art G 3, 55
Arts J–J 11 2
Art J 293
Art J 8
Arts K–K9 . . . . 3, 293
Art O 55
Art Q 63
Art VI 8
Treaty of Rome 1957 (EEC
Treaty) 4, 7, 9, 13,
                                64, 183, 224
Arts 8–8e 183

Table of Statutes

Equal Pay Act 1970 101

European Communities Act 1972 102
  s 2(1) 100, 101
  s 2(4) 102
  s 3(1) 102

Merchant Shipping Act 1988 101

Sherman Act 1870 (USA) 191

1   Introduction

I   EU law defined

The law of the EU can be defined both positively and negatively, ie in terms of what it is and what it is not. Viewed from a positive angle, EU law can be defined as all such rules, regardless of their sources, which govern the workings and policies of the European Union. In the narrowest sense, it takes the form of:

- inter-governmental treaties and conventions;
- legislation enacted by the Community institutions;
- the general principles of law which serve to clarify and supplement the treaties and the legislation; and
- the decisions by the judicial bodies, both at the EU and national levels, applying such legislation.

On a broader interpretation, it also includes the following:

- non-binding instruments such as recommendations and opinions;
- rules which are internal to the institutions;
- the debates on Community legislation in the European Parliament;
- the various communications, some more formal than others, which pass between the EU institutions and third parties; and
- such principles of international law as apply to the Community.

As defined by exclusion, Community law does *not* include the following:

- The rules governing the institutions and policies of other European organisations. This may seem the clarification of the obvious, until one discovers how many authors include in their works on Community law chapters on the European Convention of Human Rights (which, even though it is recognised by the EU Court of Justice, falls within the sphere of the Council of Europe) and the law of other European institutions.[1]
- The national laws incorporating Community law. In some cases, the domestic authorities of the Member States are required to give effect to EU law in their legislation. Although such instruments have a substantive link with these EU instruments, and are almost always scrutinised by the

---

1   Gautron, J-C, *Droit européen* (1995) Dalloz, Opperman, T, *Europarecht* (1992), CH Beck Verlag.

Community institutions, they do not form part of Community law in the accepted sense of the term.

- National parliamentary debates on Community law and policy.

II   Community or EU law?

One of the elements which has sometimes sown confusion amongst those studying this area of the law is the manner in which it is generally referred to. 'Common Market law'[2] and 'EEC law' can now safely be consigned to the history books. 'Community law' appeared to have gained the status of accepted term of art, until the Maastricht Treaty (Treaty on European Union – TEU). This instrument 'decided to establish a European Union' which is based on a number of 'pillars', stated in Article B of the TEU. One of these pillars is formed by the Communities, ie the European Community, the European Coal and Steel Community (ECSC), and the European Atomic Energy Community (EAEC). The other two 'pillars' are a common foreign and security policy, and justice and home affairs. Accordingly, Article G amended the title of the Treaty of Rome to 'Treaty establishing the European Community'.

In principle, 'EU law' should only be used when referring to the law of the three 'pillars'. However, since the law on justice and home affairs and on a common foreign and security policy has barely been developed, EU law is, in its present state, largely coterminous with Community law. It is therefore in most cases legitimate to use the terms 'EU law' and 'Community law' interchangeably, which will be the approach adopted by this work, although some scholars will have reservations about this practice.

III   The general foundations of the European Union

As has been mentioned in the previous paragraph, the Treaty on European Union has expanded the scope of action of the Community. Whereas previously the objectives were almost entirely economic (in the broadest meaning of the term), the TEU has added a more general and ideologically value-free set of objectives to Community activity. They are listed in Article B, and comprise the following:

Promotion of economic and social progress

Here, the objective is to record improvement in standards, but in such a way as to be 'balanced and sustainable'. The realisation of economic and monetary

---

2   Even though the name lingers on in such publications as the *Common Market Law reports* and the *Common Market Law Review*.

union (below, p 188) and the strengthening of economic and social cohesion (below, p 253) are seen as key elements in achieving this goal.

Assertion of EU identity on the international scene

This is to be achieved on two fronts: in the short-to-medium term, through the realisation of a common foreign and security policy, and in the long term by establishing an EU defence policy. This objective has already run into difficulties, judging by the evasiveness with which the subject was approached at the Amsterdam Summit of June 1997, and in the resulting Amsterdam Treaty.

The strengthening of rights and interests of the Community citizen

The main element here is the introduction of the notion of citizenship of the Union, which will be dealt with later (below, p 183).

Closer co-operation on justice and home affairs

The relevant provisions are set out in Articles K to K9 of the TEU. The areas falling within the ambit of this objective include asylum policy, immigration rules, the combating of drug addiction and international fraud, judicial co-operation in civil and criminal matters, customs co-operation, and co-ordination of police action for the prevention of terrorism. The Amsterdam Treaty contains a number of important provisions seeking to complement the TEU, more particularly in the area of police and judicial co-operation in criminal matters.

Maintenance of the 'acquis communautaire'

This is a concept which is explained in full at p 10.

Article F of the TEU adds that the Union must respect the national identities of its Member States, whose governmental systems are based on the democratic principle (Article F(1)). Under Article F(2) TEU, it must also have regard for fundamental rights as laid down in the European Convention of Human Rights and as they result from the constitutional traditions of the Member States and from the general principles of Community law (below, p 73).

The Amsterdam Treaty has substantiated the aspiration laid down in Article F(1) TEU by laying down certain penalties which may be imposed on Member States which are in breach of this provision. By inserting a new Article Fa into the TEU, it has provided its chief legislative body, the Council of Ministers, with the power to decide to suspend some of the rights conferred by the TEU on the Member State in question.

IV   The economic foundations of the Community

In spite of the changes brought about by such fundamental instruments as the Treaty on European Union (TEU), the objectives of the European Community[3] remain those of the Treaty or Rome, signed on 25 March 1957 between the original six Member States.[4] In spite of the references made in the Treaty Preamble to such general aims as 'an ever closer union among the peoples of Europe', the objectives of the Community are essentially economic. They can be broken down into the *general* and the *specific* objectives.

The general objectives are contained in Article 2 EC Treaty. In the first instance, the object added by TEU is to create 'a common market and an economic and monetary union'. Second, the Community must seek to promote 'a harmonious and balanced development of economic activities, sustainable and non-inflationary growth respecting the environment, a high degree of convergence of economic performance, a high level of employment and social protection, the raising of the standard of living and quality of life, and economic and social cohesion and solidarity among Member States'. This is regarded as a 'declaration against sin' rather than a definitive statement of policy.

It is in Article 3, which deals with the *specific* objectives, that an insight is provided into the manner in which the Community seeks to achieve these lofty ideals. They coincide with the major areas of Community policy-making which will be examined in greater detail elsewhere:

- the removal of customs duties and quantitative restrictions between the Member States, as well as any measures with equivalent effect;

- the setting up of a common commercial policy;

- the removal of obstacles to the free movement of goods, persons, services and capital;

- measures regarding the entry and movement of persons in the internal market;

- the adoption of common policies in agriculture and fisheries, as well as transport;

- the adoption of rules on fair competition;

- the approximation of laws to the extent required for the achievement of the common market;

- the social policy, including the creation of the Social Fund;

- the strengthening of the competitiveness of European industry;

3   Here, the term 'European Community' should be understood in its restrictive sense, as distinct from the term 'European Union'.

4   Belgium, France, Germany, Italy, Luxembourg and the Netherlands.

- the promotion of research and technical development;
- the setting up of trans-European networks;
- a contribution towards a high level of health protection;
- a contribution to education, training and culture;
- a policy on development co-operation;
- economic and social involvement of overseas countries and territories;
- strengthening consumer protection;
- Community action in the field of energy, civil protection and tourism.

Almost inevitably, Community action has not given equal weight to all these objectives, preferring to focus on those which were considered to be fundamental to its basic purpose. Thus the completion in 1992 of the programme set out in the Single European Act[5] constituted a major step in the achievement of one of the main economic objectives of the Community, which was to create an internal market with free movement of all factors of production.[6] The introduction of a single currency in 1999 should achieve yet another such economic landmark, even though at the time of writing there remain some doubts on its feasibility. The realisation of the other objectives, particularly in the field of social policy, have lagged some way behind these achievements.

From the objectives stated above, it will be clear that Community law is not a value-free system. It translates the desire of its founders to give expression to, and promote, an economic system based on the free market. Although the provisions on social policy and such matters as environmental and consumer protection mitigate this emphasis on economic liberalism, Community law is, broadly speaking, expressive of a capitalist economy and ideology.

V   The political foundations of the EU

Preamble to the TEU

The only political objective of any kind to appear in the original Treaty was the commitment to 'ever closer union' mentioned earlier. This solitary statement has since been supplemented by the TEU Preamble, which sets out a wide range of political foundations of the new Community. Although preamble statements have no binding effect and are not enforceable, those of the TEU provide a distinct idea of the general direction in which the EU is moving politically.

---

5   This is a fundamental instrument, signed in 1986, which not only had an economic objective, but also made certain institutional changes; below p 157.

6   These are capital (finance), labour and goods.

In the first place, the Member States confirm their 'attachment to the principles of liberty, democracy and respect for human rights and fundamental freedoms, and the rule of law'. The commitment to human rights protection is a recognition of the fact that the EU institutions – particularly the European Court of Justice – had already been assessing a number of issues with which they were required to deal in the light of human rights. This will be returned to in the section dealing with general legal principles (below, p 73).

The desire to 'deepen the solidarity between their peoples while respecting their history, their culture and their traditions' is a new and socially-conscious commitment which is not part of the philosophy behind the original Treaty. It finds practical expression in the policies on social cohesion (below, p 253).

The Preamble also contains a commitment towards the 'democratic and efficient functioning of the institutions so as to enable them better to carry out, within an institutional framework, the tasks entrusted to them'. Clearly the intention here was to signal a resolve to bridge the 'democratic deficit' within the EU, ie to ensure that the institutions are representative of the peoples of the Member States and that those institutions which come closest to this ideal be entrusted with as many decision-making powers as possible. The increased powers bestowed upon the European Parliament under the TEU (below, p 31) constitute a clear expression of this trend.

The commitment towards the establishment of 'a citizenship common to nationals of their countries' confirms a gradual change in the manner in which the nationals of the Member States had come to perceive the Community. Under the earlier arrangements, they were invited to consider themselves national citizens benefiting from an inter-governmental arrangement in which the Member States had merely agreed to pool their sovereignty. Under the influence of such developments as the direct elections to the European Parliament in 1979, the introduction of the European passport in the late 1980s, and the increasing emphasis by the European Court of Justice (EC) on the human rights dimension of Community action, the notion of European citizenship gradually took shape, and was confirmed by the TEU.

Article 3b, introduced by the TEU, further explains that the notion of subsidiarity involves action taken by the Community 'only if and in so far as the objectives of the proposed action cannot be sufficiently achieved by the Member States and can therefore, by reason of the scale or effects of the proposed action, be better achieved by the Community'. It was not until the Amsterdam Treaty, however, that an attempt was made to lay down some detailed criteria for the application of this principle. This will be explained more fully later (below, p 96).

Federalism

It is quite significant that this notion, which is perhaps the most controversial political term connected with the Community, is not mentioned in any of its founding or derived instruments, not even in their preamble. Alternatively referred to as 'the F-word', or the political objective that dare not speak its name, the notion of federalism has always been at the centre of any debate concerning the political direction to be taken by the Community.

It should be noted from the outset that the notion of federalism is almost as ambiguous as that of subsidiarity. In some countries (eg Belgium and Italy) federalism has been the political battle cry of those wishing to split a centralised nation state into its component parts. In others, such as Germany, it has meant the merger of formerly independent units into a state structure which, although falling short of outright centralism, nevertheless gives the most important decision-making powers to the central authorities. It is in the latter sense that federalism has tended to be used in a Community context.

As a concept, federalism has always been contrasted with and compared to the notion of 'functionalism'. Federalism seeks to achieve integration amongst formerly independent units across as broad a range of areas as possible, mainly in the economic sphere. Functionalism, on the other hand, also seeks to achieve such integration, but restricts this endeavour to certain sectors of the economy, preferably those which best lend themselves to integration under a supranational authority. The best example of European functionalism in practice has been the European Coal and Steel Community Treaty, which placed two key industrial products under the authority of joint legislative, executive and judicial institutions. The question whether there has ever been a serious attempt at federalism is a matter of continued debate. It could be argued that the Treaty of Rome was federalist in view of the broad sweep of its scope, yet some key policy areas (eg direct taxation) were not covered by its provisions. On the other hand, there is a case for arguing that, although the original Treaty of Rome was not federalist, it has been made so by the TEU because of its ultimate goal of economic and monetary union.

European political co-operation

Although the momentum towards European integration has been, and continues to be, driven by economic considerations, the prospect of achieving co-operation in political matters, particularly foreign and defence policy, has always exercised the minds of Community policy makers. The fact that the founding treaties did not make provision for such co-operation has proved no obstacle to such endeavours, since most initiatives in this field have taken place outside the framework of these treaties.

Early attempts at achieving co-ordination in the political area took the form of the Fouchet plan (1961) and the summit meeting of The Hague in 1969, at which the foreign ministers of the Member States were invited to formulate proposals for political co-operation. One such proposal was that the Foreign Ministers should meet every six months to discuss issues of foreign policy. This paved the way for the setting up of the European Council in 1974, which integrated European political co-operation (EPC) into the general framework of Community policy-making. Another major landmark was the 1981 London Report, which gave a more structured and formal appearance to the EPC procedures, which had hitherto tended to be somewhat loose and informal.[7] The Single European Act ensured that EPC had a legal basis in the founding treaties. In addition, a secretariat, based in Brussels, was established in order to assist with the preparation of EPC activities. Finally, the TEU, in Article J, established the principle of Common Foreign and Security Policy, thus giving a very specific focus to European political co-operation.

The 'third pillar' of the EU – being co-operation in the fields of justice and home affairs – also serves the purpose of European political co-operation. Article VI of the TEU requires the Member States to regard as 'matters of common interest' such issues as asylum policy, immigration, combating drug addiction and fraud, and judicial co-operation in civil and criminal matters. Such co-operation is bound to contribute not only towards improved co-ordination, but also towards greater political consensus in these areas.

VI   The legal foundations of the EU

Direct effect, direct applicability and supremacy

The Community legal system has emancipated itself from the law developed by other international treaties through in three important ways:

- It has made the Community citizen a legal subject in his own right, capable of deriving rights from Community law and of relying on these before the national courts. This is known as the *direct effect* of Community law. It has also given the individual access to the Court of Justice, both directly through the annulment procedure of Article 173 EC Treaty, and indirectly through the preliminary rulings procedure provided under Article 177 EC Treaty.

- It makes provision for the enactment of certain rules which take effect in the internal legal orders of the Member States without requiring any further measures on the part of the latter's authorities. This is known as the *direct applicability* of Community law.

- It is designed in such a way as to ensure that, in the event of a conflict between Community law and domestic law, it is the former which will

7   Nicoll, W and Salmon, T, *Understanding the New European Community* (1994), Harvester Wheatsheaf, pp 190–91.

prevail. This is regardless of the constitutional arrangements which may apply in the Member States. This is known as the *supremacy* of Community law.

It is these aspects of Community law which have made it into a legal system *sui generis*, which is neither national nor federal law, but a system which mirrors the very specific relationship between national law and the law developed under the founding treaties which is specific to the EU. These concepts will be studied in greater depth in Chapter 5. Suffice it to say at this stage that they are central to any understanding of the operation of Community law, and of the effect which it has produced on the legal systems of the Member States.

EU law: a civil law system

When the founding Treaties were signed in 1952 (ECSC) and 1957 (EEC and Euratom), there were six Member States. All had codified law systems, five of which were based on the French civil law model. The latter was the result of the major legal reforms brought about in France following the 1789 Revolution, mainly on the initiative of Napoleon Bonaparte. It is hardly surprising, therefore, to learn that Community law bears a strong imprint of the French legal system. This influence manifests itself in various ways:

- **the structure of the institutions.** This is particularly true of the Court of Justice, which is based very closely on the Conseil d'Etat (the French Supreme Administrative Court);

- **the 'administrative law' of the Community.** Thus the grounds for review of administrative action under Article 173 EC Treaty are virtually identical with those which arise under French administrative law;

- **Community procedures.** This is especially noticeable in the prominence of the written procedure before the Court of Justice and the structure of the agenda at Council of Ministers meetings;

- **the legislative techniques.** Most Community legislation follows the *loi-cadre* format, under which the legislature contents itself with laying down the main outlines of the measure to be adopted, leaving it to the executive to fill in the details;

- **the techniques of legislative interpretation.** As will be discussed more fully in Chapter 2, the Court of Justice applies the 'teleological' (or purposive) method when interpreting Community legislation. Although Anglo-Saxon systems have been moving in this direction in recent years, this technique was developed in the civil law countries;

- **the substantive law.** The contents many Community law provisions have strong civil law overtones – as can be seen, for example, from its competition law.

This is not to deny the contribution made by the legal orders of the other Member States. Thus EU company law (below, p 181) has been strongly influenced by German law, and the participation of Common Law-trained judges in the Court of Justice has allowed a more discursive and less formalistic approach towards judicial decision-making. Nevertheless, EU law remains very much a civil law system.

The *acquis communautaire*

The term *acquis communautaire* is as difficult to translate as it is to explain. The word *acquis* is a French term denoting the entire body of Community rules and the rights and principles derived from them. Applied to the Community, this amounts to what certain authors have described as the 'legal assets' of the Community, to wit the entire body of rules consisting of:

* founding treaties and international instruments of the Community;

* derived legislation;

* judicial rulings (by the ECJ) and quasi-judicial decisions (eg Commission competition rulings) made by the Community institutions; and

* the non-binding instruments such as the opinions and recommendations described in Article 189 EC Treaty, as well as the resolutions adopted by such institutions as the European Parliament and the Council of Ministers.[8]

The *acquis communautaire* is more than an academic concept. It is set of rules and principles which must be maintained and developed further. This aspect of the acquis was emphasised in the TEU, more particularly Articles B and C, which require the Union to 'maintain in full ... and build on' the *acquis communautaire*.[9] As has been mentioned earlier (above, p 3) it has been elevated by the Amsterdam Treaty to the status of fundamental principle underlying the Community. However, as is the case with other fundamental concepts of the Community encountered earlier, neither the scope nor the full meaning of this term are described in the fundamental Community law instruments.

The Community as a legal person

Legal (or corporate) personality is a legal term which is applied to persons other than natural persons – eg recognised companies, associations and societies. They are given legal personality in order to enable them to acquire and dispose of goods, and conduct such transactions as enable them to fulfil the purpose for which they were established.

8   Toth, AG, *The Oxford Encyclopaedia of European Community Law*, vol 1, 'Institutional Law' (1991). See also the Opinion of Advocate-General Reischl in Case 161/78, *Conradsen v Ministeriet för Skatter og Afgifter* (1979) ECR 2221, at 2248.

9   Charlesworth, A and Cullen, H, *European Community Law* (1994) Pitman, p 58.

The EU is also a legal person. This is expressly recognised by Article 211 EC Treaty, which provides that 'in each of the Member States, the Community shall enjoy the most extensive legal capacity accorded to legal persons under their laws; it may, in particular, acquire or dispose of movable and immovable property and may be a party to legal proceedings'. It is therefore the Community itself, and not its individual institutions, which has legal personality.[10] It is the Commission which will act on behalf of the Community for the purpose of exercising this legal personality (Article 211 EC Treaty). Thus if the Community is being sued under its tort liability, it is the Commission which will represent the Community, even though the tortious act may have been committed by the Council of Ministers.

VII The historical foundations of the EU

The early years

Contrary to popular belief, the notion of European unity did not arise exclusively from the ashes of the First World War. Although the devastation wrought by this human calamity added a certain degree of urgency to the project, the notion of co-operation between the nations of Europe can be traced back to much earlier times.

At the beginning of the first millennium, the Roman empire had succeeded in imposing its authority on a vast area which covered most of present-day Europe. After the fall of Rome in 476 AD, Charlemagne attempted to recreate this massive structure in the 9th century, by founding the Holy Roman Empire, which lasted until 1806. At its height, it included much of western and central Europe. The 19th century was very much the preserve of the nation state, which was deemed to be equal to any challenge which humankind could devise. However, there were thinkers such as Victor Hugo, Mazzini, Proudhon and Cattaneo who had advocated closer union amongst the peoples of Europe, without, however, making any practical proposals as to how this could be achieved.

One of the first authors to advocate a federal structure for Europe was the Italian author Einaudi. Although his writings did not give rise to any political movement, they gave encouragement to those who were prepared to convert such ideas into practical action, such as Count Coudenhove-Kalergi, founder of the 'Pan-Europe' movement. This was an association consisting mainly of intellectuals which had little popular support, and therefore was not translated into political action. During the late 1930s, Winston Churchill who viewed with alarm the threat posed to the rest of Europe by German fascism, proposed a

---

10 Cases 7/56 and 3–7/57, *Algera v Common Assembly of the ECSC* (1957–58) ECR 39.

federal union between Britain and France, which would have united the two countries by means of a common citizenship and a joint parliament.[11] Because of its suddenness, this proposal was never realised, but was instrumental in planting the federalist idea in the minds of statesmen.

The immediate post-war period

Once the allied powers secured victory against Nazism in 1945, the full scale and implications in this exercise in human folly became clear. Europe was entirely devastated, not only because of the toll taken of its human life, but also in economic terms. Immediately, the statesmen of Europe set about the task of devising ways of avoiding the re-occurrence of this monumental tragedy. One indispensable element was the creation of common institutions which would make it virtually impossible for the nations of Europe ever to go to war with each other again.

The first of these institutions took the form of an organisation which sought to assist with the task of rebuilding the economies of those involved in the conflict. In 1947, a senior American political figure, George Marshall, conceived a plan whereby the US would provide the countries of Europe substantial economic aid, which they would be required to use for the purpose of economic reconstruction and poverty relief. The organisation which was set up in order to administer this aid was called the Organisation for European Economic Co-operation (OEEC), established in April 1948 with 16 Member States. This body continued its existence once its original purpose was fulfilled. Under its current name of Organisation for Economic Co-operation and Development (OECD),[12] it is now the leading world organisation for economic analysis and forecasting.

In the area of defence, the 1948 Treaty of Brussels together the allied European powers. This was succeeded the following year by an organisation linking the defence of Western Europe to the military assistance provided by the US and Canada, and took the form of the North Atlantic Treaty Organisation (NATO). Germany was originally excluded from this organisation, but was allowed to joint it in 1955. For the purposes of achieving co-operation in the cultural, political, legal and social fields, the Council of Europe was established in 1949.

From ECSC to EEC

However invaluable their contribution towards the European ideal, the organisations referred to above were essentially inter-governmental. In order to

---

11 Spinelli, A, 'The Growth of the European Movement since the Second World War', in: Hodges, M (ed), *European Integration* (1972), Penguin, pp 44–45.

12 The organisation was renamed in 1961 to take account of the accession to its ranks of non-European states, such as Japan and Australia.

strengthen the links between the nations of Europe even further, it was deemed necessary to establish a body on which supranational powers would be conferred. This prompted the French Minister for Foreign Affairs, Robert Schuman, to propose the establishment of an organisation whereby two key industrial areas, ie coal and steel, would be placed under the authority of an organisation which was independent of the governments of its Member States. Initially, the plan would involve France and Germany, but any other European state would be invited to join. Thus was born the European Coal and Steel Community, established under the Treaty of Paris, which placed the production and marketing of these two products under the control of the High Authority, which thus became the first ever supra-national organ. When it commenced its activity in 1952, it had six Member States: the Benelux countries, France, Germany and Italy.

Although the ECSC represented a major breakthrough in the construction of European unity, there were those who wished to see progress in European co-operation in other fields. This was particularly the case in the area of defence. The Korean War of the early 1950s focused attention on this issue once again, and prompted an attempt to establish an exclusively European army among the ECSC Member States, called the Pleven plan. Although signed by all the Member States, the Treaty establishing the European Defence Community (EDC), under whose control this army would have operated, fell at the hurdle of the national parliaments. In 1954, the French National Assembly withheld ratification of the EDC Treaty, as a result of a strange marriage of convenience between the Right and the Left of French politics.

This gave rise to a major rethink of the future of European co-operation and integration. For this purpose, a top-level meeting, to take place in Messina (Italy), was convened in 1955. This conference signalled the beginning of the *Relance européenne* (the relaunching of Europe). It was decided that the future of European co-operation lay in economic integration, more particularly through the achievement of a common market amongst the Member States. For this purpose, an inter-governmental committee was established, chaired by the Belgian Minister for Foreign Affairs, Paul-Henri Spaak. The final report issued by this Committee contained the major outlines of the institutional structure and main policy areas of the organisation which was to achieve this objective. These were incorporated into a draft treaty establishing the European Economic Community (EEC), signed in Rome on 25 March 1957. At the same time, a functionalist treaty relating to nuclear energy, to wit the Euratom Treaty, was signed.

Birth pains and adolescent angst

The EEC Treaty provided the Community with a structure which closely mirrored that of the ECSC. It had an independent executive in the shape of the Commission, a legislature in the Council of Ministers, a judicial authority in the

Court of Justice, and a European parliamentary assembly which was to play a largely consultative role. Within this framework, work began in earnest for the elaboration of EEC policies. The first major area to which the institutions turned their attention was agriculture. After a major consultation exercise, the Commission produced a blueprint for agricultural support which was aimed at securing adequate food supplies whilst at the same time providing the European farmer with a respectable income. This was discussed at a meeting held in Stresa (Italy) which brought together Commission officials, farmers' representatives and national experts. The resulting system was to constitute the framework for the Common Agricultural Policy.

At the time of its birth, the Community was relatively small, consisting of a mere six Member States. One of the European countries which had initially refused any participation in this exercise, ie Britain, began seriously to reconsider its position in 1961. Under the impulse of the then Prime Minister, Harold McMillan, the United Kingdom made a formal application for membership in 1962. In spite of the manifest enthusiasm displayed by the Commission and the majority of the existing Member States, Britain's attempted accession was frustrated by the implacable opposition of President de Gaulle of France, who considered that the presence of the UK, with its strong transatlantic connections, would deprive the Community of its exclusively European character. De Gaulle was to repeat his veto to British accession when the UK, this time under the Labour government of Harold Wilson, made a second application to join in 1967.

The mid-1960s also witnessed an institutional crisis within the Community. Its origins lay in the increasingly fraught relationship between the Community institutions and the French government. The latter took exception to the supranational leanings of the former. These had taken the form of attempts to increase the scope of majority voting within the Council, the extension of the budgetary powers of the European Parliament, and the proposal that most Community expenditure should be financed by means of its own resources. When the French government considered that action spoke louder than words, it withdrew all co-operation by refusing to take up its seat within the Council. This became known as the 'empty chairs policy', and lasted until the inevitable compromise was reached. This took the form of the so-called 'Luxembourg agreements', which provided that whenever decisions involved vital national interests, discussions should continue until such time as agreement was reached – in other words, giving each Member State a *de facto* power of veto in Community decision-making.

The mid-1960s, however, also brought some cheer for the supporters of further integration when it was decided to merge the Council and the Commission of the three Communities (EEC, ECSC and Euratom). This was brought about by the 1965 Merger Treaty. Previously, it had been difficult to

14

achieve coherent and rational decision-making in such areas as energy and industrial policy, since the legislative and executive bodies concerned were organisationally divided. Geographically, too, the merger simplified matters, since the Community Executive (ie the Commission) was now based in Brussels,[13] whereas the ECSC High Authority had been based in Luxembourg prior to the merger.

The 1970s: extension and innovation

In 1969, President De Gaulle left office, having failed to obtain a positive verdict during a referendum on constitutional change. His successor, Georges Pompidou, proved considerably more amenable to the prospect of British accession. The following year, the British people elected a Conservative government headed by an enthusiastic supporter of European integration, Edward Heath. The combination of these developments led to the third, and successful, British application for Community membership. This resulted in the accession, not only of the UK, but also of Denmark and Ireland, in 1973. The Norwegian government had also planned to take part in this first wave of Community extension, but was frustrated by a referendum which rejected Community membership. The decade ended with negotiations for accession with Greece, which became a member in 1981.

The 1970s were also a period of innovation. At the Paris Summit held in December 1974, the Community's Heads of State and Government agreed to meet three times per year as the European Council. That meeting also saw the establishment of the European Development Fund. In July of the following year, the Member States concluded a treaty conferring wide budgetary powers upon the European Parliament, and setting up the 'financial watchdog' of the Community, ie the Court of Auditors. The mid-1970s also witnessed a number of major reports which, although very few of their contents were actually implemented, nevertheless planted the seeds for future reforms. These were:

- the Tindemans Report of 1976, which proposed an extension of Community action in the areas of economic and monetary policy, as well as in defence, and regional policy;

- the 'Three Wise Men' Report of 1979, which recommended the reinforcement of the role of the Commission, and an extension of majority voting within the Council;

- the Spierenburg Report of 1978, which contained important proposals for the reorganisation of the internal structures of the institutions.

The decade ended with two important events which were to add a totally new dimension to the development of the Community. In June 1979, the European

---

13 Nevertheless, some of the Commission's departments are still based in Luxembourg.

Parliament was elected by direct universal suffrage for the first time, thus conferring democratic legitimacy on a body whose powers looked set to increase. Later that same year, the European Exchange Rate Mechanism became operative. This was a device aimed at obtaining currency stability with a view to possible monetary union.

It should be added that these changes were made against a background of gathering economic doom for western industrial society as a whole, in the shape of the two oil crises which hit the world in 1973 and 1978. Although there were some signs of Community solidarity cracking under the strain, as witness the isolation of the Netherlands when it came under fire from the oil-producing states for the support it gave to Israel, the Member States did not by and large resort to panic-induced protective trading arrangements, preferring to seek a solution at the Community level.

The 1980s: from stagnation to revival

Following the considerable changes in the nature and membership of the Community during the previous decade, the early 1980s saw a period of relative stagnation, thus partially vindicating Chancellor Willi Brandt's dictum that the deepening integration and geographical extension could not go hand in hand. Various signs of internal dissent left their mark the development of the Community:

• the disagreements and eventual compromise over the British contributions towards the Community budget;

• the failure to agree on the extent to which economic sanctions should be imposed on the *apartheid* régime in South Africa; and

• the difficulties experienced by some currencies, particularly the French franc, inside the Exchange Rate Mechanism.

This sense of lost direction extended even to one of the central planks of Community endeavour, ie the common market. Various legislative programmes had been devised a decade earlier in order to remove barriers to trade through harmonisation, but these had become highly cumbersome affairs which took infinitely longer to complete than originally envisaged. By the mid-1980s, therefore the EC was in the doldrums, waiting for something or someone to point it in the right direction.

The event which ended this state of sclerosis was the White Paper issued by Lord Cockfield, Commissioner for the Internal Market, in 1985. It set the scene for a rolling programme of legislation aimed at completing the internal market, which was to be adopted by a definitive deadline, which was 31/12/1992. The contents of the White Paper were incorporated into the Single European Act (SEA) 1986, which at the same time carried through a number of institutional reforms – whose main effect was to give more powers to the European

Parliament in respect of internal market legislation. With one or two exceptions, the programme was implemented on schedule. The year 1986 also saw the extension of the Community to include Spain and Portugal. This had the effect of pulling the centre of gravity of the Community towards the South, with all that this entailed in terms of economic priorities and policy choices.

The Community and the new Europe: the 1990s

A few months before the new decade, there occurred an event which completely redrew the geopolitical map of Europe, to wit, the fall of the Berlin Wall and the collapse of the Communist regimes throughout the Eastern Bloc. The immediate consequence was a further extension of the Community in the shape of the former East German states. However, it was clear that in the long term, the Community would also be facing considerable pressure for a massive extension eastwards. It was clear that this could not leave its main policy areas unaffected.

Yet for a while it seemed that the Community took very little account of this new development. In 1991, the Maastricht Treaty on European Union was signed, which envisaged the realisation of Economic and Monetary Union (EMU) by the end of the decade. Only the most optimistic of observers considered this to be compatible with the early accession of the former Eastern Bloc countries. As if to emphasise this fact, three new Member States joined the European Union, which was the new name given to the Community by the TEU. These were Sweden, Austria and Finland, all three highly industrialised and wealthy states. The TEU had also brought about considerable institutional change, once again producing the effect of enhancing the status and powers of the European Parliament.

The most recent significant development to occur took the form of the Amsterdam Treaty, signed at the Intergovernmental Conference held in June 1997. It has to be admitted, however, that the expectations made of this Treaty were greater than its actual achievements. More particularly, it had been expected that the political shift towards the Left, resulting from the election of Left-wing governments or coalitions in Italy, Britain and France, would bring about a change in the way in which European union was to be achieved. It was thought that a more socially aware agenda would replace the monetarist orthodoxy which had characterised the economic convergence criteria laid down in the TEU. Except for the inclusion of a rather vague Employment Chapter, there was little to reflect this change in the balance of political forces amongst the EU Member States. The expected institutional reforms also turned out to be of a low key nature, and resulted in some piecemeal changes rather than any sizeable reform.

VIII Approaching Community Law

It is reasonable to assume that the majority of readers of this volume will be those who are being, or have been, trained in the Common Law system. As such, they will need to approach Community law in a different manner from that to which they are accustomed, in view of the fact, mentioned earlier (above, p 9) that Community law is dominated by the civil law. They should remember the following points:

• Civil law systems are based on the supremacy of the legislature. Unlike their common law counterparts, their courts are not allowed to lay down rules for the future, even when interpreting legislation.

• Many of the legal concepts featured in Community law are civil law concepts for which there is no exact equivalent in the common law. A good example is the term *le procès contradictoire*, which means a court hearing taking place after a full hearing on both sides, but which is virtually impossible to translate into English.

• The decisions of the Court of Justice are in most cases very similar to those of the French *Conseil d'Etat*, ie fairly brief. In addition, in spite of the existence of an 'established case law' (*jurisprudence constante*), they refer relatively infrequently to previous court decisions. It is by consulting the Opinion of the Advocate General and the arguments of the parties, both recorded in full in every official case report, that a better notion can be formed of the manner in which the law has developed.[14]

• The decisions of the ECJ and of the Court of First Instance (CFI) are deemed to represent the collective viewpoint of the judges who took part in the hearing. Unlike English court decisions, they will not indicate any individual ruling or dissenting opinion by judges.

• The instruments of Community law (legislative acts, opinions and recommendations and judicial decisions) are all published, and equally authentic, in all the official languages of the Community.[15] Accordingly, the English version has very frequently (and definitely in the case of the pre-1973 instruments) been translated from another Community language. These translations are not invariably of the highest quality.

Further guidelines on the use of Community law sources can be found in the section relating to practical information (below, p 303).

14 Charlesworth, A and Cullen, H, *op cit*, p 9.
15 Danish, Dutch, English, Finnish, French, German, Greek, Italian, Portuguese, Spanish, Swedish. The Irish language enjoys a special status.

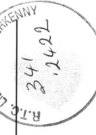
2 The Community Institutions

I Introduction

Ideally, in view of the long-term objective of 'ever closer union' amongst the people of Europe, the founding fathers of the Community would have preferred an institutional structure which had two essential characteristics. First, it should mirror that of the existing Member States, with a legislature consisting of an elected assembly, an executive which mirrors the balance of forces within that assembly, and a judiciary which hears all disputes relating to the application of Community law. In addition, all the Community institutions would have been completely independent from the national authorities of the Member States, and would be situated in one location within Community territory.

However, there were a number of considerations which prevented them from instituting such a structure. These were mainly of a political and historical nature. To carry out such a vast programme would inevitably have involved the transfer, from the Member States to the Community, of a considerable part of the former's sovereignty. In addition, the Member States themselves would have lost all control over, or even contact with, the functioning of these institutions. Third, there would have been no possibility of taking into account the national interest in the course of Community decision-making. For all these reasons – and bearing in mind that, as stated in the Introduction (above, p 9) Community law is a *sui generis* system of law – an institutional structure was devised which took into account all these considerations whilst nevertheless mirroring as closely as possible the constitutional structures which exist at the national level.

Accordingly, the institutional structure of the Communities presents the following characteristics:

- **Composite functions.** At least three of the Community institutions (the Commission, the Council and the European Parliament) have functions of different kinds which cannot be neatly accommodated into the traditional distinction between legislative, executive, judicial and advisory powers. The Commission, for example, although it is traditionally regarded as the Community Executive, has a mixture of all four of these functions.

- **Polycentric structure.** Although the centre of gravity of the Community institutions is firmly in Brussels, the latter are spread over three centres, ie Brussels, Luxembourg and Strasbourg – apart from the purely functional locations, such as the Euratom nuclear research centres at Ispra (Italy) and

Culham (United Kingdom). This may have a number of logistical disadvantages, but has enabled other major European centres to make their contribution towards the construction of Europe. This polycentric structure has been confirmed by a special Protocol attached to the Amsterdam Treaty.

- **Divided allegiances.** Ideally, all the Community institutions should have constituted and conceived in such a way that their allegiance would be only to one cause: the Community interest. However, this proved impracticable, for reasons both of principle and of pragmatism. The Commission is certainly a body which owes its allegiance purely to the EU interest – in fact, the Commissioners are required to swear an oath to that effect. The Council, however, represents the interests of the Member States, whereas the Court of Justice is required to assess all the disputes submitted to it in complete and utter impartiality.

- **Separation of powers.** This is a principle which was formulated by the French constitutional philosopher Montesquieu in the 18th century, and which inspired the manner in which the French post-revolutionary institutions were conceived. It holds that in the exercise of their powers, the legislature, executive and judiciary must be entirely independent of each other. This principle applies to the Community institutions because, although, as mentioned earlier, they have mixed functions, they are all entirely independent of each other.

II   The Commission

General

The Commission is generally regarded as the Community executive, and the most *communautaire* of the EU institutions. The scope of its powers is more wide-ranging than that of any other Community organ. It is perhaps this characteristic which has caused the Commission to be the butt of adverse comment among some sections of public opinion and in the wilder reaches of the popular press. The Commission as it were personifies the Community, with all its benefits and faults.

Composition and appointment

In its narrow sense, the Commission consists of a body of 20 members who, as is required by Article 157(1) (para 1) EC Treaty, 'shall be chosen on the grounds of their general competence and whose independence is beyond doubt'. The term 'general competence' is extremely broad, and has not been specified or clarified by any other provision of Community law. It is safe to state that in the overwhelming majority of cases, the Commissioners are national politicians of some stature. They have not invariably been chosen for their competence or interest in matters European, and at a certain point the Commission was disparagingly referred to as 'the political dustbin of Europe'.

Recently, however, there have been signs that this epithet no longer applies. This may be due in part to a number of changes which have been made in the manner in which they are appointed. Previously, the Commission was appointed 'by common accord of the Governments of the Member States' (Article 11 Merger Treaty), which often led to a process of unseemly horse-trading and jockeying for position. The president and vice-presidents of the Commission were appointed in a similar manner (Article 14 Merger Treaty). Both the TEU and the Amsterdam Treaty, however, have introduced a number of changes in the appointment procedure.

First of all, the governments of the Member States nominate the person whom they intend to appoint as Commission President. That nomination must then be approved by the European Parliament. The governments then proceed to nominate the other Commissioners-to-be, by common accord with the person whom they have nominated as President. All nominees are then subject as a body to a vote of approval to be given by the European Parliament. Once this approval has been secured, the Commission is appointed by joint agreement between the Member States' governments (Article 158(2) EC Treaty).

Nevertheless, the new procedure has not succeeded in eliminating controversy from the appointments procedure. This was very much in evidence on the first occasion when the new system was applied, ie for the Commission whose term of office commenced in January 1995. Initially, the consensus of opinion amongst the Member States' governments was in favour of Mr J Dehaene, the Belgian Prime Minister. However, the nomination was changed to Mr J Santer, of Luxembourg following objections from only one Member State, – the United Kingdom. The Parliament did not withhold its approval, although the debate on this issue reveals widespread dismay at the spirit in which the new procedure had been approached.

The Commissioners must all be nationals of one of the Member States (Article 157(1), para 2, EC Treaty). Because of the *communautaire* nature of the Commission, this should in principle have been the only restriction to be applied in terms of the Commissioners' nationality, merit being the only permissible criterion. However, political reality demands some form of national representation, which is why the Commission must include at least one citizen of each Member State (Article 157(1), para 3, EC Treaty). Unfortunately, dubious conventions have further restricted the scope for selection purely on merit. It has become the custom for the larger Member States to be represented by two commissioners, leaving the smaller states with one. Even more questionable is the British habit of ensuring that its two Commissioners are shared between a nominee of the Government and one of HM Opposition.

The membership structure of the Commission looks set to change within the foreseeable future. Under Article 1 of the Enlargement Protocol attached to the Amsterdam Treaty, the Commission will obligatorily comprise one national of each Member State as from the date on which the first enlargement of the EU takes place, provided that by then the weighting of votes within the Council (below, p 27) has been changed.

Commission members have a term of office of five years (as opposed to four under the previous system) (Article 158(1), para 1, EC Treaty). Other than this circumstance, the only way in which his or her term of office can expire is by death, resignation or compulsory retirement (Article 159, para 1, EC Treaty). The only body which may 'compulsorily retire' a Commissioner is the Court of Justice, which may do so if it considers that the Commissioner in question no longer meets the conditions for the performance of his or her duties, or that he or she has engaged in serious misconduct (Article 160 EC Treaty). Any vacancy caused by one of the circumstances mentioned above is filled by inter-governmental agreement, although the Council may decide that no such replacement is necessary (Article 159, para 1, EC Treaty). The Commission President can only be replaced by means of the normal procedure for appointing the President (above) (Article 159, para 2, EC Treaty).

The Commission may also be dismissed *en bloc* if the European Parliament succeeds in passing a motion of censure by a two-third majority of the votes cast. If this happens, a new Commission is appointed in the normal manner described above. However, its term of office will expire on the same date as that on which term of the original Commission would have ended had it remained in office (Article 144 EC Treaty). The Parliament has not yet availed itself of this power, and, frankly, is unlikely ever to do so. Whether this would be the case if the Parliament had the power to censure individual Commissioners is more debatable.

In the broader sense, the Commission consists of the Commissioners, plus its staff of approximately 19,000 officials. These are divided into 23 Directorates-General and other departments (eg the Statistical office). Each Directorate-General is divided into Directorates, which in turn consist of Divisions. The size of each Directorate-General can vary considerably (unsurprisingly, the largest of these is the one dealing with Agriculture). As is the case with the Commissioners themselves, considerations of nationality should play no part whatsoever in the appointment of these officials. However, national sensitivities have ensured that a rough 'quota system' applies, at least as regards the top posts.

Functions and powers

As has been mentioned before, the Commission is generally regarded as the Community Executive,[1] but has a range of powers which exceed that which are normally expected of an executive. Normally, the latter is expected to propose, implement and ensure the application of legislation. That the Commission's powers exceed this normal role is evident from a reading of Article 155 – which itself is not a complete statement of its functions:

In order to ensure the proper functioning and development of the common market, the Commission shall:

- ensure that the provisions of this Treaty and the measures taken by the institutions pursuant thereto are applied;

- formulate recommendations or deliver opinions on matters dealt with in the Treaty, if it expressly so provides or if the Commission considers it necessary;

- have its own power of decision and participate in the shaping of measures taken by the Council and by the European Parliament in the manner provided for in this Treaty;

- exercise the powers conferred on it by the Council for the implementation of the rules laid down by the latter.

In addition, the Commission exercises a judicial function in competition matters, acts as the legal representative of the Community, prepares the Community budget, and has a host of administrative tasks. In practical terms, its powers can be divided into five categories:

Guardian of the Treaty

In this capacity, the Commission has the power to compel Member States who fail to meet their Treaty obligations to mend their ways, if necessary by taking them to the ECJ. Under Article 169 EC Treaty, the Commission will first of all give the Member State in question the opportunity to reply to the accusation made by the Commission. The Commission then issues a reasoned opinion, to which the national authorities must reply by a given date. Where the Member State in question fails to do so, or if its reply is unsatisfactory, the Commission will bring the matter before the Court of Justice.

In the vast majority of cases, this procedure is used to enforce compliance with Council or Commission directives. The Commission's task is made easier in this respect by the fact that the Member States must provide it with regular information on the manner in which they are incorporating the contents of these directives. In most cases, the initial stages of the Article 169 procedure are

1   Some even refer to it as the 'European Government-in-waiting'.

sufficient to secure compliance by the national authorities, and it is a comparative rarity for the matter to reach the Court of Justice. The ECJ procedure in this regard is discussed further in Chapter 6 (below, p 105).

It is under this heading also that the Commission exercises its judicial functions. Under Regulation 17/62,[2] the Commission is required to investigate, and take decisions on, suspected infringements of Articles 85 and 86 of the Treaty (as well as the Mergers Regulation).[3] This topic will be returned to in Chapter 11 (below, p 214).

Participation in legislative process

Under this heading, the Commission can initiate and assist with the formulation of legislation, as well as issuing legislation in its own right. As regards the initiation of legislation, the Commission has both specific and general powers. Its specific powers derive from the large number of substantive Treaty rules requiring it to take the first step for the adoption of a regulation, directive or decision in a specific area. Such specific powers are found in, *inter alia*, Article 43(2) (agriculture), Article 51 (social security), Article 57 (co-ordination of national rules on self-employment), Article 70 (free movement of capital), Article 75 (transport policy), etc. In addition, whenever a substantive Treaty rule lays down that the procedure to be used is that of Article 189b, this necessarily involves a legislative initiative by the Commission.

Once it has made the proposal, the Commission will continue to be involved in the legislative process thus initiated. The Commission is represented at all meetings of the Council, and may at all times alter its proposals. It is frequently necessary for the Commission to do so, since any amendment by the Council to a Commission proposal must be adopted unanimously (Article 189a(2) EC Treaty). The extent of its further involvement in the legislative process will depend on the particular legislative procedure adopted. This will become clearer when these procedures are discussed further in Chapter 3 (below, p 49).

The Commission also has legislative powers in its own right, which are conferred on it by specific Treaty provisions. Thus Article 48(3)(d) requires the Commission to draw up regulations specifying the conditions in which workers may remain in the territory of a Member State after having been employed in the latter. Under Article 90(3), the Commission may address directives and decisions to Member States concerning the application of competition rules relating to public companies.

2 OJ 1962 204.
3 Regulation 4064/89 OJ 1989 L 388.

Advisory capacity

The Commission may issue recommendations or opinions on policy areas laid down in the Treaty, either where the latter specifically so provides, or on its own initiative. One of the main areas in which it has used these powers is the free movement of goods (Articles 30–36 EC Treaty), particularly once the Commission had decided to concentrate resources and efforts on solving the stream of complaints brought to it under this heading by private individuals and national governments.[4]

Representative capacity

As has been mentioned earlier, the EU is a corporate entity which has the capacity to engage in legally binding relations. It is the Commission which represents the Community for this purpose. Thus whenever the contractual or tort liability of the EU is engaged, or the latter wishes to engage that of others, it is the Commission which will act on its behalf. The Commission also represents the Community in its relations with non-Member States and international organisations. This is an extremely important function in view of the large number of bilateral and multilateral instruments concluded by the Community. Thus in the Uruguay Round of negotiations with the Community's GATT partners, it was the Commission which acted for the EU.

Financial management

The Commission is also involved in the management of the Community finances. First of all, it has a major part to play in the elaboration of the Community budget. Under Article 203(2) EC Treaty, the Commission is responsible for drawing up the preliminary draft budget which it submits to the Council. During the subsequent procedure which involves the Council and the European Parliament, the Commission will be regularly consulted; once again, its role will be to act as an 'honest broker'.

Once the Budget has been approved, the Commission must implement it, on its own responsibility and within the limits of the appropriations conferred (Article 205 EC Treaty). In addition, it must, on an annual basis, submit to the European Parliament and the Council the accounts relating to the budget as implemented for the preceding financial year (Article 205a EC Treaty). The Commission also administers the structural funds of the Community.

Administrative tasks

As befits any Executive, the Commission has a number of routine administrative tasks conferred upon it. Thus Article 156 EC Treaty requires it to

---

4   Lasok, D and Cairns, WJ, *The Customs Law of the EEC* (1984), Kluwer, p 51.

publish the annual General Report on the activities of the Community, which is normally issued around mid-February of the following year.

Prospects of change

Under a declaration made in the context of the Amsterdam Summit of 1997, the Commission has been given official blessing for its intention to make preparations for reorganisation of tasks in good time for the Commission which will take office in 2000. The object of such reorganisation will be to ensure an optimum division between the conventional 'portfolios' of the Commissioners and the specific tasks to be carried out. The Commission will also undertake a parallel reorganisation of its departments.

III   The Council

Composition and appointment

Strictly speaking, there is no such thing as *the* Council, since the composition of this body varies along with the subject area under discussion. This is embodied in Article 146 EC Treaty, which states that the Council consists 'of a representative of each Member State at ministerial level, authorised to commit the government of that Member State'. When the Council meets to discuss and decide agricultural policy, the ministers responsible for this area will constitute the Council.

Sometimes the particular nature of the subject under discussion will be of relevance to more than one ministerial area of responsibility. In that case, the Member States will be likely to be represented by more than one secretary of state. Naturally this will not increase their voting power. The Council meets whenever it is convened by its President, either at his own initiative, or at the request of one of its members or of the Commission (Article 147 EC Treaty). These meetings are held in secret. The Council's normal meeting place is Brussels, but three times per year it will also meet in Luxembourg.

The presidency obviously plays an important part in the Council's proceedings. Not only does the President convene the meetings; the country holding the Presidency is also responsible for the manner in which the meetings are conducted during its term of office. The Presidency is held for a six monthly term by each Member State in turn (Article 146, para 2, EC Treaty). In the course of the Council's existence, a number of measures have been taken in order to improve expediency and continuity at its meetings. Prominent amongst these have been the following initiatives:

- Introduction of the *troika* system. This is a permanent forum where three members meet: the current President, his or her immediate predecessor and his or her immediate successor. This ensures a maximum degree of continuity from one presidency to the next.

- Agenda planning. The Council's agenda consists of A items and B items. The former are issues on which agreement has already been reached in principle, and which merely require formal approval. The latter consist of the contentious issues. This has enabled as much time as possible to be set aside for discussion of the B points.

- Various practical measures, such as the advance planning of Council meetings, the circulation of discussion documents at least a week prior to the meeting, and the co-ordination of national cabinet meetings in order to ensure the availability of senior ministers.

The Council also has its back-up staff. The latter is more streamlined than that of the Commission, being approximately 2,500 strong.

Voting procedure

The principle underlying Council voting procedures is majority voting. This means that majority voting is the norm and can only be departed from where the Treaty expressly so provides (Article 148(1) EC Treaty). Because the Member States vary considerably as to the size of their population ranging from 380,000 (Luxembourg) to 73 million (Germany), it would be nonsensical for all the Council members to have an equal vote. Accordingly, Article 148 EC Treaty applies a weighting factor to the voting strength of each member where decisions are required to be taken by a qualified majority. However, this weighting factor only gives the faintest reflection of the size of population of the country involved. The 'big four' (Germany, France, Italy, and the United Kingdom) have 10 votes each; Spain has eight; Belgium, Greece, the Netherlands and Portugal have five, Sweden and Austria four, Denmark, Ireland, and Finland three, and Luxembourg two.

Thus weighted, acts of the Council taken by qualified majority voting require at least 62 votes in favour. If the measure is to be adopted on a Commission proposal, the distribution of these votes is irrelevant. In all other cases, however, these 62 votes must be cast by at least 10 Member States (Article 148(2) EC Treaty).

The Luxembourg Accord

One element which has devalued the principle of majority voting is the so-called Luxembourg Agreement of 28–29/1/1966, which has already been referred to (above, p 14). Considerations of space prevent a detailed examination of this document. Suffice it to say that its contents are extremely ambiguous, and sometimes even cast doubt on the question whether all its provisions actually constituted negotiated agreement. Item (b) I of the Agreement states that, where issues which are vital to one or more partners are involved, the members must endeavour, within reasonable time, to reach solutions which can be adopted by all members. Paragraph II states:

With regard to the preceding paragraph, *the French delegation considers that where very important interests are at stake, the discussion must be continued until unanimous agreement is reached* (emphasis added).

It would appear then that the famous 'veto clause' amounts to little more than a unilateral position or reservation on the part of the French Government. Nevertheless, the Council members have always treated it as though it gave the Member States, in certain areas, the power to block legislation even where the Treaty prescribed majority voting. There is some doubt as to whether the Luxembourg Agreement still applies. None of the TEU provisions expressly repealed it, although there is some authority for the view that this instrument may have abolished it implicitly.

Functions and powers

Article 145 describes the functions of the Council in the following terms:

To ensure that the objectives set out in this Treaty are attained, the Council shall, in accordance with the provisions of this Treaty:

- ensure co-ordination of the general economic policies of the Member States;

- have power to take decisions;

- confer on the Commission, in the acts which the Council adopts, powers for the implementation of the rules which the Council lays down.

This combination of policy co-ordination, decision-making powers and the right to delegate implementing powers firmly identifies the Council as the Community legislature – a profile which has survived the challenge mounted to its supremacy in this field by the additional powers conferred on the European Parliament by the TEU. Although the Council does not in principle have the right of legislative initiative, it may request the Commission to undertake any studies which it considers desirable for the achievement of the Community objectives, and may submit to it any appropriate proposals (Article 152 EC Treaty). In addition, the Council concludes the international agreements which have been negotiated by the Commission. It also decides the budget together with the European Parliament.

The role of COREPER

The Council consists of members who combine a Community role with a national mandate. There can be no doubt which task makes the greater demands on their time. Such is the pressure of the national executive and parliamentary timetable that only a fraction of the ministers' time can be devoted to their participation in the Council. In accordance with a traditional practice applied by international organisations, the national governments are represented by a body of permanent officials called the Permanent Committee of Representatives (known by the acronym COREPER).

Indeed, so important was the potential role to be played by COREPER that, when it was first established, it was greeted with some coolness by the Commission, who feared that COREPER would soon become a kind of 'second eleven' for the Council itself. These fears were never quite realised, nor have they been completely allayed by the passage of time. The terms of reference of COREPER are laid down in Article 151(1) EC Treaty, which tersely states that COREPER is responsible for preparing the work of the Council and for carrying out such tasks as are assigned to it by the latter. In fact, COREPER has a less subservient role than this provision might suggest. It plays an invaluable bridge-building part in relations between the Commission and the Council. COREPER has now split into two tiers. The Permanent Representatives proper constitute COREPER II and deal with questions of major political importance. The deputy representatives sit in COREPER II and deal with more technical matters.

IV   The European Council

The European Council is a body which is entirely distinct from the Council of Ministers. It has met regularly since the decision taken at the 1974 Summit that the Heads of State and Government, as well as the Commission President, should meet on a regular basis in order to discuss major Community issues in a less formal atmosphere than that which prevails at the meetings of the Council. Since 1986, the ministers of foreign affairs and an additional Commissioner may also be in attendance. Its legal basis is now Article D of the TEU – though why it was not formally included among the EC Treaty provisions relating to the Community institutions has never been satisfactorily explained.

The European Council meets at least twice a year, and is chaired by the Head of State or Government of the country holding the Council presidency. Its brief is described in very general terms in Article D of the TEU in the following terms:

> The European Council shall provide the Union with the necessary impetus for its development and shall define the general political guidelines thereof.

This wide remit ensures that nothing can really be excluded from the agenda of European Council meetings, as long as it is relevant to Community policy. It does not take decisions in the formal sense of the term, but issues statements or declarations which are then normally translated into Community legislation in accordance with the relevant Treaty provisions. Not all commentators have welcomed its establishment, arguing that, because of its inter-governmental nature, it tends to undermine the supranational character of the Union.

V   The European Parliament

Composition and appointment

When it came to adding an element of democratic legitimacy to the Community, its founding fathers found themselves faced with a dilemma. If they created a directly elected Parliament with full legislative powers, that would have represented a transfer of sovereignty too far for the citizens of Europe. If on the other hands they merely gave a consultative role to a directly elected assembly, they would have been accused of setting up an expensive and underemployed talking shop. The solution to this seemingly intractable problem was to make the Parliament into a largely advisory body, consisting of delegations from the national parliaments – at least provisionally. Article 138(3) EC Treaty required the Member States to formulate proposals for direct elections to the Parliament using a uniform voting system. No doubt the expectation was that by then, the Parliament would have acquired more powers and would therefore justify the energy and resources expended on such an exercise.

It was not until 1978 that the Member States agreed to hold such direct elections, which took place the following year. In fact Article 138(3) has yet to be implemented to the full, since direct elections continue to this to be organised in accordance with national voting procedures. The expectation that the Parliament would increase its powers were only partially realised, in that the 1970 and 1975 Budget Treaties conferred upon it considerable powers in relation to the Community's finances. It was only with the adoption of the SEA (1986) and the TEU (1991) that the Parliament witnessed a real extension in its functions.

Another issue which required careful thought was the question of the distribution of seats amongst the Member States. On the one hand, to have attributed an equal number of seats to each Member State would have been a travesty in view of the inequalities in the size of their populations. If seats had been allocated purely in proportion to size of population, Germany would have 127 seats and Luxembourg none – since the latter would be too small to constitute a unit of electoral representation. By way of compromise between these two extremes, seats were allocated in such a way as to reconcile the requirements of proportionality and of national sensitivities. The current distribution of the 626 available seats is as follows (Article 138(2) EC Treaty):

Belgium	25	Luxembourg	6
Denmark	16	Netherlands	31
Germany	99	Austria	21
Greece	25	Portugal	25
Spain	64	Finland	16
France	87	Sweden	22
Ireland	15	United Kingdom	87
Italy	87		

The Amsterdam Treaty has added to Article 137 EC Treaty a provision to the effect that the number of MEPs may not exceed 700. The electoral systems used differ considerably. Most countries apply some form of proportional representation (PR). Some of these are 'pure' PR systems; others make provision for the preferential vote, whereas others still are based on the Single Transferable Vote (STV). The United Kingdom uses the same uninominal system (also known as first past the post) as is applied for its national parliamentary elections. No definite proposal for a uniform voting system has yet been tabled.

The Parliament epitomises the polycentric nature of the Community institutions. The parliamentary sessions are held in Strasbourg. Its secretariat is located in Luxembourg, whereas the European political parties have their secretariates in Brussels. (In addition, some of the Parliament's Committee meetings are held in Brussels.) That this is not the most rational of arrangements is only too obvious; however, attempts at centralising the operation of the Parliament have repeatedly run into obloquy. During the parliamentary sessions, the MEPs are seated in accordance with their political grouping rather than on the basis of their nationality. These political groupings express a certain ideology. The one having the largest representation in the current 1994–99 Parliament is the Socialist group (221). The European People's Party, consisting of Christian Democrats, currently has 173 members; the Liberal Group 52, and the Confederal Left 31.

Organisationally, the Parliament has a Bureau, consisting of its 14 vice-presidents, who are elected by their peers for a period of two years. The Bureau presides over the Parliament's back-up staff, which runs to approximately 4,000 employees. The Parliament also has its committee structure. There are approximately 20 specialist committees dealing with specific areas of Community policy. Commissioners may be invited by these committees to give evidence. The Parliament has also established a number of ad hoc bodies called European Parliamentary Committees of Enquiry, which examine specific problems (below, p 33).

Powers and functions

Initially, the Parliament was a largely advisory body, although it had the power to dismiss the Commission *en bloc*. Over the years, its remit has widened substantially, and it now has considerable legislative and financial powers. These can be classified as follows:

Legislative powers

The Parliament currently has various degrees of involvement in the legislative process. At the lowest level of involvement, the Parliament has a *right to information*. This is the case, for example, in relation to any decision by the

Council to allow Member States to take unilateral measures against third countries with regard to capital movements (Article 73g(2) EC Treaty).

Second, the Parliament has retained the *right to be consulted* under various Treaty provisions. This is the case, for example, with the legislation on the common organisation of agricultural markets envisaged by Article 43(3) EC Treaty. If legislation is adopted without consulting the Parliament, it is voidable by the Court.[5] In addition, the other Community institutions may consult the Parliament even if such consultation is not obligatory.

Third, Parliamentary involvement can take the form of the *co-operation procedure*. This is the procedure which was introduced by the SEA, and is currently embodied in Article 189c EC Treaty (although the legislation covered by this procedure has changed since the SEA – see Chapter 3, below, p 53). This involves the right of the Parliament to reject the common position adopted by the Council. One of the most important areas covered by this procedure is the prohibition of discrimination based on nationality (Article 6 EC Treaty).

Fourth, the Parliament can participate in the formulation of legislation regulated by Article 189b EC Treaty.[6] This is the area of legislation in which the powers of the Parliament are at their strongest, in that it has two opportunities to reject the Council's common position. It covers most internal market legislation.

Fifth, there are items of legislation requiring the *assent* of the Parliament. Originally, this procedure was obligatory only for international agreements concluded by the Community (Articles 237 and 238 EC Treaty). However, the TEU extended the scope of this procedure to such areas as the conferral of certain supervisory tasks on the European Central Bank (Article 106(6) EC Treaty). The detailed operation of these legislative procedures will be examined in Chapter 3 (below, p 49).

Budgetary powers

Mention has already been made of the Budgetary Treaties of 1970 and 1975 (above, p 15), which increased Parliamentary involvement in the allocation of expenditure (although not in the raising of revenue). The effect of these instruments has been to make the Parliament and the Commission the joint budgetary authorities. Essentially, the Parliament has been given the last word on non-compulsory expenditure, although there are limits to the extent to which it can increase overall spending.[7] The budgetary procedure is also explained in

---

5   Case 138/79, *Roquette Frères v Council* (1980) ECR 3333.

6   By means of the *co-decision procedure* (also referred to as the 'conciliation and veto procedure').

7   Bainbridge, T and Teasdale, A, *The Penguin Companion to the European Union* (1996), Penguin, p 213.

greater detail in Chapter 3 (below, p 56). The Parliament has exercised its power to reject the Community budget on a number of occasions, more particularly in 1979 and 1984. In more recent years, it has failed to do so, probably because it feels that the effectiveness of such a rejection is subject to the law of diminishing returns.

Supervisory powers

The Parliament has a number of supervisory tasks conferred on it in relation to the other institutions. As far as the Commission is concerned, the Parliament and its members have the right to put questions to the Commission, to which the latter replies either orally or in writing (Article 140, para 3, EC Treaty). It also discusses in open session the annual report submitted by the Commission (Article 143 EC Treaty). Under Article 144 EC Treaty, the Parliament also has the right to censure the Commission. If a motion to that effect is tabled before it, the Parliament must allow three days before voting on it by open vote. If the motion is carried by a two-thirds majority of votes cast (representing a majority of MEPs), the Commission must resign as a body.

More generally, Article 138c allows the Parliament to establish a temporary Committee of Inquiry in order to investigate alleged infringements or instances of maladministration in the implementation of Community law. It may not do so, however, if the matter is still subject to judicial examination. The European Parliament can also exercise its supervisory function indirectly, by bringing an action against the Commission or the Council for failure to act, under Article 175 EC Treaty (below, p 116).

Political functions

The Parliament holds debates on the general areas of policy and topical issues. It is not bound by the Community agenda of policy areas as laid down in the Treaty. The only limitation on the scope of its debates is that it should not concern itself with defence issues. In the course of these debates, it may adopt resolutions.

VI Court of Justice

General

The Court of Justice (and its adjunct, the Court of First Instance) represents the judicial arm of the Community – at least in the narrow sense. In the broader sense, every national judicial body of the Member States is also a Community Court, since it is capable of having rules of Community law relied upon before them. These rules can confer rights on individuals which the national courts are compelled to respect and uphold (below, p 83).

The most important function expected of the Court of Justice is that it should act as a unifying force in the application and interpretation of Community law. In addition to this potentially heavy workload, the ECJ was also expected to settle all disputes between the institutions themselves, between the institutions and the Member States, and between individuals and the institutions. The latter task involves settling staff disputes. It is clear that too many demands were being placed on the Court, which is why the SEA provided it with some reinforcement in the shape of the Court of First Instance (CFI).

However invaluable has been the contribution of the CFI in providing relief for the Court, there are still signs that the Court has too heavy a workload. Exactly how this could be overcome is difficult to establish. To create several Community Courts would risk losing the unity of interpretation which forms such an important reason for the Court's existence. The number of judges – and therefore also of chambers – could be increased, but this could also have a negative effect on the unity of purpose expected of the ECJ.

Composition and appointment

As has been mentioned before, the Court now has two organs: the Court as such, and the Court of First Instance which, as is stated in Article 168a(1) EC treaty, is 'attached' to the ECJ. The former is composed of 15 judges (Article 165, para 1, EC Treaty). Although the Treaty does not lay down any requirements as to the nationality of these judges, it has hitherto been deemed politic for each nationality of the Member States to be represented.[8] These judges are assisted by eight Advocates-General (Article 166, para 1, EC Treaty)[9] and by a registrar (Article 168 EC Treaty). They appoint one of their number to act as President (Article 167, para 6, EC Treaty).

Advocates-general are representative of a phenomenon which is intrinsic to civil law systems, which is that a governmental representative should be in attendance in a court case whenever the public interest so demands. In criminal cases, this governmental representation takes the form of a public prosecutor, who brings the case against the accused on behalf of the public interest.[10] In civil and administrative cases, it takes the form of an expert opinion delivered by the representative in question, from a viewpoint representing the public interest. Before the supreme administrative court of France, the *Conseil d'Etat*,

---

8 Previously, care had always been taken to ensure that the ECJ consisted of an uneven number of judges. Thus when there were 6, 10 and 12 members, the Court consisted of 7, 11 and 13 members respectively (the 'odd' judge being called the 'floating judge'). The reason for this was to avoid a tie when the full court was in session.

9 Article 166, para 1, also provides that, until 6 October 2000, a ninth Advocate-General is in post.

10 The nearest equivalent which exists in common law jurisdictions is the Scottish Procurator-Fiscal.

this role is assumed by the *Commissaire du Gouvernement*. The Advocate-General of the Court has been modelled very closely on this French institution.

The task of the Advocate-General is to deliver reasoned submissions on all cases brought before the Court, in order to assist the latter with the discharge of its responsibilities. They must do so in open court, and in a spirit of complete independence and impartiality (Article 166, para 2, EC Treaty). These submissions (also known as Opinions) are always issued before the Court delivers judgment. In most cases the ECJ will follow this opinion, although there have been celebrated instances where this has not been the case.[11] Both judges and Advocates-General are appointed for a term of six years, by common agreement between the Member States' governments (Article 167, para 1, EC Treaty). Normally these appointments are quite uncontentious. No specific qualifications are stipulated for holding either office. The EC Treaty (Article 167, para 1) confines itself to requiring that they should be:

> ... chosen from persons whose independence is beyond doubt and who possess the qualifications required for appointment to the highest judicial offices in their respective countries or who are jurisconsults of recognised competence.

Practising judges and academics account for the majority of these appointments. In order to ensure the continuity of approach which is expected of it, the Court is renewed on a staggered basis. Accordingly, there occurs a partial replacement every three years, alternatively by eight and seven judges (Article 167, para 2 EC Treaty). Similarly, the Advocates-General are also subject to partial replacement, by four members on each occasion (Article 167, para 3, EC Treaty).

The Court of First Instance, for its part, consists of judges who are also appointed by common accord of the Member States' governments for a period of six years (Article 168a(3) EC Treaty). It has the same number of judges as the full Court, although this is not laid down in the Treaty itself. The qualifications required for judicial office with the CFI are roughly the same as those to which the judges of the full Court are subjected. Their membership is also partially renewed every three years (Article 168a(3) EC Treaty). The CFI was introduced in order to relieve the Court of Justice of some of the routine cases requiring adjudication by a Community court, thus releasing it for the more important decisions. Essentially, it deals with disputes between the Community institutions and its staff, competition cases, ECSC disputes, actions brought by individuals under Article 173(2) (action for annulment) and Article 175(3) (actions for failure to act), as well as anti-dumping and intellectual property rights cases brought by individuals. Its decisions are capable of appeal to the full Court, but only on points of law (Article 168a(1) EC Treaty).

---

11 Perhaps the best-known case in which this occurred was Case 26/62, *Van Gend en Loos v Nederlandse administratie der belastingen* (1963) ECR 1. Here, the Court conferred formulated the principle of direct effect against the express advice of the Advocate-General. See below, p85.

The President

In civil law systems, the president of a court has an extremely important function which goes well beyond the allocation of cases and a variety of administrative functions. It is normal for the President to have powers in his or her own right. This is particularly the case in relation to measures which require a good deal of urgency and for which there is no time to convene a court hearing.

This characteristic is fully reflected in the position of the President of the Court. Under Article 36 of the Statute of the Court, the President may hold summary proceedings which may differ from some of the normal rules applicable to the Court. In the course of such summary proceedings, he or she may adjudicate in applications to suspend enforcement or execution of a judgment, or to prescribe such interim measures as are allowed by the Statute.

Organisation and procedure

In principle, the Court sits in plenary session (Article 165, para 2, EC Treaty). This does not mean that for a decision to be valid, all judges must be in attendance; however, a quorum of seven judges applies. The Court may also form chambers of three or five judges (*ibid*), and it is a fact that in practice, most ECJ decisions are arrived at in chambers. However, for some types of proceeding (eg preliminary rulings) the Court must sit in plenary session. Decisions of the Court may only be said to have been validly adopted where an uneven number of judges are in attendance (Article 15 Statute of the Court). No judge or Advocate-General is allowed to take part in the adjudication of a case in which he or she had previously taken part as agent or adviser, or where he or she has acted for one of the parties. A similar estoppel arises where the that judge of Advocate-General has been required to pronounce judgment as a member of another court, tribunal, commission of enquiry, or some similar body (Article 16 Statute of the Court).

The procedure of the Court also bears all the hallmarks of civil law systems, in that there is an emphasis on the written part of the proceedings, and that the case may involve a preliminary investigation. It is described in Title III of the ECJ Statute in conjunction with Title II of the Court's Rules of Procedure, and involves four stages:

Written procedure

The case is set in motion by a written application addressed to the Registrar. It must contain various particulars, including the name and address of the applicant, the name of the defendant, the subject matter of the dispute, and the applicant's submissions. Where appropriate, it must be accompanied by documentary evidence which is specific to a particular action (eg the decision whose annulment is being sought under Article 173 EC Treaty). In the case of preliminary rulings, it is the referring court which makes the formal application. Within a month of the application having been served on him or her, the defendant must respond by providing certain particulars, including a statement of the arguments of fact and law on which he or she bases his or her defence. This may be the subject matter of a rejoinder by the applicant.

The President then fixes the date on which one of the judges involved, called the Judge-Rapporteur, will present a preliminary report to the Court. This report will contain a recommendation as to whether a preparatory investigation, or any other form of preparatory measure, must be taken before proceeding to the oral part. If no preliminary inquiry is deemed necessary, the President will fix a date for the oral hearing.

Preliminary inquiry

Cases in which the Judge-Rapporteur calls for a preliminary enquiry tend to be the exception rather than the norm. However, it is sometimes necessary to involve this stage, particularly in cases involving complex questions of a technical nature. The measures in question can take the form of a personal appearance by the parties, oral testimony, the commissioning of an expert report, etc. The Court may also decide to summon and examine witnesses and/or experts. The parties may respond by submitting written observations. The President then fixes a date for the oral hearing.

Oral procedure

The oral procedure commences with the reading of the report presented by the Judge-Rapporteur. The Court then hears Counsel for both parties, as well as any witnesses and/or experts. Finally the Opinion of the Advocate-General is read out.

The judgment

Following the conclusion of the oral proceedings, the judges retire to consider their verdict. They do so in secret, and therefore no-one is supposed to know in what language they deliberate. However, it has become a matter of common knowledge that French is used throughout. Consonant with Continental practice, the judgment is a highly formal affair, and must contain a number of particulars stated in Article 63 of the Rules of Procedure. Prominent amongst these are the grounds for the decision.

The Court decides as a collegiate body. This means that the decision is deemed to represent the collective will of all the judges taking part in the decision. There is therefore no scope here for a dissenting opinion in the common law tradition. The major advantage of this approach is that no judge can be accused of bias in favour of the nationality of any of the parties. Where a judgment is made in a preliminary ruling, the national court making the reference is bound by the Court's ruling. In all other cases, however, the rulings of the Court are not binding, either on the national courts or on the Court itself. Nevertheless, the Court has endeavoured to adhere to a consistent line in its decisions, thus giving rise to what is known as the 'established case law' of the Court.

Costs

The unsuccessful party is ordered to pay the costs of the proceedings. If there is more than one unsuccessful party, the Court decides how costs are to be shared. If each party succeeds on some points and fails on others, or in exceptional circumstances, the Court may order that the costs be shared or that the parties should bear their own costs (Article 69 Rules of Procedure).

Special review procedures

The judgment is not necessarily the last word in the case. If third parties feel that their rights have been prejudiced by a certain decision, they may challenge it on that basis (Article 97 Rules of Procedure). Second, if facts come to light which could materially affect the decision, the party affected may apply for revision of the Court's decision (Articles 98 and 99 Rules of Procedure).

Interpretation techniques

There are in principle several techniques open to the Court when interpreting provisions of Community law. The first is the literal interpretation technique, whereby the meaning of the text is derived from its wording rather than from its context. The Court has found this method to be of limited use, for two main reasons. First, provisions of Community legislation are equally authentic in all official Community languages, and differences between the various linguistic versions of an instrument obviously make it difficult for one uniform interpretation to emerge.[12] Second, Community legislation is very often framed in very broad terms, making it very difficult for the Court to gauge its intrinsic meaning. What, for example is the Court to make of the term 'worker' in Article 48 EC Treaty when applying the literal method?[13]

This is why in most cases the Court has applied a more context-based technique called the teleological method. Here, the Court attempts to establish what was the intention of the authority which issued the rule in question. This method was best expressed by the Court in the CILFIT decision,[14] where it explained that:

12   Case 29/69, *Stauder v Ulm* (1970) ECR 420, in which a difference had been noted between the German and Dutch versions of a provision.

13   Weatherill, S and Beaumont, P, *EC Law* (1994), Penguin, pp 143–44.

14   Case 283/81, *CILFIT v Italian Ministry of Health* (1982) ECR 3415.

every provision of Community law must be placed in its context and interpreted in the light of the provisions of Community law as a whole, regard being had to the objectives thereof and to its state of evolution at the date on which the provision in question is to be applied.

Functions and powers

The general role of the Court of Justice is to 'ensure that in the interpretation and application of this Treaty the law is observed'. The ECJ discharges this responsibility by means of the actions which can be brought before it. These are either direct actions, whereby an applicant brings an action to the Court on one of the grounds specified in the Treaty, or indirect actions, whereby a national court seeks from the ECJ a ruling on an issue of Community law which has arisen in a case brought before it. These are discussed in detail in the chapter dealing with judicial remedies (Chapter 6, below, p 105). The Court has certain other functions, such as acting as an appeal instance in relation to decisions made by the CFI.

Does the Court have a 'political' role?

This is an accusation which has frequently been flung at the Court, but which is hard to sustain in the light of the available evidence. Unfortunately, the Court has itself sometimes given ammunition to those who have sought to attack its role in this manner. It is certainly true that the Court has sometimes strayed from the path of judicial principle onto the uncertain wastelands of political expediency. Thus there was a suspicion in the *Van Duyn* case[15] that the Court had allowed itself to be influenced by the forthcoming referendum on British membership of the Community, and thus returned a verdict in favour of the British government in a manner which went against all its principles of interpretation. However, these are isolated events and in no way indicate a consistent departure from judicial orthodoxy for political expediency (below, p 300).

On the other hand, it must also be conceded that the Court has been responsible for developing new concepts and theories which have given a completely new dimension to Community law. The manner in which the Court developed the principle of direct effect is a case in point (below, p 83). However, in many cases the Court has no choice but to do this. Very often the provisions of Community law are very broad and, sometimes, rather vague, so that the Court is forced to avail itself of a certain degree of creativity in order to arrive at a decision. This is entirely consistent with Continental practice, and it is significant that hardly any accusation to this effect ever emanates from across the Channel.

---

15 Case 41/74, *Van Duyn v Home Office* (1974) ECR 1337.

VII The Economic and Social Committee (ESC)

Introduction

Immediately after the Second World War, a number of bodies were established which sought to secure the representation of the major social and economic groupings in society, such as trade unions and employers' organisations. This development was born from the conviction that parliamentary representation sometimes constituted an inadequate forum for the purpose of representing society in all its aspects. These bodies were not only established at the national level (which saw the establishment in France of the *Conseil économique et social*) but also saw the light of day in international organisations, as witness the Economic and Social Council of the UN.

When the Community was established, it was deemed desirable for its institutional structure to include an organ of this nature. Hence the setting up of the Economic and Social Committee, as governed by Articles 193–98 EC Treaty.[16] Since the European Parliament has now emancipated itself from its previously humble advisory status, the Economic and Social Committee can now be called the most important consultative organ of the Community. Its seat is in Brussels.

Composition and appointment

In principle, the Committee consists of representatives of the various categories of economic activity, in particular 'representatives of producers, farmers, carriers, workers, dealers, craftsmen, professional occupations and representatives of the general public' (Article 193 EC Treaty). This list has never been regarded as exhaustive, and even if it were, it would still have been sufficiently flexible to allow for new categories of representation to be included, such as consumers' organisations and environmental pressure groups. In practice, the ESC now has a tripartite structure, consisting of employers' organisations, trade unions and 'other interests'. This corresponds to the notion of 'social partnership' which has become one of the key concepts to govern EU attitudes towards social policy.

The ESC currently has 222 members, divided amongst the Member States in accordance with the formula stated in Article 194, para 1, EC Treaty. Given that Luxembourg has six members and Germany 24, there is but the most tenuous relationship between size of population and ESC membership. They are appointed by the Council, acting unanimously, for a term of office of four years

---

16   The Economic and Social Committee is sometimes referred to by the acronym ECOSOC. Strictly speaking this is unwarranted as the UN Economic and Social Committee had already appropriated this name. However, its use in this manner has become too widespread to be at all reversible.

(Article 194, para 2, EC Treaty). The members receive no remuneration for the performance of their duties; however, they are in receipt of an allowance covering travel and accommodation (Article 194, para 4, EC Treaty).

Functions

The Economic and Social Committee must be consulted on measures to be adopted whenever the Treaty expressly so provides. Examples of this compulsory consultation are Article 43 (measures establishing and implementing the Common Agricultural Policy), Article 49 (directives aimed at securing the free movement of workers), Article 54 (measures relating to the freedom of establishment), Article 75 (common transport policy measures), etc. The Amsterdam Treaty has also made consultation of the ESC compulsory in such areas as employment, social matters and public health. In addition, the ESC may be consulted by the other institutions whenever it is deemed appropriate to do so, even where there is no Treaty obligation to that effect. The Amsterdam Treaty has officially confirmed the right of the European Parliament to consult the ESC.

The members of the ESC represent their economic and social interest group rather than their countries. They may not be bound by any mandatory instruction. Accordingly they must act in complete independence in the performance of their duties, in the general interest of the Community (Article 194, para 3, EC Treaty).

VIII The committee of the regions

This is a body set up under the TEU, and which is similar in structure and purpose to the ESC. It has to be consulted by the Council or Commission whenever the Treaty so provides, and in cases where either of these institutions considers it to be appropriate (Article 198c EC Treaty). With the adoption of the Amsterdam Treaty, the European Parliament has also acquired the right to consult the Committee.

IX   The Court of Auditors

General

The Court of Auditors was established in 1977, when it was decided that the finances of the Community needed to be monitored and supervised by a specialist court. Its status was raised to that of an institution of equal rank with the others when it was incorporated into the EC Treaty by the TEU.

Composition and appointment

The Court consists of 15 members (Article 188b(1) EC Treaty). The latter must have belonged to external audit bodies at the national level, or must have other qualifications which make them suitable for such office (Article 188b(2) EC Treaty). They are appointed for a period of six years by the Council after having consulted the European Parliament (Article 188b(3) EC Treaty). There members of the Court are subject to a number of restrictions aimed at guaranteeing their independence. Thus they are prohibited from taking any instructions from any government or other body, and must refrain from any action which may be inconsistent with the performance of their tasks (Article 188b(4) EC Treaty). Nor may they engage in any other occupation, whether paid or unpaid (Article 188b(5) EC Treaty).

Powers and functions

The Court is required to examine all revenue and expenditure accounts of the Community and of all bodies set up by the Community. It must provide the European Parliament and the Council with a statement giving assurance of the reliability of the accounts and the legality and regularity of the underlying transactions (Article 188c(1) EC Treaty, as amended by the Amsterdam Treaty). In addition, the Court must verify whether all revenue has been received and all expenditure incurred in a lawful and regular manner, and whether the financial management has been sound. In doing so, it must report in particular any cases of irregularity (Article 188c(2) EC Treaty as amended by the Amsterdam Treaty).

After the close of the financial year, the Court must draw up an annual report which is sent to the other Community institutions and published in the Official Journal together with the comments of these institutions. It may also at all times submit observations on special issues and deliver opinions at the request of a Community institution (Article 188c(4) EC Treaty).

X   European Investment Bank

The Community does not restrict its activity to the issuing of rules. It also provides a wide range of funds in support of those objectives which are considered worthy of financial assistance within the framework of Community policy. This is done mainly through the so-called 'structural funds', such as the European Social Fund (ESF) and the European Agricultural Guidance and Guarantee Fund (EAGGF). However, it was also considered appropriate to establish a financial institution which could provide loans on easy repayment terms for projects which contribute towards the development of the Community. This institution is called the European Investment Bank (EIB).

The EIB has its own legal personality. Its members are the Community Member States (Article 198d EC Treaty). Its task is to contribute to the 'steady and balanced development of the common market in the interest of the Community', and for this purpose it uses both the capital markets to which it has access and its own resources (Article 198c EC Treaty). The following projects are eligible for loans and guarantees from the EIB:

- projects for the development of less-developed regions;

- projects aimed at modernising or converting businesses or for developing fresh activities required for the progressive establishment of the common market;

- projects of common interest to several Member States which are of a size or nature which would make it impossible for them to be financed by the means available to Member States (Article 198e EC Treaty).

XI   Conclusion

It has become a cliché to maintain that the Community institutions are currently in a fluid state, but even the most hackneyed expressions contain an element of truth. The one thing that characterises the current institutional structure of the EU is the uncertainty of its future development.

The Council remains the most powerful body within the Community, yet it has to contend with greater involvement on the part of the European Parliament than before. The Commission remains very firmly the Community Executive, yet there are question marks over its future role, particularly if the European Parliament assumes greater legislative powers. Will it become closely integrated with the Parliament, as is the case with executives at the national level in many states? Or will be succeed in maintaining its independence and its position of 'guardian of the Treaty' in such circumstances?

All this assumes that the European Parliament will actually increase its involvement in the legislative process. Yet this cannot be taken for granted. The Parliament remains a body which is remote from the everyday experience of the

Community citizen, as can be seen from the low electoral turn-out in those countries where voting is not compulsory. Also, such voters as make an effort to participate in the European elections very often express their sovereign will on the basis of domestic, rather than European, issues.

Finally, the Court. It has the express brief of ensuring uniformity of application and interpretation of Community law, yet cannot compel the national courts to follow its rulings. Accusations of judicial policy based on political rather than judicial considerations, however unjustified, may prompt a reassessment of its role as guardian of Community law. Quite apart from the above considerations, it is clear that any significant geographical extension of the Community will involve reforming an institutional set-up which has essentially remained the same as that which applied when the Community was but six nations strong. This is why Article 2 of the Enlargement Protocol attached to the Amsterdam Treaty has pledged that, at least one year before the membership of the EU reaches 20, a conference will be organised in order to carry out a comprehensive review of the composition and functioning of the institutions. Exactly which institutions will gain or lose from this process is as yet unclear.

3 The Community Decision-Making Process

I Introduction

The most charitable qualification of the Community's decision-making procedures is that they are 'byzantine'. Less kind are those who state that the Ancient Britons had a clearer system of rule-making, or who simply refer to Dante's Inferno – more particularly the passage which cries out *Lasciate ogni speranza voi ch'entrate* ('Abandon all hope all ye who enter this place').

Even before the TEU, the decision-making procedures of the Community tested the memory of all but the most diligent of swots. Post-Maastricht, however, even the most diligent scholar is tempted to throw up his or her hands in undisguised horror. Attempts to involve the European Parliament more deeply in the rule-making process have produced a somewhat cumbersome legislative machinery which is almost unwieldy in its complexity. In this chapter, an attempt is made at shedding some light on this procedural maze. It is intended to proceed from the general to the particular. This means commencing with the policy-making stage, and ending with the enactment of delegated legislation. The bulk of its contents, however, will be taken up by the various legislative procedures, more particularly those which dominate present-day Community legislation, to wit the co-operation and co-decision procedures. In addition, some space will be devoted to the budgetary procedure, which is also highly complex and technical.

One aspect of the decision-making process which is not dealt with in this chapter is the judicial supervision of Community legislation. In order to ensure that the Community institutions do not exceed their constitutional brief when exercising their legislative powers, the Treaties have laid down a number of safeguards in the shape of judicial review by the Court of Justice. This aspect will be dealt with in the chapter relating to judicial remedies (below, p 105).

II Policy-making

Policy-making and the treaties

The framework for Community policy is formed by the founding treaties. In this connection, a sharp distinction needs to be drawn between the EC Treaty on the one hand, and the ECSC and Euratom Treaties on the other hand. The latter are definitely law-making treaties (*traité-loi*), in which the policy lines are set out in considerable detail, leaving the Community institutions relatively little scope for discretion in their implementation. The EC Treaty, on the other hand, is a framework treaty (*traité-cadre*) which in most cases contains but the broadest outline of the policies to be enacted and implemented. The formulation of policy in this case will entail making hard choices between various policy options, which require careful thought and thorough preparation. Thus when it came to elaborating the Common Agricultural Policy on the basis of Article 43 EC Treaty, the policy-makers had several options at their disposal. They could have arrived at a completely different system of agricultural subvention, eg income support rather than price support, whilst remaining fully and legitimately within the scope of Article 43.

In fact, the only limitation imposed upon the policy-making Community authorities is that the resulting legislation be based on an Article of the Treaty. Even this requirement, however, can be circumvented in view of the 'catch-all' clauses of the EC Treaty: Articles 235, 100, 100a, and 220.

Article 235

This provision was inserted as a safeguard against a situation whereby legislation was necessary in order to attain one of the objectives of the Community, and the Treaty had failed to provide the necessary powers to do so. In such cases, the Council is empowered to take the appropriate measures on a proposal by the Commission, after due consultation of the European Parliament. This provision has proved an extremely flexible way of updating the scope of Community policy without requiring a Treaty revision. Thus when the Community leaders decided at the 1972 Paris summit to include environmental protection within the scope of Community action, Article 235 proved a suitable vehicle and legal basis for such an extension of Community policy.

The use of Article 235 as a legal basis for Community legislation is, however, subject to the supervision of the Court. On a number of occasions the latter has struck down legislation which in its view had wrongly taken Article 235 as its legal base. Thus in *Commission v Council*,[1] the Court held that:

It follows from the very wording of Article 235 that its use as the legal basis for a measure is justified only where no other provision of the Treaty gives the Community institutions the necessary powers to adopt the measure in question.

In this particular case, it held that the measure challenged was capable of being adopted under Article 113 EC Treaty, and that the use of Article 235 was unjustified. The measure in question was therefore held to be void.

---

1   Case 45/86 (1987) ECR 1493.

Articles 100 and 100a

Article 100 is an important source of general policy-making in that it requires the Council to issue directives for the approximation of such national laws, regulations and administrative rules as directly affect the establishment or functioning of the common market. It has proved an extremely useful vehicle for harmonising legislation where no specific basis for such harmonisation exists in the Treaty. Article 100 EC Treaty is, however, more restricted in scope than Article 235, in that it restricts the scope of the measures to be adopted to directives.[2] As a result, directives have become the classic instrument of harmonisation. Since directives are less immediately binding on the Member States' authorities than regulations, harmonisation has been largely an indirect mechanism, involving as it does the national authorities in the rule-making process. The implications of this factor will be examined more closely in Chapter 4 (below, p 61).

Article 100a has a somewhat more restricted focus. It was introduced by the SEA and was aimed at assisting the process of enacting all the legislation necessary to complete the achievement of the internal market. It requires the Council to issue harmonising legislation which has as its purpose the establishment and functioning of the internal market (Article 100a(1) EC Treaty). However general in scope Article 100a may appear, it does exclude certain areas. Fiscal measures, legislation on the free movement of persons and social legislation are excluded from its ambit (Article 100a(2) EC Treaty). On the other hand, as regards legislation on health, safety, environmental standards and consumer protection, the legislation in question must seek to attain high levels of protection (Article 100a(3) EC Treaty).

Article 220

This is a provision frequently neglected by the leading authors, but which has in its own way proved a significant source of policy. It concerns a number of issues for which approximation of legislation amongst the Member States is considered to be desirable, but in which such harmonisation is best achieved by means of international conventions rather than Community legislation. These areas include:

- the protection of persons and the enjoyment and protection of rights under the same conditions as those granted by each state to its own citizens;

- the elimination of double taxation within the EU;

---

2   Directives, as will be explained more fully on p 66, are Community instruments which are binding only as to the object to be achieved and leave the Member States some discretion in their incorporation into national law.

- the mutual recognition of businesses, the retention of their legal personality if they move from one Member State to another, and the possibility of mergers between businesses governed by the laws of different countries;

- the simplification of formalities governing the mutual recognition and enforcement of court judgments.

Although some have expressed regret at the fact that these areas thus elude the scope of Community legislation, it is a fact that the format of international conventions have made possible agreement and approximation which would have been practically impossible to achieve through ordinary Community legislation. It is this provision, for example which made possible the extremely important convention on the mutual recognition of national court judgments of 27 April 1968.

The policy-making process

It is mainly the Commission which is cast in the role of initiator of Community policy. It is true that the Council may, under Article 152 EC Treaty, request the Commission to undertake any studies which it considers desirable for the achievement of the common objectives, and to submit to it any appropriate proposals. However, it will be the Commission which will bear the responsibility for any policy which emerges from this process. When making policy proposals, the watchword invariably observed by the Commission is 'consultation'. The Commission will first enter into discussions with those likely to be affected by the proposals, at the political, trade union or civil service level. It will then proceed to give detailed consideration to the policy proposals with the assistance of its specialist divisions, in particular the Legal Service. This enables it to reach its final position which is then transmitted to the Council. Once the principal outlines of the policy have been agreed, the Commission will consider the practical details of implementing these proposals. Meetings are organised with experts from the national civil services in order to consider the practical implications of the proposals. These experts will be fully aware of the wishes of their governments and will therefore be in a good position to inform the Commission whether or not these proposals will be acceptable at the national level. This then will be the basis for the legislation implementing the policy proposals.[3]

Once the policy has been agreed, work can commence on its implementation. Rarely is a policy proposal translated into just one legislative instrument. Very often a considerable amount of legislation will flow from it. This requires co-ordinated action as well as timetables for their realisation. Sometimes a White Paper is published which sets out the proposed programme of legislation, but which still requires formal endorsement. The most famous example of this was

3   Lasok, D, *Lasok & Bridge – Law and Institutions of the European Union* (6th edn, 1994), Butterworth, p 190.

the Cockfield White Paper on the Single Market. Its conclusions were endorsed by the meeting of Heads and Governments in 1985, and incorporated into the SEA 1986. For policies which have already been endorsed, a general legislative programme may be adopted. This was the case with the 1969 General Programme on the removal of technical obstacles to trade, and with the 1961 programme on the abolition of restrictions on the freedom to provide services.

III Adopting legislation

Division of work

Only very rarely is the adoption of Community legislation the task of one sole institution. Thus the Commission sometimes has legislative powers in its own right (above, p 24). However, in the overwhelming majority of cases, Community legislation is the result of interaction and dialogue between two or more institutions. The following division of labour will then apply:[4]

- The Commission has the right of legislative initiative, and will propose the legislation;

- The Council is the organ having the ultimate decision-making power, except in those cases where its will can be frustrated by the European Parliament (below, p 53);

- The European Parliament has a role which varies according to the legislative procedure adopted, and which can range from mere consultation to a right of veto;

- Other organs such as the ESC and the Committee of the Regions may have a consultative function.

This division of work is reflected in the various legislative procedures. The latter have increased considerably, both in number and in complexity, during the past decade. In the present state of Community law, it is necessary to distinguish between (a) the traditional procedure, (b) the consultation procedure, (c) the conciliation procedure, (d) the co-operation procedure, (e) the co-decision procedure, and (f) the assent procedure. These, as well as the procedure involving the Commission acting alone, are examined in turn below. At this stage, it is necessary to point to a formal requirement which applies regardless of the procedure used. Under Article 190 EC Treaty, all Community legislation must state the reasons on which it is based, and must refer to any proposals or opinions which are obligatory under the Treaty. Here again, the stamp of the civil law is in evidence. In the countries which apply this system, the duty to give reason for any decision – be it legislative, administrative or judicial – is woven deeply into the fabric of the law and of the fundamental principles underlying it.

---

4   Serie Manuali Giuridici, *Diritto delle Comunità europee* (1995), pp 159–60.

The traditional procedure

As its name indicates, this was the procedure originally used for virtually all Community legislation prior to the changes wrought by the SEA and the TEU. Although its scope has been considerably reduced by these changes, there remain a number of areas in which it continues to apply, such as the movement of capital to or from third countries (Article 73c EC Treaty), minimum import prices under the CAP (Article 44(6) EC Treaty) and the autonomous alterations or suspensions of duties charged under the common customs tariff (Article 28 EC Treaty). The traditional procedure involves the Council and the Commission acting alone, without needing to consult the European Parliament or any of the other institutions. This does not mean, however, that these institutions could not be consulted if the Commission or Council saw fit to do so.

Under the traditional procedure, it is the Commission which takes the initiative and the Council which takes the ultimate measure. For ease of reference, this process is often known by the formula 'the Commission proposes, the Council disposes'. However, the European Parliament can also play its part in taking the legislative initiative. Under Article 138b EC Treaty, which was inserted by the TEU, the Parliament may request the Commission to make any suitable proposals on issues on which it considers that a Community act is required in order to implement the Treaty. For this purpose, the Parliament must act by a majority of its members. It must also be pointed out that, in the course of time, the 'purity' of the Council-Commission dialogue under the traditional procedure has been diluted by the intervention of other bodies and considerations. As has been noted earlier, COREPER now plays an important part in mediating between these two bodies. In addition, the Commission is restricted to a certain extent by the guidelines of the European Council on the measures which are to be adopted. The freedom of these bodies is also limited by financial considerations, since under Article 201a EC Treaty the Commission must give an assurance that this proposal is capable of being financed within the limits of the Community's own resources.[5]

It is under this procedure that the Council's legislative power is at its highest point. This does not mean, however, that once a proposal from the Commission is placed before it, the Council has unfettered discretion in taking the resulting decision. Under Article 189a(1) EC Treaty, any act constituting an amendment to that proposal requires unanimity within the Council. Whilst the proposal is being considered by the Council, the Commission may also at all times alter the terms of its proposal (Article 189a(2) EC Treaty). This gives expression to the role as honest broker which the Commission is required to play at Council meetings, and gives it the necessary flexibility to act in order to salvage that which can be salvaged from a proposal rather than see it abandoned or voted down altogether.

5   Serie Manuale Giuridiche, *op cit*, p 161.

The consultation procedure

Here, the Council is still the sovereign decision-making power, but can only adopt (or fail to adopt) the proposed act after having consulted the European Parliament. The scope of this procedure has also been reduced by the SEA, the TEU and the Amsterdam Treaty, but remains applicable to some important areas of Community policy, including European citizenship (Article 8e EC Treaty), industrial policy (Article 130 EC Treaty), the right of establishment (Article 54(1) EC Treaty), etc. The cynical mind might be disposed to make light of this consultation, since there is no obligation on the part of the Council to follow any advice proffered. Yet there are certain safeguards built into the system which protect this consultation exercise against tokenism. First, as has been mentioned earlier, consultation of the Parliament is a formal requirement which, if infringed, will lead to the annulment of the resulting act.[6] Second, it is not sufficient for the Council to have invited the opinion of the Parliament; that opinion must also have been issued. Third, the opinion given by the Parliament must substantially reflect the act subsequently adopted. Therefore the Parliament must be reconsulted if major changes are made to the proposal between the time when the Parliament's opinion is issued and that at which the Council is about to adopt the act.[7]

The conciliation procedure

This is a little-used procedure, introduced as a result of the Joint Declaration of the Commission, the Council and the Parliament of 4 March 1975.[8] It is a variant on the consultation procedure, and can only be used where (a) the legislative measure is of general application, (b) it has considerable financial implications, and (c) it comes within the scope of non-compulsory Community expenditure. As Beaumont and Weatherill point out,[9] this procedure is rather ineffective because Parliament is in an extremely weak bargaining position, which accounts for its scant use.

The co-operation procedure

This procedure was introduced by the SEA, and for the first time gave the Parliament a major influence in the decision-making process. When first introduced, it was intended as a means of processing legislation on the internal market in accordance with a reasonably strict timetable, thus enabling the 1992 deadline to be achieved more easily. The adoption of the TEU, however, completely changed the focus of the co-operation procedure. Most of the areas

6   Case 138/79, *op cit*, at 3361.
7   Case C-65/90, *European Parliament v Council* (1992) ECR I-4593.
8   OJ 1975 C 89.
9   Weatherill, S and Beaumont, P, *EC Law* (1993), Penguin, p 124.

hitherto covered by the co-operation procedure were subjected to a new legislative machinery, known as the co-decision procedure (Article 189b EC Treaty – below, p 53). The areas to which the co-operation procedure continued to apply were supplemented by a number of measures which previously had only required the consultation procedure. In addition, the co-operation procedure was moved from Article 149(2) to Article 189c EC Treaty.

As a result, it can be maintained that the TEU has somewhat devalued the co-operation procedure. The Amsterdam Treaty has reduced its scope even further by upgrading some of the main areas to which it applied under the TEU to the co-decision procedure. The co-operation procedure is somewhat complex, and takes place over the following stages:

(a) The Commission puts forward its proposal.

(b) The European Parliament issues its opinion. This is the so-called 'first reading'.

(c) The Council adopts a common position, acting by a qualified majority.

(d) The common position is communicated to the Parliament. At the same time, the Council and Commission inform the Parliament (i) of the full reasons which prompted the Council to adopt this common position, and (ii) of the Commission's position.

(e) The communication of this common position triggers off a three-month period. During this period, the following possibilities arise:

• The Parliament approves the common position or fails to take a decision: the Council adopts the act in accordance with the common position.

• The Parliament proposes, by an absolute majority, one or more amendments to the common position.

• The Parliament rejects the common position by the same majority.

(f) The outcome of these proceedings is communicated to the Council. If the Parliament has rejected the common position, unanimity is required for the Council to act on a second reading. If amendments have been proposed, the Commission has one month in which to re-examine the proposal on the basis of which the Council adopted its common position. In so doing, the Commission must take account of the amendments proposed by the Parliament.

(g) The Commission communicates to the Council both the re-examined proposal and such amendments put forward by the Parliament as it has not accepted, on which it must express an opinion. The Council may adopt these amendments unanimously.

(h) The Council adopts the proposal as re-examined by the Commission. It does so by a qualified majority, but unanimity is required for the Council to amend the proposal as re-examined by the Commission.

(j) If the Parliament has proposed amendments to the common position or rejected it, the Council is required to act within a period of three months. If no decision is taken within that period, the Commission proposal is deemed not to have been adopted.

As has been mentioned before, the deadlines in question are all quite strict. However, the three month periods referred to above are capable of being extended by a maximum of one month, if both the Council and the Parliament agree to such an extension. By being in a position to reject the Council's common position, the decision-making influence of the Parliament has been considerably enhanced. However, experience thus far shows that the Parliament has not abused this power, and has only rejected the common position on a limited number of occasions. What it has done, however, is to table a large number of amendments, both at the first reading and at the second reading stage.[10]

The co-decision (or conciliation and veto) procedure

This was a completely new procedure which was introduced by the TEU, and inserted in the EC Treaty under Article 189b. As has been mentioned before, it covers most of the areas originally covered by the co-operation procedure. The measures adopted under Article 100a (harmonisation assisting the completion of internal market), Article 57 (mutual recognition of diplomas), Article 54(2) (measures implementing the general programme aimed at achieving freedom of establishment), and the free movement of workers (Article 49). However, it also includes such matters as cultural policy (Article 128), health policy (Article 129) and research and technical development (Article 130i).

The Amsterdam Treaty has increased the scope of this procedure even further, by making it applicable to:

(a) certain new Treaty provisions as inserted by the Amsterdam Treaty, such as Article 5 of the new Title on Employment (incentive measures), Article 119 (Social Policy – Equal Opportunities and Treatment), Article 191a (General Principles of Transparency), and Article 209a (countering fraud affecting the financial interests of the Community);

(b) areas which previously were subject to the co-operation procedure, such as the prohibition of discrimination on grounds of nationality (Article 6), vocational training (Article 127(4)), ERDF implementation measures (Article 130e), the environment (Article 130s(1)), and development co-operation; and

(c) areas such as social security rules for Community immigrant workers (Article 51) and the co-ordination of rules on the taking up and pursuit of activities as self-employed persons (Article 57(2)), which were previously covered by the consultation procedure. (All articles referred to are those of the EC Treaty.)

10   Craig, P and de Burca, G, *EC Law – Text, Cases & Materials* (1996), Clarendon Press, pp 123–24.

The co-decision procedure enhances the legislative power of the Parliament even further than the co-operation procedure. The main difference between these two mechanisms is that the co-decision procedure enables the Parliament, acting by an absolute majority, to veto a measure at the final stage if agreement cannot be reached with the Council through the involvement of the Conciliation Committee. This is a body consisting of an equal number of representatives of the Parliament and the Council. The procedure is conducted over three broad stages, as recently amended and simplified by the Amsterdam Treaty:

First stage

The first stages are similar to those encountered under the co-operation procedure. The Commission submits its proposal to both the European Parliament and the Council. The Council, acting by a qualified majority after obtaining the opinion of the European Parliament, may do one of three things. If it approves all the amendments contained in the opinion of the Parliament, it may adopt the proposed act thus unamended. Where the Parliament has failed to propose any amendments, the Council may adopt the proposed instrument. If none of the above options are chosen, it shall adopt a common position which is then communicated to the Parliament. At the same time, the Council informs the Parliament of the reasons which led it to adopt its common position, and the Commission also informs the Parliament fully of its position.

Second stage

Once again, the communication of the common position triggers off a three-month period. During this period, a number of possibilities arise:

* The Parliament approves the common position. In this case, the Council definitively adopts intended act in accordance with the common position.

* The Parliament takes no decision. If that is the case, the Council adopts the act in question in accordance with its common position.

* The Parliament rejects the common position by an absolute majority of its component members. In that case, the proposed act is deemed not to have been adopted.

* The Parliament proposes amendments to the common position. The amended text is then forwarded to the Council and the Commission, which delivers an opinion on these amendments.

If, within three months of the matter having been referred to it, the Council approves all the amendments of the Parliament, the act in question is deemed to have been adopted in the form of the common position thus amended. If the Council does not approve all the amendments, the Council President and the president of the Parliament must call a meeting of the Conciliation Committee, and the second reading is set in motion.

Third stage

The Conciliation Committee is involved at this stage because its task is to reach agreement on a joint text. The Commission takes part in the Committee's proceedings, acting once again in its 'honest broker' capacity. If a joint text is agreed within a period of six weeks, the Parliament and the Council have a further six weeks in which to adopt the act in question in accordance with the joint text. If either institution fails to do so, the act is deemed not to have been adopted. If the Conciliation Committee fails to approve a joint text, the proposed act is deemed not to have been adopted. Here again, the three month and six week periods referred to above may be extended by a maximum of one month and two weeks respectively by joint agreement between the Parliament and the Council.

Assent procedure

This mechanism was introduced by the SEA (Articles 8 and 9). Although narrow in terms of the areas affected by it, this procedure is perhaps the one which gives the European Parliament the most powerful say in decision-making, as it gives the latter infinite powers of delay and total power of rejection.[11] Under the SEA, the assent procedure was introduced into Articles 237 and 238 EC Treaty. The TEU and the Amsterdam Treaty, however, both changed and widened the scope of this procedure to cover such matters as the penalties to be applied in the event of a serious and persistent breach of fundamental rights by a Member State (Article Fa TEU), the procedure for the accession of new Member States (Article O TEU), the functioning of the structural funds (Article 130d(1)), the establishment of a Cohesion Fund (Article 130d(2), the procedure for direct election to the European Parliament (Article 138(3)), and certain international agreements (Article 228(3)) (all Articles referred to are in the EC Treaty).

The Commission acting as sole legislature

It has already been noted that the Commission is given certain powers under the EC Treaty to act as a legislature in its own right, as is the case, for example, under Article 90(3) in relation to the position of public enterprises in EU competition policy. Neither the Treaty nor any other Community legislation lays down any procedures to be followed by the Commission in such cases. However, there is plenty of evidence to show that here too, the Commission consults as widely as possible before enacting the relevant rules. This has not prevented certain Member States from challenging the validity of such rules.[12]

11 Westlake, M, *The Commission and the Parliament: Partners and Rivals in the European Policy-making Process* (1994), Penter Publishers, p 95.

12 Craig, P and de Burca, G, *op cit*, p 121.

IV   The Community budget

From national contributions to 'own[13] resources

Originally, the Community's activity was financed solely by the contributions emanating from the Member States. However, Article 201 EC Treaty held out the prospect of having the Community operate on the basis of resources levied by the organisation itself. The Council decision of 21 April 1970[14] made provision for the gradual replacement of national contributions by the Community's own resources. These break down into five categories:

- agricultural levies imposed on food products imported from outside the Community;

- sugar and glucose levies;

- customs duties charged under the Common Customs Tariff;

- at least 1 per cent of VAT receipts levied by the Member States;

- the revenue from any other levy charged under a common policy laid down by the Treaties.

The implementation of this system took longer than originally anticipated, and it was not until the 1980 budget that the 'own resources' system became fully operational.

Budgetary principles

The Community budget makes provision for all income and expenditure of the Community as a legal personality, including the Social Fund. It also includes any administrative expenditure incurred by the institutions as a result of the common foreign and security policy, and of co-operation in justice and home affairs, as laid down in the TEU (Article 199 EC Treaty). In order to ensure that those initiating Community legislation at all times remain mindful of the financial constraints within which the EU must operate, the TEU introduced the principle of 'budgetary discipline' (Article 201a EC Treaty). This entails that the Commission may not propose or alter any proposal, or take any implementing measure, which will have serious implications for the budget unless it can give an assurance that the proposal or measure in question is capable of falling within the limits of the Community's own resources. The seriousness of intent with which the Community institutions approach this principle was clearly shown in the agreement concluded by the Parliament, the Council and the

---

13   The inverted commas are used here because the expression 'the own resources of the Community' represents one of the many assaults of Community parlance on the English language.

14   OJ Special Edition 1970, L 94.

Commission in 1993 to prevent Community expenditure from exceeding certain limits.[15]

The Community budget is also subject to the 'annuality' principle. It applies for the forthcoming year, and the expenditure included in the budget is authorised for one financial year (Article 202 EC Treaty). The financial year runs from 1 January to 31 December (Article 203(1) EC Treaty). This principle is not universally greeted as a virtue, since every year, the Budget could founder on the objections raised by one of the budgetary authorities, mainly the European Parliament. If such objections result in the Budget being rejected, as has happened on a number of occasions, the Community, whilst not being reduced to bankruptcy, nevertheless is forced to operate under severe constraints.

Compulsory and non-compulsory expenditure

This is a distinction which is not contained in the Treaty as such, but resulted from a Joint Declaration by the Commission, Parliament and Council dated 30 June 1982. Compulsory expenditure was defined as that which the Community was obliged to enter in the budget in order to be able to meet its internal obligations under the Treaty and the legislation made under it. As Bainbridge and Teasdale point out,[16] this distinction between compulsory and non-compulsory expenditure is essentially a political one, since it concerns the power relationship between the Council and the Parliament, and the question as to which of these two bodies has the last word on the major items of the Budget. The Common Agricultural Policy is by far the most important item of compulsory expenditure.

Budgetary procedure

The procedure for the adoption of the Community budget is somewhat cumbersome, but a model of clarity compared to some of the legislative procedures described earlier. It is described in Article 203 EC Treaty, and is essentially divided into four main stages.

Drawing up the draft budget – first Council reading

Before 1 July, all the Community institutions draw up estimates of their expenditure. The Commission then consolidates these estimates into a preliminary draft budget, which must contain an estimate of revenue and an estimate of expenditure. This preliminary draft budget is then placed before the Council before 1 September. If the latter intends to depart from the preliminary draft, it must consult the Commission and, where appropriate, the institutions

---

15 OJ 1993 C 331.
16 *Op cit*, p 74.

concerned. The Council then adopts the draft budget by qualified majority voting, and submits it to the Parliament, by 5 October at the latest.

First reading by Parliament

During its scrutiny of the draft budget, the Parliament's scope of action varies according to whether it is dealing with the compulsory or with the non-compulsory expenditure. As to the former, it only has the right to propose modifications. As regards the non-compulsory expenditure, it may adopt amendments, but only within a maximum rate of increase which must be notified to it by the Commission. If the Parliament approves the draft budget, or fails to amend or suggest modifications to it, within a period of 45 days, the Budget is deemed to have been finally adopted. However, if, as is mostly the case, the Parliament does suggest these changes, the draft budget, together with the amendments and proposed modification, returns to the Council for its second reading.

Second reading by the Council

The Council must first discuss the draft budget with the Commission or any other institution which may be involved. It may then modify any of the Parliament's amendments to the non-compulsory expenditure. As regards the proposed modifications to that part of the Budget which concerns compulsory expenditure, a distinction needs to be drawn between those which have the effect of increasing the total amount of the expenditure of an institution, and those which have the opposite effect. In the former case, the proposed modification is deemed to have been rejected unless the Council expressly accepts it; in the latter case the proposed modification is deemed to have been accepted unless expressly rejected by the Council. The draft budget is then changed on the basis of the proposed modifications accepted by the Council. If the Council has failed to modify any of the Parliament's amendments and has accepted the latter's modifications within a period of 15 days, the budget is deemed to have been finally adopted. If not, the draft returns to the Parliament for its second reading.

Second reading by the Parliament

Within 15 days of the draft budget having been placed before it, the Parliament may amend or reject the modifications to its amendments made by the Council, and will adopt the Budget accordingly. If the Parliament fails to act within this period, the Budget is deemed to have been adopted. However, the Parliament may also reject the draft Budget and request a new draft.

How has the Parliament used these powers?

Given that the Budget is one of the few areas in which the Parliament, until relatively recently, could really flex its muscles, it should come as no surprise to learn that it has used its power to reject the budget on several occasions (1979 and 1984). However, from time to time the Parliament has been compelled to face up to the limitations of these powers. The sharpest reminder came in 1986, when the Court ruled that, in exercising these powers, the Parliament must operate in partnership with the Council and adhere to the terms laid down in the EC Treaty.[17] This followed the procedure for the 1986 Budget, in which the Parliament had refused to comply with the limits placed on the non-compulsory expenditure. The Council took the Parliament to the ECJ over this issue, and won. However, the Budget in question did to a large extent take into account the Parliament's wishes for more non-compulsory expenditure.

Ever since, relationships between the Parliament and the Council have improved considerably on this issue, which is the main reason why the Budget has not been dismissed in recent years. One of the events which has consolidated this sense of partnership has been the Inter-Institutional Agreement between the Council and the Parliament in 1993,[18] which established a conciliation procedure for compulsory expenditure. This has served to secure some influence for the Parliament over an item of expenditure for which the Council is ultimately responsible.[19]

Consequences of rejection of draft budget

Once the Parliament decides to reject the draft budget, the financial situation of the Community institutions becomes quite parlous. By the time a new draft budget will have been submitted, the new financial year will have commenced; yet somehow the EU machinery has to keep going. This it does by applying Article 204 EC Treaty. Under this provision, where the budget has not been voted by the beginning of the financial year, an amount not exceeding one-twelfth of the budget may be spent in respect of any Budget heading. As a result, the Community institutions have to operate on the basis of financing which has failed to take inflation into account. True, Article 204 EC Treaty does enable the Council to increase the expenditure in question to an amount exceeding this one-twelfth. However, the Parliament may once again throw a spanner in the works by adopting a different decision on that part of the expenditure in question which exceeds one-twelfth.

---

17 Case 34/86, *Council v European Parliament* (1986) ECR 2155.
18 OJ 1993 C 331.
19 Lasok, D, *op cit*, p 227.

Implementing the budget

In its capacity of Community Executive, the Commission implements the Budget (Article 205 EC Treaty). It must do so in accordance with the Financial Regulations. These are rules adopted by the Council laying down the procedure to be adopted for establishing and implementing the budget, and for presenting and auditing accounts (Article 209 EC Treaty). The Commission must implement the budget on its own responsibility and remain within the limits of the relevant appropriations. Rather pointlessly, the TEU also inserted into Article 205 EC Treaty the requirement that in discharging this duty, the Commission should 'have regard to the principles of sound management'.

For the implementation of the budget the Commission is accountable to the Parliament, acting on a recommendation of the Council acting by a qualified majority (Article 206(1) EC Treaty as amended by the Amsterdam Treaty). To this end, the Council and the Parliament examine in turn the accounts and the financial statement which must be submitted annually by the Commission (Article 205a EC Treaty), as well as, *inter alia*, the annual report by the Court of Auditors and the replies of the institutions under audit to the observations made by the Court of Auditors.

V   Conclusion

The easiest of criticisms to make of the Community decision-making procedures as outlined above relates to their complexity. It is true that to remember all the details of even one of the procedures introduced by the SEA and TEU challenges the memory of even the most enthusiastic 'crammer'. Such criticisms should, however, be tempered by two considerations. The first is that the 'new' procedures have been accompanied by stringent time limits, which has increased the legal certainty attaching to the decision-making process. The second is that the complexities involved have been inspired mainly by the desire to involve as much as possible in the Community decision-making process the organisation's sole democratically-elected body. To have given the latter full legislative powers would not have been a realistic proposal to table at the time, particularly in view of the evidence that a certain degree of 'Eurocoolness' has affected the electorates of Europe ever since the early 1990s. The next best alternative was to attempt to involve the Parliament as much as possible, whilst leaving the main balance of power firmly with the Council. This seems to be an acceptable compromise.

4 The Sources of Community Law

I Introduction

In addition to their professional skill, craftsmen/women need raw materials and tools in order to realise their products. For the lawyer, these materials and tools are called 'legal sources', ie the rule-making apparatus which will enable him or her to solve legal issues as they arise in everyday practice. Lawyers belonging to the Common Law tradition have invariably interpreted the notion of 'legal sources' in a much broader way than their Civil Law counterparts. The latter being thoroughly imbued with the notion that legislation is the only valid source of law, they tend to exclude court decisions from the ambit of this term. However, even the most hardened defender of this thesis would have to admit that it is the decisions of the courts – both national and European – which have given substance to Community rules which are often characterised by their general, and at times even vague, nature. In the view of the present author, that is sufficient reason for their inclusion as a legal source.

Accordingly, a broad view will be taken in this chapter of the question as to what constitutes a 'source of Community law' – as was already apparent from the list featured earlier in Chapter 1 (above, p 1). It will successively deal with Community legislation (both the primary and the derived), court decisions, international law and the general principles of law. No distinct hierarchy has as yet been established between all these sources, although it is generally admitted that legislation takes precedence over all the others. Prior to this, however, a number of preliminary observations are in order.

First of all, it should be pointed out that the term 'Community act' means any legislative or administrative instrument issued by the Community authorities. Therefore a Commission 'comfort letter' issued under EU competition law (below, p 214) is just as valid a Community act as a basic Regulation issued by the Council. The term 'act' must therefore not be confused with the term 'act' in the Common Law sense, ie as a legislative instrument adopted by the constitutionally designed legislature (such as the United Kingdom Parliament or the US Congress).

Another point worth making at this juncture concerns the linguistic versions of the Community acts. Here, the broad principle is that all Community legislation is equally authentic in the eleven languages of the Community, which are Danish, Dutch, English, Finnish, French, German, Irish, Italian, Portuguese, Spanish and Swedish. There are a number of exceptions to this. First of all, although Irish is an official language of the Community, only the major Community treaties and conventions[1] have authentic value in the Irish language. Second, the Treaty of Paris was drafted in one language only, which was French. Although versions of this instrument have appeared in the other Community languages, the French version remains the only authentic one.

The fact that these linguistic versions are all 'equally authentic' entails that no version is to be given preference over the other. This can sometimes give rise to problems. However professional and conscientious the translation departments of the Community institutions may be, discrepancies sometimes arise between the linguistic versions of Community legislation. The question then arises as to which version, if any, will take precedence. The Court of Justice has tended to solve such difficulties by deciding the issue in the light of the objectives and spirit of the act in question.[2]

II   Primary legislation

Definition

The 'primary legislation' of the EU can be described as all instruments governing the Community which have been adopted as a result of inter-governmental action, and which have been ratified by the national legislatures in accordance with their constitutional procedures. As such it covers the following instruments:

- the founding Treaties, which are the EC, ECSC and Euratom Treaties;

- important instruments such as the Single European Act, the (Maastricht) Treaty on European Union, the 1975 Budget Treaty, the 1965 Merger Treaty, the Statute of the European Investment Bank, and the various Acts and Treaties of Accession. In most cases, these instruments have caused amendments to be made in the founding Treaties;

- the various protocols and similar attachments to the Treaties (eg the Social Protocol and the Protocol on Economic and Social Cohesion attached to the TEU);

- the conventions and other instruments concluded between the Member States. Some major items of Community legislation have been given this form, either because there was no basis for them in the founding Treaties, or because their contents were such as to require the full consent of the Member States' legislatures, which were required to ratify them. The 1968

---

1   These include not only the founding Treaties, but also such instruments as the 1968 Brussels Convention on the Mutual Recognition of Court Judgments.

2   Case 13/61, *de Geus v Bosch* (1962) ECR 45 at 49–50; Case 61/72, *PPW International v Hoofdproduktschap voor Akkerbouwprodukten* (1973) ECR 301 at 310; Case 6/74, *Moulijn v Commission* (1974) ECR 1287 at 1293.

THE SOURCES OF COMMUNITY LAW

Brussels Convention on the mutual recognition of judgments is a good example of this type of instrument.

Scope in time

In principle, all primary Community legislation has unlimited duration. In the case of the major primary instruments, this is stated expressly.[3] Where no specific mention is made of the duration of the act in question, it is assumed that it also has unlimited duration, even though many of their provisions may become redundant in time. (This is particularly the case as regards the various acts and treaties of accession.) The term 'unlimited' has been preferred to the more usual 'indefinite' in order to emphasise the irrevocable nature of the Member States' commitment.[4]

The one major exception to the unlimited nature of the primary legislation is the ECSC Treaty, which is concluded for a period of 50 years only (Article 97). This is perhaps unsurprising, considering the speculative and experimental nature of this pioneering instrument. Whether the ECSC Treaty will be renewed in 2001 is anyone's guess, although it is not inconceivable that the expiry of this 50 year deadline could be used simply to incorporate those provisions of the ECSC Treaty which are still relevant into the EC Treaty.

Territorial scope

It is difficult to extract a general principle on this issue from the provisions of the founding Treaties, in view of the differences in wording between them. The ECSC Treaty is restricted to the European territories of the Member States (Article 79).[5] That means that the non-European territories of such countries as France are excluded from its scope. No attempt has ever been made to extend the Treaty to these non-European areas, whether expressly (through Treaty amendment) or by analogy (through the ECJ). The Euratom Treaty extends its scope to the 'European territories of the Member States and to non-European territories under their jurisdiction'. The EC Treaty, on the other hand, makes its provisions applicable to each Member States, which it specifically mentions by name (Article 227). This means that the territorial scope of the Treaty is determined by reference to the constitutional arrangements of the Member States.[6] More specifically in relation to the French overseas *départements* this means that Community law automatically applies to them, inasmuch as they

---

3   See, *inter alia*, Article 240 EC Treaty, Article 208 Euratom Treaty, Article Q TEU.

4   Louis, JV, *The Community Legal Order* (2nd edn, 1990) European Perspectives, p 74.

5   Article 79 also states that the Treaty applies to those European territories for whose external relations the Member States are responsible, but this provision has lost all practical meaning today.

6   Constantinho, P and Dony, M, *Le droit communautaire* (1995), Armand Colin, p 75.

are an integral part of the French Republic. This is, however, on the understanding that it remains possible in the future to adopt specific measures which meet the particular needs of these territories.[7]

The position is complicated further by a set of exceptions and rules governing specific cases. Thus certain dependent territories of the Member States, such as the Faroe Islands and the United Kingdom Sovereign Base areas of Cyprus, are not covered by the Treaties. Other territories, such as the Isle of Man and the Channel islands, are only subject to a limited number of Treaty rules. Others still, such as Greenland, New Caledonia and French Polynesia, have a similar status to that enjoyed by the countries which are linked to the Community by association accords such as the Lomé and ACP agreements. The rules governing the territorial scope of the Treaties are therefore extremely confused, and require clarification and rationalisation at the earliest possible opportunity.

The Treaties as a constitutional framework for Community law

As has been noted before (above, p 46), the Treaty of Rome is a framework treaty. As such, it merely provides the bare outlines for the policies to be followed. The detailed implementation of these policies is to be enacted by means of the legislation laid down in Article 189, which is dealt with in the section concerning derived legislation (below, p 65). The best example of the manner in which the Treaty has merely acted as a law-making framework is the Common Agricultural Policy. Articles 38–46 merely set the general objectives; the policies themselves have been the product of regulations, directives and decisions.

The other two founding Treaties (ECSC and Euratom) are law-making treaties, and have attended to a good deal of policy detail themselves. Even these treaties, however, require derived legislation in order to realise some of the policies laid down in them. Although there is no rule which expressly prohibits any Community provision from being adopted outside the framework of the Treaties, it is generally accepted that, as a result of the combined provisions of Articles 3 and 189 EC Treaty, any rule of Community law must be based on a Treaty provision. It is for this reason that the founding Treaties are often referred to as 'the Constitution of the Community'. This is only true up to a point. Constitutions normally organise the institutions of a nation, regulate their mutual relations, and set out the fundamental guarantees for the citizen, in a manner which, from an ideological viewpoint, is entirely value-free. This cannot be said of the Community treaties, which clearly lay down a set of values which enshrine economic liberalism and the market economy.

---

7   Case 148/77, *Hansen v Hauptzollamt Flensburg* (1978) ECR 1787, at 1805.

III Derived legislation

Definition

Derived legislation is the body of Community rules adopted in accordance with the founding treaties. The term 'derived legislation' is preferred to 'secondary legislation', because it often includes instruments which, far from being secondary, have given shape and substance to certain Community policies (eg in the field of agricultural policy). There are essentially two types of derived legislation: that for which provision is made in the Treaties (the so-called 'standard acts'), and that which falls outside this category (the so-called 'non-standard' or 'innominate acts'). These will be examined in turn below. It should be pointed out beforehand that the ECSC makes provision for different types of derived legislation from those available under the EC and Euratom treaties. For the purpose of this work, however, we will concern ourselves exclusively with the legislation for which provision is made in the EC Treaty.

It is, in the opinion of the present writer, a matter for regret that no attempt has been made to bring these non-standard acts under the umbrella of the Treaty – an exercise for which the TEU surely presented an excellent opportunity. That instruments outside the Treaty framework were to see the light of day was almost inevitable. It is, however, sound legislative practice, as well as serving the interests of legal certainty, to formalise the use of these acts once their use has become widespread. Another criticism which can be levelled in this respect is the sloppy and confusing use which is sometimes made of the relevant terminology in the Treaty. Thus in Article 228(1) EC Treaty, it is stated that a special Council-appointed committee must assist the Commission in negotiating international treaties 'within the framework of such directives as the Council may issue to it'. It is clear from the context that it is not intended to use 'directives' within the meaning of Article 189 for this purpose. Surely the word 'directions' or even 'guidelines' would have been more appropriate.

Standard acts

These are laid down in Article 189 EC Treaty, and consist of regulations, directives and decisions (binding acts) and opinions and recommendations (non-binding acts).

Regulations

Article 189 EC Treaty describes these as having 'general application', as being binding in their entirety and as being directly applicable in all the Member States. Each of these characteristics is worth examining in greater detail. The fact that regulations have general application is meant to convey their abstract and general nature. They therefore apply to all those people and entities which have legal personality under Community law, ie the Member States, natural persons and legal persons.[8]

Regulations being binding in their entirety, neither the Member States' authorities nor private individuals may depart from any of the rules contained in them. Thus Member States may not unilaterally grant exemptions from an import levy which may have been imposed by a regulation.[9] It also means that a Member State may not refuse to put a regulation into effect because it expressed major reservations against it at the draft stage.[10] Although no Treaty provision specifically so provides, regulations are 'directly applicable' instruments. This means that they do not require any national measure which incorporates them into the domestic legal system of the Member States. In fact, the Court of Justice has expressly held that any national measure which actually attempts to incorporate regulations into the legal system of the state which issued such legislation is unlawful, as it detracts from the legal nature of regulations. All that the Member States may do is to adopt any implementing measures the regulation may require.[11] This topic will be returned to in Chapter 5 (below, p 89).

Regulations are not all equal amongst themselves. Under Article 145 EC Treaty, the Council has the power to delegate legislative powers to the Commission. These powers are contained in basic (or outline) regulations, which are then put into effect by the Commission in the form of implementing regulations. The latter must therefore conform to the former. If they do not, they are open to review and annulment by the Court.[12] Regulations adopted by the Council and the Commission must be published in the Official Journal. They enter into effect either on the date specified in the regulation itself, or, where no such date is provided, 20 days following the date of publication (Article 191(2) EC Treaty).

Directives

Article 189 EC Treaty defines directives as binding as to the result to be achieved on each Member State to which it is addressed, but leaving the national authorities to choose the appropriate form and methods of incorporation. They were included in the range of Community instruments in order to increase the sense of partnership between the Community and the national authorities in the decision-making process. Directives accordingly allow the national authorities to take part in the enactment of Community

8   Serie Manuali Giuridici, *op cit*, p 151.

9   Case 18/72, *Granaria v Produktschap voor Veevoeder* (1972) ECR 1163 at 1171.

10 Louis, J-V, *op cit*, p 84.

11 Case 39/72, *Commission v Italy* (1973) ECR 101 at 109–10.

12 Case 264/86, *France v Commission* (1988) ECR 973 at 996–98.

legislation. Their discretion in so doing, however, is subject to three essential limitations. First of all, the contents of the directive must be faithfully reflected in the relevant domestic measures. Second, the national authorities must observe the time-limit which the directive lays down for its incorporation. Third, they must choose the most appropriate form and methods of incorporation available.

Obviously the discretion enjoyed by the national authorities will depend on the precision of the directive in question. It should be observed at this point that some directives are more detailed than others; indeed, some are so detailed that they form a self-sufficient body of rules which merely require the national authorities to transcribe, rather than transpose, their contents into the national legislation. According to some authors, this tendency is due to the wariness displayed by certain Member States, who fear that leaving their partner states with too much discretion might give rise to distortions in competition.[13] This tendency was reduced to a certain extent by the Internal Market programme introduced by the SEA. The directives adopted under this instrument are based on the principle of mutual recognition rather than across-the-board harmonisation, and therefore content themselves with essential regulatory outlines rather than detailed provisions.

The manner in which Member States incorporate Community directives is subject to monitoring and supervision by the Commission, acting in its capacity of 'watchdog' of the Treaty. To this end, the Member States are required to supply the Commission with details of the measures which they have taken to transpose directives. Failure to incorporate directives or to incorporate them correctly can lead the Commission to take out proceedings against the Member State in question before the ECJ under Article 169 EC Treaty (below, p 105). Directives cannot by definition be directly applicable, but may in certain conditions be credited with direct effect. This aspect will be examined in greater detail in Chapter 5 (below, p 89). Those directives which are addressed to all the Member States are published in the Official Journal, and enter into effect either on the date specified, or, in the absence of such a date, on the twentieth day after their publication (Article 191(2) EC Treaty). Other directives are notified to their addressees, and take effect on the date of this notification (Article 191(3) EC Treaty).

Decisions

Decisions are binding in their entirety on those to whom they are addressed (Article 189, para 4, EC Treaty). They are therefore individual measures, whose addressees can be either Member States or private individuals. In view of their lack of general scope, they are essentially administrative, rather than rule-

13 Constantinho, P and Dony, M, *op cit*, p 77.

making, instruments. They can either impose obligations or confer rights on those to whom they are addressed.

Since decisions are binding in their entirety, they have direct effect (below, p 93). There are no requirements as to what form a decision must take, so that doubts can sometimes arise as to whether the instrument in question is a decision or not.[14] However, it is fair to say that in the overwhelming majority of cases, the institution in question will give a clear label to those instruments which it wishes to designate as decisions.

Decisions are notified to their addressees, and take effect upon such notification (Article 191(3) EC Treaty). A broad distinction can be made between administrative and quasi-judicial decisions. The former are purely executive acts which are adopted in the context of Community policies – such as decisions on dispensing monies under the various structural funds – and those which are necessary for the purposes of the Community as a large-scale administrative machinery, such as the appointment and promotion of officials. Quasi-judicial decisions, on the other hand, cover the decisions which are adopted by the Commission following adjudication proceedings – eg the various decisions taken in the context of competition policy.[15]

These are not the only binding Community acts, since the ECJ has added to their number (see below, p 68).

Opinions and recommendations

Article 189 provides no qualification of such instruments other than to stipulate that they have no binding force. The EC Treaty makes both specific and general provision for their adoption. Specific provision for them is made in measures such as Article 118b, which empowers the Commission to deliver opinions on the dialogue between the 'social partners' at the European level, or Article 128(5), which enables the Council to issue recommendations on cultural policy. A more general basis is provided by Article 155 EC Treaty, under which the Commission may adopt recommendations and opinions where it considers it necessary to do so.

Although they are non-binding instruments, recommendations and opinions are not without legal significance. Thus in *Grimaldi*,[16] the ECJ ruled that the national courts had to taken account of recommendations when handling lawsuits, particularly where these are capable of clarifying the interpretation of such domestic provisions as have been adopted for the purpose of implementing them, or where they are intended as being complementary to

14 Mathijsen, PSRF, *A Guide to European Union Law* (1995), Sweet & Maxwell, p 140.

15 Lasok, D, *op cit*, p 134.

16 Case 322/88, *Grimaldi v Fonds des maladies professionnelles* (1989) ECR 4407 at 4421.

binding Community legislation. Some authors, however, challenge the validity of this viewpoint.[17]

Non-standard acts

These are what Italian authors tend to call 'atypical acts'. They can generally be described as instruments which have no legal effect in principle, although in exceptional circumstances they could be regarded as such. An example of such exceptional circumstances was provided by the ECJ in relation to a Council of Ministers Resolution of 3 November 1976.[18] The United Kingdom had taken certain unilateral measures on fish conservation in contravention of the procedural requirements set out in this Resolution. These were considered by the ECJ to be sufficiently important to provide a valid defence, not only for France[19] and the Commission,[20] but also for a private person accused of infringing the UK rules in question.[21]

Non-standard Community acts include the following:

- Acts which regulate the internal workings of the institutions. These have occasionally been found to produce legal effects. On one particular occasion, a Community directive was annulled for having infringed such internal rules.[22]

- General harmonisation programmes, such as that which provided for the removal of barriers to trade in industrial products (1969),[23] or that which sought to abolish restrictions on the freedom of establishment[24] and the freedom to provide services (1961).[25]

- General declarations or inter-institutional agreements made by the Parliament, the Council and the Commission. These have also been found to have legal effects.[26]

---

17 Steiner, J, *Textbook on EEC Law* (1993), Blackstone, p 39.

18 Bulletin EC 1976/10, item 1502.

19 Case 141/78, *France v United Kingdom* (1979) ECR 2923.

20 Cases 32/79, *Commission v United Kingdom* (1980) ECR 2403, and 804/79, *Commission v United Kingdom* (1981) ECR 3079.

21 Case 269/80, *R v Tymen* (1981) ECR 3079.

22 Case 68/86, *United Kingdom v Council* (1988) ECR 855 at 902.

23 General Report 1969, p 55.

24 OJ 1962, p 7.

25 OJ 1962, p 2.

26 Case 204/86, *Greece v Council* (1988) ECR 5323 at 5356 *et seq.*

IV   Court decisions

The official bodies which are required to apply legislation to individual cases are normally referred to in general terms as 'the judiciary'. It has already been noted earlier (above, p 33) that, for the purpose of applying Community law, the judiciary is a very wide one, consisting as it does of the ECJ and CFI on the one hand, and the national courts before whom EU law is relied upon on the other. Many Continental works will not feature the decisions of the judiciary among the sources of Community law.[27] The reason for this is that in countries which apply the codified law system, the courts are servants rather than masters in the rule-making process. Their role is restricted to applying legislation, and the only binding effect of their decisions is produced upon the parties involved in the disputes brought before the courts. Unlike the Common Law system, the codified law does not admit of 'rule by precedents'.

However, the drafters of the EC Treaty implicitly recognised that this secondary role of the judiciary is more valid in theory than in practice. 'The Court of Justice', states Article 164, 'shall ensure that in the interpretation of this Treaty the law is observed'. How can a body whose authority is, in principle, restricted to the parties involved in a case have any such general role? In reality, the role of the ECJ in this respect is no different from that of the French *Cour de Cassation*, which was also set up in order to 'ensure' the uniformity of interpretation of the law – in spite of the non-hierarchical nature of the French courts. Acting in accordance with its task brief as set out in Article 164 EC Treaty, the Court, as well as the CFI, have amassed a body of decisions. The main lines of interpretation which emerge from this body are known as the established case law (*la jurisprudence constante*). It is no exaggeration to state that this case law has exercised as great an influence on the development of Community law as has the legislation adopted by the Council of Ministers. Indeed, many concepts of Community law, such as the direct effect and precedence of Community law (not to mention the general principles of law, to be discussed later, below, p 73), have been the exclusive product of the ECJ case law.

The fact that the ECJ does not recognise the doctrine of precedent also means that it cannot be bound by its own decisions. Were this not the case, it would be very difficult for the Court to adjust its case law in the light of developing circumstances. Thus it would have been hard for the Court to have retreated from its initial position on the public policy exception to the free movement of persons, laid down in Article 48(3) EC Treaty, a change in stance which, as will be noted later, was entirely justified, if only in order to enable the Court to be consistent with other escape clauses of this nature (below, p 174). This does not,

27   See, *inter alia*, Gautron, J-C, *op cit*, Constantinho, P and Dony, M, *op cit*, and Serie Manuali Giuridici, *op cit*.

however, prevent the Court from frequently restating certain formulations which it considers to be fundamental to the interpretation of Community law.[28] As to the decisions of the Member States' courts, these are obviously a much less persuasive source of Community law. Indeed, sometimes their contribution has been downright counterproductive, as was clearly shown in the decision issued by the French *Conseil d'Etat* in the *Cohn Bendit* case,[29] in which the *Conseil* denied the possibility of directives producing direct effect, in spite of a clear earlier ruling by the ECJ to the contrary.[30] Their main value resides in their contribution towards the relationship between Community law and national law – as was the case, for example, with the decision by the Belgian *Conseil d'Etat/Raad van State* in the *Fromageries Le Ski* decision,[31] or with the English *Factortame* ruling.[32]

V   International law

The long-term objective of the Community treaties is to achieve some kind of European federation. Community law constitutes an autonomous and *sui generis* legal system. Nevertheless, EU law remains to a certain extent inter-state law, which is why some rules of international law have been accepted by the ECJ as a valid source of Community law.[33] There are four types of international law: (a) treaties and conventions, (b) customary law, (c) general principles of international law, and (d) court decisions and the writings of the leading authors (Article 38 Statute of the International Court of Justice).

The fourth category is of no consequence in Community law. Customary law and general principles of international law, however, have some relevance to EU law, as has been regularly emphasised by the ECJ. In *Officier van Justitie v Kramer*,[34] the Court stated that once the Community had assumed jurisdiction for the Member States in such matters as fishing in international waters, it had thereby to assume the same obligations as those which had previously rested on

28   Perhaps the best example of this is the formula whereby any national measures 'which are capable of hindering, directly or indirectly, actually or potentially, intra-Community trade are to be considered as measures having an effect equivalent to a quantitative restriction', first formulated in the *Dassonville* decision (Case 8/74 (1974) ECR 837 at 852).

29   (1980) 1 CMLR 544.

30   Case 41/74, *Van Duyn v Home Office* (1974) ECR 1338.

31   (1972) CMLR 330.

32   *R v Secretary of State for Transport, ex parte Factortame* [1990] 2 AC 85.

33   Cases 21–24/72, *International Fruit Company v Produktschap voor Groenten en Fruit* (1972) ECR 1219 at 1226.

34   Case 3/76, (1976) ECR 1279 at 1310.

the Member States. The Community is also bound by the general rules relating to the law of treaties and to those relating to the privileges and immunities of international organisations.[35] However, it is especially the first category, more particularly the treaties concluded by the Community and its Member States, which are the main focus of our interest here.

Treaties concluded by the Community

Since the Community has international legal personality, it is empowered to conclude agreements with (a) non-Member States (b) groups of non-Member States, and (c) other international organisations. The Community has mainly exercised this power in the context of its Common Commercial Policy. The procedure for their conclusion is laid down in general terms in Article 228 EC Treaty (subject to a number of specific procedures such as that laid down in Article 113(3) EC Treaty).

Under this procedure, it is the Commission which takes the first step by making recommendations to the Council. The latter then authorises the Commission to open and conduct the required negotiations, which it does with the assistance of a special Council-appointed committee. The Commission then makes a formal proposal to the Council, which concludes the agreement (in some cases after the European Parliament has been consulted, or even given its consent). The Court of Justice can also be involved in the Treaty-making process, since the Commission or a Member State may request its opinion as to whether a planned international agreement is consistent with the EC Treaty or not (Article 228(6) EC Treaty). The Court has done so on a number of occasions.[36] It has been mentioned earlier (above, p 72) that Community law is bound by the general principles of international law regarding the law of treaties. One of these principles is contained in the rule *pacta sunt servanda* (agreements must be honoured).[37] It therefore follows that international agreements concluded by the EU also take precedence over its derived legislation.[38]

Treaties concluded by the Member States

Although the Community is empowered to conclude international agreements on behalf of the Member States, the latter are not thereby prevented from becoming parties to international treaties in their own right. It is generally agreed, however, that they must not do so in areas which fall within the

35 Louis, J-V, *The Community Legal Order* (1990) European Perspectives, p 92.

36 See, *inter alia*, Opinion 1/76, *Re Laying-Up Fund*, (1976) ECR 741; Opinion 1/78, *Re Rubber Agreement* (1979) ECR 2871; *Re Draft Agreement on a European Economic Area*, (1991) ECR I-6079.

37 Case 104/81, *Kupferberg* (1982) ECR 3641 at 3662.

38 Cases 21–24/72, *op cit*, at 1227.

exclusive treaty-making jurisdiction of the Community. Special problems are posed by international agreements entered into by the Member States before the EC Treaty entered into force (or before it became binding on states which subsequently acceded to EC membership). These are not affected by the provisions of the Treaty. However, Member States must take steps to remove any inconsistencies between these agreements and Community law. In addition, when applying these treaties, the Member States concerned must at all times take into account the Community, its institutions and the advantages conferred by the latter on its members (Article 234 EC Treaty).

VI   General principles of law

General

The legal sources examined hitherto could be described as formal sources of Community law. However comprehensive these may be, they are not equal to every issue to which Community law gives rise. This is particularly the case as regards the protection of individual rights – an important consideration, given that Community law confers rights and imposes obligations on private parties as well as on the EU institutions and the national authorities. It is particularly in this regard that the Court of Justice has applied what are known as the 'general principles of law'.

To a certain extent, the EC Treaty made provision for the application of these general principles. In Article 164, the ECJ is required to ensure that 'the law is observed' when interpreting and applying the Treaty. Under Article 173, one of the grounds for review of Community acts is the infringement of the Treaty 'or any rule of law relating to its application'. 'The law' means a good deal more than simply the formal rules described above. In addition, Article 215 requires the tort liability of the Community to be decided in accordance with 'the general principles common to the laws of the Member States'. They can be brought under five headings: (a) the general principles derived from the nature of Community law; (b) those which are common to the legal orders of one or more Member States; (c) fundamental human rights, and (d) general principles of international law. They are examined in turn below.

It is the Court of Justice which is responsible for introducing these general principles into the ambit of Community law. One of the reasons for this is the fact that most of its judges were trained in codified legal systems, where the courts have been more inclined to apply them than has been the case in Common Law jurisdictions.

General principles derived from the nature of Community law

These are the principles which are the inevitable corollary of the provisions of Community law. They include:

Equality

This notion is inherent in a number of Treaty provisions, both general (Article 6, which prohibits any discrimination on grounds of nationality) and specific (eg Article 119 requiring equal pay for equal work). However, 'equality' as a general legal principle has a much broader meaning than that conveyed by these provisions. Essentially, it prohibits the unequal treatment of comparable situations or the equal treatment of unequal situations, unless such differential treatment can be justified on objective grounds.[39] The equality principle, used in this generalised manner, was expressed for the first time by the ECJ in an early ECSC case.[40] Here, the Court required all comparably placed consumers within the common market to have equal access to sources of production. In that case, the equality principle was applied in a commercial context. However, the principle has been applied on a wider basis than the purely commercial, as is exemplified by a staff case which arose in the late 1980s.[41] An ECSC employee had, under Luxembourg law, been excluded from a private pension fund available to EEC and Euratom officials. The Court held that to do so would entail a fundamental inequality between ECSC officials on the one hand, and EEC and Euratom employees on the other.

Solidarity

This is the principle which holds that, since the Member States enjoy the advantages of membership, they must also observe its rules. The decision in which this was most clearly expressed was made in Case 39/72.[42] Here, the Commission had accused Italy of misapplying a Community regulation which instituted a system of payments made for slaughtering cows and withdrawing dairy produce from the market. The Court held that by unilaterally breaking the link between the advantages and the obligations resulting from EC membership, a Member State was endangering the equality between the Member States and their citizens, and was failing to observe the solidarity which was required of the Member States.

General principles common to the legal orders of several Member States

As the number of Member States has risen, it has been increasingly difficult to discern principles which they have in common. However, there are a considerable number of principles which are applicable in several Member

---

39   Constantinesco, P and Dony, M, *op cit*, p 125.

40   Case 8/57, *Hauts Fourneaux et Aciéries Belges v High Authority* (1958) ECR 245 at 256.

41   Case 130/87, *Retter v Caisse de pension des employés privés* (1989) ECR 865.

42   *Commission v Italy* (1973) ECR 101.

States, especially those which have separate courts proceedings arising from administrative disputes.

Legal certainty

Although most European legal systems have developed this notion, it is fair to state that it is mainly the German law model which inspired the Court of Justice to include this general principle among the sources of Community law. Legal certainty can be described as the obligation on the part of the public authorities to ensure that the law should be readily ascertainable by those to whom it applies, and that the latter should be able, within reason, to predict its existence, as well as the manner in which it will be applied and interpreted.[43] The fundamental importance of this requirement was emphasised by the Court where it held that the criteria of certainty and forseeability 'are requirements which must be observed strictly in the case of rules liable to entail financial consequences'.[44]

More particularly, this principle has been invoked by the ECJ in order to ensure that the Community institutions enable those individuals who have legal relations with them to ascertain their exact position. Thus in *BASFG and Other v Commission*,[45] the Commission had found against several companies for having infringed Community competition law. The CFI held this decision to be unlawful on a number of grounds, one of which was that the Commission was unable to present an original version of the decision, properly authenticated as required by Rules of Procedure. The CFI found that this failure represented an infringement of the principle of legal certainty. Another aspect of the notion of legal certainty takes the form of the principles of non-retroactivity and of vested rights. The former is a principle which is common to virtually all Member States. As the ECJ stated in the *Racke* decision,[46] its main purpose is to ensure that no measure taken by the public authorities be applicable to those concerned before the latter have been able to become aware of it. However, the same judgment also states that retrospective measures are exceptionally permissible if the purpose to be achieved demands it, and provided that the legitimate expectations of those affected have been respected. The notion of 'legitimate expectation' will be dealt with later.

As to 'vested rights', an inevitably unsatisfactory translation of the French term *droits acquis*, these concern such rights as have been conferred upon the individual by the law, and which subsequent legislation may not be allowed to remove or diminish. As such, they are an extension of the non-retroactivity rule.

---

43 Charlesworth, A and Cullen, H, *op cit*, p 122.

44 Case C-30/89, *Commission v France* (1990) ECR-I 691 at 717.

45 Cases T-79, 84–86, 89, 91–92, 94, 96, 98, 102 and 104/89, (1992) ECR II-315.

46 Case 98/78, *Racke v Hauptzollamt Mainz* (1979) ECR 69.

Unless there is clear evidence to the contrary, legislation is invariably deemed to be non-retroactive. This rule prevents Community legislation from entering into effect before its date of publication.[47] The term 'date of publication' means the actual date of publication, rather than that on which publication was intended. In one particular case,[48] the planned date of publication of a Community regulation was frustrated for reasons beyond the control of the institution which issued it. The Court held that the regulation could not be considered to have entered into effect before the true date of publication.

Legitimate expectation

This concept is very much a corollary to the principle of legal certainty, and is once again the product of German administrative law (*Vertrauenschutzprinzip*). It seeks to ensure that, where the legal system induces the belief on the part of the individual that he or she will achieve a certain result if he or she acts in accordance with the rules, this expectation must be protected. It was applied for the first time in the *Staff Salaries* decision,[49] in which the Commission applied for annulment of a Council measure. This measure had itself reversed a previous decision setting the criteria on which salaries of EC officials were to be based. The new salary scales thus set by the Council were held to be invalid. The main reason advanced by the Court was that the decision annulled by the Council had created certain valid expectations on the part of the officials concerned.

The principle of legitimate expectation is, however, subject to a number of limitations. The first is the reasonableness test. Community law will only protect the legitimate expectations of the cautious and reasonable individual. If a 'prudent and discriminating' trader should have anticipated the adoption of a Community act capable of affecting his interests, he or she cannot rely upon the legitimate expectation rule if the measure in question is adopted.[50] Secondly, the principle may only be relied upon if the expectation is legitimate. In *Mackprang*,[51] the applicant had purchased a quantity of grain in France. His sole purpose in doing so was to sell it to a German agricultural intervention agency in order to take advantage of the devaluation of the French franc. The Commission forestalled this kind of speculative activity by allowing the German government to refuse to buy non-German grain. The Court held that the speculative expectation of the applicant in concluding this transaction was not a legitimate one, and therefore disallowed the challenge.

47 Kent, P, *Law of the European Union* (2nd edn, 1996) Pitman, p 36.
48 Case 88/76, *Société pour l'exportation des sucres v Commission* (1977) ECR 709.
49 Case 81/72, *Commission v Council* (1973) ECR 575.
50 Case 265/85, *Van den Bergh en Jurgens BV and Van Dijk Food products (Lopik) BV v Commission* (1987) ECR 1155.
51 Case 2/75, *Einfuhr- und Vorratstelle für Getreide und Futtermittel v Mackprang* (1975) ECR 607.

Proportionality

Although this notion was once again inspired by German law (*Verhältnismäßigkeitsgrundsatz*), it can be found, albeit under a different formulation, in various other legal systems. It requires the public authorities to observe a due sense of proportion between the objectives to be achieved and the means placed at their disposal for achieving them. This principle was formally adopted as a general rule of Community law when the TEU inserted Article 3b, para 3 into the EC Treaty, which requires that 'any action of the Community shall not go beyond what is necessary to achieve the objectives of this Treaty'. Prior to that, however, it already had specific application in the EC Treaty by means of such provisions as Article 40(3) (common organisation of agricultural markets), Article 85(3) (exemptions from the prohibition on restrictive agreements) and Article 92 (permissible state aids).

To make an assessment of what is 'proportionate' is almost as difficult as deciding what is 'reasonable'. It is obvious that a great deal will depend on the specific circumstances of each particular case. This is well-illustrated by a few cases in which the applicants challenged decisions making them forfeit deposits paid on the issuing of a export licences. In *Internationale Handelsgesellschaft*,[52] a German trader, on being granted a licence to export cereals, was required to pay a deposit of DM 17,000. This deposit was forfeited when the trader in question failed to export the full amount of corn-flour involved. The ECJ did not consider this to be a disproportionate penalty. In Case 181/84,[53] on the other hand, the trader involved forfeited a deposit of £1,670,000 on the grounds that its application for an export licence was received by the Commission four hours past the time limit specified. The ECJ considered the forfeiture of such a sizeable sum for such a relatively trivial infringement to be entirely disproportionate.

Fundamental human rights

Originally, the area of human rights was regarded as totally alien to a legal order based firmly on economic foundations. Any European attempt in this direction was regarded as the preserve of the European Court of Human Rights, established within the framework of the Council of Europe, whose task it was to apply the European Convention on Human Rights (ECHR). Gradually, however, the ECJ recognised the need to observe certain fundamental rights when applying Community law, even though it never specifically referred to the ECHR for this purpose.

The SEA was the first Community instrument to give official recognition to the ECHR, even though it merely did so in its Preamble. The TEU was more forthcoming on this issue. In Article F(2), it states:

---

52 Case 11/70, (1970) ECR 1125.
53 *R v Intervention Board for Agricultural Produce, ex parte Mann (Sugar) Ltd* (1985) ECR 2889.

The Union shall respect fundamental human rights, as guaranteed by the European Convention for the Protection of Human Rights and Fundamental Freedoms signed in Rome on 4 November 1950 and as they result from the constitutional traditions common to the Member States, as general principles of Community law.

The Amsterdam Treaty has gone even further by raising the respect for human rights to the status of one of the general principles underlying the EU (new Article F(1)). The first case in which the Court made use of fundamental human rights was *Stauder v Ulm*.[54] Under a Commission decision of 1969, the Member States were authorised to make butter available at cheap rates to certain low-income groups. In order to take advantage of this system, the applicant had to present a voucher issued in his or her name. This provision was ambiguous because of a difference in wording between the French and the Dutch text. The Court decided to give preference to that version which did not require the beneficiaries to be actually identified by name when applying for the butter in question. Interpreted in this manner, concluded the Court, the provision in question would not contain anything 'capable of prejudicing the fundamental human rights enshrined in the general principles of Community law and protected by the Court'.

In *Stauder*, the Court studiously avoided making any references to any international instrument for the protection of these fundamental rights. In the *Nold* case,[55] however, it conceded that international human rights treaties could 'supply guidelines which should be followed within the framework of Community law'. By now, the Court has not only recognised the ECHR as the main source of legally protected human rights, but also stipulated that 'the Community cannot accept measures which are incompatible with observance of human rights thus recognised and guaranteed'.[56] The scope of this work unfortunately prevents an in-depth exploration of the various individual human rights to which the Court has given protection through its case law. Briefly, it has been possible for the ECJ to protect the right to privacy,[57] the right to due legal process,[58] the right to privacy in the relationship between the legal adviser and his client[59] and religious rights.[60] It has even upheld these rights in

---

54 Case 29/69, (1969) ECR 419.

55 Case 4/73, *Nold v Commission* (1974) ECR 491.

56 Case C-260/89, *Elliniki Radiophonia Tileorassi AE v Dimotiki Etairia Pliroforissis and Sotirios Kouvelas* (1991) ECR I-2925 at 2963–64.

57 Case 136/79, *National Panasonic (UK) v Commission* (1980) ECR 2033.

58 Cases 100–103/80, *Musique Diffusion Française v Commission* (1983) ECR 1825.

59 Case 155/79, *Australian Mining and Smelting Europe Ltd v Commission* (1982) ECR 1575.

60 Case 130/75, *Prais v Council* (1976) ECR 1589.

the criminal law – an area which does not, in principle, fall within the scope of Community law.[61]

Procedural rights

The enforcement of Community law necessarily involves the institution of court proceedings. These must also be seen to be fair, even in the absence of specific guarantees to that effect in Community legislation. For this purpose, the general principles of law have once again proved a useful remedy. It is in this area that English administrative law has made a considerable contribution.[62] The principle that such rights must be guaranteed, and that the defendant has a right to a fair hearing and natural justice, was established by the ECJ in the *Transocean* decision.[63] This right to due process of law involves a number of guarantees. First of all, it means that the party concerned has a right to be clearly and properly informed of the issues involved in the court proceedings.[64] It also involves the principle known in English law as *audi alteram partem*, ie the right to make one's views known to the court.[65] In addition, it requires the court or judicial body involved to give reasons for its decision[66] (bearing in mind that in certain codified jurisdictions, this is an almost constitutional requirement).

VII Conclusion

Community law has a wide variety of legal sources which reflect the various legal traditions on which it is based. It has to be said that these sources continue to bear the hallmark of the codified legal systems, even though the influence of the Common law jurisdictions has been increasingly felt over the past few years. This is particularly the case with the increasing emphasis on the observance of general legal principles, which form part of the 'unwritten law' of the Community. On a more critical note, it has to be said that the Community authorities could do a good deal more in order to introduce a greater note of rationality in its legal sources. It is surely time for some of the 'non-standard acts' to be given some 'constitutional' recognition in the primary law, if only to avoid any disputes as to what constitutes Community legislation. In addition, the continued existence of three fundamental Community treaties appears to be an anachronism, particularly in view of the terminological differences between

61 Case 63/83, *R v Kirk* (1984) ECR 2689.

62 Charlesworth, A and Cullen, H, *op cit*, pp 126–27.

63 Case 17/74, *Transocean Marine Plant Association v Commission* (1974) ECR 1063.

64 Case 34/77, *Ozlizlok v Commission* (1978) ECR 1099 at 1116.

65 Case 17/74, *op cit*, at 1080–81.

66 Case 222/86, *Union nationale des entraineurs et cadres techniques professionnels du football (UNECTEF) v Heylens* (1987) ECR 4097.

them which, in spite of the TEU, continue to prevail. As regards the general legal principles, it would be useful for the Community to adopt, albeit in summary form, a statement featuring an exhaustive list of those principles which should be applied and protected under Community law.

5 Community Law and National Law

I Introduction

That Community law represents a legal order in its own right is a proposition which was accepted almost from the outset by all those involved in its elaboration and application. Less straightforward was the task of defining the exact relationship between Community law and the law of its Member States. One of the main difficulties in this respect was the absence of precedents. Even after the TEU, the Community is far removed from being a federation in the accepted sense of the term. The legal models of such countries as the US, Australia and Germany were therefore of little relevance here, since the Community Member States had, and continue to have, considerably more freedom of action in relation to the Community authorities than a US state or a German *Land* has in relation to the federal authorities.

In the absence of any suitable role models or precedents, the assumption has to be that, just as Community law represents a unique and special legal order, so the relationship between it and national law is also unprecedented and *sui generis*. It has to be explored through a number of factors capable of throwing light on this unique nature. These are the division of powers between the Community and the Member States, the direct effect, direct applicability and supremacy of Community law, and the principle of subsidiarity. It must also be viewed through the prism of the constitutional arrangements by which Community law becomes part of the national legal orders. All these aspects will be examined in turn in this chapter.

II Division of powers between the Community and the Member States

General

When establishing the relationship between Community law and its members, it is essential to establish exactly where the demarcation of powers lies between them. At a relatively early stage of its case law, the Court of Justice had confirmed that the Community had acquired 'real powers stemming from a limitation of sovereignty or a transfer of powers from the states to the Community'.[1] The question then arises as to whether this transfer of powers

---

1   Case 6/64, *Costa v ENEL* (1964) ECR 585 at 593.

entails that the Community has acquired exclusive jurisdiction in the policy areas covered by the Treaties. The answer to this question is supplied by the ECJ case law, which has conferred on the Community exclusive powers, concurrent powers and parallel powers in relation to the national authorities. Whether an area will fall under either of these powers will depend not only on the substantive provisions of the Treaty, but also on the whole of its scheme.[2]

Exclusive jurisdiction

The areas in which the Community has acquired exclusive jurisdiction are those for which it emerges from the express wording of the Treaty provisions, or from their context, that the latter fully intended to confer on the Community full and definitive powers, whilst at the same time excluding any possibility of unilateral action by the Member States, even before the Community institutions have used these powers by adopting the appropriate provisions.[3]

Hitherto, the Court has claimed exclusive jurisdiction for the Community in a number of areas. Thus in its *Local Cost Standard Opinion*,[4] the Court held that the common commercial policy was a matter in which the Community only could act, to the exclusion of any concurrent actions on the part of the Member States. In another ruling,[5] it held that the Community had exclusive jurisdiction to become a party to an international Convention on the Protection of Nuclear Materials, not only because of its international legal personality, but also because of the objectives of the Euratom Treaty.[6] In *Kramer*,[7] the Court ruled that policy on maritime resource conservation was also a matter for which the Community had exclusive responsibility.

The existence of areas falling within the exclusive jurisdiction of Community action gives rise to the question as to what happens if the Community has failed to adopt the required measures in this area. On this issue, the Court has ruled that the transfer of powers to the Community in these areas was complete and definitive, and could neither entail the return of these areas to the jurisdiction of the Member States nor give the latter the freedom to act unilaterally.[8] If the Community institution in question had failed to act, the Member States' authorities could proceed to take the necessary measures, but only on a

2   Case 22/70, *Commission v Council* (1971) ECR 263 at 274.
3   Constantinho, P and Dony, M, *op cit*, p 22.
4   Opinion 1/75, (1975) ECR 1355 at 1363; see also Case 41/76, *Donckerwolcke v Procureur de la République* (1976) ECR 1921 at 1936; case 179/78, *Procureur de la République v Rivoira* (1979) ECR 1147.
5   Ruling 1/78, (1978) ECR 2151.
6   Lasok, D, *op cit*, p 61.
7   Cases 3, 4 and 6/76 (1976) ECR 1279 at 1308.
8   Case 804/79, *Commission v United Kingdom* (1981) ECR 1045 at 1073.

temporary basis, and after having consulted, and obtained the consent of, the Commission. The question as to what areas fall within the exclusive jurisdiction of the Community is a particularly important one when it comes to determining the field of application of the subsidiarity principle. This will be returned to later (below, p 96).

Concurrent jurisdiction

For a long time, the Eastern European countries refused to recognise the Community as an international legal personality. For relations with these areas, the Community and the Member States were said to have 'concurrent jurisdiction'. This kind of jurisdiction was always regarded as exceptional and transitory.[9] There are also a number of areas which have not been specifically allocated to Community jurisdiction by the Treaty, but which are potential areas of Community responsibility. Until such time as the Community institutions adopt legislation in this field, the Member States have concurrent jurisdiction in it. Even here, the Member States' powers are not unlimited, as they may not infringe the Community rules on discrimination, or detract from the principle of the free movement of goods, persons, services and capital.[10] A good example of this is those areas of company law which have not yet been harmonised by Community law (and for which there exist a number of drafts which, for one reason and another, have failed to be adopted, below, p 182). As the pace of European integration increases, these areas are becoming increasingly rare.

Parallel jurisdiction

These are areas in which Community law is complementary to national law. Thus EU competition law only prohibits abuse of dominant position where it is 'incompatible with the common market and in so far as it may affect trade between Member States' (Article 86 EC Treaty). Therefore firms which merely account for a substantial share of the national market are not covered by Article 86. The national authorities may exercise their parallel jurisdiction in relation to the anti-competitive behaviour of such companies.

III Direct effect

General

One of the factors which separates Community law from the law developed by other international institutions is its impact on the individual. Whereas the UN, WTO and OECD are organs which are mainly concerned with the relations between states, and merely confer rights and obligations on the latter, the

9   Lasok, D and Cairns, WJ, *The Customs Law of the EEC* (1984), Kluwer, p 227.
10 Constantinho, P and Dony, M, *op cit*, pp 23–24.

Community has sought to involve its citizens in the operation of its legal rules.[11] This is why Community law provided the latter with the opportunity of challenging certain Community acts before the Court of Justice, and enabled them to enforce their rights before their domestic courts.

It cannot be claimed that the Community was the first system of supranational law to give individual citizens access to an international court, or to confer rights which were enforceable before the national courts. The European Convention on Human Rights had already given the individual access to the European Court of Human Rights, albeit only after all national remedies had been exhausted. As to the recognition by national courts of treaties enforceable by individuals, or 'self-executing treaties' as they are called – this had already been accomplished in, *inter alia*, the US in the early 19th century.[12]

However, it can justly be claimed that Community law provided the framework for the first systematic attempt by an international organ, co-operating with the public authorities of its Member States, at providing the individual with a general set of rights which are protected in as uniform manner as possible by the domestic courts. The systematic element is provided by the objective criteria which any provision of Community law must satisfy in order to become enforceable in this manner – in other words, in order to acquire direct effect. These objective criteria will be examined in greater detail later (below, p 85 *et seq*).

Definition

In the broadest of terms, direct effect can be defined as the mechanism enabling the citizen to rely upon a provision of Community law before his or her national courts, which are required to acknowledge, protect and enforce the rights conferred by that provision. It should be pointed out immediately that this is not an 'official' definition which can even be inferred from a provision in the Treaty or in any other Community legislation. It is based on the criteria which the ECJ has developed for this purpose in, *inter alia*, the *Van Gend & Loos* decision.[13] In fact, it can be said that by developing the notion of direct effect, the ECJ has made one of its most important law-creating contributions towards the Community legal system.

11 Even the European Convention on Human Rights does not make the Council of Europe into an organ aimed at the individual, since it does not confer on the latter directly enforceable rights before the national courts.

12 Evans, A, 'Some Aspects of the Problems of Self-executing Treaties in Municipal Law', in *Proceedings of the American Society of International Law* (1951) p 68. See also Maresceau, M, *De directe werking van het Europees Gemeenschapsrecht* (1978) Kluwer, p 9 *et seq*.

13 Case 26/62, *van Gend & Loos v Nederlandse Administratie der Belastingen* (1963) ECR 1.

Conditions for acquiring direct effect

It was in the said *Van Gend & Loos* decision that the Court not only identified the notion of direct effect, but also laid down the basic conditions which provisions of Community law must meet if they are to acquire direct effect. These criteria have subsequently been refined and supplemented by the ECJ case law. The action prompting this case was brought by a major Dutch transport company against the Netherlands fiscal authorities, for having imposed, on a quantity of chemicals imported from Germany, a customs duty which was higher than that which applied when the EC Treaty entered into force. This practice infringed Article 12 EC Treaty. The Netherlands court referred the issue to the ECJ, which ignored the opinion of the Advocate-General, and ruled that the Dutch company could rely upon Article 12 before its national courts, on the grounds that this provision:

> contains a clear and unconditional prohibition which is not a positive but a negative obligation. This obligation, moreover, is not qualified by any reservation on the part of states which would make its implementation conditional upon a positive legislative measure enacted under national law. The very nature of this prohibition makes it ideally adapted to produce direct effects in the legal relationship between Member States and their subjects.[14]

In its subsequent case law, the Court has developed and refined these criteria further.

The rule must be clear

The ECJ has tended to take a fairly broad view of this requirement, in that it has considered the latter to have been satisfied even if the consequences of the rule are difficult to anticipate. Certainly it dismissed the view expressed by the German Government in the *Lütticke* case,[15] that the clarity requirement meant that the provision in question had to be so clear and unambiguous as to be capable of being applied without difficulty.

The rule must be unconditional

This criterion means that the right conferred by the rule in question may not be dependent on any discretion on the part of an official authority. By 'official authority' is meant not only the Community institutions themselves, but also the authorities of the Member States. On the subject of this requirement, the ruling given by the Court in *Ministère Public Luxembourg v Müller*[16] is extremely instructive, in that it provides a clear idea of the type of provision which is not

---

14 Case 26/62, *op cit*, at 13.
15 Case 57/65, *Lütticke v Hauptzollamt Saarlouis* (1966) ECR 327 at 352.
16 Case 10/71 (1971) ECR 723 at 730.

unconditional. The provision under review was Article 90(2) EC Treaty, which stipulates that public undertakings are subject to the competition law of the EC Treaty unless the performance of its task is thereby obstructed. This rule, according to the ECJ, could not be unconditional because

> its application involves an appraisal of the requirements, on the one hand, of the particular task entrusted to the undertaking and, on the other hand, the protection of the interests of the Community. This appraisal depends on the objectives of general economic policy pursued by the states under the supervision of the Commission.[17]

Accordingly, the Court ruled that Article 90(2) could not produce direct effect.

There may not be any reservation making its implementation dependent on further action taken by the authorities

Initially, the 'further action' in question was held to be national legislation. However, this has been considered to be too narrow an approach. It is now accepted that the Community rule must not be dependent on any action (whether legislation or otherwise), taken by either the national or the Community authorities.[18] Although the Court has sometimes tended to equate this condition with the requirement, mentioned earlier, that the rule be 'unconditional', it has mostly treated this as a specific additional condition. Its decision in the *Capolongo* case[19] is a good example of this. The provision under review was Article 13(2) EC Treaty, which stipulates that charges with equivalent effect to customs duties are to be removed by the end of the transitional period. The ECJ conferred direct effect on this provision because it concerned a prohibition to which no reservation on the part of the Member States was attached, in the sense that the prohibition in question could only be implemented by means of a positive national legal instrument or by the intervention of a Community institution.[20]

Treaty provisions with direct effect

Thanks to the criteria developed by the ECJ, the latter has been able to attribute direct effect to a considerable number of Treaty provisions. There is insufficient space at our disposal to list them individually. However, it is possible to highlight some significant developments in the ECJ case law when assessing the direct effect of Treaty provisions.

---

17 *Ibid*, at 730.
18 Opinion of Advocate-General Mayras in Case 2/74, *Reyners v Belgium* (1974) ECR 631 at 661.
19 Case 77/72, *Capolongo v Maya* (1973) ECR 611 at 623.
20 *Ibid*, at 623.

Positive and negative obligations

Originally, the ECJ only conferred direct effect on provisions which imposed an obligation to refrain from something. This was certainly the case in *Van Gend & Loos*,[21] where the disputed provision was an obligation not to increase existing customs duties (Article 12). Another landmark decision, *Costa v ENEL*,[22] concerned the direct effect of (a) Article 37(2) EC Treaty, which prohibits the introduction of any new measures enabling the Member States to distort intra-Community trade by manipulating their national monopolies, and (b) Article 53 EC Treaty, which forbids the Member States from introducing new restrictions on the establishment of citizens of other member countries.

However, in the *Lütticke* decision,[23] the ECJ went a stage further by also attributing direct effect to provisions imposing positive obligations. The provision in question was Article 95 EC Treaty. Subsections 1 and 2 of this Article contain 'negative' obligations in relation to indirect taxation. However, Article 95(3) requires the Member States to repeal, by the end of the transitional period, any national legislation which imposes discriminatory indirect taxation. The Court held that this paragraph gave the national authorities no discretion as to the date by which these national rules had to be repealed, which was 1 January 1962. Once this date had passed, Article 95(3) EC Treaty, which represented a positive obligation, was transformed into a directly effective provision.

This rule was clearly an important benchmark as regards the direct effect of rules requiring Member States to fulfil an obligation by a certain date. However, those provisions which require the Community institutions to adopt positive legislation within a certain time limit are also capable of having direct effect. This was amply confirmed by the ECJ in its *Reyners* decision.[24] This case concerned a number of Treaty provisions on the freedom of establishment, which required the Council to issue directives. No such directives were forthcoming when the time limit expired. The Court ruled that Article 52 EC Treaty accordingly was directly effective because:

by laying down that freedom of establishment shall be attained at the end of the transitional period, Article 52 thus imposes an obligation to attain a precise result, the fulfilment of which had to be made easier by, but not made dependent on, the implementation of a programme of progressive measures. The fact that this progression has not been adhered to leaves the obligation itself intact beyond the end of the period provided for its fulfilment.[25]

---

21 Case 26/62, *op cit.*
22 Case 6/64, *op cit*, at 598.
23 Case 57/65, *op cit.*
24 Case 2/74, *op cit.*
25 *Ibid*, at 651.

These rulings of the ECJ which hold Treaty Articles to be enforceable in the national courts, following the transitional period, thus mitigate the implications of the failure on the part of the Community institutions and the national authorities to perform the obligations undertaken before the expiry of the transitional period.[26]

Vertical and horizontal direct effect

If a Treaty obligation is imposed on the national authorities, the rule in question is capable of creating vertical direct effect, ie the individual is entitled to rely on them before his or her courts against the state. The ECJ has tended to interpret the notion of 'organs of the state' quite broadly. Thus, for example, in *Foster v British Gas*,[27] the Court ruled that the British Gas Corporation[28] fell within this category.

However, Community law also imposes obligations on private individuals which may be relied upon by other individuals. A good example of this is Article 85 EC Treaty, which requires individuals from abstaining from the conclusion of any private arrangement which distorts competition. These provisions therefore give rise to direct effect as between individuals. This is known as 'horizontal direct effect'. The Court acknowledged the direct effect of Article 85 (and Article 86) in *BRT v SABAM*.[29]

There are other EC Treaty rules, however, whose horizontal direct effect is less obvious. This was certainly the case in relation to the ECJ decision in *Defrenne v SABENA*.[30] In this case, an air hostess brought court proceedings against the Belgian airline which employed her, claiming that the higher pay awarded to male stewards than to air hostesses constituted an infringement of Article 119 EC Treaty, which seeks to ensure that men and women should receive equal pay for equal work (below, p 261). The ECJ held that this prohibition on discrimination applied not only to the activities of public authorities, but also to all collective labour agreements and contracts between individuals. Otherwise it would be impossible to achieve the 'complete implementation of the aim pursued by Article 119'. Article 119 EC Treaty therefore had vertical and horizontal direct effect.

26 Louis, J-V, *op cit*, p 113.

27 Case C-188/89 (1990) ECR I-3313.

28 At that time, the production and distribution of gas in the United Kingdom was operated by a publicly-owned concern.

29 Case 127/73 (1974) ECR 51 at 62.

30 Case 43/75 (1976) ECR 455.

Direct effect of regulations

Since Article 189 EC Treaty states that regulations are of general application, binding in their entirety, and directly applicable in all Member States, it will come as no surprise to learn that the overwhelming majority of regulations have direct effect. In addition, this direct effect can be both vertical and horizontal.[31] However, the presumption that regulations have direct effect is a rebuttable one, since some of them fail to meet the conditions for direct effect laid down by the ECJ, or even because they are, by their very nature, incapable of conferring rights on individuals. In the *Tachographs* case,[32] the Court makes specific reference to 'the implementation of Regulation 1463/70'[33] by the United Kingdom. Obviously this regulation cannot produce direct effect, as it fails to meet the requirement that the measure in question may not be dependent on further action taken by the public authorities. The reason for this was the fact that this Regulation required the Member States to take certain implementing measures.

Direct effect of directives

At first sight, directives also appear to be a category which is easily assessed in terms of their direct effect. In view of the fact that Article 189 EC Treaty (a) states that they are only binding as to the object to be achieved, (b) gives the Member States discretion in their implementation, and (c) pointedly omits to qualify them as having 'direct application', directives are in principle incapable of having direct effect. The Court, however, identified two categories of directive which were capable of having direct effect.

The first consisted of directives which had failed to be implemented, correctly or otherwise, by the time limit stipulated. In *Pubblico Ministero v Ratti*,[34] the disputed measures were two directives which had not been implemented by the Italian government. In relation to one of these, the time limit for implementation had already expired. The Court ruled that this directive was capable of having direct effect. However, it cannot produce direct effect before the deadline for implementation by the national authorities has expired.[35] Even after a directive has been implemented by the national authorities, it is always possible that the national authorities have failed to implement it correctly. In such cases, the directive in question should also have

31 Steiner, J, *op cit*, p 28.
32 Case 128/78, *Commission v United Kingdom* (1979) ECR 419 at 428.
33 OJ 1970 L 164.
34 Case 148/78 (1979) ECR 1629.
35 *Ibid*, at 1646.

direct effect, since its effectiveness would be removed if individuals were incapable of relying on it before their national courts.[36]

The second category concerns directives — or certain parts of directives — which require no implementation. In *Van Duyn v Home Office*,[37] a Dutch citizen wished to take up residence in Britain in order to fill the post of secretary to the Church of Scientology. She substantiated this claim by invoking Article 3(1) of Directive 64/221,[38] which regulates the conditions in which Member States may plead the public policy exception stated in Article 48(3) EC Treaty. The ECJ found that this subsection of the directive met the criteria for direct effect.[39] Not only did it contain an obligation admitting of no exception or condition, but also considerations of legal certainty required that individuals could rely on this obligation even if contained in an instrument which, taken as a whole, did not have direct effect. The direct effect of directives gives rise to a number of issues and problems to which the ECJ has been required to address itself — once again confirming its law-creating role.

Exclusion of horizontal direct effect

One of the issues which was bound to arise from the recognition of the direct effect of directives was the question whether the latter were capable of having horizontal as well as vertical direct effect. In the *Marshall* case,[40] the ECJ excluded the probability that directives should have horizontal direct effect, on the grounds that:

according to Article 189, the binding nature of a directive, which constitutes the basis for the possibility of relying on the directive before the national court, exists only in relation to 'each Member State to which it is addressed'. It follows that a directive may not of itself impose obligations on an individual and that a provision of a directive may not be relied upon as such against such a person.[41]

In *Faccini Dori*,[42] the Court reiterated its opposition to the granting of horizontal direct effect to directives. If it were to do so, said the ECJ, it would be tantamount to giving the Community authorities the power to impose obligations on individuals which hitherto had been restricted to regulations.

Unusually, the court appears to have applied the literal, rather than purposive, method of interpretation in ruling thus. The denial of horizontal

36 Case 51/76, *Verbond van Nederlandse Ondernemiingen v Inspecteur der Invoerrechten en Accijnzen* (1977) ECR 113 at 127.

37 Case 41/74 (1974) ECR 1337.

38 OJ (Special Edition) 1963–64, p 117.

39 Case 41/74, *op cit*, at 1348.

40 Case 152/84, *Marshall v Southampton Area Health Authority* (1986) ECR 723.

41 *Ibid* at 749.

42 Case C–91/92, *Faccini Dori v Recreb Srl* (1994) ECR I–3325.

direct effect to directives gives rise to as many problems as it solves. Quite apart from the problem that individuals could thus find themselves discriminated against, this ruling creates a number of anomalies. For example, it could give rise to a situation whereby a Treaty provision has both horizontal and vertical direct effect, whereas a directive implementing it would only have vertical direct effect. Conscious of these difficulties, the ECJ has endeavoured to mitigate their impact. One way to achieve this was to interpret the notion of 'public authority' as widely as possible. Thus in *Marshall*,[43] the Court contented itself with stating that the Health Authority – the defendant in the main action – was a public body, without specifying the criteria which such a body had to meet for the purposes of enabling a directive to be pleaded against it before the national courts. This omission was rectified in the *Foster* decision,[44] where the ECJ held that any organ which has been given responsibility for providing a public service under the supervision of the state, and which for this purpose has special powers beyond those which normally apply in relations between individuals, will constitute such a public body.

It should perhaps be added that not all the expert opinion is opposed to conferring horizontal direct effect on directives. More particularly A-G F Jacobs, advising in *Vaneetveld*,[45] considers that to do so would be consistent with the need to secure the effectiveness and uniform application of Community law. Nor would such an outcome prejudice legal certainty.

Indirect effect

It has already been noted that directives cannot produce direct effect before the expiry of the implementation deadline, and that they do not admit of horizontal direct effect. This constitutes a potential restriction on the effectiveness of directives.[46] The ECJ has attempted to overcome this difficulty by imposing on the national courts an obligation to interpret national legislation in the light of directives. This obligation is also referred to as the 'indirect effect principle', and it was laid down for the first time in the *Von Colson* decision.[47] The Court based this obligation on the duty imposed by Article 5 EC Treaty on the Member States to take all appropriate measures, both general and particular, to ensure the achieve the result envisaged by the directive in question.

43 Case 152/84, *op cit*, at 748.
44 Case C-188/89, *op cit*, at 3349.
45 Case C-316/93, *Vaneetveld* (1994) ECR 763 at 774.
46 Owen, R, *Essential European Community Law* (1995), Cavendish Publishing Ltd, pp 33–34.
47 Case 14/83, *von Colson and Kamann v Land Nordrhein-Westfalen* (1984) ECR 1891 at 1908. See also Case 79/83, *Harz v Deutsche Tradax* (1984) ECR 1921 at 1939.

The decision in *Marleasing*[48] took the principle of indirect effect a stage further. This concerned a case brought against a Spanish company by one of its creditors who alleged that the company in question was null and void. The main argument in support of this contention was that the contract on which the company was formed had no valid cause, as is required by Spanish civil law. However, the First Company Law Directive[49] did not mention this ground as a reason for annulling a company. At the time at which the main action was brought, Spain had not as yet implemented the Directive. The Court repeated the rule stated in *Von Colson*, but added that the obligation on the part of the courts to interpret national law in the light of the directive applied regardless of whether the national legislation concerned was adopted before or after the directive. Thus it was national provisions themselves which, interpreted in compliance with the directive, had direct effect.

State liability

The third issue to which the direct effect of directives gives rise concerns the damage caused by the failure on the part of the Member State to implement the directive. The Court was faced with this problem for the first time in *Francovich*.[50] The applicants in this case were owed outstanding remuneration by the company which had employed them, and which had gone bankrupt. They brought proceedings against the Italian state for its failure to implement Directive 80/987,[51] which gives protection to employees following the insolvency of their employer.

The ECJ held that, in principle, individuals were entitled to obtain compensation if their rights were infringed by a breach of Community law for which the Member State was liable. If this were not the case, the full effectiveness of Community law would be impaired, and the protection of those rights conferred by the rules of Community law would be weakened. This was the case regardless of whether the directive in question had direct effect or not. The ECJ at the same time laid down the criteria which must be met for such a claim for compensation to succeed:

- the directive must have had the object of creating rights for individuals;
- the contents of these rights can be identified from the wording of the directive; and

---

48 Case C-106/89, *Marleasing SA v La Comercial Internacional de Alimentacion SA* (1990) ECR I-4135 at 4157.

49 Directive 68/151, JO 1968 41.

50 Cases C-6/90 and C-9/90, *Francovich, Andrea, and Bonifaci, Daniela v Italian Republic* (1990) ECR I-5357.

51 OJ 1980 L 283.

- there exists a causal link between the damage incurred and the failure on the part of the Member State to implement the directive.[52]

The Court also laid down a number of other fundamental rules regarding state liability. The compensation payable should be determined in accordance with the national rules on tort liability. In the present state of Community law, it is also for the Member States to designate the appropriate courts to which such claims must be brought. In addition, the substantive and procedural rules stipulated by the national authorities on state liability may not be less favourable than those which govern similar internal claims.[53]

Recent ECJ case law has served to sharpen the focus of the *Francovich* decision. In two recent joined cases,[54] the Court held that compensation was available from the state, not only where a directive had not been transposed, but also when it had been transposed negligently. However, a number of conditions must be met if negligent transposition is to give rise to such compensation: the Community rule in question must have the object of conferring rights on individuals; the infringement must be sufficiently serious, and there must be direct causation between the infringement by the Member State and the damage incurred by the claimant.[56]

Direct effect of decisions

Even before acknowledging the possibility that directives could have direct effect, the ECJ had recognised the potential direct effect of decisions in *Grad*.[55] Here too, the Court considered that the effectiveness of decisions would be diminished if persons affected were not allowed to rely upon them. This was particularly the case where decisions imposed obligations on the Member States. Whether or not decisions can have horizontal as well as vertical direct effect is not as yet clear.[56]

Direct effect of international agreements

Since the international agreements concluded by the Community form part of its legal order, there is no reason why, in principle, they should not have direct effect if they meet the criteria stipulated. The Court has, albeit rarely, conferred direct effect on some such agreements. Thus in *Kupferberg*,[57] it held that Article 21(1) of

52   *Ibid*, at 5415.

53   *Ibid*, at 5416.

54   Cases C-46/93, *Brasserie du Pêcheur v Germany*, and C-48/93, *R v Secretary of State for Transport, ex parte Factortame (No 3)*, not yet reported.

55   Case 9/70, *Grad v Finanzamt Traunstein* (1970) ECR 825 at 837–38.

56   Weatherill, S and Beaumont, P, EC Law – *The Essential Guide to the Legal Workings of the European Community* (1994), Penguin, p 307.

57   Case 104/81, *Hauptzollamt Mainz v Kupferberg* (1982) ECR 3644.

the Free Trade Agreement between the Community and Portugal had direct effect.

IV Direct applicability

The enforcement of Community law can only be realised to the full where there is a clear understanding as to how rules of Community law can become part of the legal order of the Member States. This is an aspect for which direct effect by itself does not provide a full answer, and raises the issue of the applicability of Community rules. The issue of direct applicability concerns more particularly the question of how the derived legislation becomes part of the domestic legal order of the Member States. In fact, it should be mentioned at the outset that the notion of direct applicability is a concept which is distinct from, although related to, the notion of direct effect – even though the Court of Justice at times seems blissfully unaware of this. In fact, it is fair to state that we have the leading authors on Community law, more particularly the Dutch scholar JA Winter,[58] to thank for bringing this distinction to public attention.

Unlike the notion of direct effect, the concept of direct applicability is specifically referred to in the EC Treaty, more particularly Article 189. As has already been explained earlier (above, p 89) this provision states clearly that only regulations are 'directly applicable in all the Member States', and by omitting this qualification from directives and decisions, it denies the latter this qualification. As a result, regulations become part of the domestic legal system of the Member States without requiring any incorporating enactment on the part of the national authorities.

Such is the force of this rule that even where a Member State reproduces in one of its legislative instruments the exact contents of a regulation, that instrument must be held to be unlawful as it detracts in some way from the unhindered manner in which regulations become part of the national legal order.[59] The only circumstance in which Member States are entitled to adopt measures in relation to a regulation arises where the regulation itself allows this. Some regulations require the national authorities to implement their provisions by means of administrative measures. This practice has been accepted by the Court.[60] In such cases, regulations are not fully independent measures. This is an inevitable result of the fact that the Community institutions do not have full executive control over the manner in which their provisions are carried out. This is why the argument, put forward by some authors,[61] that

---

58 'Direct Applicability and Direct Effect' (1972) CML Rev 425.

59 Cases 89 and 93/71, *Leonesio v Ministry of Agriculture* (1972) ECR 287 at 293.

60 Case 94/77, *Zerbone v Amministrazione delle Finanze dello Stato* (1978) ECR 99.

61 Charlesworth, A and Cullen, H, *op cit*, p 78.

regulations which allow for such national measures are not true regulations appears to be somewhat specious.

Directives, decisions and Treaty Articles cannot be directly applicable since they require national or Community legislative action to implement them.[62] This is why it is essential to make the distinction between direct effect and direct applicability, even though the ECJ tends to use these terms interchangeably. Only regulations are capable of having direct applicability; however, this does not mean that all regulations have direct effect, as has already been mentioned before (above, p 89). Conversely, although directives, decisions and Treaty Articles are excluded from the scope of direct applicability, they can, as has been noted earlier (above, p 86–90) have direct effect if they meet the relevant conditions.

V Supremacy /rule of Comm Law + Precedence

In order to be fully enforceable, the rule of Community law needs to satisfy two requirements. First, the rights contained therein must be capable of being relied upon before a national court, which must protect these rights. As has been seen earlier in this chapter, the direct effect mechanism meets this requirement. However, this court will also need to give precedence to this Community law rule in the event of it entering into conflict with a national rule. This is known as the principle of supremacy, or precedence, of Community law.[63] Like the concept of direct effect, the supremacy of Community law was not specifically regulated in the Treaty. It is true that it was always implicit in the scheme and purpose of the Treaty, but this fact needed to be identified, confirmed and developed by the case law of the ECJ.

As well as laying down the principle of direct effect, the *Van Gend & Loos* decision[64] established that the Community had created a new legal order for the benefit of which its Member States had limited their sovereign rights. However, this still left unanswered the question as to what would happen if a conflict arose between an EC rule and a domestic legislative instrument. The answer was provided in a case which followed shortly after the *Van Gend & Loos* case, to wit *Costa v ENEL*.[65] This case concerned a dispute between the Italian nationalised electricity industry and a shareholder in one of the companies taken into public ownership. The Court, having confirmed its ruling in *Van Gend & Loos* as to the limitation of the Member States' sovereign rights, went on

---

62 Rawlinson, W and Cornwell-Kelly, MP, *European Community Law* (1990), Waterlow, p 14.

63 Some authors also refer to this mechanism as the 'primacy' of Community law.

64 Case 26/62, *op cit.*

65 Case 6/64, *op cit.*

to consider the potential conflicts between national law and Community law in the following terms:

The integration into the laws of each Member State of provisions which derive from the Community, and more generally the terms and the spirit of the Treaty, make it impossible for the states, as a corollary, to accord precedence to a unilateral and subsequent measure.[66]

The Court ruling in the *Simmenthal* decision[67] was even more explicit, in that it held that the nature of Community law precluded the 'valid adoption of new national measures to the extent to which they would be incompatible with Community provisions'. Therefore, concluded the Court, any domestic court were under an obligation not to apply any national rule capable of preventing that court from enforcing the rights conferred by Community law on individuals.[68] The principle of supremacy was refined even further by the *Factortame* decision.[69] The applicants were a number of Spanish fishing fleets wishing to challenge United Kingdom legislation which reserved the right to register a boat as British to persons having a genuine link with Britain. The Court ruled that in the event of a conflict between Community law and national rules, not only must the latter be ignored; it must actually be 'set aside' by the courts.[70]

VI Subsidiarity

Thus far, the reader of this chapter could be forgiven for forming the impression that the trend in the relationship between Community law and national law is one which continuously moves the centre of gravity away from the national authorities towards the Community institutions. This was certainly the case until the mid-1980s, when public opinion started to show a certain degree of alarm over this trend. This threatened to undermine the degree of popular consent which the European project needs in order to sustain its momentum.

Given that Community law takes precedence over national law as a matter of principle, the Member States also have an obligation to ensure that no national legislation should present any impediment to its full effectiveness. If it failed to do so, the Member State in question could face a challenge from the Commission under Article 169 EC Treaty (below, p 105). *judicial review*

66 Case 6/64, *op cit*, at 593–94.
67 Case 106/77, *Amministrazione delle Finanze dello Stato v Simmenthal* (1978) ECR 630 at 640.
68 *Ibid*, at 644.
69 Case C-231/89, *R v Secretary of State for Transport, ex parte Factortame* (1990) ECR I-243.
70 *Ibid*, at 2474.

It was in an effort to give reassurance to these concerns that the concept of subsidiarity was born. It was introduced into Community law by the SEA, which stipulated that the Community should act only to realise the objectives of its environmental policy where these objectives could not be attained better at the level of the national authorities. It was raised to constitutional status by the TEU, which inserted Article 3b into Part One of the EC Treaty, which lays down the principles of the Community, the second paragraph of which reads:

In areas which do not fall within its exclusive competence, the Community shall take action, in accordance with the principle of subsidiarity, only if and in so far as the objectives of the proposed action cannot be sufficiently achieved by the Member States and can therefore, by reason of the scale or effects of the proposed action, be better achieved by the Community.

The principle of subsidiarity is as yet extremely broad. Nor was there initially any derived legislation which could shed any light on its more specific meaning. An attempt to remedy this was made with the adoption of the Protocol on the application of the principles of subsidiarity and proportionality, attached to the Amsterdam Treaty. This contained the following clarifications:

(a) The principle of subsidiarity does not call into question the powers conferred on the European Community by the Treaty, as interpreted by the ECJ. The criteria stated in Article 3b(2) TEU, referred to above, relate to areas for which the Community does not have exclusive jurisdiction. The principle of subsidiarity provides a guide as to how those powers are to be exercised at the Community level. Subsidiarity is a dynamic concept and should be applied in the light of the objectives set out in the EC Treaty. It allows Community action within the limits of its powers to be expanded where circumstances so require; conversely, it enables them to be restricted or even discontinued where it is no longer justified.

(b) For Community action to be justified, both aspects of the subsidiarity principle must be met: the objectives of the proposed action cannot be adequately achieved by the Member States in the framework of their national constitutional system, and can therefore be better achieved through Community action. The following guidelines are to be followed in examining whether this condition is fulfilled:

(i) the issue under consideration has transnational aspects which cannot be satisfactorily dealt with by national action;

(ii) actions by Member States alone, or lack of Community action, would conflict with the requirements of the Treaty;

(iii) action at Community level would produce clear benefits by reason of its scale or effects compared with action at the national level.

(c) The form of Community action should be as simple as possible, consistent with the satisfactory achievement of the objective pursued by the measure and the need for effective enforcement. The Community should only legislate to the extent which is necessary. Other things being equal, directives should be preferred to regulations, and framework directives to detailed measures.

(d) Regarding the nature and extent of Community action, Community measures should leave as much scope for national decision as possible, consistent with securing the objective of the measure and observing the requirements of the Treaty.

(e) Where the application of the principle of subsidiarity results in no action being taken by the Community, Member States are required to comply with the general rules laid down in Article 5 EC Treaty, by taking all appropriate measures to ensure fulfilment of their obligations under the Treaty and by refraining from taking any measure which could imperil the achievement of the objectives of the Treaty.

However useful, this Protocol does not answer all the questions which arise in this context. One of these unresolved issues is that which seeks to establish whether, and to what extent, subsidiarity is a justiciable concept. The answer to this question will depend on two factors. The first is the extent to which the Community is prepared to work out in greater detail what the concept of subsidiarity actually entails in practice, which is the issue examined in the previous paragraph. The second factor will be the political direction in which the Community is likely to progress. If it reaches the stage where the allocation of powers becomes an issue which affects the legal position of the Community citizen, pressure will obviously be forthcoming to make the notion of subsidiarity one which the citizen can rely upon before the courts, both national and European. This will probably only be the case if the Community assumes the federal model.[71]

VII EU Law through the national looking glass

Situating the problem

If the Community was based on a truly federal model, the question of how EU law fits into the national constitutional arrangements would hardly arise. No-one ever devotes any serious study to the issue of how Utah assimilates American Federal law, or how German legislation (*Gesetzgebung*) is accommodated by the constitutional structures of Baden-Württemburg.[72] In its

71 Emiliou, N, 'Subsidiarity: an Effective Barrier against the Enterprises of Ambition?' (1992) ELR 383.
72 The only – and slightly eccentric – exception to this is Bavaria, where some brave souls continue to maintain that German Federal law does not apply because it was never formally accepted by the Land authorities!

current state, the Community model remains tilted towards the inter-governmental rather than to the federal model. As such, its legal system remains to a considerable extent dependent on the manner in which the legal orders of the individual states accommodate it. This in turn is dependent on the national constitutional arrangements which relate to Community law.

Monism and dualism

The legal systems of the Member States, and of the vast majority of states in the world community, for that matter, can be divided into two categories in terms of the manner in which they accommodate international treaties: monism and dualism. Monism starts from the assumption that international law and national law form part of the same legal order. Within that legal order, international law takes precedence over domestic law. Dualism, on the other hand, makes the opposite assumption, to wit that international law and domestic law constitute two separate legal orders. International law can only become part of the domestic law by specific incorporation by domestic legislation. Most EU countries (France, Belgium, the Netherlands, Spain) have adopted the monist approach. Some, like the United Kingdom and Italy, apply the dualist mode.

The monism/dualism split affects the manner in which the national constitutions accommodate Community law. Two points should be made at this stage. The first is that this difference of approach has not to date yielded any significant practical problems in the enforcement of Community law, more particularly in terms of its direct effect and supremacy. The second point is that it should not necessarily be assumed that where difficulties have arisen, these have materialised mainly in the countries which apply the dualist system. The difficulties which some courts in monist countries have experienced in recognising the supremacy of Community law bears this out. This has been the case in, for example, France, whose supreme administrative court had, until relatively recently, frequently been at odds with the case law of the ECJ.[73]

It should also be noted that even in those countries which have codified constitutions, the relationship between Community law and national law is not invariably governed by a specific constitutional provision. Some constitutions (eg that of Netherlands) have this relationship regulated by a constitutional provision entirely devoted to Community law. Others (eg France) have a constitutional provision regulating the constitutional position of international treaties – including the Community treaties. Others still, such as the Luxembourg constitution, make no provision whatsoever for the relationship between international law and domestic law, and have relied on their courts to develop the notion of the supremacy of Community law. The United Kingdom has no written constitution. The position of Community law in this country is

---

73 See Lasok, D, *op cit*, pp 326–32.

governed by ordinary legislation, and forms the subject matter of the next section of this Chapter.

The position under United Kingdom law

As has been mentioned before, the United Kingdom approach towards international treaties is governed by the dualist principle. (It should, however, be pointed out that the British courts have invariably endeavoured to interpret national legislation in such a way as to comply with the country's international obligations.)[74] Legislative action was therefore required in order to make Community law applicable in Britain. This was forthcoming in the shape of the 1972 European Communities Act, s 2(1) of which states:

All such rights, powers, liabilities, obligations and restrictions from time to time created or arising by or under the Treaties, and all such remedies and procedures from time to time provided for by or under the Treaties, as in accordance with the Treaties are without further enactment to be given legal effect or used in the United Kingdom shall be recognised and available in law, and be enforced, allowed and followed accordingly ...

This provision was so worded in order to ensure that any Community enactment automatically becomes applicable in the United Kingdom. If it had not been adopted or worded in these terms, every instrument of Community law would have required a validating Act of Parliament, which would have been a practical impossibility. However, because of the particular nature of Parliamentary sovereignty in Britain, s 2(1) of the 1972 Act cannot be regarded as an irrevocable commitment by the United Kingdom to maintaining the supremacy of Community law over domestic law. The British Parliament cannot, in principle, bind its successors. Therefore Community law only enjoys its present status of supremacy for as long as the European Communities Act remains on the statute book. If Parliament at some later stage sought to repeal, amend or expressly contradict s 2(1) of the Act, there can be little doubt that the British courts would be obliged to follow the express wishes of Parliament. It is important to make this point, because some authors now cleave to the view that some recent decisions by the House of Lords have constitutionally entrenched Community law in Britain. The present author believes this not to be the case, for the reasons set out below.

The first major decision in which the issue of the supremacy of Community law arose came in the case of *Macarthys v Smith*.[75] Here, an action had been brought by a stockroom manageress who was paid less than her predecessor, who had left his employment four months earlier, for performing the same

74 Akehurst, MB, *A Modern Introduction to International Law* (5th edn, 1985), George Allen & Unwin, p 44.

75 [1979] 3 All ER 325.

work. Proceedings commenced before an industrial tribunal and found their way to the Court of Appeal. The latter took the view that this raised a fundamental conflict between the Equal Pay Act 1970 on the one hand, and Article 119 EC Treaty and the EC Equal Pay Directive 1975 on the other.[76]

Lord Denning held that where such a conflict arose, the Commission was entitled to bring proceedings against the United Kingdom under Article 169 EC Treaty (below, p 105). It was, however, not necessary to await such litigation, since s 2(1) of the European Communities Act would give effect to the directly effective Article 119, as well as to any other directive which had direct effect. Should English legislation infringe such directly effective law, the courts were under an obligation to give precedence to Community law. Lord Denning did, however, also consider, *obiter*, the wider constitutional issue referred to earlier, to wit the position of the courts in the event of Parliament deciding to repudiate the EC Treaty or even legislate with the full intention of acting inconsistently with it. In that case, ruled Lord Denning, it would be the duty of the courts to follow the British Act in question.

This ruling only dealt with the problem presented by a conflict between Community law and an earlier Act of Parliament. The British courts were, however, bound to be confronted sooner or later with a conflict between Community law and subsequent national legislation. This was one of the main issues involved in the *Factortame* case.[77] The case resulted from the changes brought about by the Merchant Shipping Act 1988, banning the registration of fishing vessels as British by companies whose shareholders were not British citizens. This gave rise to a court action brought against the UK government by a number of Spanish companies which were registered in Britain but consisted of Spanish shareholders. The latter claimed that the Merchant Shipping Act infringed Community law.

The Divisional Court referred the Community law issue to the ECJ for a preliminary ruling, whilst granting interim relief to the applicant companies which enabled their vessels to continue to be registered as British pending the Community Court ruling. This was overruled by the Court of Appeal, which held that, in view of the supremacy of Parliament, the courts had no right to interfere with the applicability of an Act. The matter reached the House of Lords, which sought assistance from the ECJ on this point. The latter was asked to rule on the general issue whether a domestic court could, in reliance upon national law, be prevented from provisionally disapplying domestic legislation in order to give interim protection to a potential right under Community law. The Court of Justice replied in the negative, on the grounds that Community law could not take full effect if national law could prevent a court from

76 Directive 75/117, OJ 1975 L 45.
77 *R v Secretary of State for Transport, ex parte Factortame and others (No 2)* [1991] 1 AC 603.

providing interim relief in order to ensure the full effectiveness of a decision to be made on the existence of Community law rights.[78]

The extent to which this ruling has undermined the doctrine of Parliamentary sovereignty is unclear. It could be argued that the ECJ ruling is fully consistent with the terms of the European Communities Act 1972. After all, s 2(4) of this Act lays down that 'any enactment passed or to be passed, other than one contained in this Part of the Act, shall be construed and have effect subject to the foregoing provisions of this section'. In addition, s 3(1) expressly recognises the Court of Justice as the supreme interpreter of Community law. It is therefore fair to state that the 1972 Act had already made provision for Community law to prevail should Parliament adopt an Act which conflicted with it.

However, it must be stressed again that the position would be totally different if Parliament chose to amend, repeal or derogate expressly from the 1972 Act. It would therefore seem that Community law is entrenched against implied repeal, but not against express repeal. If the *Factortame No 1* decision had been given in connection with such an Act, a conflict would arise between the position adopted by the ECJ and the doctrine of Parliamentary sovereignty. This would be a conflict of such a fundamental nature that it could only be solved at the political, rather than at the legal, level. It should however, be pointed out that no such Act has ever been contemplated, even by governments whose commitment to the cause of the Community has sometimes been less than wholehearted.

VIII Conclusion

Community law seeks to involve the EC citizen by allowing him or her to plead certain rights before his or her domestic courts, albeit under the watchful eye of the Court of Justice. Supremacy ensures that any conflict between such rights and a national rule will result in precedence being given to those rights. As such, this combination between direct effect and supremacy constitute a radical departure in the legal aspects of the relationship between national law and the law of an international institution to which that country belongs. Although the Community is not the first legal system under which rules of international law confer rights on individuals which national courts must protect, it is the first system of international law requiring all the courts of the signatories to a Treaty to protect and enforce certain rights conferred on individuals – unlike the 'self-executing treaties', under which such rights were merely protected on the initiative of one of the Member States.

78 Case C-213/89, R. *v Secretary of State for Transport, ex parte Factortame (No 1)* (1990) ECR I-2433 at 2471.

Not all Community law provisions, however, are directly effective. To do so, the rule in question must satisfy the criteria developed by the ECJ, ie it must be clear and unconditional, and there may be no reservations making its validity depend on further legislative action at either the national or the Community level. Measured against these criteria, the Court has been able to confer direct effect on a large number of provisions, not only the most obvious category, ie regulations, but also Treaty articles, decisions and, perhaps the least likely candidates of all, directives. Two trends are particularly noticeable in the Court's case law: on the one hand, it has not restricted direct effect to negative obligations and, on the other hand, it has ensured that direct effect gives citizens rights not only against the national authorities, but also against other individuals. Direct effect should not, however, be confused with direct applicability.

6   Judicial Remedies in Community Law: Direct Actions

I   Introduction

Substantive rights and obligations without effective judicial remedies are of very little practical value to those whose interests are involved. Without these remedies, the interested party is almost entirely dependent on the goodwill of the institutions and citizens on whom the obligation rests. This goodwill cannot be guaranteed at all times, which is why the performance of these obligations by those bound by them needs to be subjected to the independent scrutiny of an independent referee, ie the judiciary. It is order to ensure such scrutiny that the EC Treaty has instituted a broad range of judicial remedies. They are extremely broad because:

- they can be either direct (where the action is brought by the applicant directly before the ECJ/CFI) or indirect (where a national court seeks the assistance of the ECJ in cases before it involving Community law);

- they involve both the European Court of Justice and the national courts; the latter in particular through the mechanism of the preliminary rulings procedure;

- they allow a wide range of plaintiffs and applicants to take the initiative and set the court action in motion; that is to say, not only institutional applicants such as the Commission, but also the private citizen;

- they are both general (eg the actions under Articles 169, 173 and 175 EC Treaty) and specialised (eg the actions brought under Article 93(2) regarding state aids).

The chapter concerns the direct actions before the ECJ; the indirect actions, which take the form of the preliminary rulings procedure, are discussed in Chapter 7.

II   Actions against Member States

General

Because the application and implementation of Community law is a matter of partnership between the Community institutions and the Member States, the public authorities of the latter are required to play a full part in its operation. This is particularly the case as regards the implementation of directives, which, with the rare exceptions discussed under the section devoted to direct effect, cannot be put into operation without the action undertaken by the national authorities. The latter are, however, sometimes careless and/or reluctant in performing this role, which is why the Treaty makes provision for calling them to account before the Court of Justice. This can be done at the initiative of either the Commission (Article 169 EC Treaty) or of the other Member States (Article 170 EC Treaty). In addition, specific action may be taken by the Commission against the Member States under Article 93(3) EC Treaty (state aids).

Actions brought by the Commission

Acting in its capacity of 'watchdog of the Treaty', the Commission is empowered by Article 169 EC Treaty to monitor the manner in which the Member States meet their obligations under Community law, call them to order in its own right, and, if this fails to secure compliance, wield the ultimate weapon of taking them to the ECJ. In principle, action by the Commission takes place over three possible stages: the formal notice of default, the action before the ECJ, and the enforcement of any decision taken by the latter. In practice, however, the formal stages are invariably preceded by an informal stage.

Mediation

Where the Commission considers that a Member State has been deficient in performing its Treaty obligations, it will first engage in a series of discussions with the national authorities, usually through the good offices of the Permanent Representation of that state with the Community. To prevent this informal stage from causing undue delay in the monitoring process, the Commission makes it clear that it intends to complete this stage by a certain time limit which usually does not exceed one year. In most cases, this informal procedure will serve to bring the matter to a satisfactory conclusion. The Member State will remedy its mistakes, and the Commission will discontinue its action.

Formal notice of default

If the Commission remains dissatisfied after the informal stage, it will serve a formal notice of default on the Member State concerned, in which the latter is invited to submit its observations. This stage is an important one, not only because it sets off the official part of the proceedings, but also because it defines the terms of reference of the dispute. The Commission may not thereafter extend the scope of the complaint brought against the national authorities.[1]

Reasoned opinion

The formal notice of default will also be sufficient to prompt the Member State into rectifying the omission complained of by the Commission. If this is not the

---

1   Case 51/83, *Commission v Italy* (1984) ECR 2793 at 2804.

case, and the national authorities resists the challenge issued by the Commission, the latter will issue a 'reasoned opinion' in which it sets out the reasons why it considers the Member State to be in default. It will also set a time limit by which the national authorities must reply. Disputes have sometimes arisen as to what constitutes (a) a 'reasoned opinion', and (b) a reasonable period in which the Member State can be expected to respond to the Opinion. The Court has tended towards a broad interpretation of both these concepts.[2]

Proceedings before the Court

If the Member State concerned fails to comply with the terms of the reasoned opinion within the period set by the Commission, the latter may bring proceedings against that state before the ECJ (Article 169, second sentence, EC Treaty). Even where the dispute has reached this stage, however, the issue can be settled without requiring a decision by the Court. In fact, approximately 44 per cent of cases actually brought to the ECJ are concluded in this way.[3] In the vast majority of cases, the Court finds against the Member State. The Member States' authorities have served up a wide variety of reasons/excuses for failing to meet their Treaty obligations. In the first place, they frequently plead internal difficulties. The Court hardly ever accepts this defence. Thus the government of a Member State cannot disclaim responsibility by placing the blame for the delay on the national parliament.[4] The action is not brought against the government as such, but against the government as representing the Member State, which is a legal person in its own right. Still less therefore can trade union objections to a particular directive serve as a valid defence for failing to implement it.[5]

Another defence which is frequently raised is that of *force majeure*, in other words, circumstances beyond the control of the national authorities in question. In one particular case, Italy was arraigned for having failed to provide statistical information regarding transport by road, as required by Directive 78/546.[6] The reason given by the Italian government for this omission was the circumstance that the data base which should have provided the answers was destroyed in a bomb attack on a Ministry of Transport building. The Court did not accept this defence. It argued that since that bomb attack, the Italian authorities had had ample time to replace the destroyed equipment and supply the relevant data.[7]

---

2   Case 7/61, *Commission v Italy* (1961) ECR 317 at 322; Case 74/82, *Commission v Ireland* (1984) ECR 317 at 338.

3   Weatherill, S and Beaumont, P, *op cit*, p 172.

4   Case 77/69, *Commission v Belgium* (1970) ECR 237 at 244.

5   Case 128/78, *Commission v United Kingdom* (1979) ECR 419 at 441.

6   OJ 1978 L 201.

7   Case 101/84, *Commission v Italy* (1985) ECR 2629, at 2537.

Reciprocity is another excuse which has been pleaded by defendant governments. Certain countries – for example France[8] – make the performance of their Treaty obligations conditional upon the other party or parties meeting theirs. When France was arraigned before the ECJ for having unlawfully banned exports of lamb, its government argued that the United Kingdom had failed to meet its obligations without being subjected to Commission action. The ECJ did not accept this argument, pointing out that the EC Treaty contained adequate mechanisms in order to address such problems.[9]

Enforcement of ECJ decision

Prior to the TEU, the decisions of the ECJ made under Article 169 EC Treaty were incapable of being enforced. Any decision made against a Member State was accompanied by the requirement that the national authorities in question should take the necessary steps to comply with the terms of the judgment. If the Member State in question continued to fall foul of its obligations, the Commission had no option but to recommence the entire Article 169 procedure afresh. The new Article 171, however, opens up new possibilities in this regard. Henceforth, if the Commission considers that the Member State in question has failed to take the necessary corrective action, it will issue a reasoned opinion to that effect, specifying the points on which the national authorities have failed to comply with the ECJ decision. If the Member State then fails to regularise its position within the time-limit laid down by the Commission, the latter may bring the case before the ECJ and specify the financial penalty which it considers to be appropriate. If the Court rules that the Member State is still in breach of its obligations, it may impose a financial penalty. It remains to be seen whether the ECJ has the will to do so.

Actions brought by other Member States

Under Article 170 EC Treaty, Member States have the right to bring proceedings against other Member States if they consider that the latter are in default of their Treaty obligations. This was always intended to be an exceptional procedure, because it is the Commission which is the proper guardian of the Treaties and which should, under Article 169 EC Treaty, bring defaulting Member States to book. However, the Article 170 procedure remains a useful safeguard against errors of judgment made by the Commission in this regard. It should, however, be pointed out that the Member State bringing the action must involve the Commission very closely during the run-up to proceedings before the ECJ.

8   See Article 55 of the 1958 Constitution of the Fifth Republic.

9   Case 232/78, *Commission v France* (1979) ECR 2729 at 2733. See also cases 90 and 91/63, *Commission v Belgium and Luxembourg* (1964) ECR 625.

Thus far, only one case of this nature has ever been taken to the ECJ. It was brought by the French Government (supported by the Commission) against the United Kingdom,[10] claiming that British rules on the mesh size of fishing nets constituted unlawful unilateral action. The Court awarded the action to France. The provisions of the new Article 171 EC Treaty, relating to the enforcement of such decisions, discussed under the previous section, also apply to this procedure.

Actions under Article 93(2) EC Treaty

The drafters of the Treaty considered that infringements by the Member States of the provisions relating to state aids warranted a separate, and more streamlined, procedure. If the Commission considers that such an infringement has been committed, it instructs the Member State in question to rectify its position within a certain time limit. If this instruction is not complied with, the Commission refers the matter to the ECJ 'in derogation from the provisions of Articles 169 and 170'. It should be noted, however, that the Commission may, if it so chooses, have any infringements of this nature dealt with under Article 169 EC Treaty.[11]

III   Actions for annulment

General

In Article 173, the EC Treaty makes provision for the judicial review of Community instruments, by organising a procedure by which they can be annulled. It is important to point out that this is one of the very few procedures by which the individual has access to the ECJ, even though the terms on which the individual can bring an action for annulment are considerably more restricted than those which apply to proceedings brought by institutional plaintiffs. In order to be successful, the action for annulment brought under Article 173 EC Treaty must clear two hurdles. The first hurdle is the admissibility requirement, which means that the applicant must first satisfy the Court that he or she or it is allowed to bring the action in the first place, and that he, she or it did so within the required time limit. The applicant must then convince the ECJ that his, her or its challenge complies with one of the substantive grounds for review. This means that the act against which the action has been brought must be capable of annulment on one of the grounds for review specified in Article 173(1) EC Treaty.

---

10   Case 141/78, *France v United Kingdom* (1979) ECR 2923.

11   Case C-35/88, *Commission v Greece, re KYDEP* (1991) ECR I-3125.

Admissibility test

To pass the admissibility test, the following questions must all be answered in the affirmative: (a) does the applicant have title to sue; (b) is the act capable of being challenged, and (c) was the challenge brought within the time limit set?

Title to sue (locus standi)

Here, a distinction needs to be drawn between institutional and private applicants. The former are the institutions specified in the second and third paragraphs of Article 173 EC Treaty – ie the Member States, the Council, the Commission, the European Parliament and the European Central Bank. The *locus standi* of the two last-named institutions is more limited than that of the three first-named. Whereas the Member States, the Council and the Commission have virtually unlimited rights of challenge, the only terms on which the Parliament and the European Central Bank are allowed to bring an action are 'for the purpose of protecting their prerogatives'.

As for private applicants, natural or legal persons also have the right to challenge Community acts, but may only do so 'against a decision addressed to that person or against a decision which, although in the form of a regulation or a decision addressed to another person, is of direct and individual concern to the former' (Article 173, para 4, EC Treaty). If the decision is directly addressed to the individual, the latter's right of action is obvious and straightforward. However, proving that a regulation or a decision addressed to someone else is, in reality, a decision which affects the individual directly and individually is quite a different proposition altogether. The ECJ has tended to be restrictive in its approach towards the individual applicant's right of action. There are several reasons for this: one is that, unlike the Community institutions, individuals are not 'guardians of lawfulness'; the other is that individuals have other means of redress available to them, particularly by bringing actions before their domestic courts which may then require the ECJ to give a preliminary ruling.[12] None of these reasons are entirely convincing.

The three main issues raised by the *locus standi* of private applicants are (a) the notion of 'individual concern', (b) the notion of 'direct concern', and (c) when is a regulation not to be regarded as a regulation, but as a *de facto* decision. Each will be dealt with in turn.

Individual concern

In one of its first decisions on this issue,[13] the Court was given the opportunity to lay down a general test for this requirement. The applicant was one of 30 German importers who challenged a refusal by the Commission to allow

---

12   Gautron, J-C, *op cit*, p 131.

13   Case 25/62, *Plaumann v Commission* (1963) ECR 95.

Germany to suspend customs duties on tangerine and mandarine oranges imported from third countries. The Court refused to concede that the applicants had been 'individually concerned' by this refusal, on the grounds that:

> Persons other than those to whom a decision is addressed may only claim to be individually concerned if that decision affects them by reason of certain attributes which are peculiar to them or by reason of circumstances in which they are differentiated from all other persons and by virtue of these factors distinguishes them individually just as in the case of the person addressed.[14]

This formula provided the framework for the approach by the Court, to be supplemented and refined in subsequent decisions. In *Toepfer*,[15] the applicants challenged a measure which allowed Germany to maintain certain protective measures based on a Community agricultural regulation. The Court held that the 'individual concern' test had been met, since it had already been possible to determine the number and identity of the importers affected on the date of adoption of the challenged decision. In the *International Fruit Company* ruling,[16] the ECJ held the application to be admissible because the decision had created a closed group of applicants which was not open to any other importer.

The combined criteria specified by the Court in *Toepfer* and *International Fruit Company*, ie that of belonging to an identifiable and closed group – were to dominate the Court's approach towards the notion of 'individual concern'. Unfortunately, the ECJ has not been entirely consistent in its judicial policy on this issue. Thus in the case of Greek exporters of cotton yarn to France,[17] the applicants challenged a decision authorising the imposition of a quota system on imports of cotton yarn from Greece decided by the French government. The ECJ ruled that what made the applicants identifiable as a separate group was the fact that they had entered into contracts which were to be performed during the period in which the quota system applied. Therefore the decision was of individual concern to them. This ruling may be consistent with the *Plaumann* criteria, but is not at all in harmony with the *International Fruit Company* ruling, since the exporters in question could hardly be said to belong to a 'closed' group of persons affected.

Direct concern

Here too, the case law of the Court is not remarkable for its consistency. The first serious test of this requirement was the *Alcan* case.[18] Here, several aluminium refining companies applied for the annulment of a refusal by the

14 Case 25/63, *op cit*, at 108.

15 Cases 106 and 107/63, *Toepfer v Commission* (1965) ECR 405.

16 Cases 41–44/70, *International Fruit Company v Commission* (1971) ECR 411.

17 Case 11/82, *Piraiki-Patraiki v Commission* (1985) ECR 207.

18 Case 69/69, *Alcan Aluminium Raeren et al v Commission* (1970) ECR 385.

111

Commission to meet a request by Belgium and Luxembourg for additional national tariff quotas for aluminium. The ECJ held that the Commission decision had no effect other than to confer a power on the Member States concerned, and did not bestow any rights on any potential beneficiaries of such measures as the states concerned could adopt under this decision. Therefore the award of the tariff quota in question could not have any effects directly concerning the applicants.[19] The existence of a discretion on the part of a third party appeared to have been a decisive factor in the Court's decision. However, the Court relaxed this somewhat strict stance in later decisions.[20]

When is a regulation not a regulation?

The mere fact that Article 173 EC Treaty gives individuals the opportunity to challenge decisions which may have the outward form of a regulation is a clear indication that the drafters of the Treaty wanted the ECJ to adopt a non-formalist approach when interpreting this concept. This means that it has always endeavoured to consider the reality behind the outward appearance. Accordingly, whenever a challenge is brought by an individual against a regulation, the ECJ will need to establish whether the challenged act is a regulation or not. This was confirmed by the first case in which this issue was raised,[21] in which the Court held that it could not content itself with the official label given to the instrument, but that it should in the first place take account of its object and content. In the aforementioned *International Fruit Company* case,[22] the Court held that the regulation under challenge was not a provision of general application within the meaning of Article 189 EC Treaty, but a bundle of individual decisions taken by the Commission, each of which, although taken in the form of a regulation, affected the legal position of the applicant. Naturally, genuine regulations are not capable of challenge by individual applicants.[23]

Particularly anti-dumping regulations have been the subject matter of challenges by individuals.[24]

Acts capable of being reviewed

Although Article 173 EC Treaty states that the Court may annul acts of the Council and Commission other than recommendations and opinions, this does not mean that only regulations, directives and decisions are capable of being

19 Case 69/69, *op cit*, at 396.

20 Case 62/70, *Bock v Commission* (1971) ECR 897. See also Case 11/82, *op cit*, at 241–42.

21 Cases 16 and 17/62, *Confédération Nationale des Producteurs de Fruits et Légumes v Council* (1962) ECR 471 at 479.

22 Cases 41–44/70, *op cit*, at 423.

23 Cases 789/89 and 790/79, *Calpack v Commission* (1980) ECR 1949 at 1962.

24 See Case 113/77, *NTN Toyo Bearing v Council* (1979) ECR 1185; Cases 239 and 275/82, *Allied Corporation v Commission* (1984) ECR 1005.

challenged. Here again, the ECJ will have regard to the contents of the act rather than its form; as long as the Community instrument is binding, it will be open to challenge.[25] Clearly the Court felt that the drafters of the Treaty, when excluding recommendations and opinions from the scope of reviewable acts under Article 173 EC Treaty, had in reality sought to ban all non-binding acts.

Applicable time limits

The final paragraph of Article 173 EC Treaty requires any action for annulment to be brought within a period of two months following the date on which the measure was published, the date on which it was notified to the plaintiff or, if these conditions do not apply, the date on which it came to the attention of the plaintiff, as the case may be. No doubt considerations of legal certainty prompted the drafters of the Treaty to lay down such a relatively short time limit. Applicants have sought to circumvent this time limit by resorting to other actions, such as the plea of illegality (Article 184 EC Treaty) or the action for failure to act (Article 175 EC Treaty), which are not constricted by any time limits. The ECJ has, however, disallowed such manoeuvres.[26]

The Court also appears to have foreclosed the possibility of using Article 177 as a way of consciously circumventing the strict time requirement under Article 173. In the *TWD* case,[27] the Commission ruled that a certain subsidy paid by the German Government was illegal under Article 92 EC Treaty. The Government informed the would-be beneficiary of this, adding that the Commission decision in question was capable of being challenged under Article 173. However, the firm in question preferred to challenge the lawfulness of the decision indirectly, ie by raising the issue in the domestic courts, which could then bring the issue to the ECJ through a preliminary ruling under Article 177. The Court held that, since the firm had been informed of the possibility of bringing a challenge under Article 173, this indirect challenge was inadmissible. However, it is likely that the Court will be less severe on this kind of indirect challenge if there is some doubt whether the would-be applicant had title to sue under Article 173, or if it was established that the person in question did not know of the relevant measure in sufficient time to be able to meet the deadline for bringing an action under Article 173.[28]

---

25 Case 22/70, *Commission v Council (Re European Road Transport Agreement* (ERTA)) (1971) ECR 263 at 277.

26 Case 156/77, *Commission v Belgium* (1978) ECR 1881 at 1897; see also Case 18/68, *Eridania v Commission* (1969) ECR 459.

27 Case C-188/92, *TWD Textilwerke Deggendorf GmbH v Germany* (1994) ECR I-833.

28 Craig, P and de Burca, G, *op cit*, p 496.

Substantive grounds for review

Once the admissibility hurdle has been overcome, the applicant must demonstrate that the act under challenge meets one of the grounds for review set out in Article 173, second paragraph, EC Treaty. These grounds are: (a) lack of competence; (b) infringement of an essential procedural requirement; (c) infringement of the Treaty or any implementing rules thereof; and (d) misuse of powers. Each will be examined in turn.

Lack of competence[29]

This is a ground for review which has no exact equivalent in English administrative law. However, Lasok and Bridge[30] are probably right where they describe it as 'broadly comparable to the English doctrine of *ultra vires*'. It is the natural corollary of Article 4 EC Treaty, which requires each of the Community institutions to act within the limits of the powers conferred upon it. However, the Treaty gives no further indication as to the scope of this ground. It is probably safe to define this ground for review as one which concerns the capacity of the authority which issued the act, of whom it is alleged that it either improperly conferred its powers on others, arrogated to itself non-existing powers, or encroached on the powers of another authority.

It is naturally the case law of the ECJ which has been instrumental in giving substance to this ground for review. Rarely has the Court been required to deal with conflicts of jurisdiction between two Community institutions, essentially for two reasons. First, the Treaty normally sets out the powers of each institutions in fairly clear terms. Second, although the Court recognises that the institutions may only exercise those powers which have been expressly conferred upon them, it tends to interpret the scope of these powers in a fairly broad manner. Thus in the *ERTA* case,[31] the Court had no difficulty in dismissing the Commission's contention that the Council lacked the power to take part in the shaping of the European Road Transport Agreement, even though Article 228 states that the Commission negotiates international agreements and the Council concludes them. Disputes regarding the delegation of powers have been less straightforward to solve. In an early case,[32] the delegation in question was challenged on the grounds that the appropriate institution had delegated its powers to a body which lacked the powers to exercise them. The Court upheld the challenge, ruling that delegation of powers was only allowed for implementing measures, subject to the body to whom the

29   The present author is not entirely happy with the terminology used, preferring the term 'lack of powers'.

30   Lasok, *op cit*, p 263.

31   Case 22/70, *op cit*, at 282.

32   Case 9/56 *Meroni v High Authority* (1957–58) ECR 133.

powers had been delegated observing the same conditions of legality as were expected of the institution which had delegated these powers.

Infringement of an essential procedural requirement

It has already been noted earlier (above, p 79) that Community law makes provision for various mechanisms to ensure that certain requirements of natural justice and fairness be observed in procedural matters. It is particularly these procedural safeguards which have been relied upon under this ground for review. One such safeguard is the duty to give reasons (Article 190 EC Treaty). The importance of this requirement was stressed by the ECJ at an early stage in its case law,[33] not only for purely formal reasons, but also because the duty to give reasons allows all those affected by the measure in question to ascertain the manner in which the institution in question has applied the Treaty. Naturally, the duty to give reasons must not be interpreted so strictly as to constitute an obstacle to the application and implementation of Community law.[34]

Infringement of the Treaty and any implementing rule

This ground should be interpreted broadly, in the sense that it covers not only the Treaties and their implementing legislation, but also the general principles of law referred to earlier (above, p 73). One such general principle to be accepted by the Court was that of legitimate expectation. In *Töpfer*,[35] the applicant claimed that under the terms by which certain sugar export licences had been granted to him, he could expect either to receive export refunds or to exercise the right of cancellation, and that he had been deprived of this choice by the Commission decision complained of. Although the ECJ awarded this decision to the Commission, it ruled that the notion of legitimate expectation was one which could in principle be taken into account by the Court.[36]

Misuse of powers

Here, the Court has applied the traditional definition of this notion provided by French administrative law, to wit, an attempt to achieve an objective which is contrary to that for which the powers were conferred.[37] In other words, it is generally interpreted as an attempt to deflect the act under challenge from the purpose for which the power to make it was conferred.[38] It should be noted that challenges to Community acts have very seldom been awarded on this ground.

33 Case 24/62, *Commission v Germany* (1963) ECR 63 at 70.
34 Case 16/65, *Schwarze v Einfuhrstelle für Getreide und Futtermittel* (1965) ECR 877 at 889.
35 Case 112/77, *Töpfer v Commission* (1978) ECR 1019.
36 Case 112/77, *op cit*, at 1030.
37 Case 6/54, *Netherlands Government v High Authority* (1954–56) ECR 103 at 116.
38 Maresceau, M, *Europese rechtspraak en rechtspleging Story-Scientia* (1975), p 70.

IV Actions for failure to act

General

Just as the EC Treaty contains a mechanism for ensuring that the Member States perform their obligations under Community law, so it seeks to obtain that the Community institutions do not fail to act whenever the Treaty requires them so to do. Hence the inclusion of Article 175, which gives the Member States and the Community institutions the right to call the Council, Commission, European Parliament and, within certain limits, the European Central Bank to account before the ECJ. To a certain extent, Article 175 EC Treaty is the mirror image of the action for annulment under Article 173, to the point where some authors qualify them as being complementary to each other. As is the case with the action for annulment, there are two hurdles to overcome, that of admissibility and that of substance.

Admissibility test

The admissibility test under Article 175 EC Treaty is both wider and narrower than is the case with actions for annulment. It is wider because there is no time limit for bringing the action (at least in its initial stage); it is narrower because the applicant cannot set the action in motion without first having applied to the institution whose inaction is being alleged. Three conditions must be met simultaneously if the admissibility test is to be met:

Title to sue

Once again, a distinction must be drawn between institutional and private applicants. The former are described in very general terms in the first paragraph of Article 175 as being 'the Member States and the other institutions of the Community'. The term 'other institutions' includes the European Parliament, as was confirmed by the ECJ in 1988.[39] To this list, the TEU added the European Central Bank, but only in those areas which fall within its jurisdiction (Article 175, fourth paragraph, EC Treaty). As to individual applicants, natural and legal persons' these are allowed to bring an Article 175 action against a Community institution which failed to address to that person any instrument other than a recommendation or opinion. The exact scope of this 'failure to address an act' is not entirely clear. With certain reservations it is probably safe to agree with Charlesworth and Cullen[40] that it requires the private applicant to meet two criteria. The first is that the instrument in question falls within the scope of the legally binding acts referred to in Article 175 EC Treaty.[41] The second is that the

---

39 Case 377/87, *Parliament v Council* (1988) ECR 4017 at 4046.

40 *Op cit*, p 154.

41 Case 15/70, *Chevalley v Commission* (1970) ECR 975 at 980.

act which, allegedly, the challenged institution should have adopted for the purpose of meeting its Treaty obligations would have been addressed to the private applicant had it actually been enacted.

Indictable institution

The action must be brought against an alleged shortcoming of the European Parliament, the Council, the Commission, or, within its field of application, the European Central Bank.

Prior approach to the indicted institution

Before applying to the Court, the applicant must approach the institution complained of in order to prompt it to act. This approach to the institution must be explicit and must make it clear that, in the absence of a reply within a two-month time limit, the institution in question will be subjected to a challenge under Article 175 EC Treaty.

Grounds for review

Once the admissibility hurdle has been overcome, the applicant must convince the Court that that of which it accuses the institution in question amounts to a failure to act 'in infringement of this Treaty'. Because very few challenges under this Article clear the admissibility hurdle, the ECJ case law is does not provide a great deal of clarification. The Court did, however, lay down some useful policy guidelines in *Parliament v Council*.[42] The Council had been accused of failing to ensure the freedom to provide services in the field of international transport, and to establish the conditions in which non-resident transporters may operate transport services within a Member State. The ECJ held that there was definitely a result to be achieved in this area, which was determined by the combined effects of Articles 59, 60, 61 and 75(1)(a) EC Treaty. The only discretion enjoyed by the institution concerned related to the means employed in obtaining this result. These obligations were therefore sufficiently well-defined for any attempt to disregard them to constitute a failure to act under Article 175. The Council had been required to extend the freedom to provide services to the transport sector, in so far as the extension related to transport between two or more countries. It was generally agreed that these measures had not been adopted; therefore the Council was guilty of a failure to act in this regard.[43]

---

42 Case 13/83 (1985) ECR 1513.
43 Case 13/83, *op cit*, at 1601.

V   Plea of illegality

The procedure described under this section is not an 'action' within the true sense of the term, since it merely amounts to an indirect challenge to a Community act made in the course of proceedings which were not brought with the intention of challenging that act – even if these proceedings take place well beyond the two month time limit for bringing an action under Article 173 EC Treaty. The possibility of bringing such a challenge is laid down in Article 184 EC Treaty. Its scope is restricted to regulations adopted jointly by the Parliament and the Council (above, p 51), by the Council on its own, by the Commission or by the European Central Bank. It must be made on the same grounds for review stated in Article 173 EC Treaty. The consequences of a successful challenge of this nature are restricted to the ECJ declaring its inapplicability rather than its annulment.

It cannot be emphasised too strongly that this indirect challenge cannot be used in order to circumvent the strict deadlines and other criteria set out in Article 173 EC Treaty: it is very much an incidental remedy. The challenge must be made in the course of proceedings before the ECJ itself. At a relatively early stage of the ECJ case law, the *Milchwerke Wöhrmann* firm[44] tried to challenge a Commission decision under Article 184 EC Treaty before the Court, a challenge which they tried to present as an incidental plea to a national court action in which the Commission decision was at issue. Wöhrmann did so on the ingenious grounds that Article 184 did not indicate the specific court before which the main proceedings had to be instituted. Therefore they were entitled to consider that in this case, the ECJ was merely the forum for bringing the incidental plea, whilst the main action was proceedings before the domestic court.

The ECJ, however, did not accept this argument. It ruled that if it were to do so, this would create a remedy parallel to that provided by Article 173 EC Treaty, which was not at all the intention of Article 184. Its wording and intention clearly suggested that it was meant to make possible a plea of inapplicability of a regulation involved in a dispute pending before the ECJ on the basis of another Article – and then only incidentally, and with limited effect.[45] Various other attempts to use Article 184 EC Treaty as a means of evading the strict conditions stipulated in Article 173 EC Treaty have also met with failure.[46]

Since the plea of illegality is merely an incidental remedy, its effects must necessarily be limited. The only possible outcome of a successful challenge is

---

44   Cases 31 and 33/62, *Milchwerke Wöhrmann v Commission* (1962) ECR 501 at 506.

45   Cases 31 and 32/62, *op cit*, at 507.

46   See, for example, Case 156/77 *Commission v Belgium* (1978) ECR 1881.

that the measure is held inapplicable – and then only *inter partes* (as between the parties to the dispute), and not *erga omnes* (in general terms). Still less is there any obligation on the part of the institution which adopted the offending act to repeal or amend it. The fear that the Court could strike down any implementing measures adopted on the basis of the act in question could provide the necessary incentive for the institution to be galvanised into action, although there is little evidence to support such lofty expectations.

VI   Actions in liability

General

The Community is an entity which has legal personality. As such, its activities are capable of having civil, as well as administrative and constitutional, implications, which could engage the liability of the Community. This means that the Community could be faced with court actions seeking a private law remedy for any erroneous actions which it may have engaged in, which in the vast majority of cases takes the form of civil damages or compensation. Under this heading, the Community could be faced with two types of action: actions in contract and actions in tort. The first-named are dealt with by Article 215 EC Treaty, which provides that contracts involving the Community are governed by the law which applies to the contract concerned.[47] In the vast majority of cases, contracts to which the Community, or one of its institutions, is a party contain a clause indicating which law of contract applies, usually the provisions of the Belgian Civil Code, as well as the court before which any disputes arising from the contract will be settled (which is never the ECJ). The actions in tort in which the Community can be involved, however, present greater difficulties and challenges, which are examined below.

Tort liability: basic principles

The fundamental rules governing the Community tort liability is the second paragraph of Article 215 EC Treaty, which states:

In the case of non-contractual liability, the Community shall, in accordance with the general principles common to the laws of the Member States, make good any damage caused by its institutions or by its servants in the performance of their duties.

The third paragraph makes the same principles applicable to any damage caused by the European Central Bank or by its officials. This provision must be

---

47   The European Central Bank is subject to specific rules regarding the contracts in which it is involved, which are laid down in Article 35.3 of its Statute.

supplemented by Article 178 EC Treaty, which lays down that it is the ECJ which has jurisdiction in disputes arising from Community liability. As with other judicial remedies at Community law, it is necessary to make a distinction between the admissibility criteria and the substantive grounds on which the action can be awarded. These aspects form the subject matter of the next two sections.

Tort liability: admissibility criteria

In the first instance, it is necessary to establish who has *locus standi*, ie who has the right to bring the action. It is generally recognised that there are hardly any restrictions which apply here: any natural or legal person may bring an action in tort against the Community, on condition that he or she can make out a *prima facie* case that he or she has suffered damage through the actions or omissions on the part of a Community institution or one of its officials. However, it is necessary that the applicant has suffered the damage. Any actions brought by a trade union or staff association on behalf of its members would be held to be inadmissible.[48]

As to the party against whom the action may be brought, the Court has ruled that this can only be the Community as represented by the institution accused of having committed the tortious action, rather than the Community as a whole.[49] This is in spite of the ECJ ruling in *Algera*,[50] which held that only the Community, and not its institutions, possesses legal capacity. It has been suggested that, since the Commission represents the legal *persona* of the Community, every action in tort should be brought against it, regardless of the institution to which the damage is attributed. This view was not shared by the Court[51] in the interests of the proper administration of justice. As for the time limit in which the action can be brought, this is set at five years as from the occurrence of the event which gave rise to the action (Article 43 of the Statute of the Court of Justice).

Tort liability: grounds on which the action may be awarded

Article 215 EC Treaty requires the ECJ to settle claims for damages on the basis of the principles of tort liability which are common to the Member States. However, the formative years of the Court's case law in this regard covered the first 15 years of the operation of the Community, when the latter consisted of six Member States, five of whom applied civil law systems based on the French model. It is therefore the case law of the ECJ has been shaped largely by the

48 Constantinho, P and Dony, M, *op cit*, p 103.
49 Cases 63–69/72, *Werhahn Hansamühle v Council* (1973) ECR 1229 at 1247.
50 Cases 7/56 and 3–7/57, *Algera v Common Assembly of the ECSC* (1957–58) ECR 39.
51 Cases 63–69/72, *op cit*, at 1246.

French law of torts.[52] Particularly the formula of Article 1382 of the French *Code Civil* has dominated the approach of the ECJ on this issue. This is a very general statement of liability, which requires that anyone who, through his or her own fault, has caused damage to another person is under an obligation to repair such damage. Three elements must therefore be established: (a) the occurrence of damage; (b) the commission of a fault on the part of the defendant; and (c) the causal relationship between (a) and (b). This was confirmed by the ECJ in a recent case.[53]

Occurrence of damage

In principle, the actionable damage is restricted to economic loss, taking into account both the loss actually incurred (*damnum emergens*) and any loss of earnings (*lucrum cessans*).[54] All that is required is that the damage be certain, real and provable. In some cases, however, the ECJ has hinted that immaterial loss cannot be excluded from the scope of Article 215, second paragraph, EC Treaty.[55] The amount of the loss is to be assessed in accordance with the general principles of law as they apply in the systems of the Member States.[56]

Commission of fault

Here, it is necessary to demonstrate both that a certain duty was owed to the applicant, and that the duty was breached. Both these elements were found to be present in the Stanley Adams decision.[57] In this case, the plaintiff was an employee of a Swiss pharmaceuticals firm who surreptitiously communicated to the Commission documents which proved conclusively that his employer had breached Community competition law. The Commission communicated the relevant documents to the firm (Hoffmann-Laroche), in spite of Mr Adams's request to keep his identity confidential. This allowed the firm to conclude that the information in question had emanated from Mr Adams, causing him to be charged with economic espionage. The Court held that there was indeed a duty of confidentiality on the part of the Commission, given that Article 214 EC Treaty requires Community officials not to disclose any information covered by the obligation of professional secrecy. Since the Commission must have been

52   For a general introduction to these rules, see Cairns, W and McKeon, R, *Introduction to French Law* (1995), Cavendish Publishing Ltd, Chapter 5.

53   Case C-358/90, *Compagnia Italiana Alcool v Commission* (1992) ECR 2457.

54   Cases 5, 7 and 13–24/66, *Kampffmeyer et al v Commission* (1967) ECR 245 at 266.

55   Case 145/83, *Adams v Commission* (1985) ECR 3539 at 3556.

56   Cases 261 and 262/78, *Interquell Stärke-Chemie v Council and Commission* (1979) ECR 3045.

57   Case 145/83, *op cit*.

aware of the risk involved in handing over photocopies of the relevant documents to the Swiss firm, it must also have breached this duty.[58]

The Community institutions are sometimes required to make difficult policy choices when enacting their rules. These choices have been known to be mistaken, and to cause damage to individuals. Do such mistakes engage the liability of the Community? The Court has, on the whole, been disinclined to reply in the affirmative, and has set extremely stringent conditions for allowing such actions to succeed. In *Schöppenstedt*,[59] the act complained of was a regulation laying down the measures which were required in order to offset the difference between national sugar prices and Community reference prices which applied as from a certain date (1 July 1968). The applicant complained that this regulation had been based on criteria which ran counter to those which should have been applied under Article 40(3) EC Treaty. This had caused a mistaken assessment of the difference between the reference price and the former German price of raw sugar, causing the plaintiff to incur severe losses. The action was dismissed by the ECJ because the plaintiff's case did not meet the criteria which, according to the Court, must be satisfied if legislative action involving measures of economic policy is to give rise to tort liability. In what has now become known as the 'Schöppenstedt formula', the Court ruled that an action brought on these grounds will not succeed:

unless a sufficiently flagrant violation of a superior rule of law for the protection of the individual has occurred.[60]

Causal link between fault and damage

The applicant must establish a direct link between the action complained of and the damage which he or she claims to have incurred. Therefore the remoteness and speculative nature of the causal link will be factors which limit the plaintiff's chances of success. In *Pool v Council*,[63] an English cattle farmer

This criterion is extremely difficult to meet, and most actions in tort brought in respect of such economic policy choices have foundered,[61] although the odd action has been known to succeed.[62] It is not difficult to see why the ECJ has been very strict in such matters, since policy-making would become an almost impossible task for the Community institutions if they were hampered in this task by constant considerations of tort liability.

58   Case 145/83, *op cit*, at 3590.
59   Case 5/71, *Zuckerfabrik Schöppenstedt v Council* (1971) ECR 975.
60   Case 5/71, *op cit*, at 984.
61   Case 83/76, *Bayerische HNL Vermehrungsbetriebe v Council* (1978) ECR 1209; Case 143/77, *Koninklijke Scholten-Honig v Council and Commission* (1979) ECR 3583.
62   Cases C-104/89 and C-37/90, *Mulder et al v Commission* (1992) ECR 2337.
63   Case 49/79 (1980) ECR 569.

claimed that the conversion rates of the Pound Sterling in the agricultural sector (the so-called 'green rates') had caused him damage. The Court dismissed his claim, on the grounds that the unrealistic and speculative nature of his claims made it impossible to establish a causal link.[64]

---

[64] *Ibid*, at 581–82.

7 Community Judicial Remedies: Indirect Actions

I Introduction

EU law is aimed principally at the individual, who is encouraged to enforce it and rely upon it before his or her national courts. However, to have allowed the latter to interpret and apply Community law independently of each other or of any other judicial authority would soon have led to a sizeable body of widely divergent case law. It is in order to avoid this contingency that the domestic courts were given the opportunity to call upon the assistance of the ECJ whenever they were faced with issues of EU law. This will ensure that the domestic courts will apply the necessary degree of unity when dealing with such questions.

The provision which regulates this judicial co-operation between the national and the European judiciary is Article 177 EC Treaty, which reads:

> The Court of Justice shall have jurisdiction to give preliminary rulings concerning:
>
> (a) the interpretation of this Treaty;
>
> (b) the validity and interpretation of acts of the institutions of the Community and the ECB;
>
> (c) the interpretation of the statutes and bodies established by an act of the council, where those statutes so provide.
>
> Where such a question is raised before any court or tribunal of a Member State, that court or tribunal may, if it considers that a decision is necessary to enable it to give judgment, request the Court of Justice to give a ruling thereon.
>
> Where any such question is raised in a case pending before a court or tribunal against whose decisions there is no judicial remedy under national law, that court or tribunal shall bring the matter before the Court of Justice.

The issues and questions which arise from this procedure are many and complex. They can be summarised as follows:

(a) what is actually meant by a 'court or tribunal' for the purpose of this procedure?

(b) what is the place of the national law, national courts and national procedures in the preliminary rulings procedure?

(c) what is the distinction between the opportunity to refer and the obligation to refer?

(d) what are the effects of a preliminary ruling?

Each will be dealt with in turn.

II   The notion of 'court or tribunal of a Member State'

It is generally agreed that the Court's interpretation of this term has been a broad one, even though it has been marred by the odd inconsistency. Curiously, the ECJ has never really formulated a watertight criterion by which this notion was to be interpreted. The closest it has ever come to doing this was in the *Pretore di Salo* case.[1] The Italian Government, whilst not disputing the *Pretore's* status as a judge, nevertheless argued that the latter was not acting in a judicial capacity in the matter for which a reference was being sought. The Court dismissed this argument, ruling that the request for a ruling may emanate from any court or tribunal which acts in the general context of its duty to settle, independently and in accordance with the law, cases which fall within the jurisdiction conferred on it by law, even though its role in a case which is referred for a preliminary ruling is not of a strictly judicial nature.

What this general statement does tell us, however, is that the ECJ has an extremely generous conception of what constitutes a court. This has enabled it without difficulty to validate the judicial status of administrative courts,[2] social security arbitration tribunals,[3] and the Italian *giudice conciliatore*.[4] The ECJ even recognises the right of certain professional associations to refer. In *Broekmeulen*,[5] the plaintiff in the underlying action had been refused registration as a general practitioner in the Netherlands by the relevant registration authority. The Netherlands Government challenged the ability of that committee to request a preliminary ruling. Because this Committee was a body which, with the consent of the public authorities, issued decisions after an adversarial procedure which were recognised as final, it was recognised by the ECJ as a 'court or tribunal', but that was more a function of the underlying dispute, which was a request for a declaration in a dispute between a member of the Bar Association and the courts and tribunals of another Member State.[6]

The position of arbitration panels is interesting. The Court has accepted these as 'courts or tribunals' as long as they present an element of public

---

1 Case 14/86, *Pretore di Salo v X* (1987) ECR 2545.

2 Such as the Netherlands Raad van State, in Case 36/73, *Nederlands Spoorwegen v Minister van Verkeer en Waterstaat* (1973) ECR 1299.

3 Case 61/65, *Vaasen v Beambtenfonds Mijnenbedrijf* (1966) ECR 261.

4 Case 6/64, *op cit*, at 596.

5 Case 246/80, *Broekmeulen v Committee for Registration of Medical Practitioners* (1981) ECR 2311.

6 Case 130/78, *Re Borker* (1980) ECR 1975.

involvement. Two cases illustrate this perfectly. In the first,[7] a dispute arose between a Danish white-collar trade union and the association of Danish employers on the interpretation of a collective bargaining agreement. It was referred to the Danish Industrial Arbitration Board for settlement. The Court held that this board fell within the scope of the term 'courts or tribunals'. The reference to the Board had not been in implementation of an arbitration clause in a contract, but resulted from a Danish law which stipulated that in disputes of this nature, either party could seize the Arbitration Board. The latter's composition and procedure were governed by Danish law; furthermore, its decision was final.

In the *Hochseefischerei* case,[8] however, the Court was faced with a private arbitrator. The case had been assigned to him pursuant to an arbitration clause in a contract concluded between various German shipbuilders. This clause not only referred all such disputes to the arbitrator, but also excluded the jurisdiction of the ordinary courts. When the arbitrator attempted to make a reference for a preliminary ruling, the Court refused to accept it. The main reasons for this were that: (a) the parties had not been obliged to involve the arbitrator and to exclude the ordinary courts – this they had done entirely voluntarily; (b) there was no public involvement whatsoever in the decision to refer the dispute to arbitration; and (c) it was not axiomatic that the public authorities would be involved at some stage of the arbitration procedure.

These two decisions go a long way towards clarifying the position of arbitrators, both public and private. Yet they do not provide all the answers. For example, exactly how much 'public involvement' is required before the arbitrator in question can be regarded as a valid 'court or tribunal'? In countries where even private arbitrations require some blessing on the part of the courts, will this suffice to confer judicial status on them for the purpose of Article 177?

III   The position of national law, national courts and national procedures

General

It was almost inevitable that questions of national law and national procedures should from time to time arise before the Court in the context of the preliminary rulings procedure, if only because of the conscious policy of constantly and increasingly integrating the Community legal order into that of the Member States. Three issues arise in this context. What is the position of the Court when

7   Case 109/88, *Handels- og Kontorfunktionaererens Forbund: Danmark v Dansk Arbejdsgiverforening, ex parte Danfoss* (1989) ECR 3199 at 3224–25.

8   Case 102/81, *Nordsee Deutsche Hochseefischerei GmbH v Reederei Mond* (1982) ECR 1095.

an appeal is made against the decision to refer? Can the ECJ involve itself in national law? Has the Court any control over the manner and circumstances in which the domestic courts make a reference?

Appeals against decisions to refer

Not all the parties involved in a dispute see the possibility of a reference for a preliminary ruling as an undiluted blessing, and sometimes appeals are lodged against decisions by national courts to make the reference. What should be the attitude of the Court of Justice if that happens? From the very outset, the Court's position has been one of non-involvement. The issue arose for the first time in the *Bosch* case.[9] Both the defendants and the French Government, intervening, were of the opinion that the request made to the ECJ by the national court warranted a preliminary ruling, because an appeal had been made for annulment of the order under which the request was made. This opinion stemmed from their interpretation of Article 177 of the Treaty, according to which such a request could only be granted if the order or decision under which it was made had become *res judicata*. The Court held that not only was such an interpretation at odds with the letter of Article 177 of the Treaty; it also failed to recognise that the law applicable to the referring court and Community law were systems of law which were totally distinct and different.[10] The jurisdiction of the Court of Justice was therefore entirely purely a factor of the existence of a request, and it did not behove the Court to examine whether or not that particular decision had become *res judicata*.

It soon appeared, however, that the very nature of the relationship between national law and Community law made such a sharp distinction between the two legal orders hard to maintain, or even to justify. In the *Chanel* case,[11] a similar problem to that which had arisen in *Bosch* was visited upon the ECJ, in that an appeal was lodged against the decision by the Rotterdam *Arrondissementsbank* (district court) to make a reference under Article 177. However, on this occasion the appeal was made after the request for a preliminary ruling had been received by the ECJ. In addition, the national court informed the ECJ that as a result of the appeal, the enforcement of the decision to refer had been suspended. The Court of Justice decided that in view of the circumstances of the case, and in view of the communication made by the national court, a decision in this case would be postponed until the appeal in question had been settled.[12] This appeal succeeded, and the request for a preliminary ruling annulled by the Court of Appeal. Accordingly, the *Chanel* case was removed from the cause list of the ECJ.

9   Case 13/61, *De Geus en Uitdenbogerd v Bosch en Van Rijn* (1962) ECR 45.

10 Case 13/61, *op cit*, at 50.

11 Case 31/68, *Chanel v Cepeha Handelsmaatschappij* (1970) ECR 403.

12 Case 31/68, *op cit*, at 405–06.

Exactly what these circumstances of the case were was never clarified by the Court. At first sight, these circumstances do not differ by much from the facts underlying the *Bosch* case. The impression is created that the Court had in fact abandoned the strict separation approach which it had proclaimed in Bosch; at the very least this approach became much harder to justify as a result of the *Chanel* judgment.[13]

Courts bound by a higher authority

A further problem which can arise in this regard is the question whether a domestic court which is bound by a decision issued by a higher judicial body may still make a reference. This was the bone of contention in the *Rheinmühlen* case.[14] Here, a decision from a lower fiscal court had been appealed before the German *Bundesfinanzhof* (Federal Fiscal Court). The latter, after having made a reference for a preliminary ruling, set aside the lower court's decision, and referred the matter back to the latter for a final ruling. The lower court was dissatisfied with the Federal Court's ruling, and decided to request a preliminary ruling itself. This resulted in the ECJ being asked to rule on the question whether the lower court had the right to make a reference. The Court replied in the affirmative. The objective of the preliminary rulings procedure was to obtain that Community law has the same effects in all EC Member States. Therefore a lower court must remain free to make a reference to the ECJ if it considers that the dispute before them gives rise to issues requiring clarification, and that the higher court's ruling would bring it into conflict with Community law. The position would be different only if the questions referred by the lower court were essentially the same as those asked by the higher court.[15]

The ECJ and national law law

As for the question whether the Court may interpret questions of national law, the answer is, in principle, in the negative. The Court is only authorised to issue rulings on matters of Community law. If it is asked to interpret domestic law, it will reword the question in such a manner as to give a broadly framed reply which is not country-specific. Here again, however, the separation between national law and Community law is sometimes hard to maintain in practice. Let us take the example of the *Deserbais* case.[16] The reply given by the Court to the French court was that:

Article 30 *et seq* of the Treaty must be interpreted as precluding a Member State from applying national legislation making the right to use the trade name of a

---

13   Maresceau, M, *op cit*, at 106–07.

14   Case 166/73, *Rheinmühlen v Einfuhr- und Vorratstelle* (1974) ECR 33.

15   Case 166/73, *op cit*, at 38–39.

16   Case 286/86, *Ministère Public v Deserbais* (1988) ECR 4907.

type of cheese subject to the observance of a minimum fat content to products of the same type imported from another Member State when those products have been lawfully manufactured and marketed under that name in that Member State and consumers are provided with proper information.[17]

Given that the reference emanated from a French court, could anyone entertain the slightest doubt that the Court is interpreting French law in the light of Community law? Yet in *Costa v ENEL*,[18] the Court had specifically ruled that the decision by the Court 'should (not) be given by the Court (...) on the validity of an Italian Law in relation to the Treaty'. However generally the manner in which preliminary rulings are worded, the Court can very often simply not avoid doing exactly that.

Formulation of the reference

It has already been noted (above, p 129) that the Court is sometimes moved to reword the preliminary reference in such a way as to avoid involving itself in issues of national law. However, this rewording will not affect the contents of the reference itself. The Court cannot examine whether or not the reference is relevant in the context of the proceedings before the referring national court.[19] Nor can the ECJ bring any judgment to bear on the reasons which prompted the national court to make the reference, or the importance which the national court attaches to the reference for the purpose of the proceedings before it.[20]

IV The opportunity to refer and the obligation to refer

General

Article 177, paragraph 3, EC Treaty makes it compulsory for the national court to make a reference if there is no judicial remedy available under national law against the decision of that court. In all other cases, the reference is optional.

Optional reference

National courts which are not caught by Article 177, paragraph 3, EC Treaty have complete discretion in the manner in which they choose to exercise their right to refer or not to refer. This means that (a) even if any of the parties involved in the case have requested a reference, the national court is under no obligation to make it, and (b) if the national court is willing and feels able to

17   Case 286/86, *op cit*, at 4926.
18   Case 6/64, *op cit*, at 597.
19   Case 43/71, *Politi v Ministry of Finance of the Italian Republic* (1971) ECR 1408.
20   Case 26/62, *op cit*, at 22.

interpret Community law without requiring the assistance of the Court, it may do so. Particularly the last-named option, which is known as the doctrine of *acte clair*, has been the subject matter of a good deal of controversy.

The term *acte clair* has been widely misunderstood and misinterpreted. Some believe[21] that this doctrine arose in the context of compulsory references under Article 177 paragraph 3 EC Treaty. The error is excusable in a certain sense because (a) it was elaborated by the First Conseil d'Etat (and to a certain extent by the Cour de Cassation), two courts which are caught by Article 177 paragraph 3, and (b) it is in the context of Article 177, paragraph 3, that this theory came to prominence (see discussion of the implications of the CILFIT decision, below). However, the *acte clair* doctrine has enjoyed wider application. It can be described as the theory (which had already been applied to international treaties before the Community treaties were adopted)[22] according to which there is no need to ask a preliminary ruling from the ECJ if the issue of Community law is so clear as to require no further explanation. In these circumstances, the national court is perfectly capable of applying Community law itself.[23]

Compulsory reference

In principle, the rule concerning compulsory rulings is clear: if a question of Community law arises before a court against whose decision no further remedies are possible, that court must make the reference. However, two issues have clouded the apparently clear-cut nature of this obligation.

The first is the issue of what constitutes a court 'against whose decisions there is no judicial remedy under national law'. In its interpretation of this concept, the Court has let itself be guided by the reality of the national court's jurisdiction rather than by its place in the judicial hierarchy. Thus in *Costa v ENEL*,[24] the reference had emanated from a mere Italian *Giudice conciliatore*. However, the Court noted that this court had jurisdiction to try a number of disputes involving modest sums in first and last instance. Accordingly, it had to be considered as a court of last resort within the meaning of Article 177, paragraph 3 of the Treaty.[25]

The position of the English Court of Appeal in this respect is somewhat ambiguous. In principle, it is not a court of last resort since its decisions are capable of review by the House of Lords. However, no application can be made

21 See, for example, Charlesworth, A and Cullen, H, *op cit*, at 202. Weatherill, S and Beaumont, P, *op cit*, at 260–61.

22 Steiner, J, *op cit*, at 296.

23 *Droit communautaire et droit français, op cit*, at 42–43.

24 Case 6/64, *op cit*.

25 *Ibid*, at 592.

to the House of Lords unless leave for appeal has been obtained from the Court of Appeal. Does this make the latter a court of last resort? The Court of Appeal itself does not consider this to be the case. In *Generics (UK) Ltd v Smith, Kline and French Laboratories Ltd*,[26] it stated unambiguously that the circumstance that leave for appeal to the Law Lords had to be obtained from it did not make it a final appellate court within the meaning of Article 177, para 3 EC Treaty. However, in a tell-tale phrase, it added 'But we have discretion'. Do we detect here the subjective view of a court wishing to assert its independence rather than seeking the best administration of justice? In any case, it lends credence to the view of a number of authors who express the view that the Court of Appeal should be regarded as a court of last instance.[27] Of course a ruling by the ECJ itself on this issue would put an end to the controversy.

The other issue which has introduced a note of ambiguity into the rule contained in Article 177, para 3, is the understandable reluctance on the part of the national courts of last resort constantly to make references on issues for which the ECJ has already made the position clear *ad nauseam*. Obviously this is where the *acte clair* theory once again becomes relevant. At an early stage already, the Court gave an indication that it was not inclined to take the strict view and to give some recognition to the *acte clair* theory. In *Da Costa en Schaake*,[28] the facts of the case and the legal issues involved were very close to those which arose in the *Van Gend & Loos* case, yet because it arose before the Netherlands *Tariefcommissie* (Upper Customs Court), against whose decisions no further remedies are possible, this court felt it necessary to make the reference. The Court, sensing the futility of this exercise, stated that although Article 177, para 3, clearly required courts of last resort to make a reference whenever a question involving the interpretation of Community law arose, it would be without purpose to make a reference where the ECJ had already made an interpretation on the same issue.[29]

Any remaining doubts on the Court's intentions in this regard were swept away by the *CILFIT* decision.[30] Here, the *Corte di Cassazione* (Supreme Court) of Italy had specifically asked the ECJ to give a ruling on the question whether courts of final resort needed to make the reference in all circumstances. The Court replied that such courts had to comply with their obligation to refer:

unless it has established that the question raised is irrelevant or that the Community provision in question had already been interpreted by the Court, or

26 (1990) CMLR 416.

27 See, for example, Wyatt, D and Dashwood, AA, *European Community Law* (1993), Sweet & Maxwell, pp 149–50.

28 Cases 28, 29 and 30/62 (1963) ECR 31.

29 *Ibid* at 38.

30 Case 283/81, *CILFIT v Ministro della Sanità* (1982) ECR 3415.

that the correct application of Community law is so obvious as to leave no scope for any reasonable doubt.

However, the Court also warned that the existence of this opportunity to by-pass the Court of Justice had to be assessed in the light of the specific characteristics of Community law, the particular difficulties raised by its interpretation, and the risk of disparities in the case law as between the Member States.

The *CILFIT* decision has given rise to a great deal of comment and debate, both inside and outside the courts. In the vast majority of cases, the decision was welcomed, although some have sought to cast doubt on the question whether in fact the Court has incorporated the *acte clair* theory into its case law.[31] It appears to the present writer, however, that such fine points of distinction owe more to academic fastidiousness than to practical reality.

V   The effects of a preliminary ruling

General

At this stage, it should be pointed out that when acting under Article 177 EC Treaty, the Court is not restricted to the mere interpretation of Community law. The national court may also refer to it a question relating to the validity of a Community act. Thus the preliminary rulings procedure completes the judicial control exercised over Community acts and to a certain extent compensates the very restricted remedies which individuals have against community action.[32] The effects of a preliminary ruling are different depending on whether it interprets Community law or makes a ruling on its validity.

Interpretation rulings

The interpretation given by the Court is binding on the court which made the reference. However, the other courts are also obliged to follow the Court's interpretation, in view of the unifying role of the preliminary rulings procedure. Should these other courts entertain any doubts as to the applicability of the ruling to the facts before them, or indeed as to the validity of the interpretation itself, they can always request a preliminary ruling themselves.[33]

The question of the temporal effect of a preliminary ruling is also a matter requiring clarification. In a leading decision, the Court stated that its interpretation of Community law clarifies and defines the meaning and scope of

31   See, for example, Rasmussen, H, 'The European Courts' (sic) *Acte Clair* Strategy in CILFIT' (1984) ELRev 242.

32   Maresceau, M, *op cit*, p 117.

33   Constantinho, P and Dony, M, *op cit*, p 113.

133

the rule in question as it should be, or should have been, understood and applied from the time at which the rule was adopted.[34] Accordingly, a ruling on the interpretation of Community law applies even to legal relationships which arose before the preliminary ruling in question.[35] However, the Court mitigated this apparent departure from the general principle of non-retroactivity by adding that the retrospective effects of a ruling can be mitigated because of considerations of legal certainty, and because of the serious effects which such a decision might have on legal relationships entered into in good faith before the ruling had been made.[36]

Rulings on the validity of community acts

These rulings are obviously not on a par with annulment decisions given under Article 173 EC Treaty. They merely entail that the national court may not apply the measure in question in the case before it. However, the ECJ has emphasised that its rulings under Article 177 should be consistent with the annulment decisions given under Article 173. Accordingly, the other courts may also regard the measure in question as invalid, even though the ruling which declared it invalid was restricted to the underlying dispute which gave rise to the reference.[37]

VI   Conclusion on Chapters 6 and 7

The Community is the first organ which has conferred upon individuals the means of using judicial remedies to enforce the rights which EU law confers upon them, either directly to the ECJ or indirectly through the preliminary rulings procedure. For this fact alone, it deserves unqualified plaudits. However, the question which could now be raised is whether a system of judicial remedies which has changed very little since the early days of the Community remains equal to the present challenges and demands of Community law. More particularly the following three issues deserve closer attention:

Access to justice

One of the principal objectives of any legal system must be to make its judicial remedies as widely available to its citizens as possible. How true is this of the Community? If the citizens are to improve their access to justice, the courts must be located as geographically close to them as possible. Yet the EU has only

34   Case 52/76, *Benedetti v Murani* (1977) ECR 166.
35   Case 61/79, *Amministrazione delle Finanze dello Stato v Denkavit Italiana* (1980) ECR 1205.
36   *Ibid.*
37   Case 66/80, *ICI v Amministrazione delle Finanze dello Stato* (1981) ECR 1191.

one judicial forum which is located in Luxembourg. In a Community spreading from southern Spain to northern Finland, this fact makes the judicial structures of the Community extremely remote for all but a relatively small number of people.

This appears to be an obvious argument in favour of judicial decentralisation. The main objection raised against this proposal is that to establish a network of Community Courts throughout the EU would be to dilute and damage the unity of purpose and of interpretation of Community law. This is not necessarily the case. The ECJ could act as a kind of European *Cour de Cassation*, whose case law would be sufficiently authoritative for the lower Community Courts to follow. If necessary, judicial policy could be determined by a European Ministry of Justice.

Procedural economy

This issue is closely related to the first. Particularly the preliminary rulings can take a very long time to be resolved. The action is first brought to the national court, which then suspends proceedings whilst the ECJ deals with the issue of Community law raised before it. The matter then returns to the national court for the final decision with the benefit of the preliminary ruling. It is an extremely long winded procedure which has two unfortunate side-effects. The first is that, in most cases, only those with substantial resources at their disposal are able to take advantage of the remedies in question. The second is that in some cases, European law is invoked in criminal trials with the sole intention of obtaining a preliminary procedure and delaying the entire proceedings.

Enforcement of court decisions

Judicial bodies which are not given the full support of the forces of law enforcement lose a great deal of their effectiveness. At the national level, payment orders are virtually ineffective without the means to enforce them – involving if necessary the services of a bailiff in order to obtain payment. At present, the Community lacks its own enforcement agencies, except in the case of its competition policy (and even here its services cannot operate independently of the national authorities – below, p 217). Even the new power to fine Member States which have persistently offended against Article 169 EC Treaty will be ineffective if the ECJ cannot call upon an enforcement agency in order actually to collect the payment. There is a limit to the extent that the Court can rely on the goodwill of the national enforcement agencies.

135

8 The Free Movement of Goods

I Introduction

The aspiration to create a barrier-free internal market is the logical outcome of the economic philosophy underlying the founding treaties. This philosophy is very much that of the free market economy, which is assumed to be the most efficient mechanism for the allocation of goods and services. It is true that the drafters of the Treaty made provision for a number of exceptions, mainly out of social considerations. Thus the prohibition of state aids may be waived in circumstances which are justified mainly from a social point of view. Nevertheless, these instances remain very much the exception, and it will be recalled that the Court of Justice has as one of its fundamental principles of interpretation that exceptions to a general rule should be strictly interpreted.

The notion of the internal market is narrowly linked to, but not fully coterminous with, the so-called Four Freedoms which are enshrined in the EC Treaty. Being essentially concerned with the freedom to circulate throughout the Community, they lay down the principle of the free movement of goods, the free movement of persons, the freedom to provide services and the free movement of capital. This chapter is restricted to the free movement of goods; the three other freedoms are dealt with in Chapters 9 and 10.

In this chapter, an attempt is made at conveying as comprehensive a picture as possible of the manner in which the EU institutions have attempted to create a barrier-free Community market in goods. It will focus on (a) the removal of customs duties, quantitative restrictions and obstacles which are equivalent in their effect; (b) measures taken to ensure that indirect taxation does not distort intra-Community trade; and (c) the positive legislation enacted under the Single European Market programme aimed at removing barriers to trade by harmonising standards.

II   Customs duties and similar obstacles

General

Customs duties represent one of the oldest forms of national trade protection, to the point of having an almost debilitating effect on trade at times.[1] Not surprisingly, therefore, it is one of the first obstacles to trade which the EC Treaty set about removing. However, in order to prevent the national authorities from circumventing this prohibition, either through negligence or protectionist intent, the drafters of the Treaty also decreed a ban on 'charges with equivalent effect', levies which, although they do not carry the official label of customs duties, nevertheless have the same inhibiting effect on trade.

Legislators intent on removing barriers to trade have two options available to them. They can either impose a straightforward prohibition and penalise infringements as they arise (reactive approach), or adopt positive measures which harmonise conditions in such a way as to make a prohibition superfluous (proactive approach). In relation to customs duties and charges with equivalent effect, the Community legislature has opted for the former approach. The only concession to the proactive approach was made during the initial period of removing customs duties as such. Under Articles 14 and 15 EC Treaty, the Council adopted legislation aimed at completing the first stage in this removal process. However, as customs duties as such were abolished well within the transitional period stipulated, these measures are no longer of any interest other than academic.

In order to be fully effective, the ban on customs duties and charges with equivalent effect must be enforceable not only by the Community institutions, but also by the individual before his or her national courts. The Court of Justice has assisted this process considerably by conferring direct effect on the relevant Treaty provisions, ie Articles 12,[2] 13(2)[3] and 16.[4] In fact, it was in relation to Article 12 that the principle of direct effect was formulated for the first time by the Court of Justice in *Van Gend & Loos*.[5]

1   It is estimated that towards the end of the 18th century, there were around 1,800 customs frontiers covering the territory now known as Germany. Traders wishing to carry goods along the Rhine from Strasbourg to the Netherlands border had to pay over 30 tolls.

2   Case 26/62, *Van Gend & Loos v Nederlandse Administratie des Belastingen* (1963) ECR 1.

3   Case 77/72, *Capolongo v Azienda Agricola Maya* (1973) ECR 611.

4   Case 18/71, *Eunomia di Possor v Italian Ministry of Education* (1971) 811.

5   Case 26/62, *op cit*.

The standstill provision

The first obligation imposed by the Treaty in order to achieve 'customs disarmament' amongst the original Member States was not to introduce any new customs duties on imports from or exports to other EC states – or charges with equivalent effect – as from the entry into effect of the Treaty. In addition, they were prohibited from increasing those customs duties which they were imposing in their trade with other EC member countries. This type of provision is known as the 'standstill' rule, and it is set out in Article 12.

This provision has from the outset been strictly interpreted by the ECJ. In the *Gingerbread* case,[6] it ruled that there could be no implied, but only express, exceptions to it in view of its fundamental nature. Such express derogations as were laid down had to be interpreted strictly.[7] It is not subject to the public policy exception of Article 36 of the Treaty, which is restricted exclusively to the provisions of Articles 30–34 of the Treaty.[8] It applies to agricultural products even if the products in question have not as yet been brought under the Common Agricultural Policy system.[9] The standstill provision remains relevant today, as it deters new Member States from introducing any new customs duties as such or increasing existing ones.

Abolition of customs duties and charges with equivalent effect

Customs duties as such were eliminated in accordance with the procedure and timetable set out in Articles 14 and 15 of the Treaty. Similar provisions have been inserted in the various acts of accession applicable to new Member States (see, for example, Articles 31–33 of the Act of Accession relating to Britain, Ireland and Denmark). Charges with equivalent effect were also to be abolished over this period. For this purpose, Article 13(2) specified that the Commission 'shall determine by means of directives the timetable for such abolition'. However, no such legislation ever materialised. It was therefore left to the ECJ to clarify the meaning of the term 'charges with equivalent effect' through the actions brought by the Commission against erring Member States (Article 169) and through the preliminary rulings procedure (Article 177). 234

The Court had very little assistance from the provisions of the Treaty in order to settle these cases. Nowhere does the Treaty define the concept of 'charges with equivalent effect'. Article 12 EC Treaty tersely stipulates that they are prohibited, whereas Article 13(2) requires the authorities of the Member

6   Cases 2 and 3/62, *Commission v Belgium and Luxembourg* (1962) ECR 425.
7   *Ibid*. See also Cases 2 and 3/69, *Sociaal Fonds voor Diamantarbeiders v Brachfeld* (1969) ECR 211.
8   Case 7/68, *Commission v Italy* (1968) ECR 423.
9   Cases 90 and 91/63, *Commission v Luxembourg and Belgium* (1964) ECR 625.

States to abolish them. The ECJ was therefore free to determine the scope and meaning of this prohibition. True to its wider responsibility for assisting and harmonising the interpretation of Community law, the Court has not restricted itself to giving a series of individual rulings, but has taken advantage of these cases to lay down a series of interpretative guidelines, thus contributing towards the creation of an established case law in this area.

The first opportunity to clarify this concept came when Germany challenged two Commission directives requiring it to remove a number of charges imposed on imports of certain agricultural products.[10] It claimed that these charges were administrative fees imposed in consideration for tasks undertaken by the administration in the interest and at the request of individuals. The Court, however, ruled that the purpose of Article 13(2) was to ban all unilateral measures which, regardless of their label and the means by which they were introduced, had the same discriminatory and protective effect as customs duties. The action by Germany was accordingly dismissed.[11]

The next opportunity for laying down general criteria for clarification came a few years later, when the Court was asked to give a preliminary ruling on a levy imposed under Belgian law on uncut diamonds.[12] The object of this levy was to confer additional benefits on workers in this industry. The Court ruled that the charge in question infringed Article 13(2). The concept of charges with equivalent effect covered any pecuniary charge, other than a customs duty in the strict sense, levied on goods circulating freely within the Community by reason of their crossing a national frontiers, insofar as such a charge is not permitted by a specific rule in the Treaty.

The Court repeated this general definition in a number of subsequent cases; it also added further criteria and refinements in order to cover as wide a range of situations capable of being caught by this concept as possible. Perhaps the most complete definition was given in the *Bauhuis* case.[13] Here, the ECJ ruled that any pecuniary charge, whatever its assignation and mode of application, which is levied unilaterally on goods by reason of the fact that they cross the frontier and which is not a customs duty in the strict sense, constitutes a charge with equivalent effect unless it relates to a general system of internal taxation applied systematically in accordance with the same criteria and at the same stage of marketing to domestic products alike.[14] This also served to distinguish the prohibition in Article 13(2) from the ban on discriminatory taxation laid

140

10 Case 52 and 55/65, *Germany v Commission* (1966) ECR 159 at 169–70.

11 *Ibid*, at 172.

12 Cases 2 and 3/69, *op cit*.

13 Case 46/76, *Bauhuis v Netherlands State* (1977) ECR 5; see also Case 35/76, *Simmenthal v Italian Minister for Finance* (1976) ECR 1871.

14 *Ibid*, at 1888.

down in Article 95 EC Treaty. This will be returned to in the section devoted to discriminatory taxation (below, p 152).

However, the Court has not yet occasion to define or clarify the notion of 'charge' as such. The available literature suggests that this term must be understood to have a Community meaning, and that it cannot therefore be defined in terms of domestic fiscal or other legislation. Accordingly, it is legitimate to interpret the concept of 'charge' as any financial charge which impedes the free movement of goods, irrespective of the way in which it is defined or labelled in national laws.[15]

Sometimes the definitions given by the Court, and the terms used in so doing, have themselves needed clarification. This was particularly the case with regard to the requirement that, to be caught by this prohibition, the charge complained of must have been introduced unilaterally.[16] In *Commission v Italy*,[17] the Court held that a charge was unilateral when it has been imposed by a Member State in its own interest. Naturally, it does not affect charges ordered by the Community authorities in the interests of the Community and of the products concerned.[18] However, even if the Community authorities allow a Member State to impose a charge in the national interest and contrary to the free movement of goods, this charge should be regarded as having been imposed unilaterally and therefore prohibited.[19]

III   Quantitative restrictions and similar obstacles

General

Import and export quotas have not been as important weapon as customs duties in the battle which the nation state has fought down the ages in order to favour the domestic market. However, where they have been adopted they have hampered trade between countries sufficiently to prompt the drafters of the Treaty to make provision for their elimination. The treatment of these barriers to trade is very much the same as is the case with customs duties and similar obstacles: the first stage consists of a standstill provision, the second seeks to remove quantitative restrictions as such, and the third seeks to abolish such measures as are considered to have the same outcome as quantitative restrictions.

15   Groeben, Boeckh, Thiesing, Ehlermann, *Kommentar zum EWG Vertrag* (1984), p 273.
16   See Cases 52 and 55/65, *op cit.*
17   Case 24/68, (1969) ECR 193.
18   Case 46/76, *Bauhuis v Netherlands* (1977) ECR 5 at 17.
19   Cases 80 and 81/77, *Société Les Commissionnaires Réunis v Receveur des Douanes* (1978) ECR 927 at 947.

The standstill rule

This rule appears as a combination of Articles 31 and 32, para 1 of the Treaty. The first-named provision prohibits Member States from introducing between themselves any new import restrictions or measures with equivalent effect. In Article 32, para 1, the Member States undertook to refrain from making any existing quotas and measures with equivalent effect more restrictive. The standstill obligation of Article 31 is absolute and admits of no exceptions whatsoever.[20]

Abolition of quantitative restrictions

The second stage consisted in removing all quantitative restrictions as such, in accordance with the timetable set out in Article 33 EC Treaty. The method used for this purpose was the gradual extension of bilateral quotas to global quotas which would become open without discrimination to the other Member States. All quotas were thus eliminated by 31 December 1961. Similar provisions have required new Member States to remove any quotas applied by them within a certain time-limit.[21]

Removal of measures with equivalent effect: Commission initiatives

As was the case with charges with equivalent effect to customs duties (Article 13(2), second sentence), the Treaty required the Commission, in Article 33(7), to lay down a timetable for the removal of measures with equivalent effect. However, as in the case of Article 13(2), the Commission failed to rise to the occasion. The Commission did, however, use Article 33(7) in order to issue a number of measures seeking to remove individual or general measures having equivalent effect. The most important directive of this kind was Directive 70/50,[22] which sought to eliminate all remaining measures with equivalent effect. It listed a number of specific provisions which had to be deemed to fall within this category.

Once the transitional period had ended, all measures with equivalent effect were deemed to be abolished, and any Member State still applying them was in breach of Article 30 EC Treaty, which lays down the fundamental prohibition of quantitative restrictions and measures with equivalent effect. In principle, it was once again for the Commission to intervene by applying to the ECJ. The Commission did not, however, invariably resort to this weapon. It also used its

---

20 Case 7/61, *Commission v Italy* (1961) ECR 317 at 328; see also Case 13/68, *op cit*, at 460.

21 See for example Article 42 of the Act of Accession for the United Kingdom, Ireland and Denmark.

22 OJ 1970, L 13.

power to issue recommendations and opinions under Article 155 EC Treaty in order to give the Member States the opportunity of removing any offending legislation. Acting on a wide variety of complaints brought to it by national authorities and private individuals, it investigated a number of alleged infringements. In most cases, the initiative taken by the Commission was followed by a constructive dialogue with the national authorities and ended in a mutually satisfactory settlement. In a number of cases, however, the Commission was not satisfied with the outcome and initiated proceedings under Article 169 EC Treaty.[23]

Removing measures with equivalent effect: Court of Justice decisions

The ECJ decisions on this issue were brought about not only on account of the Article 169 procedure, but also as a result of national cases referred to the ECJ for a preliminary ruling.

Defining and clarifying the concepts

In its first decision on this issue,[24] the Court laid down the formula which to this day defines the scope of the concept of 'measures with equivalent effect'. Criminal proceedings had been brought by the Belgian Public Prosecutor against a number of traders who had imported a consignment of whisky from France without having a valid certificate of origin issued by the British customs authorities, as is required by Belgian law. The Court discovered that it was very difficult for someone importing whisky from a country other than the United Kingdom to obtain such a certificate, and therefore this requirement impeded trade. The ECJ took advantage of this opportunity to set down a general formula defining the scope of the prohibition of Article 30:

All trading rules enacted by Member States which are capable of hindering, directly or indirectly, actually or potentially, intra-Community trade are to be considered as measures having an effect equivalent to quantitative restrictions.[25]

This has become known as the 'Dassonville formula', and its importance is such that it has almost acquired the status of an additional Article in the EC Treaty. It unambiguously indicated the strict nature of the prohibition and the uncompromising approach which the Court was to adopt on the issue. It has been restated in numerous later decisions.[26] The subsequent case law of the

---

23 For more details of these initiatives taken under Article 155, see Lasok, D, The Customs Law of the EC (1990) p 97.

24 Case 8/74, *Procureur du Roi v Dassonville* (1974) ECR 837.

25 *Ibid*, at 852.

26 See eg Case 65/75, *Tasca* (1976) ECR 291 at 307–08; Case 13/77, *Inno v Aftab* (1977) ECR 2140 at 2144; Case 82/77, *Openbaar Ministerie v Van Tiggele* (1978) ECR 25 at 39.

Court has at times sent out contrasting signals. On the one hand, certain decisions have tended to consolidate and even intensify the strictness apparent in the *Dassonville* rule. In *Blesgen*,[27] the Court held that the prohibition in Article 30 covered domestic measures governing the marketing of goods even though equally applicable to domestic and imported products, where the restrictive effect of such measures on the free movement of goods exceeds the effects intrinsic to trade rules.[28] (In spite of this, the ECJ held that the measure complained of in this case was lawful.) The Court seemed to add a further turn of the screw in *Jan van de Haar*,[29] where it ruled that the degree to which trade between Member States was hindered was irrelevant to the question whether or not a particular national measure constituted a measure with equivalent effect. As soon as a domestic measure was deemed capable of hindering intra-Community trade it was contrary to Article 30, even though the obstacle is slight and even though it remains possible to market the goods in question in other ways. On the other hand, there is some authority for the view that the severity of this formula was subsequently mitigated by the *Cassis de Dijon* decision,[30] which will be dealt with later (below, p 146).

Price-fixing rules

In a number of decisions, the measure complained of consisted in a set of rules imposing certain price levels. The Court has been very strict in its assessment if such arrangements. Thus in *Tasca*,[31] an Italian trader had been charged with the offence of selling sugar at a higher price than was allowed by Italian law. The Court ruled that a maximum price – at least to the extent to which it applies to imported goods – constituted a measure prohibited by Article 30, particularly where it is fixed at such a low level that, having regard to the position of imported goods relative to domestic goods, traders wishing to import the product in question into the Member State concerned could only do so at a loss.

In *Van Tiggele*,[32] a licensed victualler had infringed legislation which established in the Netherlands a system of minimum retail prices, which were intended to promote the adaptation of the wine and spirit trade to normal competitive conditions. The ECJ considered that although it applied without distinction to both domestic and imported products, the minimum price in question was capable of having an adverse effect on imports in so far as it

27 Case 75/81 (1982) ECR 1211.
28 *Ibid*, at 1229.
29 Cases 177 and 178/82 (1984) ECR 1797.
30 Case 120/78, *Rewe v Bundesmonopolverwaltung für Branntwein* (1979) ECR 649.
31 Case 65/75, *op cit*.
32 Case 82/77, *op cit*.

prevented their lower cost price from being reflected in the retail selling price.[33] Similar rulings were given in regard to a French measure imposing a price freeze[34] and a Belgian Ministerial Decree which regulated price increases.[35]

Protecting the consumer

In a number of cases, the defence advanced by the national authorities has been that the disputed measures were aimed at protecting the consumer and avoiding a situation whereby the latter might otherwise be misled. Generally speaking the Court has tended not to accept this argument, ruling that the desired effect could be achieved by other means. Thus in *Cassis de Dijon*,[36] the measure in question was a ban on the sale of certain spirits if their alcoholic strength was less than 25 per cent. One of the justifications advanced by the German authorities was that in the absence of the ban, the consumer might mistake the lower strength drink for the stronger spirit. The Court held that the same effect could be reached by proper labelling.

The Court has been particularly severe on this type of measure if the main, although unstated, purpose of the measure was the protection of domestic production. This was the case in *Gilli and Andres*,[37] in which the challenged measure was an Italian law prohibiting the sale of apple vinegar – ostensibly in order to protect the consumer. The Court, however, considered that the real reason was the protection of its wine vinegar production, and that the consumer could be adequately protected by suitable labelling.[38]

Measures not affecting imports

At a certain point, a number of complaints were made under Article 30 against national measures which had no particular impact on imports but merely restricted the freedom of action enjoyed by traders. In *Marchandise*[39] and *UDS v Conforama*,[40] the measure complained of was a French rule prohibiting the employment of workers on Sundays in certain areas of the retail trade. The Court failed to declare these measures unlawful, but only on the grounds that they were not excessive in relation to the objective pursued – ie without any reference to the impact of such measures on trade.

---

33 *Ibid*, at 40.
34 Case 5/79, *Procureur-Général v Buys* (1979) ECR 3203.
35 Cases 16–20, *Joseph Danis* (1979) ECR 3327.
36 Case 120/78, *op cit*, at 651.
37 Case 788/79 (1980) ECR 2071.
38 *Ibid*, at 2078.
39 Case C-332/89 (1991) ECR I-1027.
40 Case 312/89 (1991) ECR I-997.

However, subsequently a gradual shift began to take place in favour of excluding these measures from the scope of Article 30. Particularly the *Keck* ruling[41] removed any doubt on this issue. In this case, criminal proceedings had been taken against two traders who had resold goods at a loss, thus infringing French legislation banning such trading practices. The traders in question claimed that this law was contrary to Article 30. The Court showed in its ruling an awareness of the unease at the increasing number of traders relying upon Article 30 against measures which had a purely national impact, and that it was therefore necessary to reappraise its case law. Accordingly, the Court unambiguously stated that:

> the application of such rules to the sale of products from another Member State meeting the requirements laid down by that state is not by nature such as to prevent their access to the market or to impede access any more than it impeded the access of domestic products. Such rules therefore fall outside the scope of Article 30 of the Treaty.[42]

Accordingly, the national authorities may decide their own rules governing sales methods, as long as these do not have any effect on imports.

Cassis de Dijon and its aftermath

The decision in this case,[43] which has already been referred to, proved a landmark and a turning point, not only in the interpretation of Article 30, but also in the entire approach towards the removal of trade barriers. It arose when a firm was refused permission to import a consignment of Cassis de Dijon liqueur because of its inadequate alcoholic strength. This rendered it incompatible with German legislation which fixed a minimum alcohol percentage for that type of liqueur.

The Court held that the legislation in question offended Article 30. One of the reasons for this has already been dealt with earlier: the claim that the national legislation in question was necessary, the better to inform the consumer. Another defence refuted by the Court was that there was an issue of public health to consider, in that fixing a minimum alcohol content for liqueurs discouraged the 'proliferation of alcoholic beverages on the national market, in particular alcoholic beverages with a low alcohol content', being products which are capable of inducing greater tolerance towards alcohol than stronger spirits. The Court did not accept this argument, stating that there were plenty of other low-alcohol drinks available on the market, and that in any case drink containing a higher degree of alcohol was usually consumed in diluted form.

---

41   Cases C-267 and C-268/91 (1993) ECR I-6079.

42   *Ibid*, at 6131.

43   Case 120/78, *op cit.*

However, the full impact of the *Cassis de Dijon* decision was produced by a more general formula which was intended by the Court to give an indication of its interpreting policy. In the now-famous Paragraph 8 of its decision, the Court made two statements which were to have a profound impact on the general approach towards the Internal Market. On the one hand, it held that in the absence of a Community set of rules on the production and marketing of alcohol (and therefore, presumably, of any product whatsoever), it was for the national authorities to regulate the production and marketing of this product on their own territory. In more general terms:

Obstacles to movement within the Community resulting from disparities between the national laws relating to the marketing of the products in question must be accepted in so far as those provisions may be recognised as being necessary in order to satisfy mandatory requirements relating in particular to the effectiveness of fiscal supervision, the protection of public health, the fairness of commercial transactions and the defence of the consumer.

The Court also ruled that a product which has been lawfully produced and marketed in one Member State should be able to circulate fully throughout the Community. By making these pronouncements, the Court sent some important signals regarding its future policy. The first was to mitigate somewhat the strictness of the *Dassonville* formula. It will be recalled that this statement of policy – particularly in view of the words 'actually or potentially, directly or indirectly' – cast its net as widely as possible in order to catch any national measure which had any discernible effect on trade between Member States. Let us take the case of *Commission v France*.[44] Here, the measures indicted by the Commission were rules which placed advertising restrictions on two of the five categories into which the law divides intoxicating drinks. These restrictions were not based on the origin of the products; yet the Court outlawed them on the grounds that they discriminated in practice against imported alcoholic drink, particularly natural sweet wines and grain spirits such as whisky and geneva (which just happen to be drinks for which there is hardly any French production).

Measures such as these are indirectly discriminatory measures, because on the surface they apply indistinctly to imported and domestically-produced goods alike. If the French measure complained of in *Commission v France* had imposed the advertising restrictions complained of on, say, spirits emanating from the United Kingdom and Germany, it would have been a directly discriminatory measure. It would appear that, by conceding that in certain circumstances obstacles to trade resulting from disparities between national rules are acceptable subject to certain conditions being fulfilled, the *Cassis de Dijon* decision has signalled that indirectly discriminatory measures can be justified *without needing to resort to the safeguard clause of Article 36* (below, p 149).

44 Case 152/78 (1980) ECR 2299.

Presumably, as Charlesworth and Cullen suggest, they could be justified on the basis of the reasonableness test.[45]

The impact of *Cassis de Dijon* was, however, much wider and affected the entire approach adopted by the Community institutions towards the achievement of the internal market. The first indication of this impact came in a letter addressed by the Commission to the Member States' authorities and containing a set of guidelines which followed the *Cassis de Dijon* decision.[46] However, it was the Single Market programme which was to bear the clearest imprint of the *Cassis de Dijon* principles.

The White Paper presented by the Commission in 1985, entitled *Completing the Internal Market*, confirmed this new approach. It proposed that a distinction be drawn between those areas of the internal market in which harmonisation is essential and those in which it suffices to acknowledge the principle of mutual recognition of the various fundamental requirements imposed by national law. Since the Single European Act (SEA), which sought to complete the internal market, flowed directly from this White Paper, the majority of directives adopted under the SEA are based on this approach.[47] Consequently the EU institutions no longer seek to harmonise every aspect of trading activity, but confine themselves to laying down essential requirements, leaving the detailed standardisation measures to the various European standardisation bodies.[48]

Measures with equivalent effect to export quotas

Article 34 EC Treaty lays down a general prohibition of quantitative restrictions on exports and all measures having equivalent effect. From the outset, the Court has dealt with such restrictions on trade in a totally different manner from restrictions on imports. The temptation was perhaps considerable for the Court simply to apply the *Dassonville* formula to export restrictions as well, which would have presented the convenience of harmony.

The ECJ has not, however, done so. In the first case decided under Article 34,[49] the measure complained of was the Netherlands 1973 Meat Processing and Preparation Regulation, which was adopted in order to protect exports of meat products from the Netherlands to countries imposing restrictions on horsemeat imports. For this purpose, meat manufacturers were prohibited from having in stock, preparing or processing horsemeat. The Court ruled that the purpose of Article 34 related to national measures which had the specific purpose of

---

45 *Op cit*, at 228.
46 EEC Bulletin 1980, No 7/8, p 13.
47 See also below, p 157.
48 Cairns, W, 'The Legal Environment', in Nugent, N and O'Donnell, R, *The European Business Environment* (1994) McMillan, p 108.
49 Case 15/79, *Groenveld v Produktschap voor Vee en Vlees* (1979) ECR 3409.

imposing a difference in treatment between the domestic trade of a Member State and its export trade, in such a way as to confer a specific advantage for the national production of, or market in, this product at the expense of the production or trade of other Member States. This was not the case for the national measure complained of.[50] The measures complained of must be overtly or covertly protectionist.[51]

Accordingly, restrictions applying equally to domestic products for export and domestic products aimed at the national market do not infringe Article 34. This was confirmed in *Oebel*,[52] where the measure under challenge was a German Law aimed at protecting workers in small and medium-sized bakeries against permanent night duty, which would damage their health. To this end, it laid down certain times of day in which certain bakery products could not be produced or transported. The accusation that this measure was an export barrier was rejected by the Court in the same manner as in *Groenveld*.

On the other hand, direct discrimination involving distinctly applicable measures is caught by the Article 34 prohibition. This was the case in *Bouhelier*,[53] where the measure complained of was a French measure making the export of watches subject to an export licence and other formalities. Since watches sold on the domestic market were not subject to such strictures, the latter were suffering discrimination and therefore in breach of Article 34 of the Treaty.[54]

The exemption clause of Article 36 EC Treaty

The drafters of the Treaty did not completely prevent the national authorities from banning foreign goods from their national territories. By way of exception to Articles 30 to 34, Article 36 allows them to maintain or introduce prohibitions on imports, exports or goods in transit, as long as these could be justified on a number of grounds, including public morality, public policy or public security, and the protection of health and life of humans, animals and plants. This does not, however, provide the Member States with an easy way of circumventing the rules on quantitative restrictions, as can be seen from the case law described below.

Public morality, public policy and public security

These are concepts which are easily recognisable to lawyers and policy makers in any Member State, having since time immemorial been used as a justification for public intervention into activities which normally are left to the free

---

50 *Ibid*, at 3415.
51 Steiner, J, *op cit*, p 91.
52 Case 155/80, (1981) ECR 1993.
53 Case 53/76, (1977) ECR 197.
54 *Ibid*, at 205.

disposition of individuals (eg the law of contracts). There are considerable variations – even among the legal systems based on the civil law model – in the manner in which these concepts have been interpreted by the national courts.

Public morality is obviously a very sensitive issue, in view of the wide variety in cultural and ideological values which prevail in the various Member States. What passes as an indecency in Milan will not necessarily be regarded as such in Copenhagen. It is here that the Court has experienced the greatest difficulty in arriving at a Community interpretation. Interestingly, virtually the only references to the ECJ under this heading have come from English courts.[55]

In the first case of this nature,[56] the defendants had been convicted of fraudulently evading the prohibition of importing indecent or obscene material, which they had shipped to Felixtowe from Rotterdam. On appeal to the House of Lords, the defendants argued that this prohibition was contrary to Article 30, against which the British authorities invoked the safeguard clause of Article 36. The Court described the scope of action of the national authorities under the 'public morality' with an enthusiasm which almost belies the exceptional nature of Article 36. It was for each Member State to determine the scope of this concept in accordance with its scale of values and its requirements in terms of public morality.

The defendants argued that the difference in the scope of the prohibition as between imported goods and domestically-produced goods entailed that the British legislation in question was arbitrarily discriminatory, contrary to the requirements of the last sentence of Article 36. The Court conceded that there was indeed a difference in the degree of severity with which imported and domestic obscene material was penalised. However, this did not constitute arbitrary discrimination, since the purpose of these rules was the same: to prohibit or restrain the production and sale of indecent publications or articles. Therefore the relevant provision of the Customs and Excise Act was justified under Article 36.

A few years later, a similar problem arose in *Conegate*.[57] Once again, pornographic materials in the shape of so-called 'love dolls' were seized at the frontier, having been imported from Germany. Once again, the UK relied on the 'public morality' plea of Article 36. This time, however, the legal background was different. The sale of these articles were not in principle prohibited within the UK; therefore the UK could not rely on Article 36 to justify the legislation for which it sought to convict the importer in question. The fact that, as the UK authorities stressed, no comparable articles to those imported by Conegate were manufactured on British territory was irrelevant.

55 Psychologists will make of this what they will!
56 Case 34/79, *R v Henn and Darby* (1979) ECR 3795.
57 Case 121/85, *Conegate v Customs and Excise Commissioners* (1986) ECR 1007.

This decision was not met with universal enthusiasm. Thus some authors have argued that because the operation of importation takes place at the same level of manufacture, the UK legislation was not perhaps discriminatory.[58] It should also be noted that, although the ECJ adopted a stricter tone than was the case in *Henn and Darby*, it still made not the slightest attempt at forging a Community concept of 'public morality'.

On the public policy ground, the Court has shown itself commendably strict in its interpretation, but has still not succeeded in creating a 'Community concept'. The ECJ has, however, specified and defined a number of circumstances which could not be regarded as justifying a public policy exception. One of the circumstances which has frequently been invoked by the Member States is the economic interest of the consumer. Thus in the *Sekt* case,[59] the measure under scrutiny was a German rule that only German wines could describe themselves as *Weinbrand* or *Sekt*. The German authorities justified this measure on the grounds that it protected the consumer against misleading information. The Court did not agree, ruling that measures such as these, which concerned with 'indirect appellation of origin', were not strictly necessary in order to protect the consumers against deception (and other producers against unfair competition).[60] Here again, the Court applied the proportionality principle.

Protecting humans, animals or plants

The issue of public health is as important as public policy, morality and security, yet here the Court appears to have been both clearer and more consistent in its approach. The ECJ has generally required Member States invoking it to satisfy it that its actions were truly prompted by public health concerns, that they are capable of achieving the objective pursued, and that that there are no other means of achieving the same result by methods which are less restrictive.[61]

In most cases, this ground has been relied upon by the national authorities in order to justify phyto-sanitary and other health inspections of imported products, which would otherwise very probably be held to be a measure with equivalent effect. With the passage of time, of course, this ground is destined to become a much less happy hunting ground for the national authorities, since inspections of this kind are increasingly becoming the subject matter of harmonising Community legislation adopted under Article 100 EC Treaty. Once

58 Van Rijn, T, *Review of case law* (1988) CMLRev, p 590 at 593.
59 Case 12/74, *Commission v Germany* (1975) ECR 181.
60 *Ibid*, at 199. See also Case 13/78, *Eggers v Freie Hansestadt Bremen* (1978) ECR 1935 at 1957.
61 Weatherill, S and Beaumont, P, *op cit*, at 405.

this happens, systematic inspections by the Member States become unjustified, and must be restricted to a few isolated spot checks; only an administrative inspection procedure, ie the presentation of the appropriate documents, may continue to be systematically operated.[62]

In proceedings brought by the Commission against the UK,[63] the measure which was held to infringe Article 30 was a set of regulations introduced in 1981 which was ostensibly aimed at preventing the spread of Newcastle disease, which affected poultry. In practice, these measures prevented imports of poultry from all EU Member States except Ireland and Denmark. In fact, the Court held that 'the real aim of the 1981 measures was to block, for commercial and economic reasons, imports of poultry products from other Member States, particularly from France. The United Kingdom Government had been subject to pressure from British poultry producers to block these imports'. In addition, at no time had the UK authorities consulted the Community institutions about these measures, and even failed to inform the Commission about them in a timely manner.

The Court also found that there were less stringent ways of achieving the desired objective, quoting the case of the corresponding Danish measures as an example. Reliance upon Article 36 was therefore not justified and the UK was found to be in breach of its obligations under Article 30.

One of the difficulties encountered by the Court in interpreting Article 36 in the light of the public health defence is the subjective element of ascertaining the reason why a particular restrictive measure had been adopted. This aspect was fully highlighted in Case C-324/93.[64] The measure attacked was a prohibition on the importing of narcotic drugs. The ECJ ruled that a country's need to have available reliable supplies of narcotic drugs for essential medical purposes could justify a measure based on Article 36, provided that the object of the exercise was to protect public health. If, however, the measure was taken in order to ensure the survival of a domestic firm, no such justification existed.[65]

IV Fiscal discrimination

General

The differences between the tax systems applicable in the various Member States also constitute a potential obstacle to the achievement of a barrier-free

---

62 Druesne, G, *Droit matériel et politiques de la Communauté européenne* (1991), PUF, p 71.
63 Case 40/82, *Commission v United Kingdom* (1982) ECR 2793.
64 *The Queen v Secretary of State for the Home Department, ex parte Evans Medical and Macfarlane Smith*, Bulletin 4-1995, not yet reported.
65 General Report 1995, item 1126.

internal market. Higher tax rates in a Member State will not prevent goods from crossing frontiers, but will act as a disincentive for traders from other Member States to seek markets there. Alternatively, a tax rate which is lower in state A than in state B can also distort trade because of the unfair advantage it gives to products marketed there and the attraction it offers to investors from other states. Because direct taxation is one of most potent instruments of national economic policy, it was deemed best to concentrate on indirect taxes. It should be added that these provisions on fiscal discrimination have been supplemented by positive legislation aimed at harmonising indirect taxation, as is required by Article 99 EC Treaty.

Discriminatory internal taxation: the Treaty rules

The provisions on discriminatory taxation are contained in two provisions of the EC Treaty, Articles 95 and 96. The former reads:

- No Member State shall impose, directly or indirectly, on the products of other Member States any internal taxation of any kind in excess of that imposed directly or indirectly on similar domestic products.

- Furthermore, no Member State shall impose on the products of other Member States any internal taxation of such a nature as to afford indirect protection to other products.

- Member States shall, not later than at the beginning of the second stage, repeal or amend any provisions existing when this Treaty enters into force which conflict with the preceding rules.

This Article must be considered as a whole, and not on the basis of its different paragraphs. This was established in a recent ECJ decision, in which the Court stated that any system of taxation which had a discriminatory of protective effect within the meaning of Article 95 had to be condemned.[66] Article 96 requires any repayment of internal taxation levied on exported goods not to exceed, either directly or indirectly the actual taxation imposed.

The meaning of the term 'internal taxation'

The Treaty provisions in question do not specifically use the term 'indirect taxation'. However, it is quite clear that this is the target of the provisions prohibiting fiscal discrimination – if only because the latter refer throughout to 'internal taxation' on products. Direct taxation is applied to incomes and earnings, and therefore as such falls outside the scope of Articles 95–98. Within this limitation, however, the ECJ has entertained a very broad interpretation of the type of levy which falls within the scope of these provisions. It covers not only indirect taxation as such, but also all product-related charges levied by the

---

66 Case C-345/93, *Fazenda Publica v Americo* (1995) ECR I-479.

authorities, such as certain charges levied as a percentage of imported products, which are not absorbed into the general taxation system, but are charged by specific public bodies.[67] The Court has also specified charges which may not be taken into account, such as the higher cost of domestic raw materials[68] or heavier manufacturing costs.[69]

The meaning of the term 'discrimination'

This concept is not featured in Article 95 as such. It has been deduced by the Court from the combined effect of the first two sentences of this Article. In *Humblot*,[70] for example, the ECJ was required to pass judgment on the compatibility with Article 95 of differential rates of car tax. Such a system, stated the Court, was 'compatible with Article 95 only in so far as it is free from any *discriminatory or protective effect*' (my emphasis). Thus the Court has ensured that the element of discrimination is a key criterion against which the consistency of taxation systems with Community law will be assessed. The Court tends to interpret this concept broadly (ie against the Member States' authorities). Thus in one case,[71] it held that it was not only the tax itself, but also the conditions in which it was levied which could have a discriminatory effect – such as the time scale allowed for payment of the duties concerned.

Comparability of taxes

To establish whether or not Article 95 has been breached, it is necessary to make two comparisons: one between the domestic and the imported product, the other between the taxes levied on them. We are concerned here with the comparison between taxes; the comparability of products will be dealt with below, p 155. The fundamental rule as regards the comparability of taxes is laid down in *Iannelli v Meroni*.[72]

In order to apply Article 95 of the Treaty, not only the rate of direct and indirect internal taxation on domestic and imported products, but also the basis of assessment and detailed rules for levying the tax must be taken into consideration. As soon as any differences in this respect result in the imported product being taxed at the same stage of

---

67 Case 94/74, IGAV v ENCC (1975) ECR 699, Case 74/76, Iannelli v Meroni (1977) ECR 557; Case 78/76, Steinike und Weinlig v Germany (1977) ECR 595.
68 Cases 2 and 3/62, Commission v Luxembourg and Belgium (1962) ECR 425.
69 Case 28/69, Commission v Italy (1970) ECR 187 at 194.
70 Case 112/84, Humblot v Directeur des Services Fiscaux (1985) ECR 1367.
71 Case 55/79, Commission v Ireland (1980) ECR 481 at 492–93.
72 Case 74/76, op cit.

production or marketing at a higher rate than the similar domestic products, the prohibition of Article 95 is infringed.[73]

What the Court seeks to establish, in other words, is the effective tax burden, which is obtained by applying the rate of tax – expressed as a percentage or as an amount – to the relevant basis of assessment, expressed in terms of volume, quantity, or any other characteristic (eg alcoholic strength) of the product.[74] Therefore the application of a different rate of taxation to two comparable products will not necessarily be discriminatory; the same tax burden could still be achieved by applying the differential tax rate to different tax bases. The tax burden is calculated purely by computational methods, without taking into account whether or not the higher tax is reflected in the end price of the product to the consumer.[75]

Comparability of products

To pass the non-discrimination test, the tax under scrutiny must, under Article 95, meet two requirements: it must be tax neutral as between similar imported and domestic products, and it may not give indirect protection to other products. According to the ECJ, the second requirement is complementary to the first. It forbids any internal taxation which levies a heavier charge on an imported product than on a domestic product which competes with that imported product – even though it may not be similar to it within the meaning of the first requirement.[76] The question can therefore be redefined as follows: when are two products similar, and when are they in competition with each other?

As to what constitutes similar products, the case law of the Court has evolved considerably in recent years. Initially, its position was that similarity exists where the products in question are normally considered to fall within the same fiscal, customs or statistical classification, as the case may be.[77] However, since those days the Court has gradually turned away from this rather formal approach and viewed the 'similarity' factor in terms of their practical analogy, and the manner in which the products viewed by the consumer in terms of their actual or potential use. Here, the case of *John Walker v Ministeriet for Skatter*[78] is instructive. Here, the two products in question were whisky and liqueur fruit wine. The Court first tried to establish the similarity or otherwise of the products in the basis of objective criteria, such as their manufacturing

---

73 *Ibid*, at 579–80.
74 Lasok, D and Cairns, WJ, *The Customs Law of the EEC* (1984), Kluwer, p 125.
75 Case 45/75, *op cit*, at 181.
76 Case 27/67, *op cit*, at 234.
77 Case 27/67, *Fink-Frucht v Hauptzollamt München* (1968) ECR 223 at 232; Case 28/69, *op cit*, at 194.
78 Case 243/86 (1986) ECR 875.

procedures or alcohol content. The Court then proceeded to establish whether the two products satisfied similar consumer needs. In this respect, the ECJ decided that their characteristics were so different that the products could not be considered to be similar. Even the fact that both types of drink are consumed by many in diluted form was inadequate for the purpose of establishing any likeness between them.[79]

As has been noted before, Article 95 can be breached not only if the goods are similar, but also where they are in competition with each other. This aspect was well illustrated when in the late 1970s, the Commission scrutinised the fiscal charges on spirits in a number of Member States, and decided to institute Article 169 proceedings against several of them. In the action against Britain, it was alleged that its indirect taxation favoured beer to the detriment of wine.

The question whether beer and wine were in competition with each other was the subject matter of a drawn-out battle between the contending parties. The United Kingdom relied heavily on consumer habits in its contention that beer and wine were not in competition with each other. Beer, it was argued, is mainly consumed in public houses, whereas wine is mostly drunk in the home; therefore the British consumer did not regard wine and beer as being substitutable for each other. The Italian Government, intervening, argued that it was the lightest wines with an alcoholic strength of about 9° – in other words, the cheap and popular wines – which were truly in competition with beer. Therefore these wines should be taken as a basis for comparison. The Court accepted this argument and ruled that the UK excise duties on wine breached Article 95 of the Treaty. As a result, the Chancellor of the Exchequer made the appropriate adjustment in his 1985 Budget.[80]

Article 95 and charges with equivalent effect to customs duties

In the broadest sense of the term, customs duties are fiscal charges. In addition, the broad sweep of the term 'charges with equivalent effect' is likely to embrace certain charges coming within a grey area between internal taxation and customs duties. There is accordingly some potential for confusion between the field of application of these two provisions, and the Court has on occasion been required to distinguish between them.

It will be recalled that the Court had already delimited the scope of 'charges with equivalent effect' in the *Bauhuis* decision,[81] where it held that any pecuniary charge, whatever its assignation and mode of application, which is

---

79 *Ibid*, at 881–82.
80 Case 170/78, *Commission v United Kingdom* (1980) ECR 417 at 437.
81 Case 46/76, *Bauhuis v Netherlands State* (1977) ECR 5 at 17–18.

imposed unilaterally on goods because of their crossing the frontier, and which is not a customs duty as such, is a charge with equivalent effect unless it relates to a general system of internal taxation applied systematically to domestic products and imports, in accordance with the same criteria and at the same stage of marketing.

In its subsequent case law, the Court has developed criteria which a particular charge is to meet if it is to be considered as forming part of a system of internal taxation. In *Commission v Denmark*,[82] it ruled that a charge does not fall within a system of internal taxation unless it forms part of a general system applicable systematically to categories of products in accordance with objective criteria regardless of the origin of the goods.[83]

This criterion should be sufficiently clear to be able to distinguish a charge with equivalent effect to a customs duty from taxation in the strict sense of the term. Nevertheless there remains some scope for doubt in certain cases.

In *Cucchi*,[84] the ECJ held that, even where a duty appears to be a genuine tax, it could be considered to be a charge with equivalent effect if it has been individualised in such a way as to benefit exclusively the domestic product on which the tax was imposed. In the same decision, the Court ruled that the prohibition of charges with equivalent effect on the one hand, and that of discriminatory taxation on the other hand, are mutually exclusive. Therefore, in cases where the complainant is in doubt as to which category the duty complained of falls, it is safer for him or her to rely on both Articles 12 and 95, leaving it to the ECJ to define the boundaries between them.

V The internal market White Paper and the Single European Act

Target 1992

The unsatisfactory progress made with the implementation of a number of earlier harmonisation programmes was one of the reasons for the adoption by the Community authorities of a programme with a realistic agenda – the adoption of around 300 directives – and a definitive target date, which was 31 December 1992. This was the substance of the White paper Completing the Internal Market,[85] which was presented by the Commission in 1985 and approved by the European Council two months later. This White Paper was complemented shortly afterwards by the Single European Act, which laid down

---

82   Case 158/82 (1983) ECR 3572.

83   *Ibid* at 3584; see also Case 90/79, *Commission v France* (1981) ECR 283 at 301.

84   Case 77/76, *Fratelli Cucchi v Avez SpA* (1977) ECR 987 at 1007–08.

85   Commission Document COM (85) 310.

the various procedural means of realising its objectives.

The main action areas of the White Paper were the following:

- the removal of physical and technical barriers to trade;
- the free movement of capital;
- harmonisation of company law and related measures;
- conditions in which services such as banking and insurance can move freely across frontiers;
- fiscal harmonisation;
- removal of internal controls on the movement of persons.

Virtually all the directives implementing this programme were adopted by the 1992 target date, and by now, 94 per cent of them have been successfully incorporated into the Member States' legislative systems. In a recent General Report, however, the Commission stressed that this fact concealed wide disparities from one area of legislation to another.[86]

A number of these provisions will be, and have been, discussed elsewhere under the appropriate heading. Here, we will concern ourselves mainly with the removal of technical barriers to trade.

Technical barriers to trade: the new approach

Discussing the various reasons why the earlier attempts at harmonisation had been less successful than expected, the authors of the White Paper correctly identified the actual harmonisation methods themselves as one of the main factors. It also recognised the merits of the approach pioneered by the *Cassis de Dijon* decision, which is mutual recognition – the more so because the Council, in a communication made in 1984,[87] had recognised the essential equivalence of the objectives pursued by the Member States's legislation in technical matters.[88]

However, the document also cautions against excessive reliance upon the mutual recognition principle. One of its disadvantages, it is recognised, lies in the fact that it could prove to be inadequate for the purpose of building up an expanding market based on the competitiveness to which a European single market could give rise. What was needed therefore was a strategy which combined the best of both these methods – whilst allowing more rapid progress to be made than in the past.[89] This strategy is based on the following principles:

- a clear distinction between that which is essential to harmonise and that

---

86 General Report 1996, p 56.

87 Conclusions on Standardisation, 16 July 1984.

88 Doc COM(85)310, *op cit*, para 63.

89 Document COM(85)310, para 64.

which may be left to mutual recognition of national regulations and standards;

- legislative harmonisation within the meaning of Article 100 was in future to be restricted to laying down health and safety requirements which would be obligatory in all Member States;

- harmonisation of industrial standards would proceed by elaborating European standards and be promoted as much as possible; however, the absence of such standards would not be allowed as a barrier to free movement. Pending the adoption of such standards, mutual acceptance of national standards should prevail.[90]

What this approach amounts to is a strategy of concentrating on that which is regarded as the main impediment to market integration, to wit the existence of trade barriers which result from the disparities between existing national laws. This leaves the Member States with the ultimate responsibility for such matters as health and safety.[91] Some see this as an example of subsidiarity in action.[92] Others are less enthusiastic about this approach, particularly from the point of view of consumer protection.[93]

To discuss each initiative under this heading would lead us too far. There is, however, one area which has aroused considerable interest hitherto the Community had, either deliberately or unintentionally, hitherto avoided, to wit telecommunications and information technology.

One of the reasons why the EU has been galvanised into action in this area is the fact that the development of technology in this area has considerably facilitated the emergence of firms whose field of activity transcends national boundaries. The application of information technology and telecommunications have facilitated the virtually instantaneous transmission of the spoken and written word and data, as well as images.[94] This, as well as the concern of the Commission to liberalise this sector as much as possible, prompted a Commission Green Paper on the subject in 1987,[95] which contained various principles setting out ways of liberalising and improving the market

90 Document COM(85)310, *op cit*, para 65.

91 Dehousse, R, 'Completing the Internal Market: Institutional Constraints and Challenges', in: Bieber, Dehousse, R, Pinder, J and Weiler, J (eds) *1992: One European Market?* (1988), Nomos, p 323.

92 Weatherill, S and Beaumont, P, *op cit*, at 423.

93 Reich, N, 'Protection of Diffuse Interests in the EEC and the Perspective of Progressively Establishing an Internal Market' (1988) JCP 395.

94 Jacobson, D, 'The Technological and Infrastructural Environment', in: Nugent, N and O'Donnell, R, The European Business Environment (1993), p 199 at 225.

95 Development of the Common Market for Telecommunications Services and Equipment.

environment in the telecommunications industry. On this basis, a number of directives relating to the use of telecommunications networks and infrastructure, the provision of services, the supplying of equipment, and the application of rules of competition in this area, were adopted.

In 1987, a Decision was adopted dealing with the issue of standardisation in the field of information technology and telecommunications.[96] This specifies those measures which need to be taken for the achievement of the appropriate level of standardisation. Such measures include IT standards and specifications for electronic data services and information interchange transmitted by means of telecommunications networks. In addition, it lays down a schedule for the standardisation of information and telecommunications technology, specifying that public purchasers are compelled to refer to EU standards in any procurement tender calls.[97]

Another important initiative in this field was the 1994 Green Paper on mobile personal communications[98] which calls for the liberalisation of the mobile telephone market, the global system for telecommunications GSM becoming the general European standard. To this end, it proposes the freedom to develop infrastructure networks for mobile telephone users, the co-ordination of standards, licensing and award procedures, and the removal of restrictions on the provision of services across the EU, together with the encouragement of interconnections and access codes co-ordination.[99]

Technical standards creating barriers

The EU has not as yet banned Member States from applying their own national standards; indeed, as has been noted above, the mutual recognition principle tends to encourage a trend in this direction. However, this presents the danger of creating new barriers to trade, however involuntarily. This is the reason why, in 1983, a directive was adopted[100] requiring the Commission to be informed of proposals for new technical standards and regulations. This facilitates intervention by the Commission and the other Member States should the need arise. This has served to discourage the growth of new barriers and to promote European standards, and therefore was extended in 1989 to cover certain additional areas, such as agricultural products, pharmaceuticals, foodstuffs and cosmetics. Transparency proposals which go even further are now being

96 Decision 87/95, OJ 1987 L 36.

97 Charlesworth, A and Cullen, H, op cit, p 345.

98 General Report 1994, p 83, Kogan Page.

99 Roney, A, EC/EU Fact Book (1995), Kogan Page, p 186.

100 Directive 83/189 OJ 1983 L 109.

101 Roney, A, op cit, p 75.

proposed, under which goods not covered by harmonisation measures may be affected by national fiscal requirements.[101]

Does a failure on the part of the national authorities to inform the Commission of technical regulations falling within the scope of this Directive make the national rules in question inapplicable? This question was raised in the *Security International* case.[102] The ECJ replied that this was indeed the case. The Directive in question was designed not only to lay down a procedure for the provision of information to the Commission, but also to protect the free movement of goods by a mechanism of preventative control. This served to justify a temporary ban on implementing the domestic rule in question until such time as the Commission and the Member State concerned had sufficient time to examine it, propose amendments to it, or suggest a harmonising directive.[103]

---

102 Case C-194, *Security International v Signalson and Securitel Bulletin* 7/8–1996, not yet reported.
103 General Report 1996, item 1127.

9 The Free Movement of Persons

I Introduction

Community rules on the free movement of persons have outgrown their original context. Whereas initially, the free movement of persons was viewed as a necessary element in achieving the common market, its current perception tends to see this freedom as a fundamental right conferred on all EU nationals.

In fact, the provisions of the Treaty on the free movement of persons are essentially a specific expression of Article 6, which states that 'within the scope of this Treaty, and without prejudice to any special provisions contained therein, any discrimination on grounds of nationality shall be prohibited'. This principle has been applied to the free movement of workers and the freedom of establishment, and gradually the case law of the Court based on these provisions came to develop the notion of European citizenship, which was subsequently confirmed by the TEU. The non-discrimination principle is one of the general principles of law which form a valid source of Community law (above, p 74).

II Free movement of workers

Treaty provisions

The basic rules on the free movement of workers are set out in Articles 48 to 51 of the Treaty. These fundamental provisions not only set out the principle of free movement, but also stipulate the various rights which accompany this principle – equality of treatment for employment purposes and the scope of his right to move to and remain in any part of the Community – subject to the possible application of the public policy exception. Article 49 requires the Community institutions to adopt positive legislation in order to make the free movement of workers a practical reality. Article 50 of the Treaty encourages the exchange of young workers, and Article 51 of the Treaty makes provision for the transferability of social security benefits.

Scope of the term 'worker'

The principle of free movement applies to all workers of the Member States, including the citizens of the Member States' dependencies, such as the *Départements d'outre-mer* (overseas territories) of France. However, the term 'citizen' does not coincide with the term 'worker' for the purpose of Article 48 EC Treaty. Unfortunately, we cannot rely on either the Treaty or the derived legislation to provide us with a definition of the term 'worker'. Once again, it has been for the Court of Justice to determine both the meaning and the scope of this term. The first conclusive definition of this term came in the *Levin* case.[1] Here, the Court issued a general statement of principle to the effect that the rules on the free movement of workers covered only 'the pursuit of effective and genuine activities, to the exclusion of activities of such a small scale as to be regarded as purely marginal and ancillary'.[2] Therefore, concluded the court, these rules guaranteed only 'the free movement of persons who pursue or are desirous of pursuing an economic activity'. The Court, however, stopped short of providing a definition of the term 'economic activity'. Instead, it has, in a series of decisions, identified those conditions which do and those conditions which do not fall within the scope of this definition.

Thus in the *Kempf* case[3] the dispute centred round the earnings of a German working in The Netherlands, which consisted of the income from giving 12 lessons per week plus supplementary benefit payments. Rather oddly, the Netherlands Supreme Administrative Court, which made the reference, had already admitted that the income from these 12 lessons in themselves satisfied the *Levin* test; what it wanted the ECJ to establish was whether the fact that he also received supplementary benefits disqualified the German teacher from the status as 'worker'. The ECJ replied in the negative; a person in effective and genuine part-time employment could not be excluded from the scope of Article 48 because he or she earned less than minimum subsistence levels and tried to supplement this by 'other lawful means of subsistence'. Whether these other subsistence payments derived from property income, were supplied by other members of the family, or were allocated by the state was irrelevant.[4]

Having established this fundamental principle, the Court proceeded to judge several cases purely on their merits – in *Steymann*,[5] it found that someone working as a plumber for an Eastern religious sect without payment as such but in return for having his needs met by the commune qualified as a worker; in *Lavrie-Blum*[6] the same conclusion was reached in relation to a trainee teacher giving a few hours' instruction per week; whereas in the case of *Bettray*[7] a person who worked under a work placement scheme as an alternative to

1   Case 53/81, *Levin* (1982) ECR 1035.
2   Case 53/81, *op cit*, at 1050.
3   Case 139/85, *Kempf v Staatssecretaris voor Justitie* (1986) ECR 1741.
4   *Ibid*, at 1751.
5   Case 196/87, *Steymann v Staatssecretaris voor Justitie* (1988) ECR 6159.
6   Case 66/85, *Lavrie-Blum v Land Baden-Württemburg* (1986) ECR 2121.
7   Case 344/87, *Bettray v Staatssecretaris van Justitie* (1989) ECR 1622.

receiving unemployment benefit did not qualify. In principle, the notion of 'worker' is extended to cover the members of his or her family, subject to the restrictions set out in the relevant derived legislation (below, p 167).

Special cases

The ECJ has been faced with a number of cases in which a person claimed the status of 'worker' even though he or she was merely *expecting* to work. An example of this is provided by the *Antonissen* case.[8] Here, a Belgian national had come to Britain in order to seek employment. More than six months later, he had still not succeeded in finding work. This prompted the Home Office to issue a deportation order against him. The Court ruled that domestic legislation which required a foreign Community national to leave after six months' fruitless quest for employment – subject to appeal – was compatible with Community law, unless the person concerned could prove that he was continuing to find work and had a genuine chance of being offered employment.[9] Yet again, one senses that the Court was trying to shift onto the referring court the true responsibility for assessing the national rule in the light of the Community provision.

The advantages conferred

Once a person qualifies as a 'worker' in the sense described above, a range of benefits are conferred on him or her by Community law. Perhaps the most straightforward course of action would have been to issue the blanket rule that once accepted as a valid migrant worker, the person concerned shall enjoy without exception the same rights as any worker having the nationality of the host country. The Community legislators, however, rightly anticipated that a number of problems would arise even if this straightforward solution was adopted, which would have to be settled through the tortuous procedures before the ECJ. On the age old principle that prevention is preferable to cure, the Community institutions issued a number of instruments of derived legislation which give substance to the non-discrimination principle. These cover the right of entry and residence; access to conditions of employment; and the right to remain in the territory of the host country once his or her employment has terminated.

Right of entry and residence

Directive 68/360[10] was adopted by the Council in order to abolish restrictions on the movement and residence of Community nationals. However, it

---

8 Case C-292/89, *R v IAT, ex parte Antonissen* (1991) ECR 1-745.

9 *Ibid*, at 779.

10 OJ Special Edition 1968 (II) 485.

recognises that certain formalities must be complied with for this purpose, even though it seeks to reduce these to a strict minimum.

The rights involved are not entirely dependent on the host Member State. Member States must also give Community nationals the right to leave their territory in order to work elsewhere in the EU (Article 2(1)). This right must be granted on the simple production of a valid identity card or passport, which the Member States must issue to their nationals (Article 2(2)), and which must be valid for all the Member States and for the countries through which the Community national must pass in order to travel between Member States (Article 2(3)) – remembering that to travel to another EU Member State can sometimes involve passing through third countries (eg from Italy to Sweden, or from almost anywhere in the Community to Greece).

Inevitably, the question arises as to what measures may be taken by the host Member State against a migrant worker who fails to comply with these formalities. This was the subject matter of the *Pieck* case.[11] The defendant was a Dutchman working in Wales, who was found to be without a valid residence permit, and therefore had a deportation order served on him. The Court ruled that failing to comply with the formalities set out in Directive 68/360 could not be penalised in such a disproportionate way as to constitute a barrier to the free movement of persons. Such disproportionate penalties included deportation and imprisonment.[12]

Access to conditions of employment

Article 48(2) EC Treaty requires Member States to abolish all discrimination based on nationality regarding employment, pay, and other conditions of employment. To this end, Regulation 1612/68[13] was adopted. The key provisions are contained in Part I, which is divided into three Titles.

Title 1 deals with eligibility for employment. The first provision states the general principle that any Community national may, regardless of his or her place of residence, take up and pursue employment in another Member State in accordance with the applicable rules; in so doing, he or she has the same priority as nationals of the host country (Article 1). For this purpose, employer and employee may exchange applications for and offers of employment (Article 2).

Article 3 makes inapplicable any provision of domestic law which contravenes the non-discrimination principle. True to the non-formalistic approach applied by the Community institutions in other fields, this rule applies not only to those which expressly discriminate on grounds of nationality, but also those which have the practical effect of excluding foreign

---

11 Case 157/79, *R v Pieck* (1980) ECR 2171.

12 *Ibid*, at 2187.

13 OJ Special Edition 1968 (II) 475.

Community nationals from the employment offered. It does not apply to conditions which require a degree of linguistic knowledge because of the nature of the post. The Court has specified, however, that this linguistic requirement must be demanded of all applicants regardless of their nationality.[14] Member States may not make employment of a foreign Community national conditional upon medical, vocational or other criteria which are discriminatory on grounds of nationality (Article 6).

Title II lays down rules on employment and equality of treatment. Under Article 7(1), migrant workers may not receive any different treatment from domestic workers regarding such conditions of employment as pay, dismissal and reinstatement. They shall in addition enjoy the same social and fiscal advantages as national workers (Article 7(2)). The notion of 'social advantage' cannot be interpreted restrictively.[15] It covers the right to enjoy railway travel at reduced rate, if that right was accorded to domestic workers. It can even cover conditions which have nothing whatsoever to do with the employment as such. In the *Mutsch* case,[16] a Belgian public prosecutor had attempted – for reasons best known to himself – to prevent a Luxembourg national from addressing a criminal court in German ... even though the gentleman concerned lived in Eupen (a German-speaking commune of Belgium) and Belgian nationals were allowed to use that language if they wished! Presumably contriving to keep a straight face, the ECJ judges ruled that, even though this linguistic condition had nothing to do with his contract of employment, the choice of language before a court of law was an important matter; if foreign nationals were treated differently from this point of view, an obstacle to the free movement of workers could be created.

Title III concerns the workers' families. Under Article 10, the migrant worker may be accompanied by his or her spouse and their closest relatives, regardless their nationality. For other relatives not falling within this category, but dependent on the worker or living with him or her, Member States must facilitate their admission. It cannot be stressed too strongly that the rights of the worker's family are entirely dependent on his or her being a 'worker' falling within the scope of Article 48, as explained above (p 163). This leads to the absurd situation of migrant workers' families having more rights than those who stayed at home, as can be seen from the *Morson* decision.[17]

Whilst a Community national is working – in an employed or self-employed capacity – within the territory of another Member State, his or her spouse and dependent children have the right to take up employment in that state, even if

---

14 Case 378/87, *Groener v Minister for Education* (1989) ECR at 3967.

15 Case 32/75, *Cristini v SNCF* (1975) ECR 1085 at 1094–95.

16 Case 137/84, *Ministère Public v Mutsch* (1985) ECR 2660 at 681.

17 Cases 35 and 36/82, *Morson v Netherlands State* (1982) ECR 3720.

they are not Community nationals (Article 11). The relative earning power of the spouses is irrelevant. In *Gül*,[18] a Cypriot doctor was married to a British citizen. Even though he earned considerably more than his wife, he claimed to be a dependant of his wife. The ECJ agreed.

Right to remain even after termination of employment

Pursuant to Regulation 1251/70,[19] Member States may not order migrant workers to leave the country after their employment has ended because of retirement or incapacity. Retired workers obtain this right of continued residence once they have reached the age stipulated for entitlement to old-age pension. Incapacitated workers acquire this right after having been employed in the host country for a minimum of 12 months and resided in it for at least three years (Article 2(1)). The members of the retired or incapacitated worker's family are entitled to remain in the host country even after the worker's death (Article 3(1)).

Free movement of sporting professionals

Many national bodies governing professional sports impose limits on foreign players. More particularly the footballing authorities of most Member States prohibit clubs from fielding more than a certain number of professionals who are not citizens of the country in question. The transfer system between clubs also raised some issues which could have implications under Community law. Remarkably, given the nature of the business interests associated with professional soccer, it has taken more than 35 years following the entry into effect of the Treaty for a legal challenge to be brought to such rules. Although in one particular case the ECJ had ruled that football *managers* enjoyed free movement across the Community,[20] no-one felt moved to demand the same right for footballers. No doubt the fears that the professional game would be even more dominated than it is today by a handful of wealthy clubs caused a certain reticence in this regard.

This particular day of reckoning could not, however, be postponed for ever, and it dawned when, on the expiry of his two year contract with FC Liège, a leading Belgian club, Mr Bosman, a Belgian professional, attempted to move to a French club, US Dunkerque. Agreement was reached between the two clubs on the transfer fee. However, a difficulty arose when the Belgian club failed to request the necessary clearance certificate from the Belgian football authorities which would have allowed Bosman to join his new club. The reason for this was that the Belgian club entertained doubts about the ability of the French club to

18 Case 131/85, *Emir Gül v Regierungs-präsident Düsseldorf* (1986) ECR 1573.
19 OJ Special Edition 1970, 402.
20 Case 222/86, *Unectef v Heylens* (1987) ECR 4112.

pay the agreed transfer fee. Mr. Bosman undertook legal action against both clubs. The issue reached the Liège Court of Appeal, which referred two questions to the ECJ under Article 177 of the Treaty:

- did Article 48 of the Treaty prohibit a football club from requiring and receiving payment of a sum upon the engagement by a new club of one of its players who has terminated his contract; and

- did the same provision prevent national and international football bodies from including in their respective regulations provisions restricting the access of foreign players from the European Union to the competitions which they organise?

The ECJ replied to both questions in the affirmative. As to the first issue, by preventing or deterring citizens of a Member State from leaving their country or origin, the rules on transfer under challenge constituted an obstacle to the free movement of workers. Predictably, the defendants had argued that outlawing such rules were 'bad for football', on the grounds that they maintained a sporting and financial balance in the world of football. The Court rejected this argument, stating that they had not prevented the richest clubs from obtaining the services of the top players.[21]

On the second question, the Court held that Article 48 precluded national rules from requiring clubs to field a limited number of foreign players for a given fixture. The arguments used by the defendants were much the same as those put forward under the first question, and received equally short shrift from the Court. By giving this ruling, the Court gave expression to a view which had already been held by other Community institutions – thus, for example, the European Parliament in a number of resolutions on the subject.[22]

Social security provisions

Article 51 EC Treaty requires the Council to adopt instruments enabling workers to aggregate all the periods of work spent in various Member States for the purpose of calculating the benefit due to him or her, and to enable him or her to have his or her social security benefits paid in any Member State. If this did not happen, workers would be discouraged from seeking and taking up employment elsewhere in the EU, which would constitute an indirect obstacle to their freedom of movement.

The major piece of legislation which was issued in compliance with this Article is Regulation 1408/71.[23] The object of this Regulation was not the harmonisation of social security systems across the Community, but merely to

21 Case C-415/93, *Bosman*, not yet reported.
22 Farrell, R, 'Bosman Opinion – What does it Mean?' (1995) 3 *Journal of Sports Law* (a refereed journal, of course!) p 17.
23 OJ Special Edition 1971 (II) 416.

achieve the co-ordinated application of the relevant national provisions in such a way that the migrant worker is not penalised because of his working in different Member States. It is based on a number of principles, which are detailed below.

Universality

This principle covers both the beneficiaries of the system and the social security benefits covered by it. As to the beneficiaries of the system established by this regulation, these are not confined to workers within the meaning of Article 48. Under Article 2(1) of the Regulation, its provisions apply not only to the employed, but also to the self-employed, their families, stateless persons and refugees. Even this broad description of those affected has been broadened by the Court. Thus even persons who have moved across frontiers for a purpose other than work may be eligible. In *Hessische Knappschaft*,[24] a German miner was killed whilst on holiday in France. The German social security agency paid the benefits due to his dependants, then tried to recover the money from the driver who caused the accident. The latter's insurers objected on the grounds that the German miner was not actually working at the time of the accident. The Court, however, ruled that the term 'worker' in this context was not restricted to those who had to move within the Community because of their employment.[25]

The universality principle also applies to the range of benefits covered. Article 4(1) stipulates that the scope *ratione materiae* of the Regulation covers (a) sickness and maternity pay, (b) invalidity benefit, (c) old-age and surviving spouses' pensions, (d) benefits payable for industrial accidents and occupational illnesses; (e) death grants; (f) unemployment benefit and (g) family benefit. Article 4(2) adds that the system applies to all social security systems, whether special or general, contributory or non-contributory.

Non-discrimination

This principle is set out in Article 3(1), which requires all persons resident within the territory of a Member State to be treated on an equal basis. They shall, in principle, have the same obligations and enjoy the same advantages under the legislation of the host country as those to which the nationals of that host country are subjected. It does not refer to non-discrimination on grounds of gender, which is dealt with elsewhere (below, p 261).

Migrant workers cannot therefore be excluded from national social security cover[26] and cannot be prevented from making social security contributions or

---

24   Case 44/65, *Hessische Knappschaft v Maison Singer* (1965) ECR 965.

25   *Ibid*, at 971.

26   Case 33/88, *Allue and Coonan v Università degli Studi di Venezia* (1989) ECR 1591 at 1612.

taxes which are applicable to citizens of the host state.[27] This non-discrimination extends even to migrant trainee workers; their social insurance contributions must be calculated according to the same criteria as those applicable to domestic trainees.[28] As is the case with other area of anti-discrimination legislation, the Regulation is concerned with both direct discrimination – which is comparatively infrequent – and indirect discrimination, which arises when legislation apparently applies indistinctly to foreign and domestic workers, but, by imposing such conditions as residential requirements,[29] in practice works to the disadvantage of the migrant worker.

Aggregated benefits yes, concurrent benefits no

The purpose of the Regulation is to place the migrant worker on an equal footing with his or her counterpart in the host state, not to give the former an advantage over the latter. Accordingly, it enables the migrant worker to aggregate consecutive periods of social insurance, and not to give him or her the opportunity to enjoy concurrent benefits.

On the one hand, a number of Articles of the Regulation require the social security authorities of each Member State to treat each period of employment, insurance or residence completed by the migrant worker in any other EU country as though it had been completed in that Member State, whether the benefit in question concern sickness and maternity payments (Article 18 of the Regulation), invalidity benefit (Article 38), old age and surviving spouse pension (Article 45), unemployment benefit (Article 67), etc.

On the other hand, Article 13 of the Regulation states that the migrant worker may only be subject to the legislation of one Member State at any time. Because domestic legislation on social security is not as yet harmonised, this could have challenged the ingenuity of some migrant workers (and/or the negligence of some social security authorities) to enjoy concurrent benefits. That danger is avoided by Article 12(1), which states that the latter 'can neither confer nor maintain the right to several benefits of the same kind for one and the same period of compulsory insurance'.

The system laid down in the Regulation does not, however, merely aim at aggregation as such; it also seeks to guarantee aggregation without loss. Therefore it has built into it adequate safeguards to ensure that the migrant claimant does not actually suffer any disadvantage from the differences in benefit levels applicable in the various Member States. Such discrepancies are

---

27   Case 143/87, *Stanton v INASTI* (1988) ECR 3877.

28   Case 27–91, *Ursaff v Société Hostellerie Le Manoir* (1991) ECR I-5531 at 5542.

29   Steiner, J, *op cit*, at 236.

resolved by making the appropriate institution of the state award the highest benefits making up the difference between the lower and the higher payment.[30]

The public policy exception

Article 48(3) of the Treaty confers on the national authorities the right to maintain or introduce certain limitations on the free movement of workers 'on grounds of public policy, public security or public health'. A similar rule is contained in Article 56(1) of the Treaty, in relation to the freedom of establishment. Article 56(2) requires the Community legislature to issue directives in order to co-ordinate the national provisions on this exception to the free movement of persons. That this has not invariably been adhered to by the ECJ is a proposition which the most important is Directive 64/221.[32] The Council has issued a number of directives, of which the most important is Directive 64/221.[32]

It needs hardly be added that, like the public policy exception of Article 36 of the Treaty in relation to the free movement of goods, these provisions should be interpreted strictly as constituting an exception to a general, and in this case fundamental, principle of Community law, which is the free movement of persons. That this has not invariably been adhered to by the ECJ is a proposition which will be discussed below.

General rules

The Directive and the case law of the ECJ have laid down a number of principles which are common to all three grounds justifying the exception (apart from the procedural aspects, which will be dealt with separately).

The scope of the exception is once again characterised by the universality principle: the Directive covers all Community nationals who reside in or travel to another Member State as are persons who are employed, self-employed or recipients of services – as well as the members of their family as defined above[33] (Article 1 of the Directive). It applies to all measures applicable to the above persons concerning entry, residence permits, or expulsion (Article 2(1)). This principle has been extended by the Court, which has ruled that these rules apply not only to cross-border movements, but also to movements by the foreign Community national within the territory of the Member State. Thus an order served by the French authorities restricting the movements of an Italian political extremist to certain *départements* was held to be unlawful.[34] However,

---

30 Case 128/88, *Di Felice v Institut National d'Assurances Sociales pour les Travailleurs Indépendants* (1989) 923.

31 Similar rule in Article 48(3)!

32 OJ (Special edition) 1963–64, p 117.

33 Above, p 167.

34 Case 36/75, *Rutili* (1975) ECR 1219.

such restrictions may be possible if the national authorities also have the right to impose them on their own nationals.[35] Also, once a Community national has lawfully entered the territory of another Member State, the latter's authorities may not use the public policy exception against him or her in a discriminatory manner.[36]

The expiry of an identity card or passport may not be used to justify expulsion (Article 3(3)). More generally, the Court ruled that a mere failure by a Community national to complete legal formalities concerning access, movement and residence of aliens does not justify an expulsion order.[37] Any state issuing an identity card must allow the holder to re-enter its territory even if that card is no longer valid or the holder's nationality is in dispute (Article 3(4)).

Public policy

It has already been observed that this is a concept derived from the French law term *ordre public* which translates very uncomfortably into the English 'public policy'. This does not excuse the unwillingness or inability of the Court or of the Community legislature to arrive at a *communautaire* concept of public policy – or at least to have tried. Witness the following extract from the *Van Duyn* decision:[38]

the concept of public policy ... must be interpreted strictly, so that its scope cannot be determined unilaterally by each Member State without being subject to controls by the institutions of the Community. Nevertheless the particular circumstances justifying recourse to the concept of public policy may vary from one country to another and from one period to another, and it is therefore necessary in this matter to allow the competent national authorities an area of discretion within the limits imposed by the Treaty.

This, to put it mildly, is somewhat inconclusive, and not very helpful to the national court which requested the ECJ opinion in the first place. This is not to say that Community law contains no indications whatsoever as to the meaning and scope of this concept. Thus Article 3(1) stipulates that measures adopted on grounds of public policy (and security) must be based on the personal conduct of the individual concerned. Previous convictions cannot by themselves justify an expulsion measure (Article 3(2)). The ECJ has had ample opportunity to clarify these notions.

---

35 Groves, *op cit*, at 172.
36 Case 15/69, *Südmilch v Ugliogla* (1969) ECR 363.
37 Case 48/75, *Royer* (1976) ECR 497 at 515.
38 Case 41/74, *Van Duyn v Home Office* (1974) ECR 1337 at 1350.

The first true test of the scope of these provisions came in the famous *Van Duyn* decision.[39] When Ms. Van Duyn, a Netherlands national, arrived in Britain to take up a secretarial position with the Church of Scientology, she was refused entry on the grounds this position with this sect was considered to be socially harmful. The Court had to consider whether membership of an organisation or sect could constitute 'personal conduct' within the meaning of Directive 64/221. The Court first explained that, as has been mentioned earlier, the Member States retained a measure of discretion in this area.

The ECJ then turned to one of the main objections by the plaintiff to her exclusion, ie the fact that in the United Kingdom, membership of the Church of Scientology was not actually prohibited. The Court replied that, just because a Member State had stated its position by declaring an activity socially harmful and taking certain administrative measures against it, that did not mean that it was also compelled to make such activities unlawful. This argument does not, however, meet the discrimination test. It could be argued that, for Ms. Van Duyn's treatment not to be discriminatory, some administrative measure, stopping short of declaring the activity unlawful, could have been applied to UK nationals (perhaps some kind of 'Government health warning'?). In fact, a question along those lines is raised in ground of judgment 20 of the decision. The Court's response, in Ground 21, is extremely evasive. It ultimately awarded the decision to the UK authorities.

Suggestions that, with the British referendum on Community membership looming immediately ahead, the Court was motivated by considerations other than the purely legal are normally dismissed with disdain by most authorities. Yet this is not the only occasion on which such accusations have been levelled at the Court; in addition, the Court almost immediately lost no time in distancing itself from its position.[40]

This 'retreat from Van Duyn', as it is described, is well documented. In *Bonsignore*,[41] an Italian working in Germany fatally wounded his brother whilst cleaning a gun. He was convicted of causing death by negligence and for possessing a firearm without a licence, but received no prison sentence. He was served with a deportation order by the German municipal authorities. The Court disregarded the plea made by the latter that the illegal possession of a gun represented 'personal conduct' which was a serious danger to the well-being of the citizen, both German and foreign. It ruled that a deportation order, to satisfy the 'personal conduct' requirement, had to be made 'for breaches of the peace and public security which might be committed by the individual

---

39 *Ibid.*

40 Fewer than three months elapsed between the *Van Duyn* decision and the first of these recanting judgments (Bonsignore)!

41 Case 67/74, *Bonsignore v Oberstadtdirektor Köln* (1975) ECR 297.

affected'. More generally, it ruled that Article 3 of the Directive prohibited deportations of a 'general preventative nature'.

In *Bouchereau*,[42] a Frenchman working in Britain was recommended for deportation by a court after having been twice convicted of drugs offences. The ECJ held that previous criminal convictions may only be taken into account for the purposes of a deportation order insofar as the circumstances giving rise to that conviction constituted a present threat to public policy. However, it immediately went on to qualify this finding by adding that 'it is possible that past conduct alone may constitute such a threat to the requirements of policy'. This is not very helpful to a referring court, which was not informed as to whether the ECJ considered M Bouchereau's offences to fall into that category.

Finally, in *Adoui and Cornouaille v Belgium*,[43] two ladies were refused permission to reside in Belgium because they were suspected of prostitution. However, prostitution is not in itself an offence in Belgium. The national authorities argued that the two women were likely to promote criminal activity because of the well-known association of their profession with the underworld was rejected, as the Court did not consider this to come within the scope of 'personal conduct'.

Public security

Neither the Directive nor the available case law provide us with a great deal of clarification of this concept. One of the main reasons for this is that it is to all practical intents and purposes conflated with the notion of public policy, particularly because Article 3(1) of the Directive imposes the 'personal conduct' requirement on both the public policy and the public security ground for expulsion. Another reason is that the domestic legal systems do not invariably make a clear-cut distinction between these two concepts themselves.

Public service employment

Article 48(4) of the Treaty disapplies the provisions on the free movement of workers from employment in the public service. Does this term include any post held with any public body? The Court has replied in the negative. This is again an exception to a major principle, and must therefore be interpreted strictly. The Court laid down the relevant demarcation line in *Commission v Belgium*,[44] where it decided that Article 48(4) applied to posts which involve an 'association with tasks belonging to the public service properly so-called'. Therefore activities, even those of a social and economic kind, which fall within the scope of the public law of the state, and where the latter assumes

---

42 Case 30/77, *R v Bouchereau* (1977) ECR 1999.

43 Cases 115 and 116/81 (1982) ECR 1665.

44 Case 149/79, (1982) ECR 1845.

responsibility for their performance, do not fall within the scope of this provision.[45]

III   Freedom of establishment – freedom to provide services

General

The two freedoms discussed in this section are dealt with in separate Chapters of the Treaty. However, their very nature makes it appropriate for them to be dealt with together. Strictly speaking, the freedom to provide services has nothing to do with the free movement of persons, since the philosophy underlying this freedom is that anyone should be able to offer his or her services throughout the Community *even if this means that the provider himself/herself has not crossed any border*. In practice, however, those who wish to provide services in another Member State will be inclined to travel for that purpose, and therefore need the various freedoms conferred for that purpose by Community law. In addition, this joint approach is to a certain extent sanctioned by Community law itself – witness the various items of legislation which are based on both sets of provisions in the Treaty.

Definition and scope

From Article 52, second paragraph, EC Treaty, it can be concluded that the freedom of establishment is the freedom to take up permanent residence in another Community country in order to pursue a professional activity other than that which is carried out in paid employment, whether by acting as a self-employed person or by setting up a firm or company. This freedom also covers the right of so-called 'secondary establishment' in another Member State, meaning the right to set up a branch or a subsidiary of an existing firm or company in another state. However, from the wording of Article 52, first sentence, EC Treaty it follows that this right of secondary establishment is restricted to Community nationals who are already established on EU territory. However, it is generally agreed that an EU citizen who has a principal establishment in a non-Member State and a secondary establishment in a Member State enjoys the right of establishment in any other Member State.[46]

As for the freedom to provide services, Article 60 of the Treaty itself provides a detailed and self-sufficient definition. Services are deemed to fall within the scope of this freedom where 'they are normally provided for

---

45   See also case 152/73, *Sotgiu v Deutsche Bundespost* (1974) ECR 153.
46   Gautron, JC, *Droit européen* (2nd edn, 1993), Mementos Dalloz, p 166.

remuneration, in so far as they are not governed by the provisions relating to the freedom of movement of goods, capital and persons' (Article 60, first paragraph, EC Treaty). More particularly, the notion of 'services' includes (a) activities of an industrial nature, (b) commercial activities, (c) the activities of craftsmen, and (d) the activities of 'the professions' (meaning the so-called 'liberal' professions) (Article 60, second paragraph). The third paragraph states that the person providing such a service, 'may, in order to do so, temporarily pursue his activity in the state where the service is provided, under the same conditions as are imposed by the state on its own nationals'.

The Court has extended the rights of providers of services to the recipients of services, in the sense that it has decreed the right, not only of the provider to come to the customer, but also the right of the customer to travel across intra-Community frontiers to receive the service from its provider. This was established in *Luisi and Carbone*.[47] The plaintiffs were two Italian nationals who had exceeded the maximum permitted amount of foreign currency which under Italian law may be exported. They claimed that, since they needed to export the extra amount of currency in order to pay their way as tourists abroad, these Italian rules infringed Articles 59 and 60 EC Treaty. The Court ruled that:

the freedom to provide services includes the freedom, for the recipient of services, to go to another Member State in order to receive a service there, without being obstructed by restrictions, even in relation to payments, and that tourists, persons receiving medical treatment and persons travelling for the purposes of education or business are to be regarded as recipients of services.[48]

As with the free movement of workers, the applicability of Article 59 requires a cross-border element. In *Debauve*,[49] the defendant had criminal proceedings brought against him in Belgium for having broadcast commercial advertising on television, which at the time was prohibited in Belgium. The Court was unable to help him, because the provisions on the freedom to provide services were incapable of application in cases where the activity in question was restricted to one Member State.[50]

Public authority exception

Article 55 of the Treaty exempts from the provisions on the freedom of establishment and the freedom to provide services any activities which are connected, even on an occasional basis, with the exercising of official authority. This is naturally the counterpart to the 'public service exception' laid down in

47 Cases 286/82 and 26/83, *Luisi and Carbone v Ministero del Tesoro* (1984) ECR 377.

48 *Ibid*, at 403.

49 Case 52/79, *Procureur du Roi v Debauve* (1980) ECR 833.

50 *Ibid*, at 859.

Article 48 in relation to the free movement of workers. Here too, the Court has tended to interpret this exception strictly. In the *Reyners* decision,[51] it added that to be caught by Article 55 of the Treaty, the activity in question had to have a direct and specific connection with the exercise of official authority. In that case, the Belgian authorities had relied on Article 55, para 1, EC Treaty, in justifying rules restricting the access of foreigners to the Brussels Bar. It pointed out that in Belgium, barristers may sometimes be called upon to complete a panel of judges. The Court, however, ruled that this contingency was separable from the professional activity in question. The most typical activities of the profession were to give legal assistance and representation to its clients.[52]

Direct and indirect discrimination

Cases of direct discrimination are obvious examples of the kind of practices prohibited under the freedoms under review. Thus in *Reyners*,[53] the applicant was a Dutchman who possessed a Belgian law degree. Belgian rules preventing him from practising with the Brussels bar were held to be unlawful by the Court. However, the ECJ has also found ways of outlawing indirect discrimination in the field of establishment and services.[54]

Its first opportunity arose in *Thieffry*.[55] In this dispute, the plaintiff was a Belgian lawyer who had obtained his law degree in Belgium and sought access to the Paris Bar (unlike Mr Reyners, who actually had a law degree issued in the country where he sought to practise). Although the Belgian degree was recognised by France as being equivalent to the French degree required to become an avocat, his application was refused. The Court held that an unjustified restriction on the freedom of establishment would arise if admission to a particular profession were refused to someone covered by the Treaty who has a degree recognised to be equivalent to the relevant national diploma, and who had met all the other conditions for access to the French legal profession. This was the case even if no harmonising legislation under Article 57[56] had as yet been forthcoming.[57]

Those active in other walks of life have been less fortunate. Thus in *Bouchoucha*,[58] a French national was prosecuted by the British authorities for

51 Case 2/74 (1974) ECR 631.
52 *Ibid*, at 655.
53 *Op cit*.
54 The notion of 'indirect discrimination' is one which has been applied by the Court in other field, more particularly that of discrimination based on gender as prohibited by Article 119 of the Treaty; below, p 261 *et seq*.
55 Case 71/76, *Thieffry v Conseil de l'Ordre des Avocats à la Cour de Paris* (1977) ECR 765.
56 Relating to the mutual recognition and co-ordination of qualifications.
57 Case 186/87, *op cit*, at 221.
58 Case C-61/89 (1990) ECR I-3551.

pursuing the occupation of osteopath without being qualified as a doctor. At that time, harmonising legislation on the medical profession had already been adopted; however, it did not provide a precise description of a doctor's responsibilities. This prompted the Court to concede that, in the absence of any Community legislation governing the practice of osteopathy, the national authorities retained the right to regulate this activity, provided that this did not involve any discrimination based on nationality.[59]

Nevertheless, the Court has attempted to curb the prerogatives of the Member States where it felt that they imposed rules relating to certain professions, less to safeguard the public interest than to prevent nationals from other Member States from gaining access to them. Thus in Case 205/84,[60] the Commission brought Article 169 proceedings against Germany in respect of its rules requiring all direct insurers to be established in Germany and hold the necessary authorisation. The Court conceded that there might be public interest reasons for Germany to distrust the relevant rules in the state where a non-German based insurer was operating. However, the blanket requirement that all direct insurers must be based in Germany was a disproportionate restriction on the freedom to provide services. The authorisation requirement, on the other hand, was permissible under Community law subject to certain conditions.[61]

Harmonising legislation

Articles 54 and 63 of the Treaty required the Community legislature to draw up general programmes for the abolition of restrictions in the fields of establishment and services. This was done on 18 December 1961, with the adoption of General Programme 32/62 (services) and 36/62 (establishment).[62] They run parallel to each other and many of its provisions are worded in almost identical fashion.

These programmes were extremely ambitious. They set out to banish every conceivable form of discrimination based on nationality. There is simply not enough space here even to mention, let alone describe, all the various directives, decisions and recommendations which have been issued in implementation of these General Programmes. Reference can be made to Lasok's *Professions and Services in the EEC*,[63] although a good deal of legislation has been adopted since its publication. The same applies to Burrows, *Freedom of Movement in European*

59 *Ibid*, at 3568.
60 *Commission v Germany* (1986) ECR 3755.
61 *Ibid*, at 3809.
62 Reproduced entirely in Lasok, D, *The Professions and Services in the European Economic Community* (1986) Kluwer, Appendices I and II.
63 *Op cit*, published 1986.

Community Law,[64] An up-to-date digest of all the instruments adopted in the fields of banking and insurance can be found in Lasok and Bridge, pp 499–505,[65]

Educational qualifications

One potential obstacle in the path of those wishing to avail themselves of the full mobility of persons resides in the considerable differences that exist between the various educational qualifications awarded in the various Member States, and the fact that in many cases, the national authorities refuse to recognise those of other Member States. This is why Article 57 of the Treaty makes provision for the enactment of a major legislative programme aimed at removing these discrepancies as a factor inhibiting mobility.

Article 57 of the Treaty uses a twin-track approach in order to achieve its ends. Article 57(1) requires the Council to adopt directives for the mutual recognition of 'diplomas, certificates and other evidence of formal qualifications'. Article 57(2) provides for the enactment of directives for the co-ordination of the national rules on the taking up and pursuit of self-employed occupations. This the Council seeks to achieve by ensuring that the programmes of study and training leading up to these qualifications meet a number of minimum requirements. As regards the medical and related professions (including those dealing in matters pharmaceutical) Article 57(3) specifies that abolition of restrictions is dependent on the co-ordination of the conditions for their exercise.

In implementation of Article 57, the Community legislature proceeded to adopt directives which reflected the twin-track approach described earlier, and did so on a sector-by-sector basis. A number of professions were dealt with in this manner. Various professions, particularly in the medical field, were thus harmonised. This sector-by-sector method tended to be rather laborious, and therefore, as can be seen from some of the dates of the directives described above, incurred considerable delay in some areas. Nor was the frustrated self-employed person assisted by the *Auer* judgment,[66] in which the ECJ held that is a directive is adopted in implementation of Article 57 of the Treaty, individuals may not claim any rights under Articles 52 or 59 of the Treaty in relation to its contents until such time as the transitional period laid down in that directive has expired.[67] This is why a new approach was pioneered in the late 1980s, which sought to concentrate on a broad approach as regard the basic standards which must be met, instead of the detailed approach followed under the sector-

---

64 Published 1987.

65 *Op cit* (1994).

66 Case 136/78, *Ministere Public v Auer* (1979) ECR 437.

67 *Ibid*, at 451.

by-sector method. This then was the basis for Directive 89/48 on a General System for the Recognition of Higher Education Diplomas.[68]

This instrument applies to all regulated professions, ie those professions whose pursuit is subject to a degree awarded after a study programme of at least three years' duration. It also applies to salaried persons who are not civil servants. The host state may, however, require the applicant to undergo, according to his or her choice, either a period of training for adjustment purposes or an aptitude test. For the legal profession, however, the host state has the right to specify whether an adaptation period or an aptitude test is required. Directive 89/48 has now been complemented by Directive 92/51,[69] which applies to qualifications involving higher education training for three years and over.

Once a particular profession has been subjected to harmonising legislation (whether under the 'old' or the 'new' approaches), Member States may not implement the measures in such a manner as to hamper their proper functioning.[70] Although qualifications from non-Member States are not covered by any harmonising legislation, once a Member State has decided to recognise such a qualification, it must also take into account any practical training or experience obtained by the claimant when it is establishing whether a training condition imposed by national law has been met.[71]

In 1996, the Commission adopted a proposal for a directive which would establish a mechanism for the recognition of qualifications for occupations in small craft industries, commerce and services.[72]

Harmonisation of company law

The free movement of persons refers not only to individuals as natural persons, but also to those entities which assume the form of legal persons. These are artificially created persons which are established by natural persons, but acquire rights and obligations which are separate from those who have set them up. Since they are given legal personality, they too much be able to enjoy the benefits of the freedom of establishment. It is for this purpose that Article 54(3)(g) of the Treaty required the EU legislature to adopt directives which harmonise those safeguards which the national authorities impose on corporate bodies, in order to protect both the interests of the general public and those of the company members themselves.

---

68 OJ 1989 L 19.

69 OJ 1992 L 209.

70 Case 427/85, *Commission v Germany* (1988) ECR 1123 at 166.

71 Case C-319/92, *Haim v Kassenzahnärtzliche Vereinigung Nordrhein* (1994) ECR I-425.

72 General Report 1996, p 62.

Here too, the legislative programme has incurred a number of delays. One of the reasons for this is that a number of proposed directives proved to be quite troublesome from a political point of view, such as the proposed Fifth Directive, which makes provision for mandatory worker participation in the company management. The following Company Law directives have thus far been adopted:

- First Directive on the disclosure of vital information for the protection of shareholders and others.[73]

- Second Directive on the formation of public limited liability companies and the maintenance and alteration of their capital.[74]

- Fourth Directive on company accounts.[75]

- Third Directive on mergers of public limited liability companies.[76]

- Sixth Directive on the division of public limited liability companies.[77]

- Seventh Directive on consolidated accounts.[78]

- Eighth Directive on statutory auditors.[79]

- Eleventh Directive on the disclosure of documents for branches of companies established in another Member State.[80]

- Twelfth Directive on one-person limited liability companies.[81]

The procession of harmonising measures in this field looks set to continue, in spite of the political difficulties involved in certain proposals. For a number of years now, proposals have been made for a European company. One of these proposed the adoption of a European Company Statute;[82] another proposal is for a Directive seeking the involvement of employees in the European Company.[83]

73 Directive 68/151, OJ Special Edition 1968 (I), p 41.

74 Directive 77/91, OJ 1977 L 26.

75 Directive 78/660, OJ 1978 L 222.

76 Directive 78/855, OJ 1978 L 295.

77 Directive 82/891, OJ 1982 L 378.

78 Directive 83/49, OJ 1983 244.

79 Directive 84/253, OJ 1984 L 126.

80 Directive 88/627, OJ 1988 L 348.

81 Directive 89/667, OJ 1989 L 395.

82 OJ 1991 C 176.

83 OJ 1991 C 138.

Providing the European citizen with a frontier-free Community

General

Although, as has been mentioned before, the European Union continues to be an essentially economic arrangement, the last decade or so has seen a trend in favour of a Europe of the citizen, and towards providing the latter with freedom of movement within the Community regardless of economic considerations.

EU citizenship

The TEU officially changed the title of the Treaty of Rome from 'EEC Treaty' to 'European Community Treaty'. This symbolic gesture was accompanied by the insertion in the Treaty of a number of provisions laying the foundations of 'citizenship of the Union', Articles 8 to 8e. Article 8 of the Treaty lays down the principle that any national of any Member State shall be a citizen of the Union; all such citizens are bound by the rights and obligations conferred by the Treaty.

Articles 8a to 8d of the Treaty contain a number of provisions which could be described as an embryonic Bill of Rights for the Community citizen. Article 8a of the Treaty lays down the principle of free movement within the Union, and enables the Council to adopt measures in furtherance of this principle. Article 8b of the Treaty confers on the EU citizen the right to stand in municipal or European elections anywhere within the Union, and on the same conditions as the nationals of the Member State in which he or she is exercising this right.

Under Article 8c of the Treaty, whenever EU citizens find themselves within the territory of a non-Member State, they have a right to protection by the consular and diplomatic authorities of any Member State. Article 8d of the Treaty gives Union citizens the right to petition the European Parliament or address the Ombudsman appointed by the European Parliament.

The last of these new provisions, Article 8e of the Treaty, requires the Commission to report every three years to the European Parliament, the Council and the Economic and Social Committee, on the manner in which this 'Citizens' Charter' is being applied. The Council may adopt rules aimed at strengthening or supplementing the new rights referred to above. These rules must, however, be approved by the national authorities of the Member States in accordance with their constitutional rules.

Towards a frontier-free community

As long as border controls within the Community remain, the free movement of persons will be incomplete, however simplified the procedures at these control points may be. Until the mid-eighties, this aspiration had merely amounted to a few statements of intent and half-hearted principles. Then matters started moving at a considerably more energetic pace. At the Fontainebleau European Council Meeting of 14 June 1984, it was agreed in principle that all customs and police formalities should be abolished at intra-Community border points. Just over a year later, France and Germany made the first step in this direction by signing the *Saarbrücken* Agreement. Shortly afterwards, on 14 June 1985, a number or countries signed an agreement committing its signatories to the progressive removal of checks at shared borders, as well as free passage for those crossing those borders, regardless of whether he or she was a Community national or not. This was the first Schengen Agreement, and was concluded by Belgium, France, Germany, Luxembourg and the Netherlands. These five countries signed the second Schengen agreement five years later, setting out a number of conditions and guarantees for the purpose of implementing the free movement of non-Community nationals in the EU. The original signatories were later joined by Italy, Spain and Portugal.

Under the law and order and security arrangements, the agreements makes provision for more intense co-operation between the national authorities in order to improve the effectiveness of border controls. The Agreement also contains measures against terrorism and organised crime. For this purpose, provision is made for improved levels of communication and co-ordination between the judicial authorities and government departments of the Member States.

The Amsterdam Treaty has integrated Community policy on the free movement of persons, asylum and immigration into its fundamental objective, which is the establishment of an area of freedom, security and justice. A new Title to this effect has been inserted into the EC Treaty. Article A thereof requires the Council to adopt, within five years of the entry into effect of the Amsterdam Treaty, measures aimed at ensuring the free movement of persons in accordance with Article 7a EC Treaty, together with related measures regarding external border controls, asylum and immigration. It should be recalled that Article 7a requires the establishment of an internal market without any intra-Community frontiers, thus securing the free movement of goods, persons, services and capital.

Article B requires, within the same five-year period, the adoption of Council legislation aimed at ensuring the absence of any controls on person, be they EU citizens or third country nationals, when crossing internal EU borders. To this end, Article B(2) sets out a list of detailed rules which will need to be adopted to substantiate this objective.

10 The Free Movement of Capital

I Introduction

The free movement of money is widely regarded as a necessary corollary to the free movement of goods, persons and services. If payments were unable to follow goods or services when carried across frontiers, or if workers were not allowed to transfer their earnings from one Community country to another, precious little benefit would stand to be gained from these freedoms. However, money is moved for purposes other than paying for goods or services, such as investing, speculating, providing security or extending credit. It is therefore appropriate to draw a distinction between the free movement of current payments and the free movement of capital.

II Movement of payments

As to the free movement of payments, this is dealt with in several Treaty provisions. Payments connected with the movement of goods and services are dealt with in Article 106(1) EC Treaty. Under this rule, all Member States must authorise any payments in connection with these freedoms, as well as any transfers of capital and earnings, but only to the extent that the free movement of goods, persons, capital and services has been achieved in accordance with the Treaty. The rule is therefore that the extent to which goods and services are liberalised determines the extent to which people may move monies across intra-Community borders in order to pay for them.

However, this freedom is subject to certain restrictions, as the available Court of Justice case law shows the *Casati*[1] and *Luisi and Carbone*[2] cases. Both these decisions concerned Italian legislation on currency restrictions, more particularly the limit placed on the exporting of foreign monies, and criminal proceedings brought on these grounds. In *Casati*, the accused had exported foreign currency, but only after having imported it into Italy in order to pay for kitchen equipment, found the factory closed, and returned to Germany with the money still in his possession. In the other case, proceedings had been brought against two persons who wanted to export foreign currency, one for tourist purposes, the other in order to undergo medical treatment.

---

1   Case 203/80 (1981) ECR 2595.
2   Cases 286/82 and 26/83, *op cit.*

The Court held that no restrictions could be placed on intra-Community transfers or payments which would have the effect of hindering the free movement of goods or of services. However, the re-exporting of banknotes was not a normal means of paying for goods or services. Therefore the Italian legislation governing these re-exportation bans was not contrary to Community law. In *Luisa and Carbone*, the Court held that in order to enjoy their freedom to receive services (above, p 177), the plaintiffs needed to be able to bring with them the means with which to pay for these goods or services. However, where these services were paid for by means of a transfer of banknotes, the movements of money in question did not constitute 'movement of capital' protected by Community law. Article 106 EC Treaty has, however, been abolished by the TEU. Whether this makes the above case law entirely redundant in not entirely clear.

III Capital movements

Article 67 lays down the principle that Member States shall abolish between themselves all restrictions on capital movements belonging to persons residing in the Community, as well as any discrimination based on nationality or place of residence in this field. However, the obligation to liberalise is subject to one major caveat, which is that it must be achieved 'to the extent necessary to ensure the proper functioning of the common market'. Initially, the Community institutions tended to interpret this condition in an extremely cautious manner, only to step up the pace of integration once its crucial importance to the realisation of a single market became clear.

This explains why the progress made in liberalising capital movements has been achieved over two distinct and sharply contrasting stages. During the first, advances were very slow and partial, whereas the second phase has resulted in a freedom of capital movements which is virtually unlimited.

Stage One: 1960 to 1988

During this period, the Community legislature, in fulfilment of Article 69, issued a major directive aimed at liberalising national exchange regulations. It was adopted on 11 May 1960, and distinguished between four types of capital movement. For List A movements, which include the most commonly used capital transactions such as direct investment and personal capital movements, the Member States had to grant all the foreign exchange authorisations which were necessary for their completion. For List B movements, which concerned ordinary operations in securities, the national authorities had to grant general permission for their conclusion or performance. As regards List C movements, regarding more specialist types of securities transactions, Member States had to grant all such foreign exchange authorisations as were required. For List D movements, which include mainly short-term capital movements involving speculative movements of funds capable of producing unfavourable effects on the balance of payments, there was no obligation to liberalise transactions.

This directive was subsequently supplemented and extended by Directive 85/583.[3] The question has arisen as to whether this directive applied to stock exchange transactions, which remained subject to national law.[4]

Stage Two: 1988 to present

The adoption of the Single European Act highlighted the fact that no barrier-free internal market would be fully achieved unless the remaining restrictions on capital movements were completely abolished. As a result, Directive 88/361 was adopted.[5] This measure requires the national authorities not only to abolish all remaining restrictions on capital movements, but also to ensure that transfers of capital are made at the same exchange rate as those to which current transactions are subject. In addition, it requires the abolition of all discriminatory measures, such as different rates of taxation applicable to investors.

Even this directive, however, allowed the Member States to maintain some restrictions. If foreign exchange markets are being subjected to exceptionally sizeable short-term capital movements, which could cause serious disruption in the monetary and exchange rate policies of the Member States, such capital movements may be restricted for a maximum of six months. Naturally such exceptional measures are subject to the supervision of the Commission, and are surrounded by procedural safeguards. In addition, Article 4 of the Directive allows the Member States to take all such measures as are necessary to prevent violations of their laws and regulations. More particularly, it allowed the national authorities to make the export of certain means of payment, such as coins, banknotes, or bearer cheques, subject to a prior declaration, which need not be a mere formality (without constituting an actual prior authorisation). Such a declaration may be demanded prior to an export transaction, in order to enable the domestic authorities to exercise adequate supervision so as to prevent infringements of their national laws and regulations.[6]

In the wake of the SEA, the Council also adopted Regulation 1969/88,[7] which organises facilities enabling the Member States to enjoy medium term financial assistance with their balance-of-payments problems. Following the adoption of the TEU, the Council took the view that this support mechanism needed to be retained during the transition to the third stage of economic and

---

3   OJ 1985, L 372.

4   Case 143/86, *East (t/a Margetts and Addenbrooke) v Cuddy* (1988) ECR 625.

5   OJ 1988 L 178.

6   Cases C-358/93 and C-416/93, *Bordessa and Others* (not yet reported).

7   OJ 1988 L 178.

monetary union. Thus Italy, in 1992, applied for and obtained a loan of 8,000 million ECUs in order to assist it in its endeavours to overcome the currency crisis which affected the country during that year.[8] This is in spite of the new Article 73b which was inserted into the Treaty by the TEU, and which in principle imposes a total ban on any restrictions on capital movements or payments whatsoever.

Recently the Court has also to interpret strictly the Treaty rules on the free movement of capital. Thus a Luxembourg rule refusing housing aid to anyone who contracts a loan with a bank not established within the Grand Duchy was held by the ECJ to constitute an obstacle to the free movement of capital, because they were capable of deterring people from approaching banks established in other Member States.[9]

IV Towards economic and monetary union

Like the Single European Act, the Treaty on European Union contained both institutional and substantive provisions. We have already examined some of the institutional aspects in the section devoted to Community legislation (above, p 53). The substantive aspects cover a wide range of Community policies. However, it is fair to state that the most important substantive provisions are those relating to the establishment of economic and monetary union – which was to a large extent the *raison d'être* of the TEU.

Virtually all the provisions relating to EMU are contained within the new Title VI, Economic and Monetary Policy (Articles 102a to 109m EC Treaty). EMU is to be achieved over three stages. The first stage involves preparing the economies of the Member States for EMU, and requires the Member States to satisfy certain economic convergence criteria in order to be allowed to participate in the final stage of EMU. During the second stage, the machinery for bringing EMU into operation is to be established, consisting mainly in setting up the European Central Bank and giving the latter certain powers in relation to the achievement of EMU. The final stage is to consist in the gradual introduction of a single European currency.

The most controversial aspect of the establishment of EMU is undoubtedly the so-called economic convergence criteria. These impose on the Member States the obligation to align their economic policies in terms of price stability and the control of public finances. More particularly, Article 109j EC Treaty as amended requires Member States to meet the following criteria:

- the achievement of price stability, as demonstrated by an inflation rate similar to that of the three best performing Member States in this regard;

---

8 Mathijsen, PSRF, *A Guide to European Union Law* (1995), Sweet & Maxwell, p 214.

9 Case C-484/93, *Svensson* (1995) ECR I-3955.

- sustainable financial policies by the national governments as evidenced by a low budgetary deficit;
- keeping within the normal margins of fluctuation which currencies must not exceed for at least two years without devaluing against any other Community currency;
- the durability of the convergence achieved by the Member State concerned and of its participation in the Exchange Rate Mechanism of the European Monetary System, as reflected in the level of long-term interest rates.

These criteria are unambiguously deflationary, and the resulting reduction in state expenditure and rises in interest rates could aggravate an unemployment problem which has already placed the social peace under a severe strain in many countries. At the time of writing, it looks unlikely that all the Member States will be able to participate in the third and final stage of EMU. This will hasten the emergence of a two-speed Europe, which some see as a prelude to the unravelling of the entire Community. It can be doubted, however, whether the populations of the Member States will be as adversely affected by such trend as they will be by the strict application of the TEU convergence criteria.

V   Conclusion on the 'Four Freedoms'

The provisions of the Treaty and the resulting derived legislation, as well as the specific programme occasioned by the SEA, have secured for the Community an internal market which has considerably enhanced trading opportunities between the Member States. However, it would be a mistake to conclude that the internal market is now complete. The main barriers which remain are the following:

- **Fiscal barriers.** It is unlikely that direct taxation will be harmonised, at least in the near future. However, there remains plenty of scope for action in the field of indirect taxation. VAT rates are not yet fully harmonised, and therefore are capable of constituting a barrier to trade in that if Country A has higher rates than Country B, the exporters from other Member States will tend to prefer exporting to Country B, as lower VAT rates will presumably boost their sales on that market.

- **Technical barriers.** The mutual recognition approach which has characterised internal market legislation ever since *Cassis de Dijon* (above, p 146) could distort trade as well as promote it. If products from countries with low levels of government regulation can move freely to countries where such levels are high, without being subject to any minimum requirements or standards, this gives producers from the low-regulation countries a considerable competitive advantage over those emanating from high-regulation countries. Some would call this unfair competition, but of a kind which is not caught by any of the EC Treaty rules on competition (below, p 191).

• **Legal barriers.** In spite of the harmonising legislation described at p 182, company law remains subject to considerable differences as between the Member States, which could constitute a barrier towards the freedom of establishment. Differences in such legal areas as tort liability and contracts have major implications for the business world, and the absence of any harmonisation could also give rise to obstacles.

• **Administrative barriers.** These too present certain potential impediments to trade. For example, any company which establishes itself in another Member State must undergo the registration procedures of that country, even though it was already validly registered in its country of origin. Various occupations requiring licences – eg for those operating financial services – are similarly hamstrung by the need to register in every Member State in which they wish to practise.

A great deal of work therefore remains to be done before the EU can truly be said to preside over a single market.

11 Competition Policy

I Introduction

Background

Rules aimed at regulating competition in the marketplace are a relatively new phenomenon. The conventional wisdom, especially that of the liberal school of the 19th century, was that any public interference with the market mechanism would almost automatically have a harmful effect on the economy. However, the realisation slowly began to dawn that to leave market forces entirely unfettered led to precisely the outcome which free marketeers abhorred, the formation of large monopolies able to operate without feeling the pressure of competition. The United States led the way in competition regulation with the Sherman Act 1870, which was aimed at preventing stultifying cartels and monopolies. During the years that followed, virtually every industrialised country emulated this example. The nations of Europe also introduced laws aimed at restraining anti-competitive behaviour.

The drafters of the Community Treaties understood only too well that the expanded market which they were about to create would tempt some companies to circumvent these national competition rules by operating their anti-competitive practices on a European scale. Accordingly, they inserted in the primary Community instruments rules which, essentially, had three objectives: (a) to avoid restrictive agreements and practices, (b) to prevent large undertakings from abusing their economic dominance, and (c) to ensure that, within certain limits, the public sector also kept to the rules of the game. It is these rules which form the subject matter of this chapter.

The fundamental objectives of EU competition policy

In spite of its shortcomings, it is generally agreed that the Community institutions have succeeded in framing a cohesive and consistent set of objectives to be pursued in implementing EU competition policy. The clearest statement of these fundamental objectives was given by the Commission in the Ninth Report on Competition Policy, whose introduction listed the four essential aims which are being pursued in this regard:

(a) to create an open and unified market which is not partitioned by restrictive and anti-competitive agreements between firms;

(b) to realise an appropriate amount of effective competition in markets, avoiding over-concentration or any abuses exercised by dominant companies;

(c) to achieve fairness in the market place, which involves giving support to small and medium-sized firms, measures for the protection of the consumer, and the penalising of unlawful state subsidies;

(d) to maintain the competitive position of the Community towards its principal rivals in the global economy, being mainly Japan and the US.

In the conclusion to this Report,[1] the Commission emphasised the central position occupied by competition policy in the overall objectives of the Community's economic and industrial policy. It maintained that the sheer size of the common market and its close involvement in global trade meant that only a Community-wide competition policy was capable of assuming the role of a regulator of economic activity throughout the Community. If the Community policy were to yield to the temptation of retreating into self-sufficient isolation, this would simply worsen the problem beyond resolution by aggravating the trauma of the structural changes which shifting patterns of world trade are forcing upon Europe. Therefore:

if we delude ourselves that we can dispense with the forces of competition and a decentralised economy and can steer through the necessary restructuring by purely legislative means, we run the irremediable risk of cutting our Community off from the economic reality of its surroundings.[2]

Competition law and price

One of the main economic objectives of EU competition policy expresses itself at the level of prices. In the *ICI* case,[3] the Court stated that the purpose of competition is, in relation to prices, to keep them at as low a level as possible, and to promote the movement of goods between Member States in order to enable commercial activities to be allocated as efficiently as possible on the basis of the productivity and adaptability of the undertakings concerned. This was the case even though price competition was not the only form of competitive behaviour in existence. This definition has the merit of striking a balance between the interests of the consumer, the maximum degree of free movement of goods, and production structures.[4]

---

1 Ninth Competition Policy Report, pp 9–11.
2 *Ibid* p 11.
3 Case 48/68, *Imperial Chemical Industries v Commission* (1972) ECR 619.
4 Gautron, J–C, *op cit*, p 172.

II The essential characteristics of EU competition law

Universality

The general competition rules cover all items which are capable of forming the subject matter of commercial transactions. That means that they concern not only goods, but also services and even intellectual property rights. There are, however, a number of specific provisions of competition, such as those relating to transport (Articles 77–81 EC Treaty) and to which the rules of Articles 85 to 94 of the Treaty do not apply by virtue of the principle *lex specialis generali derogat* (the specific law takes precedence over the general rule).

Largely the creation of the case law

The provisions of Articles 85 to 94 of the Treaty are worded in very broad terms, and have required a good deal of interpretation by the Court. However, the influence of the derived legislation is becoming increasingly felt. This is particularly the case in relation to rules such as the Mergers Regulation, which is a major self-standing item of competition legislation (unlike, for example, the block exemption regulations, whose terms are entirely dictated by the requirements of the implementation of Article 85 of the Treaty).

Extra-territorial principle

EU competition law applies to all firms whose actions have implications for the common market, regardless of whether they are established in a Community Member State or not. This has been confirmed by the Court of Justice, where it ruled that the Commission is entitled to initiate proceedings against firms under Articles 85 and 86 where their actions have adverse effects on intra-Community trade, even if they have no registered office in the EU.[5]

Ideological pragmatism

The object of Community competition policy is to avoid distortions in trade within the Community; as such it is loyal to the market liberalism which underlies the Treaty. However, this attachment to free-market values is not pursued dogmatically – in fact, much less so than is the case with other basic trading rules, such as the free movement of goods. Accordingly, the various provisions laying down the ground rules are subject to a generous range of exceptions which are inspired either by social considerations (eg Article 92(2) of the Treaty), or by considerations of market efficiency (eg Article 85(3) of the Treaty).

---

5   Cases 89, 104, 114, 116, 117 and 125–29/85 *Re Wood Pulp* (1988) ECR 5193.

Penalises actions which affect intra-Community trade

Community law only requires penalising proceedings to be taken against firms or national authorities where their actions affect trade between Member States. This is regardless of the magnitude of the extent to which intra-Community trade has been affected. Even if the activity in question consisted in an agreement between two firms situated within one Member State, their agreement could be penalised if it affected trade between Member States.[6] As to what are the circumstances in which this condition is met, the Court laid down a general formula to that effect in *Brasserie de Haecht v Wilkin*,[7] where it stated that it must be possible for the indicted practice:

> to be capable of having some influence, direct or indirect, on trade between Member States, of being conducive to a partitioning of the market and of hampering the economic interpenetration sought by the Treaty.

III Competition law and the private sector: general context

Sources

The competition law which applies to private undertakings essentially revolves around the anti-trust provisions of the Treaty (Article 85), its rules on monopoly control (Article 86), together with the case law and derived legislation based on them. The latter covers not only the block exemption regulations, but also legislation dealing with anti-competitive situations in a manner which is more independent from the basic Treaty provisions, as well as the procedural competition rules.

EU and national competition law

Rules of competition policy exist at the national as well as at the Community level. The question inevitably arises as to the relationship between the EU and domestic rules of competition. Surprisingly, the ECJ has had relatively few opportunities to clarify this relationship. In *Wilhelm and Others v Bundeskartellamt*,[8] a number of German concerns were fined by the German Cartels Authority for having engaged in an unlawful cartel, contrary to German competition legislation. The companies affected appealed against this decision on the grounds that the German authority could not lawfully bring proceedings for an infringement which was the subject matter of simultaneous proceedings under EC competition law by the Commission. The Court ruled that EC and

---

6   Gautron, J-C, *op cit*, p 172.
7   Case 23/67 (1967) ECR 407.
8   Case 14/68 (1969) ECR 1.

national competition rules operated in two different spheres: the former sought to penalise market behaviour which affected intra-Community trade, whereas the latter operated in a purely national context. As a result, the domestic authorities were entitled to take action against an agreement pursuant to their national law, even where a dispute concerning the applicability of Community rules to that agreement is proceeding before the Commission.

The notion of 'undertakings'

The provisions of Article 85 and 86 of the Treaty apply to the behaviour of undertakings, without specifying the scope of this term. This gap has been filled by the Court and the Commission, whose interpretation of this concept has tended to be broad. Thus it is not necessary that the entity in question has legal personality; as long as it is engaged in trading activity it falls within the scope of this term.[9] It follows that a natural person could also constitute an undertaking provided that he or she engaged in commercial activity. It also follows that the entity in question must not necessarily be driven by a profit motive.[10]

Two specific problems arise in this context. First, are groups of companies to be regarded as one and the same undertaking? The Court has replied in the affirmative, provided that one of the members of that group exercises a sufficient degree of control over the other. In *Hydrotherm v Andreoli*,[11] the Court ruled that a group consisting of a man, a company and a partnership controlled by the man constituted one undertaking. The other problem concerns the relationship between a parent company and its subsidiaries. Here, the Commission and Court have allowed themselves to be guided by the principle that if a subsidiary does not form an economic entity with the parent company, it does not constitute a single undertaking together with its parent company. This can have the effect of rendering lawful agreements between parent companies and subsidiaries which, if concluded between separate undertakings, would have infringed EU competition policy.[12]

---

9 *Re Polypropylene* OJ 1986 L 230.
10 Cases 209–215, 218/78 *Heintz van Landewijck v Commission* (1980) ECR 3125 at 3250.
11 Case 170/83, (1984) ECR 2999.
12 Case T-102/92, *Viho Europe v Commission* unreported. See also Case 32/78, *BMW v Belgium* (1979) ECR 2435.

IV Competition law: arrangements between firms (Article 85)

General

Article 85(1) of the Treaty prohibits the following arrangements as being incompatible with the common market:

all agreements between undertakings, decisions by associations of undertakings and concerted practices which may affect trade between Member States and which have as their object or effect the prevention, restriction or distortion of competition within the common market, and in particular those which:

(a) directly or indirectly fix purchase or selling prices or any other trading conditions;

(b) limit or control production, markets, technical development, or investment;

(c) share markets or sources of supply;

(d) apply dissimilar conditions to equivalent transactions with other trading parties, thereby placing them at a competitive disadvantage;

(e) make the conclusion of contracts subject to acceptance by the other parties of supplementary obligations which, by their nature or according to commercial usage, have no connection with the subject of such contracts.

Arrangements within the meaning of Article 85(1) of the Treaty

To fall within the purview of this prohibition, the indicted arrangement must be either an agreement between undertakings, a decision by an association of undertakings or a concerted practice. All three notions have been interpreted broadly by both the Court and the Commission. As a result, the distinction between these three categories of arrangements has sometimes been difficult to draw.

The one element which they must all have in common is that of collusion. Unilateral action does not fall within the scope of Article 85 of the Treaty, although it may constitute an abuse of dominant position caught by Article 86 of the Treaty. Here again, the distinction between unilateral action and collusion is not always easy to draw. In *AEG v Commission*,[13] a refusal by a company to admit a trader to its distribution network was held to be an agreement rather than a unilateral act, since it formed part of a system of contracts between the company and its existing distributors.

The term 'agreements' has been interpreted by the Court as referring not only to written contracts but also purely verbal arrangements.[14] It therefore also

13 Case 107/82, *AEG-Telefunken v Commission* (1983) ECR 3151.

14 Case 28/77, *Tepea* (1978) ECR 1391 at 1415.

includes informal arrangements such as the so-called 'gentlemen's agreements' and even imposed agreements. Once again, the Court has applied a non-formal criterion, in which it is the substance of the arrangement and the intention of the parties in concluding it, rather than its form, which will be decisive. Thus in the *Quinine Cartel* case,[15] the Court held a gentlemen's agreement to constitute an 'agreement' because 'this document amounted to the faithful expression of the joint intention of the parties to the agreement with regard to their conduct in the Common Market'.

The notion of 'decisions by associations of undertakings' has been interpreted as relating mainly, but not exclusively, to the co-ordinating measures decided by trade associations. This is the case even where the measure in question merely takes the form of a recommendation.[16] Arrangements between more than one trade association tend to be regarded by the Court as 'agreements' rather than 'decisions'.[17]

'Concerted practices' can be defined as co-ordinated action between undertakings which, without amounting to an agreement, consciously substitutes co-operation for competition.[18] It is not necessary for there to have been a conscious plan; a more reliable guideline is the requirement inherent in the competition provisions of the Treaty that every economic operator must determine independently the policy which he intend to pursue within the Common Market.[19] Thus in the *Dyestuffs* case,[20] the Court upheld a ruling by the Commission that a series of uniform prices increases applied by leading manufacturers in this field amounted to concerted practices.

Conditions in which the arrangements caught by Article 85(1) of the Treaty are prohibited

There are two conditions which must be met if the indicted arrangement is to be prohibited under Article 85(1) of the Treaty. The first is that it be capable of affecting trade between Member States: this condition has already been examined earlier (above, p 194). The second condition is that the arrangement has the object or effect of preventing, restricting or distorting competition within the common market.

---

15   Cases 41, 44 and 45/69, *ACF Chemiefarma v Commission* (1970) ECR 661, at 693–94.

16   Case 8/72, *Vereniging van Cementhandelaren v Commission* (1972) ECR 977; Cases 96–102, 104, 105 108 and 110/82, *NV IAZ International Belgium v Commission* (1983) ECR 3369.

17   Case 246/86, *Belasco v Commission* (1989) ECR 2117.

18   Tillotson, J, *European Community Law – Cases and Materials Text* (1993), Cavendish Publishing Ltd, p 356.

19   Cases 40–48, 50, 54–56, 111, 113 and 114/73, *Suiker Unie v Commission* (1975) ECR 1663.

20   Case 48/69, *op cit*, at 664.

The condition that the arrangement in question must have had the 'object or effect' of undermining competition indicates that here, the Treaty is concerned as much with the practical outcome of business arrangements between companies as with the intention behind them. The terms 'object' and 'effect' are alternative to each other; therefore once it has been established that the object of an arrangement was to distort competition, it is no longer necessary to investigate the effects of indicted action.[21]

The exact extent to which competition must have been undermined is not made clear in Article 85 of the Treaty. There is considerable doubt as to whether the rule of reason, which applies under US anti-trust law, is applicable to this aspect of Article 85.[22] It is safe to say that the case law of the Court is a mixture of general and specific guidelines.

One objective which always guides the Court when assessing whether or not to prohibit a private arrangement is to avoid applying the rules in such a way as to stifle enterprise and initiative. This was expressly recognised in *Société Technique Minière v Maschinenbau Ulm*.[23] The agreement under challenge in this case was an exclusive supply contract giving *Société Technique* the sole right to sell in France heavy earth-moving equipment manufactured by Ulm. However, the agreement involved no export bans, and the distributors were not given total territorial protection; nor were there any obstacles to parallel imports. When a dispute arose from the agreement, the matter was brought to a national court which referred it to the ECJ for a preliminary ruling.

The Court stressed the actual economic context in which the agreement applied. More particularly it doubted whether competition was being undermined if the agreement under challenge was truly necessary in order to enable a firm to penetrate a new market. The ECJ went on to rule that, on the basis of the economic analysis based on factors such as the nature and quality of the products covered by the agreement, the importance of the grantor and the concessionnaire on the market for these products, etc., the agreement in question did not infringe Article 85(1). The Court also engaged in an extensive economic analysis of the context in which the agreement existed in the *Delimitis* case.[24]

Horizontal and vertical agreements

Anti-competitive agreements as prohibited by Article 85(1) may have been concluded at two levels. The first is the horizontal level, where the agreement is between firms situated at the same level of the commercial process, eg between

21 Cases 56 and 58/64, *op cit*, at 341–42.
22 Peeters, J, 'The Rule of Reason Revisited: Prohibition on Restraints of Competition in the Sherman Act and the EEC Treaty' (1989) *American Journal of Comparative Law*, p 521 and p 568.
23 Case 56/65 (1966) ECR 235.
24 Case C-234/89, *Stergios Delimitis v Henninger Bräu* (1991) ECR I-935.

manufacturers or retailers amongst themselves. Of this type, the arrangement indicted in the *Dyestuffs*[25] case is a good example, involving as it did the leading producers of this particular chemical. The second is the vertical level, involving transactions between economic agents occupying different positions in the commercial process. The example normally given of this type of arrangement is that of exclusive distribution agreements; however, it has become increasingly dangerous to do so in view of the fact that these agreements have been the subject matter of both individual and group exemptions (below, p 200).

Specific types of agreement

Article 85(1) of the Treaty sets out some types of agreement which are in principle prohibited under Article 85. These agreements are merely given by way of example and must in no circumstances be treated as an exhaustive list of prohibited agreements.

(i) Arrangements which directly or indirectly fix purchase or selling prices or any other trading conditions

Under this heading, the Commission has prohibited an agreement between the main producers of zinc,[26] and one between Italian manufacturers of flat glass,[27] and the Court has penalised a system of resale price maintenance agreed by two associations which, in Belgium and the Netherlands, included most of the traders of books in the Dutch language.[28]

(ii) Arrangements which limit or control production, markets, technical development, or investment

These are agreements whereby the firms who are parties to them undertake to restrict their own potential for growth, but which has anti-competitive consequences, which can be the raising of prices by of preventing those outside the agreement to enter a particular market. Of this type of agreement, the *Quinine Cartel* case[29] provides a good example. One of the arrangements which was outlawed by the Court in this decision was that between firms in France, the Netherlands and Germany to determine sales quotas and the prohibition of manufacturing synthetic quinine. The object of the exercise was to raise prices. See also *Re PVC Cartel*.[30]

---

25 Case 48/69, *op cit*.

26 *Re Zinc Producers Group* OJ 1984 L 220.

27 *Re Italian Flat Glass Cartel* OJ 1989 L 33.

28 Cases 43 and 63/82, *VBVB and VVVB v Commission* (1983) ECR 19.

29 Cases 41, 44 and 45/69, *op cit*.

30 Decision 89/190 OJ 1989, L 74.

(iii) Arrangements which share markets and sources of supply

These are transactions which enable competitors to share out amongst themselves a market for a particular article, either in geographical terms or on the basis of a particular product range. This type of arrangement can arise particularly in oligopolistic markets. Suppose that there were only two producers of a particular article; they could both appoint each other as an exclusive dealer in a particular area of the Community, thus keeping out of each other's way. Such a mutual dealing agreement was outlawed by the Commission in *Siemens/Fanuc*.[31]

(iv) Arrangements to apply dissimilar conditions to equivalent transactions with other trading parties

The object of this kind of transaction is to place the latter at a competitive disadvantage. Thus in *IAZ International Belgium*,[32] the agreement in question had been concluded between the Belgian National Association of Water Boards on the one hand, and producers and exclusive importers of washing machines on the other hand. Only those machines meeting Belgian standards would be connected to the water network. However, the conditions under which conformity with this standards was checked were found to be more favourable for these manufacturers and exclusive importers than for parallel importers. This was held by the Court to distort competition.[33]

(v) Arrangements requiring the performance of additional obligations

These are prohibited where, by their nature or according to commercial practice, they have no connection with the actual subject matter of these contracts. This would be the case, for instance, where a contracting party would be obliged to purchase a quantity of products which was vastly greater than was necessary to meet the needs of the user, or the obligation to order products having no connection with those which form the subject matter of the main transaction.[34]

Exemptions

It has already been noted (above, p 193) that EU competition policy attempts to steer a course between the need to maintain healthy competition and the avoidance of unnecessary restrictions on individual enterprise. It is for this reason that Article 85(3) of the Treaty makes provision the possibility of exemptions in respect of agreements, decisions or concerted practices – or

31 OJ 1985 L 376.
32 Cases 96–102, 104, 105, 108 and 110/82 (1983) ECR 3369.
33 *Ibid*, at 3411.
34 Druesne, G, *op cit*, pp 175–76.

categories thereof – which contribute towards improving the production or distribution of goods or serves the cause of technical or economic progress, whilst allowing consumers to share fairly in the benefits of such arrangements. However, any such exemption must meet two requirements: (a) it may not impose on the firms concerned any restrictions which are not indispensable in order to achieve these objectives, and (b) it may not provide the firms involved with the opportunity to eliminate competition for a substantial part of the products in question.

There are therefore two categories of exemption: individual exemptions, granted by Commission decisions, and group or block exemptions, normally adopted by means of a Council regulation. Before turning our attention to these, we must first examine the conditions which must be met if these exemptions are to apply. There are two types of condition: the positive conditions, to wit those which stipulate that the arrangement in question must constitute an improvement and benefit the consumer, and the negative, ie that no unnecessary restrictions are applied in the process, and that the arrangement does not enable the participating firms to eliminate a substantial part of the competition. All these conditions must apply for the exemption to be granted. Essentially, they amount to an assessment whether the advantages of the agreement outweigh the disadvantages.[35]

(i) Positive conditions for the granting of the exemption

In the first instance, the agreement must contribute to improvement and progress. The economic context of the agreement will obviously be the most important consideration here, although recently other criteria have been taken into account. A considerable range of agreements have been found to meet this test. Patent and know-how licences fall within this category, because they enable inventions and processes to be used more effectively. Specialisation agreements also pass this test: by agreeing to refrain from manufacturing certain product ranges and sharing them out between those involved in the agreement, they improve production to the extent that they enable those involved in it to use their resources in a more rational manner and increase their productivity. Even exclusive dealerships have been justified on this basis, on the grounds that they help to penetrate world markets. The same applies to joint research agreements which lead to economic improvements.[36] They can give rise to improvements in production and distribution if they involve exchanges of information between manufacturer and distributor.

The second positive condition, that the consumer must be allowed to share in the benefits of the arrangement, presents a number of difficulties of

35 Tillotson, J, *op cit*, p 369.

36 See, for example, the agreement concluded between the Fiat and Ford groups which set up a joint venture for the production and distribution of a certain type of vehicle (OJ 1988 L 230).

interpretation. In the first place, does the term 'consumer' mean the 'end consumer' or merely the person to whom the producer sells his goods? If the former meaning was adhered to, this could lead to a situation whereby the manufacturer sold his products to a distributor, who failed to pass onto the end consumer the benefits accrued under an agreement entered into by the manufacturer. This would obviously give rise to iniquitous results, so it would appear that it is the second meaning which is the correct one.

(ii) *Negative conditions for the granting of an exemption*

The agreement for which exemption is being sought may not, in addition, impose any unnecessary restrictions or enable the firms involved to remove their competitors from the market. The first-named condition is a specific application of the proportionality principle: every clause in the agreement will be scrutinised in order to assess whether or not the arrangement is strictly necessary in order to achieve its ostensible objective. In this regard, the Court has consistently ruled that any absolute territorial protection conferred upon a licensee in order to obtain that parallel imports be controlled and prevented leads to the artificial maintenance of separate national markets, which contravenes the purpose of the Treaty.[37]

The other negative condition is that the agreement does not give the parties an opportunity to eliminate the competition. What this entails is that the agreement may not prevent third parties from marketing similar products, ie products of the same nature or capable of being substituted for those covered by the agreement, within that part of the common market to which the agreement applies. Any assessment of this criterion will therefore need to take account of that proportion of the market which is already controlled by those concluding the agreement. The larger this share, the less likely will it be that an exemption will be granted for the agreement in question.[38]

(iii) *Individual dispensations*

It is exclusively incumbent upon the Commission to grant dispensations in individual cases. In order to qualify for such an dispensation, the undertakings involved must give official notification to the Commission of the agreement which they are about to conclude. The procedure for such notification is laid down in Regulation 17/62 (below, p 214). The dispensation can take the form of an exemption or of negative clearance. Exemptions are decisions by the Commission taken on the basis of the positive and negative criteria set out above, and which are granted for a specified period, after which the exemption may be renewed or revoked. Negative clearances, on the other hand, are

37 Case 258/78, *Nungesser v Commission* (1982) ECR 2015 at 2070.
38 Druesne, G, *op cit*, p 183.

Commission decisions stating that Article 85(1) of the Treaty does not apply to the agreement in question. This can be either because the agreement admits of no discernible competition-restricting elements, or falls within the category of *de minimis* agreements referred to above (above, p 201). They intimate to the applicants that the Commission will proceed no further in relation to their agreement; however, it reserves the right to re-open proceedings if circumstances change.

When granting an individual exemption, the Commission is required to carry out a full, detailed and impartial examination of the relevant facts, failing which the decision granting the exemption is likely to be annulled by the ECJ.[39] The Commission is in principle allowed to base its decisions to grant individual exemptions on public interest considerations. However, the Commission must do so on the basis of a specific economic analysis. This is why, in the *Métropole Television* case,[40] the Court held that the Commission had failed to demonstrate that it was in the public interest that the members of the European Broadcasting Union should have exclusive rights to the broadcasting of sports events, or that such exclusive rights were indispensable if the EBU was to enjoy a fair return on its investment.

(iv) Block exemptions

Another way in which the time-consuming procedure for the granting of individual exemptions can be circumvented is by using the opportunity provided in Article 85(3) of the Treaty of granting exemptions for categories of agreements. This procedure also serves the purpose of giving guidance and a greater sense of certainty to the business world in relation to agreements which they are about to conclude and the validity of which under competition law may be in some doubt. This has prompted Weatherill[41] to qualify them as 'charters for lawful agreements'. Naturally the onus is on the firms concerned to draft their agreements in such a way as to conform to the terms in which the relevant block exemption is set out. As they invariably take the form of regulations, they have direct effect and are therefore enforceable before the national courts.

The granting of these block exemptions does not mean that companies must tailor or amend their agreements in such a way as to fall within the scope of the legislation granting these exemptions. To do so would be to force companies into a straitjacket and potentially stifle creativity and free enterprise, which is precisely that which EU competition policy seeks to avoid.[42] However, if the

---

39 Cases T-528/93, T-542/93 and T-546/93, *Métropole Television and Others v Commission*, Bulletin 10-1996 (not yet reported).

40 Cases T-528/93, T-542/93 and T-546/93, *op cit.*

41 *Op cit*, p 364

42 Case 10/86, *VAG France v Etablissements Magne* (1986) ECR 4071.

arrangement in question wishes to benefit from the protection afforded by a block exemption, it must conform to every term and condition stated in the relevant Regulation. This does not mean that the arrangement must be identical with the block exemption in every respect; what it does mean is that the agreement in question may not contain any restriction on competition other than that allowed by the block exemption.[43]

Summarised briefly, the block exemption regulations adopted cover the following areas:

• Exclusive distribution agreements (Regulation 1983/83).[44] This Regulation stops short of giving protection to absolute territorial protection.

• Exclusive purchasing agreements (Regulation 1984/83).[45] This measure makes special provision for the brewery industry and for 'solus' petrol agreements.

• Patent Licensing (Regulation 2349/84).[46]

• Specialisation Agreements (Regulation 417/85).[47]

• Research and Development arrangements (Regulation 418/85).[48]

• Motor Vehicle Distribution Agreements (Regulation 123/85).[49]

• Franchising Agreements (Regulation 4078/88).[50]

• Know-how Licensing Agreements (Regulation 556/89).[51]

V Abuse of dominant position
Ex(Article 86 of the Treaty) #art 82.

General

The other main threat to free and fair competition as perceived by the drafters of the Treaty was the negative effect of concentrations of economic power. More particularly, it sought to control the powerful economic position held by those who were in a position to dominate markets, and the unfair advantages which

---

43   Lasok and Bridge, *op cit*, p 616.
44   OJ 1983 L 173.
45   OJ 1983 L 173.
46   OJ 1984 L 219.
47   OJ 1985 L 53.
48   OJ 1985 L 53.
49   OJ 1985 L 15.
50   OJ 1988 L 359.
51   OJ 1989 L 61.

they could derive from this position. To this end, Article 86, para 1, of the Treaty, disposes that:

Any abuse by one or more undertakings of a dominant position within the common market or in a substantial part of it shall be prohibited as incompatible with the common market in so far as it may affect trade between Member States.

The second paragraph contains the same examples of the type of market distortion envisaged as those which are featured in Article 85(1) of the Treaty. However, Article 86 makes no provision for exemptions, either at the individual or at the collective level. Article 86 also has direct effect.

In order to be caught by the prohibition contained in Article 86 of the Treaty, the indicted practice must meet three conditions: (a) the firm or firms which engage in it must have a dominant position in the Common Market or a substantial part of it; (b) that practice must constitute an abuse of this dominant position, and (c) trade between Member States must have been affected by it. Each condition will be examined in turn, followed by some examples of the specific abuses mentioned in Article 86, second paragraph.

The notion of 'dominant position'

Nowhere does the Treaty define the concept of 'dominant position'. It has therefore once again been for the Court of Justice and the Commission to fill this particular gap by means of its case law. Admittedly these institutions did enjoy some assistance in the shape of the ECSC Treaty, which contained similar provisions seeking to safeguard competition. One of these, ie Article 66(7), defines a dominant position as one in which the relevant undertakings hold a position 'shielding them against effective competition in a substantial part of the common market'. This provision was, however, only of limited assistance to the relevant authorities, since the term 'effective competition' raised almost as many questions as it answered.

It was the Commission which had the first opportunity to attempt a comprehensive definition in the *Continental Can* case,[52] in which it described undertakings enjoying a dominant position as those which are in a position to engage in independent actions which enable them to act without needing to take account of their competitors, purchasers or suppliers. It is this ability to act independently which emerged as the decisive criterion in defining this concept, as was confirmed by the Court as soon as it entered this particular fray. Thus in *United Brands*,[53] the ECJ defined the term 'dominant position' as

a position of economic strength enjoyed by an undertaking which enables it to prevent competition being maintained on the relevant market by giving it the

---

52 OJ 1972 L 17.

53 Case 27/76, *United Brands v Commission* (1978) ECR 207.

power to behave to an appreciable extent independently of its competitors, customers, and ultimately of its consumers.[54]

In their subsequent case law, both the Court and the Commission have paid particular attention to one the most efficient ways in which firms can prevent the maintenance of competition, to wit the ability to prevent other undertakings from entering the market. This notion was floated for the first time in *AKZO*.[55] Another factor which has been taken into account is the market share accounted for by the undertaking or undertakings in question. If this reaches the order of 70 to 80 per cent, the Court tends to the view that the firm in question automatically occupies a dominant position.[56] Other factors used to evaluate the market power of undertakings have been the economies of scale realised by it,[57] and the capital strength of a firm and its access to capital markets.[58]

None of the criteria mentioned above would be conclusive in assessing whether or not firms had a dominant position if these criteria were not judged in the light of the market to which they relate. This is the dimension known as the 'relevant market'. Without it, firms accused of infringing Article 86 of the Treaty would be able to defend themselves effectively by pointing to their relative lack of significance on the world, or even the national, market taken as a whole. The relevant market has to be considered from three different perspectives: the *product market*, the *geographical market* and the *temporal market*.

The *product market* is more difficult to assess than might appear at first sight. If a firm which produces and markets exclusively television sets is being accused of abusing a dominant position, the immediate reaction would be to see the relevant product market as being restricted to television sets. However, in so doing, it is assumed (a) that television sets form a market in their own right, and cannot be subsumed into another category – for example, audio-visual home entertainment equipment – and (b) that those who produce and market television sets are not in competition with producers and sellers of any other product (eg radios or hi-fi equipment). Therefore, a firm can only be said to have absolute domination in a particular market if it has total control over all the products which are essentially interchangeable.[59]

The *geographical market* is the market in which objective competitive conditions are the same for all traders.[60] This criterion recognises that the notion

54   *Ibid*, at 276–77.

55   Case 62/86, *AKZO v Commission* (1991) ECR I-3359.

56   Druesne, *op cit*, p 192.

57   Case 27/76, *op cit*, at 281.

58   *Ibid*.

59   Swann, D, *Competition and Industrial policy in the European Community* (1983), Methuen, p 83.

60   Case 27/76, *op cit*, at 273.

of dominance is dependent on the geographical distribution of producers and consumers. It is obvious that the competitive situation of a producer who operates in a busy commercial area will be totally different from someone who serves a remote rural district, even if they both have the same share of the product market. The latter will be in a much stronger position, because his customers will be less inclined or able to seek out alternative suppliers should they fail to be satisfied with him. It will therefore also be necessary to identify the territorial scope in which traders operate and consumers purchase in order to assess the degree of interchangeability of the goods or services sold.

It is not only the sheer geographical location which will be conclusive in this regard. Factors such as carriage costs, the quality and frequency of transport facilities, can place traders at a competitive advantage or disadvantage. Thus in one case,[61] the Commission held that not only the fact that Britain was separated from the Continent by the British Channel, but also the cost of freight, made Britain into a separate market.

The *temporal market* can also be a relevant factor. This will be particularly the case with regard to food products, some of which are seasonal. Thus in *United Brands*[62] the Court pointed out that, for the product in question – bananas – it was necessary, when assessing the dominance criterion, to take into account the fact that for this product, there was a time of year, ie the winter months, in which product substitutability was very low.

Collective dominant position

Thus far, we have been dealing with the dominant position exercised by one firm only. However, Article 86 stipulates that the dominant position may be exercised by 'one or more undertakings'. Does this indicate that the drafters of the Treaty intended to control the activities of firms operating in oligopolies, being markets dominated by a few large suppliers? The ECJ appeared to reject this view in *Hoffmann-Laroche*,[63] where it went to great pains to distinguish between the notion of dominant position and 'parallel courses of action which are peculiar to oligopolies' because:

in an oligopoly, the courses of action interact, while in the case of an undertaking occupying a dominant position the conduct of the undertaking which derives profits from that position is to a great extent determined unilaterally.[64]

The decision in *Italian Flat Glass*[65] appears to have qualified this position somewhat. Here, the Commission had ruled various agreements made between

---

61 *Napier Brown/British Sugar*, OJ 1988 L 284.
62 Case 27/76, *op cit*.
63 Case 85/76, *Hoffman-Laroche v Commission* (1979) ECR 461.
64 *Ibid*, at 520.
65 Cases T-68, 77 and 78/89 (1992) ECR II-1403.

firms fixing quotas and prices to be contrary not only to Article 85, but also Article 86. It claimed that, because the firms involved presented themselves as a single unit on the market, they had abused a joint dominant position. This decision was appealed before the CFI, which annulled the decision. However, the CFI did acknowledge the existence of collective dominant position. This could be the case where two or more firms jointly had, through agreements or licences, a technological lead enabling them to act to a considerable extent independently of their competitors and customers.[66]

The 'abuse' of a dominant position

Here again, no definition of this concept is provided in the Treaty, which means that, with the exception of the extremely general statements contained in Articles 2 and 3 of the Treaty, it has been the case law of Court and Commission which has clarified this notion. This it has done by means of broad definitions and principles on the one hand, and specific examples on the other hand.

The Court's approach can fairly be qualified as objective, since it has more regard to the actual effects of a particular action or set of actions rather than to the actual intentions of the enterprise being investigated. This emerges very clearly from the most comprehensive definition which the Court has given of this notion, namely in the *Hoffmann-LaRoche*[67] decision:

The concept of abuse is an objective concept relating to the behaviour of an undertaking in a dominant position which is such as to influence the structure of the market where, as a result of the very presence of the undertaking in question, the degree of competition is weakened and which, through recourse to methods different from those which condition normal competition in products or services on the basis of the transactions of commercial operators, has the effect of hindering the maintenance of the degree of competition still existing in the market or the growth of that competition.

This objective nature of the Court's approach is also evident in the *Continental Can* decision.[68] The company in question held 85 per cent of shares in a company which dominated the German market in tins and metal closures. Through one of its subsidiaries, it attempted to obtain a controlling interest in a firm which occupied a strong position on the Netherlands market in these products. The company argued that its intention was not to harm the interest of the consumer. There was therefore no causal link between its dominant position and the abuse complained of. The Court, however, stated that, regardless of its intentions, the fact that the company would strengthen its position and thus eliminate competition to a significant degree was in itself an abuse of its

66 *Ibid.*
67 Case 85/76, *Hoffmann-LaRoche v Commission* (1976) ECR 461 at 521.
68 Case 6/72, *op cit.*

dominant position.[69] Nevertheless, the fine originally imposed by the Commission was quashed because the latter had failed to prove that other firms would be inhibited in making fish and meat cans by Continental Can's actions.

Specific examples of abuses

Article 86 provides a number of such specific examples:

(a) directly or indirectly imposing unfair purchase or selling prices or other unfair trading conditions;

(b) limiting production, markets or technical development to the prejudice of consumers;

(c) applying dissimilar conditions to equivalent transactions with other trading parties, thereby placing them at a competitive disadvantage;

(d) making the conclusion of contracts subject to acceptance by the other parties of supplementary obligations which, by their nature or according to commercial usage, have no connection with the subject of such contracts.

This list is not exhaustive, and is merely provided by way of illustration. The case law has supplemented this list, which results in a very wide range of specific applications. It has become customary to classify abuses into two categories, to wit, exploitative abuses and anti-competitive abuses. Whereas the former impose unfair conditions on the consumer, the latter are aimed at preventing or reducing the possibility of other undertakings competing against the dominant firm. This is not an entirely satisfactory classification, since there are clearly abuses which fall in both categories.[70]

(i) Unfair pricing policies

These can assume several forms. In the first place, firms can apply predatory pricing strategies. This is a policy whereby firms can use their greater financial reserves in order to keep prices artificially and abnormally low with a view first to eliminating or barring weaker competitors from a particular market, then to resume charging normal, if not higher, prices. This was found to be contrary to Article 86 in the *AKZO* case.[71] The company in question occupied a dominant position in relation to the benzole peroxide substance. With a view to barring a small British competitor from the organic peroxides market, AKZO cut its prices considerably for a prolonged period. The Court found that the Commission was right to take action against this firm, but reduced the latter's fine.

Excessive prices can also be the subject matter of a challenge under Article 86. Here, we are dealing with firms taking unfair advantage of their monopoly position to charge prices to consumers who have no choice but to pay them.

---

69 *Ibid* at 246.

70 Charlesworth, A and Cullen, H, *op cit*, p 293.

71 Case C-62/86, *AKZO Chemie v Commission* (1991) ECR I-3359.

As to what constitutes an excessive price, the Court held this to be the case where the price charged bore no relation to the economic value of the product.[72]

Discriminatory pricing is also outlawed by Article 86. Thus in the *United Brands* case,[73] the company investigated was found to have committed this particular infringement by charging different prices in various Community states. In *British Telecom*,[74] the Commission found that the practice of charging different prices for message-forwarding services depending on whether the message came from a domestic caller or from another Community country was contrary to Article 86.

(ii) *Refusal to supply*

Dominant firms are capable of distorting competition to their advantage by refusing to supply their goods or services, or only doing so on unreasonable terms. The Court appears to have placed the onus of proof squarely on the firm in question: if it engages in such practices, it must demonstrate that they can be justified on objective grounds; if not, they will be regarded as an infringement of Article 86.[75] Thus in the Commercial Solvents dispute, the refusal by the indicted corporation to provide an existing customer with raw materials was held by the Court to be part of a strategy to eliminate that firm from the market, and therefore as infringing Article 86.[76]

(iii) *Tying*

This is the practice of making contracts conditional upon acceptance by the other party of obligations which are unconnected to the subject matter of the contract. A typical example of such a practice was found to exist in *Tetra Pak II*.[77] Here, the firm in question had invented a particular process by which a carton of milk or fruit juice could be filled in such a way as to prolong its shelf life to around six months. The sale of this type of machine, in which it was found to occupy a dominant position, was subject to the condition that the purchase would only use Tetra-Pak cartons, and obtain them from the company's subsidiary in the Member State concerned. The Commission held this to be an abuse of the company's dominant position, and, on the basis of this and other infringements of competition law, imposed a fine of 75 million ECUs.

72 Case 26/75, *General Motors v Commission* (1975) ECR 1367 at 000.
73 Case 27/76, *op cit*, at 294–98.
74 OJ 1982, L 360/36.
75 Case 77/77, *BP v Commission* (1978) ECR 1513.
76 Cases 6 and 7/73, *op cit*, at 250–51.
77 OJ 1992, L 72.

VI   Control of mergers

Merger control prior to the mergers regulation

Until a specific Regulation on this subject (4064/89) was adopted in 1990, the Commission was compelled to rely on Articles 85 and 86 of the Treaty in order to exercise some control over mergers which posed a major threat to competition within the Common Market. The first opportunity to do so presented itself in the *Continental Can* case.[78] It will be recalled that this firm sought to obtain a controlling interest in TDV, a Netherlands company. The Court ruled that Article 86 of the Treaty was infringed if a firm having a dominant position strengthens its dominance in such a way that the only undertaking to remain in the relevant market are those whose behaviour depends on the dominant one. This effect was achieved by the take-over in question.[79]

Towards the end of the 1980s, however, pressure grew for legislation giving the EU authorities direct control over mergers and acquisitions. In view of the limits on the Commission's powers, there was a case for introducing more rigorous procedures in order to expedite proceedings and make them more efficient.[80] This legislation took the form of Regulation 4064/89.[81]

Objective of the Regulation

The general objective of this Regulation is to identify mergers of a considerable size, both in absolute terms and in terms of the operations of the firms involved in Europe. The accent is on those mergers which have an EU-wide dimension, which are suitable for assessment by the Commission rather than by the domestic legislation of the Member States. It does this by applying thresholds above which the Community regulation applies and below which matters are left to the domestic legislation of Member States.[82]

The concept of concentrations

The regulation does not concern itself only with mergers in the strict sense of the term. More generally, it is seeking to exercise control over significant changes in ownership over companies which could distort competition. In the light of this objective, it is the notion of *concentration* which is central to this legislation. Article 3(1) of the Regulation provides that such a concentration can

---

78 Case 6/72, *op cit.*

79 *Ibid*, at 244–45.

80 Fishwick, F, *Making Sense of Competition Policy* (1993), Kogan Page, p 116.

81 OJ 1989 L 395.

82 Pearson, ES, *Law for European Business Studies* (1994), Pitman, p 342.

exist in two circumstances: (a) where two or more previously independent firms actually merge to form a single unit, or (b) where a firm acquires control or another firm, either wholly or in part, by buying its assets or shares. In most cases this will amount to the taking of a majority shareholding, but this need not automatically be the case. Even if the purchasing firm fails to obtain more than 50 per cent of assets or shares, the agreement in question could be caught by the regulation because it can still exercise 'control' within the meaning of (b) above. There is said to be 'control' where there exists the possibility of exercising decisive influence over another firm.

Article 3 also deals specifically with joint ventures. The so-called 'co-operative joint ventures',[83] are those which, although they enable the firms in question to co-ordinate their competitive behaviour, nevertheless allow these firms to remain independent. In such cases, the element of control is missing, and the ventures will not be caught by the regulation. However, a joint venture which performs on a permanent basis all the functions of an independent economic unit, and which does not involve the co-ordination of the competitive behaviour of the firms involved, will be a concentration within the meaning of the regulation.

Notifiable concentrations

As is the case with other potential infringements of competition law, it is the Commission which will play a central role in assessing the lawfulness of concentrations. For this purpose, concentrations which have a 'Community dimension' must be notified to the Commission. Under Article 1 of the Regulation, they will have this Community dimension where certain thresholds have been exceeded:

(a) where the total worldwide turnover of all the firms involved in the concentration exceeds 500 million ECUs; and

(b) where the total Community-wide turnover of each of at least two of the firms involved is in excess of 250 million ECUs.

These concentrations must, pursuant to Article 4 of the Regulation, be notified to the Commission no more than a week following the date on which the agreement was concluded, the announcement of public tender made, or the controlling interest obtained. The detailed rules governing the notification procedure are contained in Regulation 2367/90.[84]

---

83 Commission Notice regarding Concentrative and Co-operative Operations under Council Regulation 4064/89, OJ 1990 C 203.

84 OJ 1990, L 219.

Commission appraisal: the criteria applied

Notifiable concentrations will be examined by the Commission in the light of a basic criterion contained in Article 2(3), which is whether it creates or enhances a dominant position which would lead to effective competition being significantly impeded in the common market, or on a substantial part of it.

The economic assessment which the Commission is required to make is extremely wide-ranging and complex, beginning with the need to establish the relevant product and geographic markets.[85] In the case law which it has already developed on this regulation, the Commission has shown itself to have particular regard to the dynamic nature of the market, and the question whether or not the proposed merger constituted barriers to market entry.[86]

Commission appraisal: timetable of decisions taken

Once the Commission has been notified of an intended concentration, the Commission must take one of three decisions: (a) that the intended concentration falls within the scope of the regulation and must give rise to proceedings because it is potentially incompatible with the requirements of the common market; (b) that it falls within the scope of the regulation, but does not give rise to doubts as to its compatibility with the common market, and therefore does not require proceedings to be commenced; (c) that it falls outside the scope of the regulation (Article 6).

If the Commission decides to initiate proceedings, it must once again take one of three possible decisions: (a) that the concentration is consistent with the common market; this decision must be taken as soon as it is clear that no doubts remain on the consistency with the common market, and ultimately within four months of proceedings having been initiated; (b) that the intended concentration is compatible with the Common Market; this decision must be taken within four months, or (c) where the concentration has already taken place, a decision to rescind it in such a way as to restore conditions of effective competition (Article 8).

---

85 Tillotson, J, *op cit*, p 419.

86 Case IV/M57, *Re Concentration between Digital Equipment International and Mannessman Kienzle GmbH* (1992) 4 CMLR M99; Case IV/M53, *Re Concentration between Aérospatiale SNI and Alenia-Aeritalia e Selenia and de Havilland* (1992) 4 CMLR M2.

VII The procedural rules relating to competition

General

The principal instrument which lays down the rules relating to enforcement of competition law is Regulation 17/62.[87] The latter was adopted in implementation of Article 87 of the Treaty, which conferred on the Council the power to adopt the measures which were necessary to give effect to Articles 85 and 86 of the Treaty. Therefore the competition rules relating to the public sector (Articles 90, 92–93, 37 of the Treaty) do not fall within the scope of this Regulation.

The fundamental rule governing the enforcement of EU competition law is laid down in Article 1 of the Regulation, which states that the practices described in Articles 85 and 86 of the Treaty are prohibited even if there has been no prior decision to that effect. This means that firms cannot plead an absence of action on the part of the relevant authorities as a valid defence against an accusation of infringement.

Range of options

The Commission has a wide range of options when faced with agreements and practices which are potential infringements of Articles 85 and 86 of the Treaty. The first possibility is that of giving negative clearance to the agreement or practice in question. Under this procedure, the Commission may, on application by undertakings made individually or collectively, certify that, on the basis of the facts available to it, there is no reason to bring any proceedings against the firm or firms concerned (Article 2 Regulation 17/62). Secondly, the Commission may grant individual exemptions based on Article 85(3) of the Treaty. Thirdly, the Commission may institute an investigation but conclude that, on the basis of its findings, there are no grounds for imposing a penalty. Fourthly, the Commission may penalise the firm or firms concerned, by imposing a fine under Article 15 of the Regulation, or by requiring periodic penalty payments under Article 16.

The Commission will in many cases endeavour to bring its investigations to an informal conclusion – if only because it lacks the manpower and resources to proceed to formal decisions with their attendant procedures and safeguards for the defendant. The procedure will then be concluded by means of an administrative communication known as a 'comfort letter' sent to the parties, in which the Commission will state that, in its opinion, the agreement or practice in question does not violate Article 85(1) or qualifies for exemption. The file is then closed, but may be reopened if the legal or factual circumstances of the case change. Until and unless this happens, however, the parties involved are

---

[87] OJ Special Edition (1959–62) p 87.

entitled to the reasonable expectation that the Commission will refrain from taking any further action.[88]

Notification of agreements

If an individual exemption is to be granted under Article 85(3) of the Treaty, the initiative must be taken by the firm or firms concerned, by notifying any suspect agreement, practice or decision to the Commission. Those agreements which were in existence at the time at which the Treaty entered into force had to be notified by 1 November 1962 or 1 February 1963, depending on the number of firms involved (Article 5 Regulation 17/62). New agreements have to be notified to the Commission as they arise (Article 4(2) Regulation 17/62). An exception is made for certain kinds of minor agreement. Notification cannot prevent the voidance of an unlawful agreement, but may lead to immunity from fines (Article 15(5) Regulation 17/62). The forms which are to be used when making notification are set out in Regulation 27/62 (as amended by Regulation 2526/85).[89]

Investigative powers of the Commission

The Commission may initiate investigations either on its own initiative or on application by Member States or interested private parties (Article 3 Regulation 17/62). If the initiative has been taken by one or more interested parties, it is for the Commission to decide whether or not actually to carry out an investigation. The Commission may only decline to take action after having conducted an appropriate preliminary investigation, and having applied proper standards of appraisal.[90] In addition, if the Commission decides not to pursue an investigation it must notify the interested party or parties who alerted the Commission of this fact.

The Commission has extensive powers to obtain information. This information may, under Article 11(1) of Regulation 17/62, be obtained from the Governments and relevant authorities of the Member States, and from firms or associations of firms. It is largely within the discretion of the Commission to determine the scope of the information which is necessary to further the investigation.[91]

The Commission also has considerable powers to conduct inspections (Article 14 of Regulation 17/62). Thus it has the right to (a) examine the books and other business records, (b) take copies or extracts from books and business records, (c) request oral explanations on the spot, and (d) enter any premises, land and means of transport of undertakings.

88 Tillotson, J, *op cit*, p 371.

89 OJ 1985 L 240.

90 Case T-7/92, *Asia Motor France v Commission* (1994) 4 CMLR 30.

91 Case T-39/90, *Samenwerkende Electriciteits-productiebedrijven NV v Commission* (1992) ECR II-1497.

Judicial powers of the Commission

As has been mentioned before, the Commission must allow the undertakings concerned, or any other interested party, to be heard before taking a decision under Community competition rules. The procedures for organising these hearings are laid down in Commission Regulation 99/63.[92] The practice adopted by the Commission is to draw up a paper, known as the Statement of Objections, to which the parties are invited to respond within a time limit which is normally two months. The hearing is usually fixed two months after the expiry of this period. Adequate arrangements are made to enable the parties involved to have access to all the documents included in the case file.[93] On the other hand, the Commission may not have access to documents which are protected by the lawyer/client privileged relationship. For this privileged relationship to apply, however, three conditions must apply: (a) the document must have been made in the client's defence; (b) the legal counsels in question are not 'in-house' lawyers, and (c) the lawyers in question must practise within the European union.[94]

Penalties

The Commission has the power to impose two types of financial penalty: fines and periodic penalty payments. Article 15 of Regulation 17/62 makes provision for both major and minor fines. Major fines are those which are imposed for infringing Articles 85 or 86, or any conditions imposed on undertakings in a decision granting individual exemption by (Article 15(2) Regulation 17/62). These fines can range between 1,000 and 1,000,000 ECUs, or assume the form of a higher amount which does not exceed 10 per cent of the turnover recorded by the firm involved during the previous business year. The precise amount of the fine will depend on the seriousness and the duration of the infringement.

As for periodic penalty payments, these are incentive-led penalties which are commonly applied in codified law jurisdictions. By requiring defaulters to pay a certain amount for every day or week during which they remain in default, they have every incentive to discontinue their infringement as early as possible. Under Article 16 of Regulation 17/62, the Commission may impose such periodic penalties ranging from 50 to 1000 ECUs on undertakings in order to compel them to discontinue their infringement or refrain from committing any.

Review by the Court of First Instance

Under Article 17 of Regulation 17/62, the Court of Justice may review the decisions of the Commission which impose fines or periodic penalty payments.

---

92 OJ Special Edition (1963–64) p 47.
93 Korah, V, *op cit*, p 124.
94 Case 155/79, *A M & S Europe v Commission* (1982) ECR 1575.

Since 1989, the task of carrying out such reviews has been incumbent on the Court of First Instance. Actions for review take the form of individual challenges for review under Article 173 or 175 of the Treaty. For the various procedural rules governing these challenges, the reader is referred to Chapter 6 (above, p 105).

One difficulty which has arisen more frequently when challenges have been made for the review of competition decisions has been the nature of the act whose annulment is sought. The fact that Article 17 of Regulation 17/62 gives the Court jurisdiction to review decisions involving pecuniary penalties does not necessarily mean that other Community acts relating to competition policy are excluded from judicial review. Thus the Court's jurisdiction can easily be extended to cover negative clearances and findings of infringement. Other acts are less straightforward.

Enforcement by the national authorities

Enforcement of EU competition law would be virtually impossible without the co-operation of the national authorities, for reasons explained above (above, p 215). Domestic authorities are capable of being involved at various levels of the enforcement process. This role is, moreover, acknowledged by Community legislation itself (eg Article 9(3) of Regulation 17/62).

(i) Investigation

The authorities of the Member States are entitled to initiate the investigation by making an application to that effect with the Commission (Article 3 Regulation 17/62). Once the investigation has commenced, the national authorities are required to liaise closely with the Commission in order to enable the latter to proceed as effectively and efficiently as possible. Thus under Article 10(1) of Regulation 17/62, the Commission communicates a copy of any applications and notifications made, together with copies of the most important documents, in order to establish an infringement or granting an exemption. More generally, Article 10(2) requires the Commission to act in close and constant liaison with the national authorities for this purpose. The latter have the right to express their views on the procedure being followed. As regards requests for information, the Commission may obtain all the necessary information from the Member States' authorities (Article 11).

The national authorities can from time to time engage in independent investigations. Under Article 13, they must undertake investigations at the request of the Commission. The national officials responsible for such matters must produce a written authorisation whenever they carry out such investigations. The Commission officials may assist the national authorities in discharging this duty.

(ii) Judicial role

Under Article 9(3) of the Regulation, the national authorities may apply Articles 85(1) and 86 of the Treaty as long as the Commission has not initiated any negative clearance, infringement or individual exemption proceedings. The national authorities in question are obviously the domestic courts.

Does this mean that the national courts are entirely estopped from applying competition law once the Commission has started proceedings? Not according to the ECJ in *BRT v SABAM*.[95] Here, the Court held that the courts had jurisdiction to apply Articles 85(1) and 86 of the Treaty because the latter had direct effect, and not on the basis of Article 9(3) of the Regulation. This gave the courts the power to rule that agreements were void under Article 85(2) of the Treaty, that national court orders could be granted in order to enforce competition rules, and that the domestic courts could award damages for infringements of Articles 85 and 86 of the Treaty.

In effect, this entails that the national courts may operate totally independently of the Commission in applying Articles 85 and 86 of the Treaty, even to the point of applying these provisions where the Commission had issued a comfort letter.[96] However, they have no powers to grant individual exemptions, even though they may rule that firms fall within the terms on which such exemptions are normally granted.

VIII The state sector and Community competition law

General

The national public authorities operate monopolies in various sectors; they have publicly-owned undertakings which command a considerable percentage of the market; they can subsidise certain privately-owned industries, and, generally speaking, act in a discriminatory manner in such a way as to favour and protect their national industries. They are therefore extremely powerful operators in the market place, a fact which did not escape the attention of the drafters of the Treaty.

In principle, the drafters of the Treaty could have confined themselves to requiring the public sector to abide by the same rules on competition as the private sector. They did not do so because special considerations apply in the case of commercial operations of the public sector. In many cases, the public authorities apply practices which *prima facie* amount to unfair discrimination, but which actually have the compassionate purpose of assisting certain

95 Case 127/73, (1974) ECR 51.
96 Case 99/79, *op cit*, at 2553.

backward regions, industries or sections of the population. It is particularly because of this socially-conscious dimension that a separate set of rules on competition policy was devised for the public sector.

Public undertakings

In spite of the free market ethic which characterises the economic system of the European Union, there are no rules prohibiting public ownership in the Member States. Article 222 of the Treaty states that the latter 'shall in no way prejudice the rules in the Member States governing the system of property ownership'. Although Community law is not strictly neutral in this respect – as can be seen from some ECJ decisions[97] – the Member States are allowed not only to operate a public sector of their economy, but also to extend it, so long as in so doing they do not break any of the fundamental principles on which Community law is based.

In principle, public undertakings are subject to the same rules on competition policy as those which apply to the private sector.[98] They may therefore not enter into any of the arrangements prohibited by Article 85 of the Treaty, or may not abuse any dominant position which they may occupy pursuant to Article 86 of the Treaty. Thus in 1982 the Commission found that British Telecom had abused its dominant position in relation to message-forwarding services.[99]

(i) The scope of Article 90(1)

This provision states:

In the case of public undertakings and undertakings to which Member States grant exclusive rights, Member States shall neither enact nor maintain in force any measure contrary to the rules contained in this Treaty, in particular to those rules provided for in Article 6 and Articles 85 to 94.

Article 90(1) of the Treaty therefore applies to two types of company: 'public undertakings' and those 'to whom Member States grant exclusive rights'. 'Public undertakings' are defined by the ECJ as 'any undertakings over which the public authorities may exercise directly or indirectly dominant influence by virtue of their ownership of it, their financial participation therein, or the rules which govern it'.[100] The conclusive factor here is therefore the degree of control exercised over the undertaking concerned by a public body, and not the legal form assumed by the undertaking in question. No definition has as yet been

---

97 See, eg Case 6/64, *op cit.*

98 Case 155/73, *Sacchi* (1974) ECR 409 at 430. See also Eleventh Report of the Community on Competition Policy (1981), p 155.

99 Decision 82/861, OJ 1982 L 360/36.

100 Cases 188–190/80, *France v Commission* (1982) ECR 2545 at 2579.

forthcoming of undertakings to whom Member States have granted exclusive rights.

(ii) Obligations of the national authorities under Article 90(1)

The Member States are required to refrain from enacting or maintaining in force any measures which would cause the firms envisaged to infringe the principles of the internal market. The obligations imposed by this Article are therefore on the Member States' authorities, and not on the undertakings in question. These public authorities may not take advantage of the control or leverage which they have over these undertakings in order to force the latter into arrangements which are contrary to Article 85 of the Treaty or into actions which contravene Article 86 of the Treaty. Nor may they grant to such undertakings subsidies which are contrary to Articles 92 and 93 of the Treaty.

(iii) Exceptions provided for in Article 90(2)

The special treatment of public undertakings under EU competition policy comes to full expression in the exceptions to the general principle laid down in Article 90(1). To this end, Article 90(2) of the Treaty states:

> Undertakings entrusted with the operation of services of general economic interest or having the character of a revenue-producing monopoly shall be subject to the rules contained in this Treaty, in particular to the rules of competition, in so far as the application of such rules does not obstruct the performance, in law or in fact, of the particular tasks assigned to them. The development of trade must not be affected to such an extent as would be contrary to the interests of the Community.

The decisive criterion for identifying this type of undertaking was laid down by the Court in BRT v SABAM,[101] where it stated that, for a firm to fall within the scope of this concept, it was essential for the service concerned to have been entrusted to that firm by an act of a public body – regardless of whether the undertaking in question is publicly or privately owned. This act need not necessarily take the form of an official document; all that is required that the public authority took certain steps to entrust the undertaking with that particular service.[102] A good example of this type of arrangement was provided in the air transport rates case.[103] The undertaking under scrutiny here was an air carrier compelled by the public authorities to operate, for reasons of public interest, air routes which were not commercially profitable.

101 Case 127/73, op cit, at 61; cf also Case 10/71, Hein, (1971) ECR 430.
102 Case 7/82, GVL v Commission (1983) ECR 483.
103 Case 66/86, Ahmed Saeed Luftreisen and Silver Line Reisebüro v Zentrale sur Bekämpfung Unlauterer Wettbewerbs (1989) ECR 803.

State aids

One of the most powerful tools of economic policy available to the national authorities is that of granting subsidies of various kinds to such economic activities as they seek to protect and/or foster. However socially conscious may be the reasons for such public aids, they are actions which are fraught with potentially damaging effects on free competition in the common market. This is why the Treaty has adopted a number of measures aimed at bringing such state subsidies within the sphere of legitimacy under Community competition law. This was done in Articles 92–94 of the Treaty.

(i) The general prohibition

Article 92(1) of the Treaty sets out the general principle governing state aids, where it states that, unless the Treaty specifically stipulates to the contrary, aids granted by Member States, using any public money whatsoever, which actually or potentially distort competition by favouring certain firms or industrial activities, are unlawful inasmuch as they affect intra-Community trade. By laying down this general rule, the drafters of the Treaty wished to indicate that, in principle, fair competition required business entities to operate within the common market using their own resources. Therefore, any financial assistance received by them from the public authorities no longer made the market place a level playing field. Where such assistance on the part of the state is justified by social considerations, it must be limited to that which is strictly necessary in order to achieve the desired result; once this has been realised, the aid should be discontinued.

The notion of 'state aids' should be interpreted broadly, if only because Article 92(1) of the Treaty refers to 'aid granted by a Member State or through state resources in any form whatsoever'. This term therefore covers not only financial assistance given by a public body but also that given by public, or even private, firms in which the state has a controlling interest. This is well illustrated by an action brought by the Commission against France under this heading involving solidarity payments benefiting low-paid agricultural workers.[104]

It is not necessary for the aids in question to have taken the form of direct payments by the body in question. Indirect financial advantages also fall within the purview of this prohibition. Thus in *Commission v Italy*,[105] the measure under scrutiny was an Italian measure which provided for a three-year reduction in the contributions payable by employers in the textile industry, which was aimed at covering their contributions towards the family allowances of their employees. Even though no money had changed hands directly, and the

104 Case 290/83, *Commission v France* (1985) ECR 440.
105 Case 173/73 (1974) ECR 709 at 719–20.

measure in question was a tax concession rather than a subsidy, the Court held that it constituted a state aid as prohibited by Article 92 of the Treaty.[106]

As is the case with the rules of competition applying to the private sector, it must be proved that intra-Community trade has been adversely affected by the state aid in question. This implies a causal connection between these two elements, which requires that the measure in question has been targeted at a specific industry or even category of industry, rather than forming part of a general economic policy.

(ii) State aids which are, or may be, compatible with Article 92(1)

As has been mentioned before, the drafters of the Treaty were to a certain extent conscious of the social dimension of the free-market policies advocated by them. This is revealed particularly in their approach towards state aids, some of which are compatible with the Common Market as of right, and some of which may under certain circumstances be compatible.

Article 92(2) of the Treaty sets out those state aids which can in principle be reconciled with the requirements of the common market. They are:

* Aids having a social character granted to individual consumers, provided that such aid is granted without discrimination as to the origin of the products involved.

* Aid aimed at making good the damage caused by natural disasters or exceptional events.

* Aid granted to certain areas of Germany which are affected by the division of that country.

These categories are relatively straightforward and have given rise to very few disputes. It is hard to understand, however, why advantage was not taken of the TEU in order to remove the third category, which appears to have become redundant in the light of the re-unification of Germany.

Article 92(3) of the Treaty sets out those state aids which may be compatible with the common market. For these categories, the Commission (and in certain exceptional cases the Council) will have to act as a referee and authorise the aids in question. The categories of state aid which fall within this group are:

* Aid aimed at promoting the economic development of areas in which the standard of living is abnormally low or where there is high unemployment.

* Aid seeking to promote the implementation of a major project of common European interest or at rectifying serious disruption in a Member State;

* Aid aimed at facilitating the development of certain economic activities or of certain economic areas, on condition that such aids do not have an adverse

106 See also Case 253/84, *GAEC v Commission* (1987) ECR 123, and Case C-301/87, *France v Commission* (1990) ECR-I 307.

effect on trading conditions in such a way as to prejudice the general interest.

- Aid seeking to promote culture and heritage conservation where such aid does not affect trading conditions and competition in a way which would be against the general interest.

- Any other categories of aid as may be specified by a decision of the Council, acting on a proposal by the Commission.

Two broad categories of aid caught by these provisions have been the subject matter of contention before the European Court: regional aid and sectoral aid.

As regards regional aid, two elements have complicated the search for a clear and consistent policy on this issue the part of the Community authorities. First, the Community is itself active in regional policy (below, p 253) and its funds, such as the European Regional Development Fund (ERDF), European Social Fund (ESF) and European Agricultural Guidance and Guarantee Fund (EAGGF) constitute an important EU instrument in this field. The other complicating factor is the circumstance that regional aid is contained in two subsections of Article 92 of the Treaty. Subsection (a) provides for the possibility of granting assistance to areas whose population are undergoing serious hardship. This provision is not hedged by any conditions. Subsection (c), on the other hand, allows the Member State to grant development aid to certain economic areas, on condition that such aid 'does not affect adversely trading interests to an extent contrary to the national interest'. There is a clear difference in emphasis between these two subsections; yet not to an extent which is capable of eliminating all ambiguity from their combined meaning.

A good example of the Court's approach towards state aids based on regional development policy is the *Philip Morris* decision.[107] When the Netherlands government granted a certain sum to a cigarette manufacturer, the Commission decided that this aid did not fall within the terms of Article 92(3) of the Treaty. It was not satisfied that the aid in question would contribute towards the achievement of one of the objectives specified in the derogations of Article 92 of the Treaty, which under normal circumstances the beneficiaries would not attain by their own actions. The Commission also held that the area in question, Bergen-op-Zoom, was not an area having an abnormally low standard of living or experiencing serious unemployment within the meaning of Article 92(3)(c) of the Treaty. In addition, it found that, far from creating the 475 jobs which the Netherlands Government had confidently projected, the aid would only lead to the creation of five new posts.

The tobacco company appealed to the Court of Justice against this decision. The latter found that if this type of aid were to be allowed, this would result in

---

107 Case 730/79, *Philip Morris Holland v Commission* (1980) ECR 2671.

the national authorities being allowed to make payments which would enhance the financial situation of the beneficiary although they were not necessary for the attainment of the objectives specified in Article 92(3) of the Treaty. It also found that the Commission's assessment of the economic situation in Bergen-op-Zoom was correct.

As regards sectoral aid, Article 92(3)(c) of the Treaty holds out the possibility of granting national aid for 'the development of certain economic activities'. Although the criteria are clearer for this category than is the case in relation to regional aid, the Commission has also seen fit to clarify its policy by means of a communication, addressed to the Council.[108] It points out that, in spite of the prevailing economic difficulties of the time – the communication was written at the time of the second oil crisis – if aids were to be awarded in a disparate manner, without taking into account the degree of Community solidarity required, this would cause the dislocation of the Common Market. Aids could therefore only be allocated in industrial sectors where they were strictly necessary, and made subject to strict conditions as to the future competitivity of the beneficiaries.

IX Conclusion

Competition policy fully reflects the ethos of individual liberalism which underlies the entire Treaty of Rome. It regulates not only the private, but also the public sector. The latter is thus compelled to comply entirely with the free market ideology of the Community. This can be extremely unfortunate, as in most cases public intervention in the economy occurs precisely because the free competition mechanism has failed to meet the needs of certain regions or certain economic sectors. It is true that Articles 92 and 93, on state aids, make allowance for such aids as have essentially a social character. However, these are exceptions to the general rule of free competition as embodied in Articles 85 and 86, and as such the Court of Justice, in accordance with its principles of interpretation, will require such an exception to be interpreted strictly. Thus a number of state aids schemes which could have saved the jobs of workers were sacrificed on the altar of free and unfettered competition.

The business world faces another problem in relation to Community competition policy – to wit, inconsistencies between national and EU policies. As F. Fishwick states,[109] it is bad enough for business managers to be faced with two jurisdictions; it is intolerable that these should apply different rules. Sadly, this particular problem cannot be solved by an agreement among the Member States to apply policies identical to those of the EU, precisely because of the

108 Bull, 1978/5, p 29.
109 Op cit, pp 194–95.

criticism which is regularly levelled at the rules in question. One of the many criticisms aired is that the prohibition of abuse of dominant position needs to be supplemented by other policies to deal with the effects of particular market structures. Measures of this type should seek to regulate conduct, rather than impose retrospective punishment, as happens under the Treaty. As regards Article 85, the cause of transparency and consistency in the application of policy could be increased by making more explicit reference to the application of policy power of the parties to any agreement or concerted practice, since without such power the adverse effects of an agreement could be considerable.[110]

Another valid criticism which can, and has, been made of Community competition policy is its excessive legalism and inadequate economic analysis. In her excellent critique on this subject, Valentine Korah rightly castigates the 'paucity of economic analysis in the Commission's public decisions'.[111] Professor Korah rightly condemns the unpredictable nature of the Commission's decisions, and the reluctance of the Court to review the Commission's economic analysis. This can be attributed to the Court's excessive caution in reviewing, under Article 173 of the Treaty, anything other than a 'manifest error of law'. All this has been to the detriment of legal certainty, and one expects better things of the body which is presumed to be the ultimate authority on such matters.

---

110 *Ibid*, at p 195.
111 Korah, V, *EC Competition Law and Practice* (5th edn, 1994), Sweet & Maxwell, pp 267–68.

12 Customs Law: External Aspects

I Introduction

The EU has not confined its efforts at trade regulation to the creation of a barrier-free internal market which safeguards free and fair competition. It has also sought to present itself towards the outside world as a single trading unit, in the sense that anyone from outside the EU wishing to do business with anyone inside the latter will be subject to the same restrictions, payments, or entitlements regardless of the Member State in which the other party to the deal is situated.

The main tool employed by the Community for this purpose has been the introduction of a common external tariff. This is an essential complement to the free movement of goods, since, if Member States were allowed to retain their national customs tariffs, they would need to retain customs controls – if only for products coming from outside the Community. This would seriously undermine the single market, not to mention giving rise to all manner of undesirable economic side effects such as deflection of trade.

Between the entry into effect of the EC Treaty and the current legislative framework, the rules governing the CCT have undergone a good deal of change. Article 23 required the Common Customs Tariff to be put into place amongst the original Member States by the end of the transitional period. This objective was achieved ahead of schedule thanks to two speed-up decisions by the Council. The initial average of CCT duties was approximately 11 per cent, ie considerably lower than those applied by the other major trading powers.

The original CCT was contained in Regulation 950/68.[1] Subsequently, a revised and updated version of this instrument has been issued every year. In the course of its development, the CCT has been subjected to many influences, both internal and external, such as:

- the accession of new Member States;
- the Common Agricultural Policy, which has resulted in agricultural products being subject to a special system of import charges;
- the International Convention on the Harmonised Commodity Description and Coding System, which entered into effect on 1 January 1988. This was a convention which united the customs and trade classification systems. The

1 OJ Special Edition 1968(I) p 275.

- EU has implemented this convention by means of Regulation 2658/87,[2] which contains the Combined Nomenclature (CN) and the Integrated Tariff of the Communities (TARIC);

- the tariff rounds concluded under the General Agreement on Tariffs and Trade (GATT), ie the Dillon, Kennedy, Tokyo and Uruguay Rounds, which have each produced changes in the rates applied under the CCT.

- the commercial agreements concluded with non-Member States, either individually or collectively, which have exempted these countries from CCT duties, or reduced them.

The application and management of the CCT has required an extensive body of rules governing such matters as rules of origin, customs valuation, exemptions from the CCT, etc. Initially these were contained in individual instruments. Recently, however, these have all been consolidated in one Community Customs Code, which was adopted on 12 October 1992, in a regulation which will henceforth be referred to as the 'CCC Regulation'.[3] This was supplemented a year later by a regulation which implements the broadly-framed provisions of the CCC Regulation; this instrument will henceforth be referred to as the 'Implementing Regulation'.[4]

The CCT displays two columns of duty. One is for the 'autonomous' rate, being that which formed part of the original CCT. The other is for the 'conventional' rates, which are those which have been negotiated in the context of GATT rate reductions. The average level of the CCT as applied to industrial products is 4.7 per cent.

II The CCT: exemptions and special categories of products

Exemptions

Various circumstances can arise which serve to exempt certain goods from payment of CCT duties. The first of these circumstances is the end use to which products are put. Thus the product toluole will be exempt from CCT duty if used for any purpose other than serving as power or heating fuel. Once the product is admitted for such a purpose, the importer must meet a number of obligations: not only must the goods in question be used for the purpose justifying the exemption, but also keep proper records and submit to such inspection measures as are considered to be necessary (Article 293 Implementing Regulation). If the authorisation is withdrawn, the importer must

2 OJ 1987 L 256.
3 Regulation 2913/92, OJ 1992 L 302.
4 Regulation 2545/93, OJ 1993 L 253.

immediately pay import duties on those goods which have not already been used for the exempting end use (Article 292 Implementing Regulation).

There are also temporary exemptions. Article 28 of the Treaty also allows derogations or suspensions of CCT duties for products which may not exceed 20 per cent of the applicable rate for a maximum period of six months. They must be decided by the Council by a qualified majority. There are two types of circumstances in which the Council has allowed such exemptions. The first resides in the various preferential trading arrangements which have been concluded with third countries and which have the effect of reducing the CCT duties normally applied. The second set of circumstances are those in which the Council considers that EU traders will actually benefit from such reductions – eg where a particular product is not available in the EU but is required by EU manufacturers for inclusion in the production process.

There are also exemptions for particular categories of products. These exemptions are also based on Article 28 of the Treaty. Various products which foster public, rather than commercial, needs have thus been exempted from CCT duties. The provisions governing these exemptions have been consolidated in Regulation 918/83 establishing an EU system of reliefs from customs duty.[5] They include scientific instruments, educational, scientific and cultural materials, medical instruments, and goods intended for trade promotion.

It is also possible for the Member States, acting individually, to grant tariff exemptions which only apply to their national territory. Article 25 of the Treaty recognises that sometimes the availability of certain items in certain Member States is inadequate to meet demand, and that these countries may be traditionally dependent for the supplying of such goods on imports from third countries. If such circumstances prevail, the Council may allow the Member State in question to apply tariff quotas.

Special categories of products

Some categories of products have been placed outside the ambit of the CCT altogether for a variety of reasons. Agricultural products are governed by the Common Agricultural Policy, which, as will be discussed later, is a fully integrated system in which the customs treatment of non-EU produce is narrowly linked to the common organisation of the markets in this sector. Nuclear materials also fall within this category, since their customs treatment is governed by the Euratom Treaty, and Article 232(2) of the Treaty provides that any special rules in the Euratom Treaty take precedence over EU rules. Coal and steel products also fall outside the scope of the CCT, since their customs treatment is governed by Articles 71 and 72 of the ECSC Treaty.

5   OJ 1983 L 105.

III The CCT: interpretation of the combined nomenclature

Difficulties of interpretation

For the Combined Nomenclature of the CCT to have any credibility at all it must be interpreted uniformly throughout the EU. This will be a task incumbent on the Court of Justice, which, on reference from the national courts, has had to deal with a large number of interpretation disputes. The reason for this is twofold. In the first place, the authors of the Combined Nomenclature have found it necessary to use very general denominations in order to bring all conceivable products within its ambit – for example, the heading 'other goods made from wood'. The second reason is that the duties levied under the CCT vary considerably, and classifying a large consignment of goods under one particular subheading could mean that the importer will be charged a great deal more money than if that consignment had been brought under another subheading.

Fortunately, the judicial authorities currently have plenty of material at their disposal in order to give them guidance on the correct interpretation of the CCT. This material is made up of (i) the CCT nomenclature itself, (ii) the case law of the ECJ, (iii) binding sources of interpretation. Each will be examined in turn.

The CCT nomenclature

The guidance provided by the CCT Nomenclature takes the form of general rules of interpretation, which can be found in Part One of the annual version of the CCT. These rules have remained substantially unchanged since they were first adopted in the original 1968 legislation.[6]

Rule 1 states that the titles of the sections, chapters and sub-chapters are provided merely for ease of reference. For legal purposes, goods must be classified on the basis of the headings and any relevant section or chapter notes and, unless the such headings or notes require otherwise, according to Rules 2 to 5.

Rule 2(a) provides that any reference made in a heading to an article must be taken to include a reference to that article, whether complete or unfinished, on condition that the incomplete or unfinished article, as imported, has the essential character of the complete or finished article.

Under *Rule 2(b)*, any reference in a heading to a material or substance must be taken to include a reference to mixtures or combinations of that material or substance with other materials or substances.

---

6   Regulation 950/68.

Rule 3 lays down the technical rules to be followed when, for any reason, goods are in principle classifiable under two or more headings.

Rule 4 states that goods not falling within any heading of the tariff must be classified under the heading appropriate to the goods to which they are most akin.

Rule 5 provides that the above rules also apply when determining the appropriate subheading within a heading.

The ECJ case law

As in any other area of Community law, it is the ECJ which had had to ensure that the CCT is interpreted as uniformly as possible. This it has done mainly through the preliminary rulings mechanism of Article 177 of the Treaty. It is therefore only natural that the case law which the Court has built up on the basis of these references has itself become a key guide to the interpretation of the CCT. Thus in one particular case,[7] the Court found that 'flashing light circles', consisting of a circular plastic frame to which are attached incandescent light bulbs of various colours which flash when switched on, should be classified under tariff heading 97.05 ('Carnival Articles'). In another decision,[8] it was held that the expression 'discrete components' within the meaning of Note 5(B) of Chapter 85 had to be interpreted as denoting physical units consisting of a single electric circuit element and having a single electrical function such as, for example, diodes, transistors or resistors. It must be admitted, however, that the co-ordination between these decisions and the other sources of interpretation of the CCT is not always all that it should be.[9]

Binding instruments of interpretation

Sometimes the EU authorities wish to make the classification of particular items binding for the future. In that case, they will rely on binding legislation rather than on the ECJ case law. A good example of this type of instrument is Commission Regulation 3491/88 on the classification of certain goods in the combined nomenclature.[10]

7   Case 205/80, *Elba v Hauptzollamt Berlin-Packhof* (1981) ECR 2097.
8   Case 122/80, *Analog Devices v Hauptzollamt München-Mitte and Hauptzollamt München-West* (1981) ECR 2781.
9   See Lasok, D, *The Customs Law of the EC* (1990), Kluwer, p 216.
10 OJ 1988 L 306.

IV Rules of origin

Why rules of origin are necessary

It has already been explained (above, p 227) that the institution of a common external tariff makes it unnecessary for rules of origin to be applied when goods move from one Member State to another. However, it remains necessary to apply rules of origin in relation to goods entering EU customs territory from third countries. The reason for this is that, very often, one particular good has been produced in several states, which could be Member States or third countries. It was therefore necessary to lay down rules which would decide the official origin of such hybrid products. These rules of origin are governed by Title II, Chapter 2, of the CCC Regulation.

A distinction needs to be made between preferential and non-preferential rules of origin. Rules of preferential origin relate to goods traded with countries, or groups of countries, with which the EU has preferential trading arrangements, and to which preferential duties are applied. For goods traded with any other country or group of countries, non-preferential rules of origin apply.

Non-preferential rules of origin

Where goods have been wholly obtained or produced in one country, they are considered as originating in that country. Article 23 of the CCC Regulation lists those goods which are considered to fall within this category. If, on the other hand, a product is obtained in two or more countries, it is regarded as originating in the country in which the 'last substantial process that was economically justified' took place. Three criteria must be met for the product to be attributed to any particular country: (a) the last substantial process or operation which was economically justified must have been performed there; (b) that process must have been carried out in an undertaking equipped for that purpose, and (c) that process must have resulted in the manufacture of a new product or represent an important stage in the manufacturing process (Article 24 CCC Regulation).

The Implementing Regulation clarifies this basic rule by laying down what should be regarded as working or processing operations conferring origin (Articles 36 and 37) and specifies those operations which will be insufficient to confer the status originating product (Article 38).

The case law of the Court has also assisted with the process of clarifying these criteria. In the *Überseehandel* case,[11] it ruled that the last operation or process will only be considered to be substantial where the product resulting from it has its own properties and composition, which it did not have before

11 Case 49/76, *Gesellschaft für Überseehandel mbH v Handelskammer Hamburg* (1977) ECR 41.

that process or operation. In *Brother*,[12] the ECJ held that Article 5 of Regulation 802/68 (which was the instrument which was consolidated in the CCC Regulation) had failed to specify the extent to which assembly operations could be regarded as a substantial operation or process. It therefore laid down the general rule that an assembly confers origin if, from a technical viewpoint and taking account of the definition of the products in question, it represented the decisive stage of production in which the end use of the product becomes apparent and in the course of which the product acquires its specific properties.

Preferential rules of origin

As has been mentioned earlier, the EU has, as part of its Common Commercial Policy, made it possible for a number of countries, situated mainly in the Southern hemisphere, to export their produce to the EU at preferential customs tariffs. The latter are set out in the so-called preferential trade agreements, and are concluded with third countries on an individual, group or generalised basis.

The rules of origin are marginally different from those applying to non-preferential goods. The criteria which must be met by products to be regarded as 'wholly obtained products' only differ marginally from those laid down for preferential goods. The main difference, however, resides in the conditions to be met by goods produced in a country containing products which do not originate in that country. These will be regarded as originating in the country of manufacture on condition that the non-originating products have undergone 'sufficient working or processing'. The criteria for meeting condition are set out in the Implementing Regulation (Article 68 *et seq*).

V   Customs valuation

General

Most duties applicable under the CCT are imposed on an *ad valorem* basis, which means that they are expressed as a percentage of the value of the imported article. It is therefore extremely important that this value be established as correctly and uniformly as possible. The CCC Regulation (which replaced the earlier Valuation Regulation 1224/80)[13] lays down a number of rules which are to be followed for this purpose. These have been largely the product of international agreements to which the EU Member States are parties, such as GATT (Article VII), the Brussels Valuation Convention and the GATT Customs Valuation Code.

12   Case 26/88, *Brother International GmbH v Hauptzollamt Giessen* (1990) ECR 707.
13   OJ 1980 L 134.

The substantive rules relating to valuation are set out in the CCC Regulation, whereas the procedural provisions are contained in the Implementing Regulation.

The substantive rules

The system of valuation laid down in the CCC is based on the value of the goods which have been imported. This is why Article 31(2) of the CCC Regulation expressly prohibits the use of such elements as the selling price in the EU of goods produced there, the price of goods on the domestic market of the country of export, or minimum customs values.

Instead, the Regulation lays down five valuation methods which must be applied successively until such time as the appropriate method has been found: the transaction value of the goods, the transaction value of identical goods, the transaction value of similar goods, the deductive value, and the computed value.

(i) Transaction value of goods

This is the first method which must be applied. The transaction value is defined as the price which is actually paid or payable for the goods when sold for export to the EU (Article 29(1) CCC Regulation). The 'price actually paid or payable' is the total payment accruing to the seller for the imported goods. It includes payments made to third parties which meet an obligation on the part of the seller. The payment in question does not need to consist of a money transfer: it can also assume the form of a letter of credit or some other negotiable instrument (Article 29(3)(a) CCC Regulation).

If vendor and buyer are related, the transaction value will not be accepted if this relationship is held to have affected the price. However, even if such a relationship is involved, the transaction value will be acceptable where it approximates the value which would have been achieved by applying any other acceptable valuation method. Where the customs authorities believe that the price has been influenced by the relationship, natural justice demands that the importer be given the opportunity to defend himself. The authorities will then have to decide whether or not to accept the transaction value claimed by the importer.

Certain costs which are directly related to the transaction value may be added when computing the transaction value (Article 32 CCC Regulation). As regards intellectual property rights, these may be included in the price paid or payable if the application of a patented process represents the only economically justifiable use of the item in question.[14] Article 33 of the CCC regulation details a number of costs which may are deemed to be too remote from the transaction in question, and therefore may not be included in the customs value.

14 Case 1/77, *Robert Bosch v Hauptzollamt Hildesheim* (1977) ECR 1473.

(ii) Transaction value of identical goods

If it is not feasible to use the transaction value of the good in question, the next method which must be tried is to use the transaction of an identical item. A great deal will depend here on a process of consultations between the customs authorities and the importer, aimed at obtaining the information which will enable this transaction value to be established. The term 'identical goods' covers goods which are the same in all respects, including their physical properties, quality and reputation.

(iii) Transaction value of similar goods

The next best method for assessing the customs value will be the transaction value of similar goods which are sold for export to the EU and are exported at around the same time as the goods subject to valuation (Article 30(2)(b) of the CCC Regulation). The term 'similar goods' must be understood as meaning goods made in the same country as those being valued which, although not alike in all respects, nevertheless have similar characteristics and component materials enabling them to perform the same functions and to be substitutable for them (Article 142(1)(d) Implementing Regulation).

(iv) Deductive goods

If none of the above are appropriate, the deductive value must be applied. This is the value based on the unit price at which the imported goods (or identical or similar goods) are sold within the EU in the greatest aggregate quantity, to persons not related to the sellers (Article 30(2)(c) CCC Regulation).

(v) Computed value

The next in line is the computed value, being the value which is based on the sum of a number of elements which include the cost of materials and manufacture in producing the imported goods; an amount for profit and general expenses usually reflected in sales of goods of the same type; and the cost of transport and insurance to the place of entry into EU customs territory (Article 30(2)(d) CCC Regulation).

(vi) Reasonable means test

If the above methods are unequal to the situation, the customs value should be determined using such reasonable means as are consistent with the principles and general rules of the CCC and Article VII of GATT and on the basis of data available within the EU (Article 30(2)(d) CCC Regulation). The Explanatory Notes to the GATT Valuation Code have interpreted this as meaning that once the previous five methods have been unsuccessfully tried, they should still be applied but with 'reasonable flexibility'.

Procedural rules

Normally, the valuation process is conducted on the basis of information contained in a form called the 'value declaration', which must accompany the form required to obtain the release of the goods for free circulation (Article 178 Implementing Regulation). The information specified on the value declaration is aimed at determining the customs value based on the transaction value of the goods. If any of the other valuation methods specified under (c) above is applied, the customs authorities may waive production of the value declaration. This will also be the case for low-value or non-commercial goods (Article 179(1) Implementing Regulation).

Customs valuation and valuation for other purposes

Establishing the correct value of imported goods can serve purposes other than EU customs valuation. The national authorities may also use this information for the purpose of applying and enforcing national economic rules, such as income tax assessments. Because infringement of these rules may involve the imposition of criminal penalties, the question has arisen as to the propriety of using these purely EU procedures in this manner. In the *Chatain* decision,[15] the Court ruled that customs valuation data could be used in this manner, provided that the Member States' authorities did so on a purely national basis. These procedures may not, however, be used for the purpose of imposing customs duties on goods which are not capable of being put into free circulation.[16]

Exchange rate rules

Very often the data used in order to establish the customs value of goods are expressed in currencies other than those of the Member State in which the valuation is being carried out. If this is the case, the exchange rate used must be that which has been duly published by the appropriate authorities of the Member State in question (Article 35 CCC Regulation). This rate must be the rate recorded on the second-last Wednesday of each month, and published on the following day (Article 169(1) Implementing Regulation).

15   Case 65/79, *Procureur de la République v Chatain* (1980) ECR 1345.
16   Case 50/80, *Horvath v Hauptzollamt Hamburg-Jonas* (1981) ECR 385.

VI   Customs approved treatment or use

Range of customs procedures needed

Thus far, we have examined the rules which govern the application of the CCT. Equally important to an efficient and equitable system of customs clearance, however, is a range of procedures which determine the fate of the goods once they arrive at an EU external customs post. Although inevitably this will involve a certain amount of paperwork, the object of the exercise is to reduce both this aspect and the time scale involved to the barest minimum.

The procedures in question are not restricted to the formalities involved in securing for the goods safe passage through the customs administration and then allowing them to pass into free circulation. Some goods remain under customs supervision after having been declared to the customs authorities, and therefore cannot be released for free circulation. There are also certain procedures aimed at securing the unhindered passage from one Member State to another. In addition, the exporting of goods from EU territory also involve a number of formalities.

Placing goods under customs supervision

The first step which needs to be taken in order to obtain customs clearance is to place the goods under customs procedure. This is done by means of a customs declaration (Article 59 CCC Regulation). The form which this declaration may take is quite flexible (Article 61 CCC Regulation), in that it may be made (a) in writing, using approved data processing techniques, (b) by means of a normal declaration, or (c) by any other authorised act of the holder indicating his desire that the goods be placed under a customs procedure. However, where the declaration is made in writing or according to the normal procedure, the official form used must be the Single Administrative Document (SAD) (Article 205 Implementing Regulation).

Where the declaration is made in writing, either the normal or the simplified procedure will be used. Under the former, the declaration must be made on a form which corresponds to the official form provided. They must be signed and include all the particulars required for the proper implementation of the provisions governing the normal procedure. The declaration must be accompanied by all the necessary documentation (Article 62 Implementing Regulation).

If the simplified procedure applies one of three types may be used. The procedure for incomplete declarations enables the customs authorities to accept declarations which do not include all the particulars required or are not accompanied by all the necessary documentation. Naturally, a minimum number of details and documents will need to be produced (Articles 254 and 255 Implementing Regulation). The simplified declaration procedure enables goods to be entered for the customs procedure in question by using a simplified declaration, on condition that a supplementary declaration be produced (Article 259 Implementing Regulation). The local clearance procedure enables goods to be entered in accordance with a procedure to be conducted at the premises of the person in question, or on any other location approved or designated by the customs authorities (Article 264 Implementing Regulation).

Releasing goods for free circulation

These rules are aimed at ensuring that, once they have entered the EU customs territory, goods emanating from outside the EU enjoy the same treatment as Community-produced goods. They thus seek to achieve that non-EU goods receive the same status as EU goods. It is at this stage that the actual customs duties payable will be charged. It will therefore need to be ascertained not only what the applicable CCT rate is, but also whether any measures adopted under the Common Commercial policy of the EU are applicable. The term 'duty' must be understood as referring not only to CCT duties, but also the various levies charged under the Common Agricultural Policy.

The actual charging of the applicable duty is fraught with all manner of expensive and time-consuming formalities. Consignments of goods do not invariably come in convenient batches of goods which all attract the same rate. This is why, for mixed consignments, it is possible for the customs administration to impose one duty, the highest, to the entire consignment, if the declarant so wishes.

It is at this particular stage that the customs authorities are able to deal with a problem which has increasingly damaged international trade, to wit counterfeited and pirate material, especially in the case of recorded material. If the customs authorities discover such goods, these are either destroyed, disposed of in a non-commercial manner, or dealt with in such a manner as to deprive the persons indicted of any economic benefit deriving from such items (Regulation 3295/94).[17]

Suspensive arrangements and customs procedures with economic impact

Certain measures and procedures are necessary in order to ensure that, once they have entered EU territory, goods can move as freely as possible across EU Member States' borders. In addition, some goods imported into the EU attract either reduced customs duties or none at all, and remain under the supervision of the customs authorities. Once they have been presented for customs clearance, they will not be released for free circulation, but will be subject to restricted movement. This circumstance also requires special arrangements. All

17 OJ 1994 L 341.

these measures are grouped together in the CCC as 'suspensive arrangements and customs procedures with economic impact'.

(i) External transit procedure

Once goods have been released for free circulation, they should be able to move without let or hindrance throughout the Community. Unfortunately, despite the claim that an internal market now exists within the EU, goods passing from one Member State to another still experience the presence of border controls, mainly for the purpose of such public policy measures as health inspections and drug controls.

This is why a Community transit procedure was introduced. This enables any person to convey, under the cover of a single document (Community Transit Document) goods from any customs office within the EU of EFTA to one situated in the EU or in an EFTA country, without requiring any customs formalities other than the presentation of the goods and the production of an appropriate form. The transit procedure also applies to the export of Community goods to third countries, for which the relevant export formalities have already been carried out but which still need to travel across Member States' borders.

Because the object of the procedure is to facilitate as much as possible the passage of goods across Community frontiers, it is possible for EU Member States to maintain or enter into, amongst themselves, bilateral or multilateral agreements which introduce simplified procedures (Article 97 CCC Regulation).

(ii) Customs warehouses

Sometimes the fate of goods after their customs clearance is uncertain, and will need to be stored on EU customs territory as long as that uncertainty continues. Therefore Community customs law makes it possible to organise customs warehouses which will be licensed and supervised by the customs authority and used for such goods without the latter being subjected to import duties or common commercial policy measures (Article 98 CCC Regulation).

These customs warehouses may be publicly or privately owned. The warehouse keeper must ensure that the goods will not elude the supervision of the customs administration, carry out the obligations which arise from the storage of the goods, and observe the specific conditions contained in the relevant authorisation (Article 101 CCC Regulation). The customs authorities must allow certain operations, called 'usual forms of handling', to be performed on the goods whilst in storage (Article 109 CCC Regulation).

(iii) Inward processing

The international division of labour often requires goods to move across frontiers merely for the purpose of being processed, only to be re-exported immediately afterwards. To impose customs duties on such goods would mean losing the economic advantage inherent in such movements. This is why certain procedures have been built into the EU customs system to take account of these economic facts. These are called the inward processing procedures.

These procedures enable non-EU goods to enter the Community customs territory customs-free, on condition that they are subjected to some form of processing operation within the EU and are intended for re-export in the form of 'compensating products'. This exemption can only be enjoyed if the appropriate authorisation has been obtained from the appropriate customs authority. The award of this authorisation in turn is conditional upon certain conditions being met (Article 117 CCC Regulation). To qualify as a 'compensating product' the article in question must have been subject to one of the following procedures: working (including erecting and assembling the goods), processing, repair, or the use of goods which are not to be found in the compensating product, but allow or facilitate the manufacture of such products (Article 114 CCC Regulation).

(iv) Processing under customs control

If customs duties were charged on certain products which enter – and subsequently remain within – the EU for processing purposes, this could make it economically unviable for them to be used for processing purposes. If the relevant conditions are met, such goods may enter the EU duty free, but once they have been processed, the finished product thus obtained will be charged the appropriate customs duty (Article 130–36 CCC Regulation).

(v) Temporary importation

Sometimes goods are imported into the EU for a specific purpose, and with the express intention of being re-exported once they have served this purpose. Here again, there would be little sense in subjecting these goods to the payment of customs duties. This is why such goods will obtain relief from customs duties if they are used for certain specified purposes, are subject to the lodging of a deposit, and do not remain on Community customs territory for any longer than 24 months. This relief from customs duties may be total or partial.

(vi) Outward processing

Just as goods are sometimes imported into the EU purely for processing purposes, EU goods are sometimes conveyed to third countries for the same reason. The CCC contains rules aimed at ensuring that the goods which have resulted from the processing of these EU products will be released for free circulation with total or partial relief from customs duties (Articles 145–47 CCC Regulation).

'Standard exchange arrangements' – the importing into the EU of replacement goods for products exported from the EU, with the former being granted partial or total exemption from customs duties – are included in the same CCC chapter relating to outward processing arrangements (Articles 154–59 CCC Regulation).

Export

The exporting of goods from EU territory is subject to a number of formalities, if only in fulfilment of the Community's obligations towards other countries under its Common Commercial Policy. This is why a common procedure for the export of goods from the Community are included in the CCC (Article 161 CCC Regulation). The detailed rules relating to export procedure are contained in Articles 788–98 of the Implementing Regulation.

Internal transit

The internal transit procedure aims at allowing EU goods to be conveyed from one point in the EU to another whilst passing through the territory, without suffering any change in their customs status (Article 163 CCC Regulation).

Other types of customs-approved treatment

Special customs arrangements apply in certain other circumstances, such as free zones and free warehouses, and privileged operations such as goods exempted from customs duty, returned goods and sea-fishing products.

VII The customs debt

General

The customs debt is the obligation imposed on a person to pay a certain sum by way of import or export duties. The CCC lays down specific rules aimed at ensuring that the maximum amount of legal certainty surrounds its collection and payment.

Where the debt is incurred

The customs debt is incurred at the place where the events from which it arises occur (Article 215(1) CCC Regulation). If it proves impossible to identify this location, the debt will be deemed to have been incurred at the place where the customs administration considers that the goods find themselves in a situation in which a customs debt has been incurred (Article 215(2) CCC Regulation).

The customs debt and the assessment of duties

The amount of import or export duty payable will in principle be determined on the basis of the rules of assessment which are appropriate to those goods at the time when the customs debt was incurred (Article 214(1) CCC Regulation). If the time at which the customs debt was incurred cannot be established with precision, the time to be taken into account will be time at which the customs administration has arrived at the conclusion that the goods find themselves in a situation in which the customs debt has been incurred (Article 214(2) CCC Regulation).

How the customs debt is incurred on imports

The detailed rules on the circumstances in which the customs debt is incurred on the importation of goods can be found in Articles 2 and 3 of Regulation 2144/87 on customs debt.[18]

How the customs debt is incurred on exports

The detailed rules on the circumstances in which the customs debt is incurred on the exportation of goods can be found in Articles 209–11 of the CCC Regulation.

13 Social Policy

I Introduction

Evolution

The initial framework for EU social policy was Articles 117 to 122 of the Treaty, supplemented by Articles 123–25 which make provision for the establishment of the European Social Fund. The foundation stones of this policy were laid down in provisions which have been replaced by a new set of rules as a result of the Amsterdam Treaty. Originally, Article 117 of the Treaty set out the general aims and objectives of Community social policy, which is 'to promote improved working conditions and an improved standard of living for workers, so as to make possible their harmonisation while the improvement is being maintained'. Article 118 of the Treaty set out the areas in which the Commission was to achieve 'close co-operation' between the Member States, ie employment, labour law and working conditions, basic and advanced vocational training, social security, prevention of occupational accidents and diseases, occupational hygiene and the right of association and collective bargaining. Article 119 required observance of the principle of equal pay for equal work as between men and women.

The legislative framework for the achievement of EU social policy was therefore decidedly modest, as compared with the more closely-worded injunctions to the Community institutions to adopt harmonising and/or approximating legislation in other fields (eg the free movement of persons). Clearly, the authors of the Treaty considered that the achievement of the Common Market would be the main catalyst for the achievement of uniformly high levels of social protection throughout the Community. That there were limits to the potential of this approach became evident as soon as the oil crisis set off a chain of economic difficulties in the Member States. However, even once policy makers at the Community level had grasped this fact, progress on the area of social policy remained laborious and slow. The main reasons for this were (a) the fact that legislation in this field must be taken by unanimous voting, and (b) the opposition by some Member States, in particular the United Kingdom, to any extensive legislative programme in this area.[1]

Nevertheless, the general desire to extend the scope of Community action in the social field was expressed in the Single European Act, which added two

---

1 *Diritto delle Comunita europee, op cit,* p 287.

Articles to the Treaty Chapter on social policy. Article 118a requires the Member States to pay particular attention to improving the working environment as well as the health and safety of workers, and sets out the general objective of harmonisation in this field. It adds, however, that any directives implementing this objective should avoid imposing any constraints which could frustrate the creation and development of small and medium-sized businesses. Article 118b requires the Commission to promote the dialogue between employers and employees which could lead to relations based on consensus.

This is generally admitted to have introduced the notion of the 'social dimension' of the Community, ie the process whereby the business aspects of Community action are matched by action in the social sphere. The resonance of this idea was, however, rather small, since the contrast between the extensive and relatively detailed provisions of the SEA relating to the achievement of the single market were only accompanied by the two rather innocuous provisions of Articles 118a and 118b of the Treaty. This is why it was felt that the momentum towards a social dimension needed to be maintained by means of new initiatives. On the basis of a Commission working paper called 'The Social Dimension of the Internal Market', the Economic and Social Committee and the European Parliament had recommended the enactment of a European Social Charter. This instrument was adopted at that European Council meeting of May 1989. The United Kingdom, however, expressing once again its opposition to the involvement of Community action in this field, refused to recognise the Charter. This posed a major difficulty which was unprecedented in Community law. The original plan had been that the Charter should be a binding act, but the form which was ultimately chosen was that of a Solemn Declaration. To this day, mystery and confusion surround the question as to the exact legal effect of the Social Charter. The contents of the Charter are discussed in greater detail later (below, p 248).

The adoption of the TEU seemed to be another appropriate opportunity to advance the social agenda of the Community. The negotiations leading up to the TEU appeared to indicate strong support for this idea amongst all the Member States with the exception of the United Kingdom. This led to the adoption of a new tactic advanced by the Dutch President of the European Council, Ruud Lubbers: to exclude the UK from that part of the TEU agenda which concerned social policy, and to build on the aims and objectives of the Social Charter in order to give it the form of a Treaty – albeit a separate component of a Treaty. This gave rise to the inclusion in the TEU of the 'Social Protocol' (also referred to as 'Social Chapter'). This instrument lays down decision-making procedures which are those of the EU; however, the decisions implementing the Social Chapter would not be adopted by the Council, and they would not apply in the United Kingdom.[2] The Social Chapter will be

---

2   Nicoll, W and Salmon, TC, *op cit.*

returned to later (see p 247). The TEU also inserted in the Treaty a Title on economic and social cohesion (Articles 13a to 130e).

The one issue of social policy which has increasingly preoccupied EU policy makers in this field is unemployment. This was particularly noticeable in the White Paper presented by the Commission in 1993, entitled *Competitiveness and Employment: the challenges and ways forward into the 21st century*. This instrument noted the alarming increases in unemployment throughout the Community since the 1980s, in particular the worrying trend towards increased long-term unemployment. For this purpose, the Commission set a target of creating 15 million new jobs by the year 2000. This has proved too ambitious an aspiration; indeed, there are many who feel that some of the other EU policies are actually contributing towards increased joblessness (in particular the criteria for economic convergence for the achievement of Economic and Monetary Union).

EU Social policy received a new impetus with the adoption of the Amsterdam Treaty. This instrument gave greater substance and detail to the Chapters of Title VIII which concerned social policy. In addition, it added a new Employment Chapter, thus reflecting the increased urgency with which, as was seen in the previous paragraph, EU policy makers were prepared to tackle this major issue. The new Treaty framework for social policy thus created is described in the following section.

II   Social policy: the new treaty framework

The Amsterdam Treaty made a number of fundamental changes in the relevant EC Treaty provisions. The new Article 117 sets out the fundamental objectives of EU social policy. By specific reference to the Social Charter of the Council of Europe (adopted in 1961), and the 1989 EC Social Charter, which is referred to in the previous section, the Community and the Member States now have as their objectives:

the promotion of employment, improved living and working conditions, so as to make possible their harmonisation while the improvement is being maintained, proper social protection, dialogue between management and labour, the development of human resources with a view to lasting high employment and the combating of exclusion.

The second paragraph, however, contains two limitations on the extent to which these objectives are to be achieved. One has to do with the principle of subsidiarity, since the Community and Member States are to achieve these objectives by taking into account 'the diverse forms of national practices', in particular in the field of contractual relations. The other concerns what is generally described as 'economic realism', since it requires that the measures concerned take account of 'the need to maintain the competitiveness of the Community economy.

Article 118 sets out the manner in which these objectives are to be achieved. Article 118(1) lists a number of fields in which 'the Community shall support and complement the activities of the Member States'. This clearly shows that the intention is not to harmonise standards. Rather the intention is to lay down certain irreducible minima by means of directives, as is made clear by Article 118(2). This provision goes on to state that such directives 'shall avoid imposing administrative, financial and legal constraints in a way which would hold back the creation and development of small and medium-sized undertakings'. This shows once again the concern with 'economic realism' which characterises present-day EU social policy.

The areas of Community concern referred to are the following (Article 118(2) EC Treaty):

- improvement of the working environment in order to protect workers' safety;

- working conditions;

- information and consultation of workers;

- the integration of persons excluded from the labour market;

- equality between men and women regarding work opportunities and treatment at work.

The new Articles 118a and 118b enshrine a principle which for some time now has characterised the European approach towards industrial relations, to wit dialogue between the 'social partners' (management and labour). The Commission has the task of promoting the consultation of management and labour at the community level. It is to take any relevant measure aimed at facilitating this dialogue by ensuring balanced support for the parties (Article 118a(1) EC Treaty). For this purpose, the Commission must consult management and labour on the possible direction of Community action before submitting proposals in this field (Article 118a(2) EC Treaty) and on the contents of the envisaged proposal (Article 118a(3) EC Treaty). Where management and labour so desire, the dialogue between them at Community level may lead to contractual relations (Article 118b(1) EC Treaty).

Under Article 118c, the Commission is to encourage the Member States to co-operate and facilitate the co-ordination of their action in all social policy fields covered by the EC Treaty, particularly in the areas of employment, labour law and working conditions, basic and advanced vocational training; social security, the prevention of occupational accidents and diseases, occupational hygiene and the rights of association and collective bargaining between employers and workers.

III   The institutional and legislative framework

Social policy in the EU has created its own institutional framework. The main fund to have been established in the context of EU social policy is the European Social Fund (ESF). Its general brief is described in Article 123 of the Treaty as being 'to improve employment opportunities for workers in the internal market and to contribute thereby to raising the standard of living'. It is a structural fund (Article 130b EC Treaty) which is administered by the Commission, together with a committee chaired by a Commission member and consisting of representatives of the Governments, trade unions and employers' organisations (Article 124 of the Treaty).

In the course of its existence, the ESF has undergone a number of fundamental changes. The first, which took place in 1971, conferred on the ESF the task of providing financial assistance in order to mitigate some of the undesirable social effects of certain Community policies. It was also instructed to concentrate its efforts increasingly on structural unemployment in the economically backward areas of the Community. The second change, in 1983, sought to ensure that the ESF would focus its action on the fight against youth unemployment. ESF assistance is characterised by the principle of additionality, which means that it is mainly intended to complement aid emanating from the national authorities, rather than create new programmes.

Social policy also has important legislative implications, particularly as regards the voting procedure to be used within the Council when adopting measures in this field. The United Kingdom having opted out of the Social Chapter of the TEU, the other Member States concluded amongst themselves two instruments[3] which established the procedures and mechanisms by which decisions in this field were to be adopted. As a result, social policy decisions can be divided into three groups in terms of voting procedure:

(i) those which are to be adopted by qualified majority in accordance with the conciliation procedure under Article 189c of the Treaty: improvement in the working environment to protect workers' health and safety; working conditions; the information and consultation of workers; equality between men and women regarding labour market opportunities and treatment at work, and the integration of those excluded from the labour market;

(ii) those which are subject to unanimous voting: social security and protection of workers; protection of workers where their contract of employment is terminated; representation and collective defence of the interests of workers and employers, including co-determination; conditions of employment for

---

3   The 'Protocol on Social Policy' and the 'Agreement on Social Policy concluded between the Member States of the European Community with the Exception of the United Kingdom of Great Britain and Northern Ireland'.

third-country nationals legally residing in Community territory; financial contributions for promotion of employment and job-creation;

(iii) those which are entirely excluded from Community decision-making: pay, the right of association, the right to strike and the right to impose lock-outs.

IV   The European Social Charter

This act should not to be confused with the Council of Europe instrument of the same name, adopted in 1961 and consisting of 38 Articles. As has been noted earlier, the EU Social Charter was adopted by the European Council in May 1989 by all the existing Member States except for the United Kingdom. It sets out the basic rights of workers, and lays down 13 fundamental principles:

- the right to move from one EU Member State to another for the purpose of employment;

- the right to fair remuneration;

- the right to exercise any occupation on the same terms as those applied to workers employed in the host state;

- the right to improved living and working conditions;

- the right to social protection under the existing national systems, together with a minimum income for those unable to obtain employment or those who are no longer entitled to unemployment benefit;

- the right to freedom of association and collective bargaining;

- the right to vocational training;

- the right men and women to equal treatment;

- the right of workers to information, consultation and participation;

- the right to the protection of health and safety at work;

- the protection of children and adolescents;

- a guaranteed minimum standard of living for the elderly;

- improved social and professional integration for the disabled.

Under Article 27 of the Charter, it is first and foremost for the national authorities of the Member States to implement these provisions, even though Article 28 enables the Commission to make proposals for the enactment of implementing measures coming within the Community's existing jurisdiction. The Charter is backed up by an Action Programme of 47 initiatives, of which 29 require binding legislative action. Progress in implementing these has been disappointing, the only real achievement in this regard being Regulation 91/533 on the obligation of the employer to inform his employees of the terms and conditions of their contract of employment.[4] Some of the measures formally adopted under the Social Charter are in fact little more than rules adopted under policies which already existed before the Social Charter.

Mention has already been made of the ambiguous legal status of the Social Charter. Charlesworth and Cullen are probably right where they describe the implementation of the Social Charter as 'a combination of the Community approach of adopting binding measures at Community level and the international human rights law approach of Member State implementation supervised by a reporting system'.[5] The 'reporting system' in question is that provided under Article 29, which requires the Commission to submit an annual report on the implementation of the Social Charter by the Member States and the EU. Whether 'reporting systems' constitute as robust a method of enforcing the rights of citizens is open to debate.

V   Working conditions

As has been noted earlier, Article 118 of the Treaty empowers the Council to adopt measures aimed at improving the working environment, in order to protect the workers' health and safety. The most significant legislative action thus far for this purpose has been Directive 89/391[6] on measures to encourage improvements in the safety and health of workers at work. It has a very wide scope, including as it does all areas of activity in the public and the private sector – even though certain activities of the public sector, such as the armed forces and the police, are excluded from it (Article 2 of the Directive). The Directive is a framework instrument, in that it makes provision for the adoption of more detailed directives on specific points (included some listed in the Annex) (Article 16). Examples of such directives are Directive 92/85 on pregnant workers who have recently given birth or are breast feeding[7] and Directive 92/57 implementing minimum health and safety requirements on temporary or mobile work sites.[8] For the purpose of updating these directives, the Commission is assisted by a Committee consisting of Member State representatives and chaired by a Commission member (Article 17 of the Directive).

The two main sections of the Directive concern the obligations of the employer and those of the worker in this field. However, it is clear from the wording of the provisions in question that the main burden falls upon the

---

4   OJ 1991 L 288.
5   Charlesworth, A and Cullen, C, *op cit*, p 390.
6   OJ 1989 L 183.
7   OJ 1992 L 348.
8   OJ 1992 L 245.

employers. By way of general obligations, employers are bound to take all such measures as are necessary for the safety and health protection of workers, including prevention of occupational risks and the provision of information and training (Article 6(1) of the Directive). These measures must be carried out in accordance with a series of general principles of prevention, being risk avoidance, risk evaluation, combating risk at source, adapting the work to the individual, adapting to technical progress, replacing the dangerous by the non-dangerous or less dangerous; developing a coherent overall prevention policy, giving collective protective measures precedence over individual protective measures, and giving suitable instructions to the workers (Article 6(2) of the Directive).

The employers are also bound to observe specific obligations. Thus they must put into place protective and preventive services, and to this end appoint one or more workers who are competent in this field; if no such workers are available, outside forces must be brought in to discharge this obligation (Article 7 of the Directive). Employers must also take appropriate measures to ensure first aid, firefighting and evacuation facilities for the benefit of the workers (Article 8 of the Directive). In addition, they must fulfil such obligations as being in possession of an assessment of the risk to their workers, decide on the protective measures to be taken and the protective equipment to be used, and keep a list of such occupational accidents as have caused workers to be unfit for work for over three days (Article 9(1) of the Directive). They must also ensure that the workers are adequately informed of the risks they face and the measures taken to forswear them (Article 10 of the Directive), that the workers are satisfactorily involved in this exercise (Article 11 of the Directive) and provide adequate training in this regard for their workers (Article 12 of the Directive).

The workers' obligations are equally divided into the general and the specific. By way of general duties, the workers must take care as far as possible of his own safety and that of others affected by his actions (Article 13(1) of the Directive). Their specific obligations are to use correctly the machinery, equipment, tools and substances involved in their work; make proper use of such personal protective equipment as is made available to them; refrain from doing anything irresponsible with safety devices fitted to machinery, tools and equipment; inform the management of any danger to health and safety in the workplace; and to co-operate with the employer to protect health and safety and work (Article 13(2) of the Directive).

VI   Labour relations

EU action in this regard has been aimed at providing the worker with certain minimum safeguards in his or her relationship with the employer under his or her contract of employment. The first major initiative in this regard occurred in 1975, with the adoption of a Directive on the harmonisation of laws regarding collective redundancies.[9] The scope of this Directive extends to dismissals by an employer of a certain percentage of his or her workforce (normally around 10 per cent) and makes provision for extensive information and consultation of the workforce prior to such a step, as well as certain procedural safeguards. It does not apply to collective redundancies affected under short term contracts, to workers employed in the public sector, or to shipping crews.

Mention should also be made in this regard of Directive 77/187 which safeguards employees' rights in the event of transfers of a business to another employer as a result of a legal transfer.[10] The safeguards in question concern mainly protection against dismissal and the protection of the social security rights of those affected. However, in order to be applicable, the firm in question retain its identity, and its activity must be continued or resumed, even if there has been a change in the natural or legal person responsible for managing the business.[11] It does not apply where an employee terminates his or her contract with the first employer and enters into a new contract with a second firm, performing the same work, if there has been no concomitant transfer from one business to the other of important tangible or intangible assets, or a taking over by the new employer of a significant part of the workforce.[12]

Thirdly, there is the Insolvency's Directive, adopted in 1980.[13] Here again, the object is to protect the interests of the workers – in particular their remuneration – against the effects of decisions and developments beyond their control – in this case, the bankruptcy of their firm. It compels the Member States to establish an appropriate guarantee body, and to ensure that this body will be in a position to meet any outstanding claims for wages by the workers affected.

Mention should also be made of the Directive establishing the European Works Council[14] (EWC). This instrument requires firms employing at least 1,000 workers within the territory of one Member State, and 150 workers in two

---

9   Directive 75/129, OJ 1975 L 48, as amended by Directive 92/56, OJ 1992, L 245.

10   OJ 1977 L 61.

11   Case 24/85, *Spijkers* (1986) 119 at 1128–29; Joined Cases C 171–94 and C-172/94, *Merckx and Neuhuys* (1996) ECR I-1253.

12   Case 13/95, *Ayse Süzen v Zehnacker Gebäudereinigung GmbH Krankenhausservice* as yet unpublished.

13   Directive 80/987 OJ 1980 L 283.

14   Directive 94/45 OJ 1994 L 64.

Member States, to set up committees representing the workforce. The EW is entitled to be informed and consulted on any measures, such as collective redundancies and transfers of location, which affect the interests of the workers. This measure constitutes the first legislative application of the Social Chapter of the TEU. As has been mentioned before, the co-operation between management and labour has, as a result of the Amsterdam Treaty, become one of the cornerstones of EU social policy (above, p 245).

VII The new title on employment

The Amsterdam Treaty inserted a new Title on Employment after Part Three, Title VI of the EC Treaty. The general aim of Community policy under this Title is to work towards a co-ordinated strategy for employment, and more particularly to promote a skilled, trained and adaptable workforce, as well as labour markets responsive to economic change (Article 1 Employment Title). The Member States must contribute towards the achievement of these objectives in a way which is consistent with the broad guidelines of the economic policies of the Member States and of the Community (Article 2(1) Employment Title).

Every year, the European Council must consider the employment situation in the Community and adopt appropriate conclusions, on the basis of a joint report by the Council and the Commission (Article 4(1) Employment Title). On the basis of the conclusions formulated by the European Council, the Council must each year draw up guidelines which the Member States must take into account in their employment policies (Article 4(2) Employment Title). In addition, every Member State must provide the Council and the Commission with an annual report on the main measures taken to implement its employment policy in the light of the guidelines for employment (Article 4(3) Employment Title). On the basis of these reports, the Council examines the implementation of the employment policies of the Member States in the light of these guidelines. If necessary, it makes appropriate recommendations to the Member States (Article 4(4) Employment Title). On the basis of the results of that examination, the Council and the Commission draw up a joint annual report and submit it to the European Council (Article 4(5) Employment Title).

The Council may adopt incentive measures designed to encourage co-operation between Member States and to support their action in the field of employment, through initiatives aimed at developing exchanges of information and best practices (Article 5 Employment Title). The Council is to establish an Employment Committee with advisory status, in order to promote co-ordination between Member States on employment and labour market policies (Article 6 Employment Title).

252

VIII Economic and social cohesion (regional policy)

Background

Even amongst the original six Member States, there were considerable differences in the standard of living between certain regions of the Community (areas of particular concern being the *Mezzogiorno* area of Southern Italy and the old industrial basins of Belgium and France). The Treaty of Rome gave recognition to this fact in its Preamble, which seeks, *inter alia*, to reduce 'the differences existing between the various regions and the backwardness of the less favoured regions'. This declaration of intent, however, was not matched by any concrete provisions in the Treaty, let alone any legislative action on the part of the Community institutions. Initially, it was thought that the realisation of the Common Market would in itself go a long way towards ironing out these differences. However, any such illusions were dispelled by the economic crises of the 1970 and early 1980s. In addition, the number of less-favoured regions increased as the Community expanded geographically. The first step in this direction was the establishment, in 1975, of the Regional Development Fund, aimed at reducing the differences between the affluent and the less affluent regions of the Community. However, it was not before the mid-1980s that a comprehensive policy on this issue emerged.

The adoption of the Single European Act was the appropriate moment to give more substance to the notion of economic and social solidarity between the regions. It inserted a new Title in Part Three of the Treaty, entitled 'Economic and Social Cohesion' (Articles 130a to 130e). The TEU added a few refinements to these new provisions – eg by specifically including rural areas amongst the least-favoured regions, and requiring the Commission to submit regular reports on progress made in this field. In addition, the TEU introduced the notion of a specific Cohesion Fund, which, under the new Article 130d, was to be established by 31 December 1993.

Aims and objectives

The general objective of economic and social cohesion policy is described in Article 130a of the Treaty as being to reduce 'the disparities between the levels of development of the various regions and the backwardness of the least-favoured regions, including rural areas'. Article 130b of the Treaty requires the Member States to gear their economic policies to this objective, and co-ordinate them accordingly. It also demands that the Community takes this aim into account in implementing the internal market, and ensure that the various financial instruments, such as the structural funds, contribute towards the achievement of these goals.

The structural funds

The financial instruments by which the EU must support the achievement of economic and social cohesion are listed in Article 130b of the Treaty as being the Structural Funds (EAGGF, Guidance Section, the ESF, the European Regional Development Fund), the European Investment Bank, and the 'other existing financial instruments'. The EAGGF, ESF and European Investment Bank have already been examined earlier. The European Regional Development Fund (ERDF) is a fund which was established in 1975, and is intended to assist the development and redevelopment of regions presenting structural deficits and of those which have a declining industrial base. The funds provided by the ERDF support both Community programmes aimed at achieving the goals of economic and social cohesion, and such national programmes which are capable of contributing towards the achievement of this objective.

As to the 'other existing financial instruments', these include (a) the European Monetary Co-operation Fund, which keeps account of short term borrowing aimed at supporting national currencies; (b) the European Development Fund, which controls the aid provided by the Community under the Lomé Convention, (c) the New Community Instrument for Borrowing and Lending, which finances structural investment projects, (d) the European Financial Instrument for the Environment, and (e) the European Investment Fund, established in 1994, which grants long-term guarantees and supports investment in, and the development of, Trans-European Networks (TENs) in the areas of transport, telecommunications and energy.

Structural fund reform

The drafters of the Single European Act were fully aware that, if their efforts at matching the internal market with measures of economic and social cohesion were to have any effect, the existing structural funds would need to be reformed in such a way as to permit an integrated approach towards the challenges set by this policy. Up to this point, the various structural funds and other financial instruments of the Community had operated on an autonomous basis. This had led not only to a lack of co-ordination between them, but also to a tendency by these funds to spread their resources too thinly over too wide a range of actions and programmes. The new system of management of the structural funds was to ensure adequate co-ordination aimed at maximising their efficiency in achieving their objectives.

The reforms were carried out by means of an outline regulation,[15] which entered into effect on 1 January 1989. The new system has the effect of co-

---

15 Regulation 2052/88 OJ 1988 L 185, as amended by Regulation 2981/93 OJ 1993 L 193. This regulation is supplemented by a consolidation regulation (Regulation 4253/88 OJ 1988 L 374) and four sectoral regulations.

Ordinating the operation of the Structural Funds, both amongst themselves and with the European Investment Bank. These funds are now governed by five guiding principles.

(i) First principle: to concentrate resources on five priority objectives

These are objectives which are directly linked to EU social, regional and agricultural policy, and seek to concentrate resources on priority objectives to be met in those regions which are experiencing the most serious economic and social difficulties. The five priority objectives are:

- to promote the development and structural adjustment of regions whose development is at a disadvantage. The regions entitled to assistance under this heading are listed in the outline regulation;

- to convert the regions and areas which are affected by industrial decline;

- to combat long-term unemployment (defined as unemployment affecting those who are aged 25 and over, and who have been out of work for more than 12 months), as well as facilitating the employment of the young and of those who are threatened with exclusion from the employment market;

- to enable the workers to adjust to industrial change and to change in manufacturing systems;

- to mitigate the social consequences of the reforms of the CAP, by (a) expediting the adjustment of production, processing and marketing structures relating to agricultural and fisheries products, and (b) enabling rural areas to achieve economic diversification.

(ii) Second principle: partnership and involvement

The new system makes provision for extensive consultations between the Commission, the Member States involved, and such appropriate authorities as have been designated by the latter, be it at the national, regional or local level. The economic and social partners should also be involved. The focus of this partnership is the formulation and implementation of the various structural programmes.

(iii) Third principle: additionality

This principle is based on the notion that the funds in question should not be used to fund programmes in their entirety. As part of the involvement of the national authorities in the actions in question, any Structural Fund assistance must be matched by at least an equivalent amount in development aid granted by the Member State in question. At the same time, this requirement ensures that the Member States do not reduce their structural expenditure and simply rely on the Community funds for their regional development.

(iv) Fourth principle: programming

Structural aid is no longer project-based, but rests on the long-term perspective of programmes carried out over a number of years. First, the appropriate authorities designated by the Member States present the Commission with a multi-annual programme, covering a period of between three to six years, which specifies the objectives pursued, as well as an indicative financial table and environmental audit. On the basis of this programme, and in consideration with the authorities in question, the Commission sets out the priorities to be observed, as well as the means of financing them, in Community Support Frameworks (CSF). On the basis of these CSFs, the authorities formulate an Operational Programme, which provide a summary of the individual sectoral measures to be implemented within the framework of the CSFs. The POs are then submitted to the Commission by the Member State in question.

(v) Fifth principle: observance of Community law

The Commission must ensure that the actions which are financed by the various funds do so in compliance with the provisions of the Treaty and of the legislation adopted under them, as well as with EU policies. Special regard must be had to four aspects of Community law in this connection: equality of opportunity between men and women, the Community rules on public procurement, competition law and environmental policy.[16] On this last point, it should be recalled that the various development plans must contain an environmental audit.

IX   Trans-European networks (TENs)

Background

Closely related to regional policy is the opportunity to establish Trans-European Networks (TENs). The object is to enable other forms of human organisation than the nation state to enter fully into the spirit of the Internal Market. It is a recognised fact that the integration of national markets through this internal market project can only yield the desired economic and social benefits by making it possible for the economic operators to enjoy trans-European networks in transport, telecommunications and energy.

The social and economic benefits which stand to be made from these trans-European networks are considerable. It enables the EU to set in motion a comprehensive programme aimed at upgrading transport, communication and energy networks, thus complementing the various below structure policies

16   Constantinho, P and Dony, M, *op cit, p* 193.

targeted at the revisions under the various structural funds. They are also intended to buttress other initiatives seeking to improve EU competitiveness by enabling strategically important networks to be developed, and by ensuring that such networks are not choked by bottlenecks or other constraints which could have the effect of imposing needless costs on industry.[17]

The creation of such networks enables the best possible use to be made of the various legal instruments which govern the operation of the internal market.[18] It is interesting to note, however, that they pull in the opposite direction of complete liberalisation, based as they are on the principles of co-operation, co-ordination and standardisation.[19] Nevertheless, it would be a mistake to conclude, as some have done, that their purpose was to increase public spending in order to compensate for a temporary decline in private spending – in other words, a neo-Keyenisan exercise in demand management. Although the TENs involve increases in public expenditure, and therefore represent an injection of demand into the economy, the large-scale and long-term nature of the projects involved entails that their short term effect in curbing a downturn in the economy will of necessity be extremely modest.[20]

The Treaty provisions

Because of the central role which these networks were capable of playing in the internal market, the drafters of the TEU decided to provide a legal basis for the setting up of such networks. The principal object was to enable the citizens, economic operators and regional and local authorities to derive the benefit of such networks. More particularly account was taken of the need to link areas such as islands, peripheral areas and landlocked regions to the geographical centre of the EU.[21] Accordingly, a new Title XII (Articles 129b to 129d) on trans-European Networks was added to the Treaty.

In order to realise these networks, the Community institutions are required under Article 129c(1) of the Treaty to take the following initiatives:

• they are to establish a series of guidelines covering the objectives, priorities and broad lines of measures envisaged in this field; more particularly these guidelines are intended to identify projects of common interest;

• they are to implement such measures as may prove necessary to ensure the inter-operability of the networks, particularly in the field of technical standardisation;

17 Barbour, P, *The European Handbook* (1996), Fitzroy Dearborrm, pp 190–91.
18 Moussis, N, *Access to European Union* (5th edn, 1995), Edit-Eur, p 114.
19 Scott, C, 'European Community Utilities Law and Policy' in: Shaw, J and More, G, *New Legal Dynamics of the European Union* (1995), Clarendon Press, pp 213–14.
20 Barbour, P, *op cit*, p 190.
21 Moussis, N, *op cit*, p 114.

- they may support the financial efforts made by the Member States for such projects of common interest as are financed by the latter, in particular through feasibility studies, loan guarantees or interest rate subsidies. The Community may also contribute to specific projects on transport infrastructure through the Cohesion Fund (above, p 253).

The guidelines referred to above are to be adopted by the Council, applying the conciliation and veto procedure of Article 189b of the Treaty, and after having consulted the Economic and Social Committee. The other measures provided in Article 129c(1) are to be adopted using the co-operation procedure of Article 189c of the Treaty, after having consulted both the Economic and Social Committee and the Committee of the Regions (Article 129d).

In addition, the EU institutions may decide to co-operate with non-Member States for the purpose of promoting projects of mutual interest, and in order to ensure the inter-operability of networks (Article 129c(3) of the Treaty).

Subsequent developments

In principle, to be eligible for support under this programme, the projects in question must meet a number of criteria, such as their importance for the regional economy, their employment-creation potential, and not least their impact on the environment. However, in the light of recent developments, it is clear that the main object of the exercise is to support EU-wide network development. In the area of transport, for example, although the first 30 odd TEN projects to receive approval were concentrated in a few regions, their potential impact could be equally felt in the more remote regions. This is particularly true for the programme which aims to link up core areas such as London and Amsterdam, Madrid and Perpignan, Lyon and Turin, as well as Paris and Berlin. Although these are all relatively wealthy areas of the EU, the plan in question can be justified in terms of regional assistance in that it helps to reduce travel times to, and between the peripheral areas of the EU.[22] In 1996, the Commission produced a number of guidelines for the development of a TEN transport network up to the year 2010, and set out the criteria and specifications applicable to projects of common interest in this sector.[23]

Since the insertion of the rules on TENs into the Treaty by the TEU, the rules on the financing of the projects in question have also been placed on a sounder footing. The financial instruments concerned are now the Financial Instrument for Cohesion, certain actions for which provision is made in the rules on Structural Funds for the 1994–99 periods, and the temporary loan mechanism of the EIB.[24] In 1994, the Commission presented a draft Regulation setting out the

22 Barbour, P, *op cit*, pp 190–91.
23 General Report 1996, p 141.
24 Moussis, N, *op cit*, p 115.

rules for the granting of EU financial assistance under the TEN programme.[25] In 1996, approval was given for the spending of 314 million ECU's on TENs.[26] This represented an increase of 15 per cent compared to the previous year.

25   OJ 1994 C 89.

26   General Report 1996, p 141.

14 Discrimination Based on Gender

Background and fundamental concepts

Included among the social policy provisions of the Treaty is Article 119. This is a provision which has been expanded by the Amsterdam Treaty, even though the underlying principles remain the same.

Article 119(1) requires Member States to ensure and maintain the principle that men and women should receive equal pay for equal work. It should be borne in mind, however, that the object of this provision is not only social, but also economic, since it prevents Member States from deriving any competitive advantage over another through any shortcomings in this field. It is a provision which hitherto has given rise to more derived legislation and case law than any other aspect of EU social policy, which is why, in this book, it is dealt with under a separate heading.

Article 119(1) EC Treaty is an updated version of the first paragraph of the original Article 119, which was held by the ECJ to be a Treaty provision with direct effect. This direct effect is not only vertical, in that the national authorities are bound by the principle towards their citizens, but also horizontal, in that private parties – in particular private employers – are also obliged to comply with it.[1] The Community institutions have endeavoured to give Article 119(1) as wide a scope as possible. Thus it has extended the concept of 'discrimination' to cover not only direct, but also indirect discrimination. Direct, or 'overt', discrimination is at all times unlawful, and arises where similar situations are treated differently or different situations are treated similarly. Indirect discrimination, on the other hand, arises as a result of practices which, *prima facie*, are based on neutral considerations but which have the concrete effect of putting one sex at a disadvantage towards the other. Indirect discrimination is not necessarily unlawful where it is capable of objective justification. Similarly, whereas Article 199 refers to 'equal pay for equal value', the adoption of the 1975 Equal Pay Directive[2] means that Community law terminology has moved towards the more comprehensive notion of 'remuneration for work of equal value' as used in the International Labour Organisation Convention No 100 of 1951.[3]

1 Case 43/75, *Defrenne v SABENA* (1976) ECR 455 at 473.
2 Directive 75/117, OJ 1975 L 45.
3 Tillotson, J, *op cit*, p 310.

II   The scope of the notion of 'pay'

Article 119(2) EC Treaty defines 'pay' as 'the ordinary basic or minimum wage or salary and any other consideration, whether in cash or in kind, which the worker receives, directly or indirectly, in respect of employment from his employer'. Although quite specific by the standards of the Treaty, this definition still leaves plenty of scope for interpretation. In the First *Defrenne* case,[4] the question was raised as to the applicability of Article 119 of the Treaty to Belgian legislation relating to retirement pensions, and which excluded air hostesses from its scope. The plaintiff argued that there was a direct and necessary relationship between pensions and salaries. The Court of Justice, however, followed the opinion of the Commission, and ruled that, although in principle the nature of social security payments was not alien to the notion of 'pay':

> there cannot be brought within this concept, as defined by Article 119, social security schemes or benefits, in particular retirement pensions, directly governed by legislation without any element of agreement within the undertaking or the occupational branch concerned, which are obligatorily applicable to general categories of workers.[5]

Consistently with this decision, the ECJ held, in *Worringham and Humphreys*[6] and in *Barber*[7] that a private occupational pension scheme whose members had opted out of the state pension system did constitute 'pay' within the scope of Article 119. Equally, in *Bilka-Kaufhaus*,[8] 'the contractual, rather than the statutory nature' of the pension scheme in question brought it within the ambit of Article 119. Exactly why the element of agreement or contractual nature of the scheme is so important a criterion in deciding whether pensions should be included in the notion of 'pay' is not clear to the present author. This interpretation by the Court is all the more baffling because in other cases the 'non-agreed' nature of an entitlement did not appear to play a particularly decisive role in the Court's ruling. Thus in *Rinner-Kühn*,[9] statutory sick pay was held to fall within the meaning of the notion of pay; similarly, in *Bötel*,[10] indemnities statutorily payable to workers for workers attending 'day-release' training courses were also held to constitute 'pay'.

---

4   Case 80/70, *Defrenne v Belgium* (1971) ECR 445.
5   Case 80/70, *op cit*, at 451.
6   Case 69/80, *Worringham and Humphries v Lloyds Bank Limited* (1981) ECR 767.
7   Case C-262/88, *Barber v Guardian Royal Exchange* (1990) ECR I-1889.
8   Case 170/84, *Bilka-Kaufhaus GmbH v Karin Weber von Hartz* (1986) ECR 1607.
9   Case 171/88, *Rinner-Kühn v FWW Spezial-Gebäudereinigung GmbH* (1989) ECR 2743.
10 Case C-360/90, *Arbeitswohlfahrt der Stadt Berlin v Bötel* (1992) ECR I-3589.

In other decisions, however, the Court has tended to mitigate the strict line on statutory pensions taken in the First Defrenne decision. *Liefting*[11] also concerned a statutory pension scheme. However, in this case it was the fact that the pension scheme in question applied to a particular group of workers which caused the Court to distinguish *Defrenne (No 1)*.[12] Yet here again, the Court appears to make certain spurious distinctions. In *Liefting*, it held that benefits which the public authorities are required to pay become 'pay' within the meaning of Article 119 of the Treaty where they are included in calculating their employees' gross pay, on the basis of which other salary benefits were calculated. In *Newstead v Department of Transport*,[13] however, the ECJ ruled that a deduction made from a civil servant's pay fell outside the scope of Article 119 because it resulted in the reduction of the net pay of the employees in question. Here again, it is hard to grasp exactly why the gross or net nature of the salaries in question is so decisive in assessing the applicability of Article 119 of the Treaty.

Other recent decisions by the Court relating to pension schemes have only served to add a note of confusion to an area already riddled with uncertainty. In the *Neath*[14] and *Coloroll*[15] decisions, the disputed benefits were the contributions made by employers to a contracted-out occupational pension scheme. These are known as 'defined benefit' schemes, because the pension which employees receive under them is fixed in advance in accordance with certain actuarial criteria. The Advocate-General, Walter Van Gerven, had proposed that any pension scheme, irrespective of the nature of the scheme – whether statutory or contracted out, voluntary or compulsory – should constitute 'pay' within the meaning of Article 119. The Court, however, made yet another of these specious distinctions which are becoming the hallmark of its case law in this area. It ruled that the pension itself constituted pay, but that neither the contributions of the employer, nor the lump sum which was payable to the male (but not to the female) employees involved, could be covered by this notion. Thus an excellent opportunity to settle on a broad and acceptable set of criteria to determine the notion of 'pay' was lost.

Apart from pension schemes, the Court has tended to entertain a broad interpretation of the concept of 'pay'. In *Garland*,[16] the disputed entitlement was formed by the travel facilities awarded to retired railway male employees and

---

11   Case 23/83, *Liefting v Directie van het Academisch Ziekenhuis bij de Universiteit van Amsterdam* (1984) ECR 5225.

12   Steiner, J, *op cit*, p 252.

13   Case 192/85 (1987) ECR 4753.

14   Case C-152/91, *Neath v Hugh Steeper Ltd* (1993) ECR I-6935.

15   Case C-200/91, *Coloroll Pension Trustees Ltd v Russell* (1994) ECR-I 4389.

16   Case 12/81, *Garland v British Rail Engineering Limited* (1982) ECR 359.

their families, but not to their female counterparts. The Court placed these benefits within the scope of Article 119 of the Treaty, from which it may be extrapolated that non-contractual benefits, as a general rule, should in principle be regarded as 'pay'. In *Kowalski*,[17] severance pay negotiated under a collective bargaining agreement was held to fall within the purview of Article 119. Even the expatriation allowances paid by the Community institutions to their staff (*quis custodiet custodes ipsos!*) come within the meaning of this term.[18] The Court seems to have drawn the line at working conditions which, although freely negotiated as part of the contract of employment, have no direct pecuniary implications. In the *Third Defrenne* case,[19] the plaintiff complained about the fact that the age of retirement for female employees was different from that of their male colleagues. It could, however, just as plausibly be argued that a difference in retirement age does have economic consequences for those affected in terms of the extra years' entitlements which the person subjected to the lower retirement age is compelled to forego.

III The position of part-timers

The position of part-timers constitutes a good example of the condition of 'indirect discrimination' referred to earlier (above, p 261). Indirect discrimination, it will be recalled, is the effect of practices which, on the face of it, treat men and women equally, but in practice place one sex at a disadvantage compared to the other. Because women make up the majority of part-time workers, any difference in treatment to which they are subjected could be regarded as indirect discrimination against women, in the absence of any objective justification. In the case of *Jenkins v Kingsgate (Clothing Productions) Ltd*,[20] the main action had been brought by a part-timer who received, *pro rata*, 10 per cent less than full-time workers performing the same work. The Court ruled that lower rates for part-time workers did not in themselves constitute discrimination as prohibited by Article 119. However, the ECJ went on the state that if fewer women than men worked the minimum number of hours required to rank as full-timers, the inequality in pay would infringe Article 119 if, in view of the difficulties which women experience in practice in reaching this minimum working week, the only possible explanation for the difference in pay is discrimination based on gender. If there were objective factors to justify this difference, however, there would be no infringement of Article 119. The national court would have to decide whether this was the case; the onus of proof would, however, be on the employer.

17 Case C-33/89 (1990) ECR I-2591.
18 Case 32/71, *Sabbatini v European Parliament* (1972) ECR 345.
19 Case 149/77, *Defrenne v SABENA* (1979) ECR 1365.
20 Case 96/80 (1981) ECR 911.

In *Jenkins*, the ECJ fell short of explaining the criteria on the basis of which such objective justification could be accepted. This shortcoming was remedied in *Bilka-Kaufhaus*.[21] In this case, a part-timer had complained that the pension scheme operated by her employer discriminated against her. The reason for this was that she could only claim pension rights after having been employed for 15 out of 20 years, whereas full-time workers did not need to meet this condition. The employers justified the difference in treatment by the fact that part-timers were less economic as a workforce, since they were more reluctant to work unsociable hours. Although the ECJ, in the time-honoured fashion, once again held that it was for the national court to decide whether the arguments of the employer constituted objective justification, in this decision at least it provided the referring court with a set of closely-defined criteria for assessing whether or not this was the case. The criteria which had to be met by an employer claiming objective justification were that (a) the difference in treatment had to meet the genuine need of the firm; (b) that it was appropriate for achieving the objectives pursued by the firm, and (c) that it was necessary for that purpose. The Court appears to have applied the proportionality principle here in the same manner as it did in the *Cassis de Dijon* case.[22]

In *Rinner Kuhn*,[23] the Court added a further refinement to these criteria. The disputed difference here concerned sick pay, which was only available to employees working a minimum number of hours, thus in effect excluding part-timers from its scope. The employer argued that the difference was justified on the grounds that part-timers were less integrated into the business than full-timers. Such arguments, said the Court, amounted to general statements rather than objective justification. Nor did the Court accept the argument put forward by the German government, intervening, that part-time workers were less dependent on their wages than full-timers. The Court appears here to have drawn the traditional distinction between a reason and an excuse – in other words, the employer or any other interested party must provide objective justification rather than objective reasons.

Two further recent cases also illustrate the extent of the burden of proof which the Court has placed on the employers in this regard. In *Nimez*,[24] the dispute concerned the complaint that part-time workers were compelled to work twice as long as full-timers in order to have access to a higher grading. The employer, the City of Hamburg, pleaded the objective justification that full-time employees acquired more rapidly the abilities and skills relating to a particular job, whereas the German Government claimed that the greater

21 Case 170/84, *Bilka-Kaufhaus GmbH v Weber von Harz* (1986) ECR 1607. See also Case C-184/89, *Nimz v Frei- und Hansestadt Hamburg* (1991) ECR 297.

22 Case 120/78, *op cit*, p 662.

23 Case 171/88, *Rinner-Kuhn v FWW Spezial Gebäudereinigung GmbH* (1989) ECR 2743.

24 Case C-184/89, *op cit*.

experience of such workers also justified the difference in treatment. The Court held that the objective nature of such claims depended on the circumstances of each particular case. The ECJ therefore re-iterated the point made in *Rinner-Kuhn* that generalisations about the attributed of part-time workers are unlikely to constitute grounds for justifying differences which have a disproportionate impact on one gender.[25] In *Bötel*, the applicant had taken paid leave in order to attend a training course. Although this course required her attendance for periods which were longer than her part-time hours, the employer only paid her replacement wages in respect of her part-time hours. The Court ruled that there was no objective justification for this difference, which could discourage part-time workers from attending training courses.

IV   Effect in time

That legislation should not be retrospective in its effect has long been regarded as a fundamental principle of natural justice. Greater controversy surrounds the question whether the case law which interprets legislation can also have this effect. This question was raised in relation to the case law based on Article 119 of the Treaty, and the Equal Pay Directive (75/117). The issue was raised more particularly because of the potentially costly implications which the various decisions discussed above – in particular the *Barber* ruling – could have on pension schemes, particularly those which were contracted out, which saw themselves faced with the prospect of having to recalculate the amounts paid to men and women with effect from the date on which Article 119 and/or the Equal Pay directive became enforceable. This is why, in the *Barber* judgment, the Court held that, in relation to pension schemes, Article 119 of the Treaty would have direct effect only after the judgment (the only exception being those claims which had already been brought before the national courts at the time of the *Barber* ruling). Thus pension schemes became exempt from the retroactivity of the *Barber* ruling.[26]

The Court appears to have allowed itself to be swayed by some of the more histrionic claims made by the United Kingdom Government about the probable cost of such retrospective action, which it estimated at anything between £33,000 million and £45,000 million. In addition, it gave some weight to the claims made by certain governments that, by failing to take any corrective action under Article 169 against those states who had failed to bring their legislation into line with the equal pay principle of Article 119 and Directive 75/117. Since these governments were in effect pleading their own guilt in order to create an estoppel, the Court allowed itself to break the rule which states *nemo auditur suam turpitudinem allegans* (no-one is allowed to plead his

25   Craig, P, and de Burca, G, *op cit*, p 810.
26   Case 262/88, *op cit*.

own guilt as a defence). Not for the first time, the Court gave precedence to expediency over justice. At least it had the grace to recognise that it was undermining the principle of legal certainty by ruling as it did.

V   Equal pay for equal work

The principle that men and women should receive equal pay for equal work was refined and complemented by Directive 75/117,[27] known as the Equal Pay Directive. Article 1(1) of the Directive defines the equal pay principle as meaning that 'for the same work or for work to which equal value is attributed, the elimination of all discrimination on grounds of sex with regard to all aspects and conditions of remuneration'. The Court of Justice has held that this Article merely restates the principle laid down in the original Article 119 of the Treaty.[28] The principle 'Equal pay for equal work' has therefore been refined, rather than changed, to that of 'equal pay for work of equal value'. Others, however, believe that the scope of Article 1 was to extend the rule stated in Article 119 of the Treaty.[29] Certainly it is legitimate to ask the question why the Council bothered to use a different formulation if all it did was to restate the Article 119 rule. This does not mean that the two provisions are interchangeable. The relationship between the two provisions is usually clarified by the following rule of thumb: if a national court is able to identify discrimination solely on the basis of Article 119 of the Treaty, the latter will be applied and be directly effective. If, on the other hand, discrimination can only be discerned by using additional criteria, reliance will be placed on a combined effect of the Directive and its national implementing provisions.[30]

At all events, Article 1(2) of the Directive adds a useful criterion for assessing the equivalence referred to in Article 1(1) of the Directive, where it states:

> In particular, where a job classification system is used for determining pay, it must be based on the same criteria for both men and women and so drawn up as to exclude any discrimination on grounds of sex.

It is important to stress, however, that Article 1(2) of the Directive is merely illustrative. It cannot be read as meaning that there is no equal pay requirement if no such job evaluation scheme exists. This was emphasised in *Commission v United Kingdom*.[31] The British legislation in question only imposed equal pay where the work performed by a man and a woman were rated as equivalent on

---

27   OJ 1975 L 45.
28   Case 96/80, *op cit*, at 927.
29   Nielsen, R and Szyszczak, E, *The Social Dimension of the European Community* (1991), Handelshøjskolens Forlag, p 87.
30   Tillotson, J, *op cit*, p 322.
31   Case 61/81 (1982) ECR 2601.

the basis of a job evaluation scheme. Such a scheme was, however, subject to the consent of the employer. The Court held that the United Kingdom was in breach of Community law, and was subsequently compelled to amend the relevant legislation.

Indirect discrimination is also capable of rearing its head in a job evaluation scheme which, on the face of it, makes the same demands of men as of women. This was highlighted in the case of *Rummler v Dato-Druck GmbH*.[32] The job evaluation scheme was part of a collective bargaining agreement fixing wage rates in the printing industry. One of the criteria used was the ability to lift heavy parcels. It was claimed that this had a discriminatory effect on women employees in view of the muscular effort involved. The Court held that such a criterion was not necessarily discriminatory, as long as (a) the system as a whole precluded discrimination based on gender, and (b) the criterion in question was capable of objective justification, both by being relevant to the tasks carried out, and by corresponding to a genuine need of the firm in question. The condition of 'relevance', however, seems to raise as many questions as it answers. Any court called upon to take a decision taking into account this condition will need to examine very closely the requirements of each type of employment in respect of which the discrimination is being claimed.

The *Rummler* case turned on the evaluation of very precise criteria. However, broadly-worded criteria can also give rise to accusations of indirect discrimination. Thus in *Danfoss*,[33] a trade union brought an action on behalf of a group of women employees whose earnings were seven per cent lower than those received by their male colleagues covered by the same collective bargaining agreement. This difference was accounted for by bonus payments which could be earned on the basis of such criteria as flexibility and seniority. It was claimed that these criteria, which by themselves were neutral, were being applied in such a way as to produce a discriminatory effect. The Court ruled that there was nothing to prevent employers from using criteria such as flexibility or seniority when determining pay levels. However, the employees were entitled to know exactly on what basis compliance with such criteria were being assessed. The Court pointed out that it had already, in an earlier decision,[34] condemned a system of recruitment based on lack of transparency as being contrary to the principle of equal access to employment. The onus was therefore on the employer to prove that his use of these criteria is not discriminatory. Any other solution would deprive female workers whose pay was on average lower than male workers of any effective means of enforcing the principle of equal pay before the national courts.

32 Case 237/85 (1986) ECR 2101.
33 Case 109/88, *Handels-OG Kontorfunktionærernes Forbund i Danmark v Dansk Arbejdsgiverforening, ex parte Danfoss* (1989) ECR 3199.
34 Case 318/86, *Commission v France* (1988) ECR 3559.

VI Equality of treatment

Derived legislation has extended the prohibition of discrimination based on gender beyond that of pay. It was felt that Community action to achieve the principle of equality of treatment in such areas as access to employment and vocational training and promotion, as well as other working conditions, was a necessary corollary to the Equal Pay Directive. This was achieved with the enactment of Directive 76/207,[35] known as the Equal Treatment Directive, using the 'catch-all' provisions of Article 235 as a legal basis. The Directive prohibits any discrimination in the areas mentioned above, be it direct or indirect (Article 2(1) of the Directive).

The Directive does not, however, prevent Member States from excluding from the scope of the directive those occupations for which, because of the nature of the work involved, gender is the determining criterion (Article 2(2) of the Directive). Given the rules of interpretation applied by the Court, which are discussed elsewhere in this work (above, p 38), one might expect the Court to interpret this rule against those who rely on it. However, the Court has not done so, if *Commission v United Kingdom*,[36] is anything to go by. This was one of the rare cases where it was claimed that the male of the species claimed had been at the sharp end of discriminatory practice. The Commission had arraigned the UK because it considered that the restrictions which the latter placed on men as regards access to the profession of midwife constituted gender discrimination. The British Government claimed that the profession of midwife involved specific sensibilities which made these restrictions necessary. The ECJ agreed, and ruled that the UK had not exceeded its powers under this provision of the Equal Access Directive.

Equality of access to employment was the contentious issue in *Dekker*.[37] Here, the plaintiff had been offered employment, only to have it withdrawn once it was learned that the prospective employee was pregnant. The employer pleaded economic necessity, on the grounds that he would not have been able to recover from the social insurance fund the cost of the maternity benefit which he was bound to pay. Therefore, in his view, there had not occurred any discrimination. The Court was not impressed. It held that refusal to employ on grounds of pregnancy constituted overt discrimination, which could not be excused on grounds of economic necessity.

Some have seen in the *Dekker* decision an extension of the notion of indirect discrimination. The reason why the offer had been withdrawn from the prospective employee was that she was pregnant. Since only women can

---

35 OJ 1976 L 39.
36 Case 165/82 (1983) ECR 3431.
37 Case C-177/88, *Dekker v Stichting Vormingscentrum voor Jonge Volwassenen* (1990) ECR I-3941.

become pregnant, her gender must have been the reason for her failure to be recruited.[38] However, illnesses which occur as a result of pregnancy are a different matter. This was the subject matter of the dispute in yet another action brought by the main Danish white-collar workers union.[39] In this case, a female employee had been dismissed on grounds of persistent illness, which arose from a pregnancy which had occurred a few years earlier. The Court held that illnesses which resulted from pregnancy, and which arose after maternity leave, should be treated like any other ailment which could also be suffered by a man. The Court's reasoning is a little hard to follow if the rule in *Dekker* is interpreted in the general manner suggested at the beginning of this paragraph. For if dismissal for reasons of pregnancy is something which by its nature can only affect women, the same surely applies to illnesses resulting from pregnancy,

Equality of access to training was one of the issues involved in the *Danfoss* case which has been discussed earlier.[40] In addition, to discrimination in remuneration, it was claimed that the employer in question had discriminated against the female employees in question as regards access to training. The Court ruled, however, that vocational training offered only to a category of workers who were predominantly male did not constitute a discriminatory practice where the employer could prove that there was an objective justification for doing so. This was found to be the case, because the training in question had been offered for duties which had been required of employees, the vast majority of whom were male.

Reverse discrimination is also contrary to the principles laid down in Directive 76/207. In *Kalanke*,[41] the ECJ was asked to rule on the question whether certain arrangements applied by the German Land of Bremen on equality of treatment in the public services were consistent with this Community measure. The rules in question laid down that where employees are recruited or assigned to a higher position, women possessing qualifications equivalent to those of their male counterparts should be given precedence over the latter if the area in question underrepresented women – more particularly if women did not constitute at least 50 per cent of the staff.

The Court first of all pointed to Article 2(4) of the Directive, which seeks to achieve that its provisions are applied without prejudice to measures aimed at promoting equal opportunities for men and women. The object of the directive was therefore to outlaw any direct or indirect discrimination based on gender.

38 Ellis, E, 'Recent case law of the Court of Justice on the equal treatment of women and men' (1994) CMLRev 43–75.

39 Case C-179/88, *Handels- og Kontorfunktionærernes Forbund i Danmark v Dansk Arbejdsforening, ex parte Aldi Marked* (1990) ECR I-3979.

40 Case 109/88, *op cit*.

41 Case C-450/93, *Kalanke v Freie Hansestadt Bremen* Bulletin 12-1995, not yet reported.

Nevertheless, domestic rules giving absolute and unconditional priority to women who held qualifications similar to those of their male counterparts would itself result in gender-based discrimination. They constituted a derogation from the individual rights contained in Article 2(1) of the directive, and were therefore unlawful.

However, the Amsterdam Treaty has inserted a new Article 119(4) EC Treaty, which states that, with a view to ensuring full equality in practice between men and women in working life, the principle of equal treatment shall not prevent Member States from maintaining or adopting measures providing specific advantages, which make it easier for the underrepresented gender to pursue a vocational activity or to prevent compensate for disadvantages in professional careers. It remains to be seen whether the Court considers this provision to nullify its opposition to the principle of reverse discrimination or not.

Does Directive 76/207 preclude discrimination against transsexuals? The Court replied in the affirmative to this question in Case C-13/94.[42] It held that the Directive merely was the expression, in the relevant field, of the principle of equality, which was one of the fundamental principles of Community law. It was intended to preclude any discrimination whatsoever based on gender. To tolerate such discrimination in regard to transsexuals would amount to failing to respect the dignity and freedom to which such people were entitled, and which the ECJ had an obligation to protect.[43]

The Amsterdam Treaty has also added to Article 119 a positive statement as to what equal pay without discrimination based on gender entails. Under the new second paragraph of Article 119(2), it is provided that this notion means

(a) that pay for the same work at piece rates must be calculated on the basis of the same unit of measurement;

(b) that pay for work at time rates must be the same for the same job.

Obviously, the Court of Justice will at some stage be called upon to give more substance to this new provision through its case law.

VII Social security discrimination

Community action on gender equality has sought to remove discrimination from virtually every aspect of employment. This includes social security, and to this end the Council adopted two important directives.

---

42 *P v S and Cornwall County Council Bulletin* 7/8-1996, not yet reported.
43 General Report 1996, item 1125.

The first of these is Directive 79/7,[44] which deals with discrimination in social security in general. The directive casts its net very widely. It includes in its scope the employed and the self-employed, even those whose activity is interrupted by illness of other circumstances beyond their control (Article 2). It applies not only to the traditional areas of social security, such as sickness, invalidity, old age, accident and unemployment insurance, but also the social assistance which is intended to supplement these areas (Article 3(1) of the Directive). It does not, however, apply to survivors' or family benefits. In *Smithson*,[45] the Court also excluded housing benefit from the scope of this Directive. Strictly speaking the Court was right, since housing benefit is not mentioned in Article 3(1) of the Directive. However, there have been other occasions when the Court has extended the scope of a legislative provision where it considered that the list contained in that provision was not exhaustive. It is difficult to see why the Court could not bring itself to do so in this case as well.

In this area, equal treatment means that there may not occur any discrimination in the scope of and access to the schemes, the obligation to contribute to them, or the calculation of benefits. However, Article 7 of the Directive allows the Member States to exclude from its scope (a) the determination of pensionable age for the purpose of granting old-age and retirement pensions; (b) advantages regarding old-age pension schemes granted to persons who have brought up children; (c) the granting of old-age invalidity benefit entitlements by virtue of derived entitlements of a wife; (d) the granting of increases of long term invalidity, old age, accidents at work and occupational disease benefits for a dependent wife, and (e) the consequences of exercising the right of option not to acquire rights or incur obligations under a statutory scheme.

Directive 86/378[46] organises the principle of equal treatment in occupational (as opposed to statutory) social security schemes. It is worded in virtually identical terms to Directive 79/7, which it complements. Directive 86/613[47] applies the equal treatment principle to activities, including agriculture, which are exercised in a self-employed capacity. It deals with those areas not covered by Directives 79/7 and 86/378, and is therefore essentially complementary to them.[48]

44   OJ 1979 L 6.

45   Case C 243/90, *R v Secretary of State for Social Security, ex parte Smithson* (1992) ECR I-467.

46   OJ 1986 L 225.

47   OJ 1986 L 359.

48   Steiner, J, *op cit*, p 274.

15 Intellectual Property

I   Introduction

In its present state, Community law does not embrace the law of property. Yet there is one aspect of property law which has potential implications for Community law, to wit intellectual property law. Broadly defined, intellectual property concerns the valuable rights arising from the results of the intellectual activity of one or more persons. In the main, it covers patents, copyright and trademarks. The main reason why these rules have attracted the interest of Community law is that any system of rules which regulates intellectual property seeks to protect the valuable rights in question. Intellectual property law started on a national basis, which is why the protection given to these rights was essentially national. One side-effect of this is that systems intellectual property have a tendency towards splitting up the market along national lines. This presents potential dangers for the achievement of a barrier-free internal market, and therefore requires regulation at the Community level. As the Court of Justice put it in one of its early cases dealing with intellectual property rights:

> The national rules relating to the protection of industrial property have not been unified within the Community. In the absence of such unification, the national character of the protection of industrial property and the variations between the different legislative systems on this subject are capable of creating obstacles both to the free movement of the patented products and to competition within the common market.[1]

Initially, intellectual property rights were only caught by Community law inasmuch as they were mentioned in the Treaty as having implications for the free movement of goods and for competition law. It was also caught indirectly by Article 222 EC Treaty, which provides that the Treaty shall not prejudice the rules on property ownership applied by the Member States.

Gradually, however, Community policy-makers became attracted by the notion of harmonising legislation in this field, not only by adopting derived legislation, but also by issuing primary instruments (such as the 1989 Community Patent Convention).

This chapter will deal first with the implications of intellectual property rights for the free movement of goods and competition law, and subsequently describe the main initiatives taken in harmonising legislation.

---

1   Case 24/67, *Parke Davis v Probel & Centrafarm* (1968) ECR 55.

II Intellectual property and the free movement of goods

General

It has already been noted earlier (above, p 149) that the free movement of goods is subject to the exemption clause of Article 36 EC Treaty, which allows certain national restrictions on imports, exports or goods in transit on a number of grounds, one of which is the protection of intellectual property.

Under this safeguard clause, the Court has been compelled to walk a narrow tightrope between the need to safeguard the fundamental principles of the Community and to avoid stifling the inventiveness and ingenuity of intellectual creation by an excessively restrictive approach. It has done so by laying down from the outset that the sole restrictions on the free movement of goods allowed under this part of Article 36 were those which related to the specific subject matter of the intellectual property right in question. This was emphasised particularly in the *Deutsche Grammophon* ruling.[2] In the same decision, the ECJ drew a distinction between the existence of national intellectual property rights and their exercise; whereas it cannot deny their existence, it can certainly control their exercise.[3]

'Specific subject matter'

The notion of 'specific subject matter' has been applied by the Court to a number of specific intellectual property rights. In relation to patents, it defined this notion as the guarantee that, in order to reward the inventor's creative effort, the patentee is given the exclusive right (a) to use an invention with a view to producing industrial goods and placing them on the market for the first time, either directly or through the granting of licences for third parties, and (b) to oppose infringements.[4] In relation to trade marks, this term could be defined as the guarantee that the owner of the trade mark has the exclusive right to use it in order to place products protected by that trade mark into circulation for the first time; this guarantee is therefore intended to protect the holder against any competitors wishing to take unfair advantage of the status and reputation of the trade mark.[5] The Court has not pronounced itself expressly on that which constitutes the specific subject matter of copyright; it is, however, assumed to be very similar as that which applies to trade marks and patents.[6]

2   Case 78/70, *Deutsche Grammophon Gesellschaft v Metro-Grossmärkte* (1971) ECR 487.
3   Weatherill, S, *Cases and Materials on EC Law* (2nd edn, 1994), Blackstone, p 430.
4   Case 15/74, *Centrafarm v Sterling Drug* (1974) ECR 1147 at 1162.
5   Case 16/74, *Centrafarm v Winthrop* (1974) ECR 1183 at 1194.
6   Groves, P, *op cit*, p 144.

The Court has repeatedly used the specific subject matter criterion in order to asses whether various categories of intellectual property rights infringed the free movement of goods. Exactly how far this concept extends can be seen from the 'exhaustion of rights' principle. Suppose M Dupont has an intellectual property right protected by France. As long as he exercises this right in France, it will be protected by Article 36 of the Treaty, even if strictly speaking it does not meet the test of the *Dassonville* formula.[7] M. Dupont also has the right to use this intellectual property right in Germany or Belgium for the first time.[8] However, once he has chosen to sell a product protected by intellectual property in another Member State, he cannot subsequently object to the reimportation of that product into France. He has, in other words, exhausted his rights under the French law of intellectual property.

It should be pointed out, however, that the owner's rights will only be exhausted if the product in question has been sold abroad with his or her consent. This requirement can become particularly problematical in the case of so-called compulsory licences. These enable the licensee to manufacture the protected item subject to the payment of a royalty to the holder of the intellectual property right. This issue arose in the *Pharmon* case.[9]

Hoechst, a German pharmaceuticals firm, held a patent for a certain drug in Germany as well as parallel patents for the same product in the Netherlands and the United Kingdom. Before Hoechst had the opportunity to make and market its product in Britain, a company called DDSA had obtained a compulsory licence enabling it to produce the drug without Hoecht's consent. At a certain point, Pharmon, a Dutch company, wanted to import this product from the United Kingdom and sell it in the Netherlands. Hoechst opposed these sales, relying on its Netherlands patent. Pharmon argued that Hoechst had exhausted its rights in the United Kingdom, on the basis that a compulsory licence does not differ that much from a licence which has been freely granted, in view of the legal protection enjoyed by the patent holder and the compensation which is paid to the latter as a result of the compulsory licence. Hoechst denied this, pointing out that a compulsory licence differs from one which has been freely granted because of the absence of negotiations and of the relationship which normally exists between the patentee and a contractual licensee. Both the Commission and a host of national governments supported Hoechst in this contention. The Court came down in favour of Hoechst's viewpoint. It pointed out that whenever a compulsory licence is granted to a third party, it confers on the latter the ability to carry out production and

7 Case 15/74, *Centrafarm v Sterling Drug Inc* (1974) ECR 1147 at 1165.

8 Case 187/80, *Merck v Stephar* (1981) ECR 2063 at 280–82.

9 Case 19/84, *Pharmon BV v Hoechst BV* (1985) ECR 2281.

marketing activities which the patentee normally would have the right to prevent.[10]

The true contents of the exhaustion of rights principle has been brought out by the Court when it was required to examine this notion when applied to specific forms of intellectual property rights. This issue can raise particularly complex questions arising from (a) repackaged goods and (b) copyright holders seeking compensation for loss rather than to prevent goods from being reimported into the country where the original copyright was awarded. An example of both is given below.

Repackaged goods

What happens when the goods made under a particular trade mark are re-imported into the country where the original trade mark was awarded, not in their original unaltered form, as was the case in *Centrafarm v Winthrop*,[11] but in a repackaged form? This is what happened in *Hoffman-Laroche*.[12] The product in question was the well-known sedative 'Valium', which was sold in a different form in Germany and Britain. In the former, it was sold by its UK branch in larger packages and at lower prices than was the case in Germany. The Centrafarm company saw in this situation an opportunity for making the proverbial explosive, and bought up 'British' Valium which it placed in packages twice the size of those marketed by the UK branch of Hoffman-Laroche, and attached to these the Hoffman-Laroche trade mark as well as a statement that the tablets were marketed by Centrafarm. These it sold in Germany; in addition, Centrafarm announced its intention to sell smaller packages for individual use. Hoffman-Laroche sued Centrafarm before the German courts on the grounds that the latter had infringed its German trade mark. The matter was referred to the ECJ.

The Court held that in principle, Article 36 recognised the right of the trade mark holder to prevent the kind of practice engaged in by Centrafarm, having regard to the essential function of a trade mark. However, the Court very helpfully added those conditions under which the importing repackager could lawfully market his produce in the country of the original trade mark, since it held that any attempt by the original trade mark holder to prevent the practice complained of would be regarded as a disguised restriction on trade if (a) the use of the trade mark right by the holder, having regard to the marketing system which he has adopted, will be conducive to partitioning markets between Member States; (b) the repackaging of the products is incapable of adversely affecting the products; (c) the holder has been notified of the intention

10   *Ibid*, at 2296.
11   Case 16/74, *op cit*.
12   Case 102/77, *Hoffman-Laroche v Centrafarm* (1978) ECR 1139.

to market the repackaged product, and (d) the new packaging states the name of the person who repackaged the product.

Quick to understand, some firms took appropriate action by following what Weatherill[13] calls the Court's free legal advice, and successfully withstood a challenge to their practices before the ECJ.[14]

Claims of compensation for loss

This was the issue in a case where the scope of the exhaustion of rights principle was examined in relation to copyright.[15] GEMA, a German copyright management association, had brought an action against two companies which imported recordings of musical works protected by copyright from Britain into Germany. It was agreed between the parties that GEMA's rights had been exhausted, and that the latter's consent had been obtained for the marketing of the imported goods, which is why no attempt was made to ban the imports in question. Instead, GEMA claimed compensation amounting to the difference between the royalties payable on recordings sold in Germany and the royalties payable in Britain, which were much lower. The Court held this claim to be contrary to Article 36 of the Treaty, since:

no provision of national legislation may permit an undertaking which is responsible for the management of copyrights and has a monopoly on the territory of that Member State by virtue of that management to charge a levy on products imported from another Member State where they were put into circulation by or with the consent of the copyright owner and thereby cause the Common Market to be partitioned. Such a practice would amount to allowing a private undertaking to impose a charge on the importation of sound recordings which are already in free circulation in the Common Market on account of their crossing a frontier; it would therefore have the effect of entrenching the isolation of national markets which the Treaty seeks to abolish.[16]

The rationale for this decision is that the holder of an intellectual property right must accept the full consequences of expanding the market for the protected product. The German copyright holder had therefore to accept the British market together with all its peculiar characteristics.[17]

13 *Op cit*, at p 437.
14 Case 1/81, *Pfizer Inc v Eurim-Pharm* (1981) ECR 2913 at 2927.
15 Cases 55 and 57/80, *Musik-Vertrieb Membran v GEMA* (1981) ECR 147.
16 *Ibid*, at 163–64.
17 Weatherill, S, *op cit*, p 439.

Common origin principle

In situations where different persons in different Member States held trade marks having a common origin, it was until recently regarded as unlawful to prevent the marketing in one Member State of goods covered by one of the national trade marks merely because the holder of the trade mark enjoyed national protection in that Member State. To recognise the exercising of this right would be to confer legitimacy on the isolation of national markets. This had been established in the *First Hag* decision.[18]

The common origin principle was limited to trade marks. The reason for this was that trade marks protect the reputation of a product indefinitely, whereas the protection afforded by other intellectual property rights such as copyright or patents was of limited duration. Therefore trade marks were considered to represent a greater threat to the free movement of goods than other intellectual property rights.[19]

This approach has been subjected to a good deal of criticism,[20] and exposed the Court to the charge that it was seeking to promote market integration at the expense of national property rights.[21] In the *Second Hag* case,[22] the Court appeared to retreat from this earlier stance. Here, the Court stressed the absence of any consent to having the product marketed outside the country where the original trade mark was granted as a reason for allowing the holder of the mark in one state to prevent the marketing of similar products sold by an unrelated firm in another state.[23]

It may appear somewhat strange that a subject as vast as the incidence of intellectual property rights on the free movement of goods has been constructed almost entirely by the Court of Justice on the basis of a subclause in a sentence of a Treaty Article. The reason for this is probably that the drafters of the Treaty had not envisaged the possibility that private parties were capable of hampering the free movement of goods. As Community law has developed, however, it became increasingly clear – through mechanisms such as horizontal direct effect – that private parties were also bound by certain Treaty rules.

18 Case 192/73, *Van Zuylen Frères v Hag AG* (1974) ECR 731 at 743–44.

19 Kent, P, *European Community Law* (1991), Pitman, p 240.

20 Kemp, J, 'The Erosion of Trade Mark Rights in Europe' (1974) CMLRev 117.

21 Weatherill, S and Beaumont, P, *op cit*, p 748.

22 Case C-10/89, *CNL–Sucal v Hag* (1990) ECR I–377.

23 Weatherill, S and Beaumont, P, *op cit*, p 748.

III   EU competition law and intellectual property

Posing the problem

Attention has already been drawn to Article 222 of the Treaty, where it is stated that the Treaty provisions may not prejudice national rules on property ownership. The drafters of the Treaty obviously did not see the potential conflict which could exist between Article 222 of the Treaty on the one hand, and the competition rules of Articles 85–93 of the Treaty (above, Chapter 10) on the other.

Yet businesses could, in principle, use the intellectual property rights held by them in order to conclude agreements which make it difficult for potential competitors to have access to the relevant market. Intellectual property could be the means by which a dominant position is created which adversely affects competition. It has therefore been for the ECJ to determine the extent to which the use of intellectual property rights is compatible with Community competition policy. The Court has, essentially, adopted the same approach as that which governed its rulings on intellectual property in the context of the free movement of goods – that the mere existence of intellectual property rights does not in itself break competition rules, but the exercise of these rights may do so in certain circumstances.[24]

Exhaustion of rights rule

Since the existence of an intellectual property right is not in principle contrary to Community law, it follows, according to the ECJ, that its holder may protect the 'specific subject matter' of that right. This notion has been defined by the Court as:

the guarantee that the patentee, to reward the creative effort of the inventor, has the exclusive right to use an invention with a view to manufacturing industrial products and putting them into circulation for the first time, either directly or by the grant of licences to third parties as well as the right to oppose infringements.[25]

The main restriction on this right to protect the specific subject matter of intellectual property is the so-called exhaustion of rights doctrine. Under this principle, the holder of an intellectual property right may do either of two things. He or she may operate his or her right on the domestic market alone, in which case he or she is protected by national law; where appropriate, this will give him or her the right to exclude goods from another EU state. On the other hand, the holder may exercise his or her rights abroad, in which case he or she cannot rely on those rights to exclude goods from other Member States. The

---

24   Case 119/75, *Terrapin v Terranova* (1976) ECR 1039 at 1061.
25   Case 15/74, *Centrafarm v Sterling Drug* (1974) ECR 1147.

holder's consent to marketing the right, or the products covered by that right, abroad has 'exhausted' the rights he or she has under national law. In EU law terms, the specific subject matter of the patent will have been spent once the holder has consented to the products covered by the intellectual property right being marketed abroad.[26]

The element of 'consent'

The question as to when such consent has been obtained was raised in *Pharmon v Hoechst*.[27] The defendant was a German company which had patented the manufacturing processes of a drug. For this product, it owned a patent in Germany and parallel patents in both the Netherlands and Britain. This product was produced in Britain; not, however, by the patent holder Hoechst, but by DDSA, who did so as a result of a compulsory licence granted by the UK authorities. The Court agreed with Hoechst that this compulsory licence had removed this element of consent. Compulsory licences deprived the holders of the patent of their right to determine freely the conditions in which he chooses to sell his products. The various guarantees given to the holder by the compulsory licence were irrelevant in this context.

Pace Weatherill,[28] it is hard not to agree with the Court even though, strictly speaking, its ruling goes against the grain of free trade. Sometimes considerations of human rights must take precedence over the demands of unrestricted commerce.

Exhaustion of rights and trade marks

Here too, the Court has adopted a position based on the 'specific subject matter' of the right in question. In *Centrafarm*,[29] the Court defined this specific subject matter as the exclusive right of the holder to utilise that trade mark in order to place the products protected by that trade mark on the market for the first time. It is therefore intended to protect him against competitors who seek to take advantage of the status and reputation of the trade mark by marketing products unlawfully using it. It is in this sense that EU law seeks to protect the existence of trade marks. However, once the goods covered by the trade mark have been placed on the market abroad by the holder or with his consent, the latter's rights are exhausted, and any national provision to the contrary would be an obstacle to free trade.

Once again, the element of 'consent' is crucial to the understanding of the exhaustion of rights principle. This requirement has been restrictively applied

26 Weatherill, S, *op cit*, p 431.
27 Case 19/84, *Pharmon v Hoechst* (1985) ECR 2281.
28 *Op cit*, p 435.
29 Case 16/74, *Centrafarm v Winthrop* (1974) ECR 1183.

by the Court. If such 'consent' is to lead to an exhaustion of rights, the owners of the trade mark in the importing and exporting countries must be the same, or, even where they are separate, they must be economically linked.[30] This will be the case where the products in question have been placed in free circulation by the same undertaking, by a licensee, by a parent company, by a subsidiary of the same group, or by an exclusive distributor. It does not in principle cover the situation whereby goods are placed on the market by an assignee of a trade mark, where there is no legal or economic link between assignor and assignee.[31]

Exhaustion of rights and copyright

The Court has not defined the specific subject matter of copyright. This may be because of the sheer variety in the works which are protected by copyright. The specific subject matter of the copyright to literary work will not necessarily be the same as that which applies to musical compositions or paintings. In spite of this, it is generally agreed that this particular intellectual property right is governed by the same principles as those which apply to patents and trade marks.[32]

IV Harmonising legislation

General

The implications of intellectual property rights for the free movement of goods and for competition policy, which are dealt with above, made harmonisation in this field a necessity. Differences in the intellectual property rules between the Member States not only cause distortions in the common market, but also serve to confuse and restrict the trader. Weatherill and Beaumont[33] consider that there also could be a more ideological reason for preferring rule by harmonisation to rule by case law. 'The modern judicial approach', they write, 'tends to favour national protection over free trade'. Therefore it is preferable to use the steam-roller of harmonising legislation to achieve the sacrosanct objective of liberalisation. It should be noted, however, that thus far, the legislation concerned has tended to harmonise the contents of the intellectual property rights, rather than the level of protection given.[34]

The sections below will deal with the main areas of intellectual property law harmonisation, to wit trade marks, copyright and patents. In addition to those

30 Case C-93, *IHT Internationale Heiztechnik GmbH v Ideal Standard GmbH* (1994) ECR I-2789.

31 Craig, P and de Burca, G, *op cit*, p 1036.

32 Cases 55 and 57/80, *Musik-Vertrieb Membrean GmbH v Gesellschaft für Musikalische Aufführungs- und Mechanische Vervielfaltungsrechte* (GEMA) (1981) ECR 147.

33 *Op cit*, p 749.

34 *Ibid.*

harmonisation measures, the Commission has also sought to address issues relating to modern technology in such a way as to serve notice of its intention to lead the field in the development of any rules intellectual property in this area. It has done so by the enactment of rules on software protection, database protection and the regulation of intellectual property rights arising from satellite broadcasting.[35]

Trade marks

The first harmonising legislation in this field took the form of Directive 89/104.[36] Its drafters make it quite clear that the object of this directive stops a long way short of full-scale harmonisation of the trade mark law of the Member States; instead, the intention is to harmonise those national provisions which most directly affect the functioning of the common market. The Member States' national authorities remain free to continue to protect trade marks acquired through use, and to fix the procedural rules relating to the registration, revocation and invalidity of trade marks acquired by registration. Nor does it preclude the application to trade marks of national rules relating to unfair competition, tort liability or consumer protection. The main thrust of the directive is to ensure that the conditions for obtaining and continuing to hold a registered trade mark are, in general terms, identical throughout the Community.

To this end, the Directive has harmonised the following aspects of trade mark law:

(i) Signs which a trade mark may consist of

Trade marks may consist of any sign capable of graphic representation, particularly words. Not only personal names, designs and letters are permitted, but also numerals, the shape of the goods or their packaging. The decisive criterion is that these should be capable of distinguishing the goods or services of one undertaking from those of other undertakings (Article 2 of the Directive).

(ii) Grounds for refusal of invalidity

Article 3(1) of the Directive lists the types of symbol for which registration will in principle be refused or declared invalid. They include signs which cannot constitute a trade mark, trade marks devoid of any distinctive character, and those which are contrary to public policy or to accepted principles of morality. Member States may, in addition, refuse to invalidate registration on other grounds – including legal provisions other than those concerning trade marks, and signs which have religious or other symbolic significance, or represent a

35 Charlesworth, A and Cullen, H, *op cit*, p 319.
36 OJ 1989 L 40, as amended by Directive 92/10 (OJ 1992 L 6).

public interest other than that laid down in the Paris Convention[37] (Article 3(2) of the Directive). Article 4 of the Directive contains additional grounds for refusal or invalidity arising from conflicts with earlier rights.

(iii) Rights conferred by the trade mark

The exclusive rights conferred on the owner of the trade mark entitle the latter to prevent anyone else from any sign which is identical to that which forms the trade mark, or which risks causing confusion with the protected trade mark (Article 5(1) of the Directive). Here again, the Member States are allowed to introduce more stringent provisions for the protection of the trade mark holder (Article 5(2) of the Directive).

(iv) Limitation of the effects of a trade mark

Article 6(1) of the Directive lays down that the owner of a trade mark cannot prohibit others from using certain data concerning him, such as his name or address, various indications regarding the good or service being offered, and the trade mark itself where it is necessary to indicate the intended purpose of a product or service. The rights conferred by a trade mark are also exhausted in certain circumstances (Article 7 of the Directive). Article 9 sets out the limitations of a trade mark as a result of acquiescence.

(v) Use and non-use of trade marks.

Article 10(1) of the Directive provides that where, within five years of registration, the owner does not use it in the country of registration, or suspends its use for five years or more, it can be revoked. Article 11 lays down a number of penalties for non-use of a trade mark in legal or administrative proceedings. The trade mark can also be revoked where, as a result of the owner's failure to use it, it has become the common name of the product or service concerned, or where the use made of the trade mark by the owner has a misleading effect (Article 12 of the Directive).

Naturally, all the harmonising measures mentioned above would be entirely redundant if there existed a single Community Trade Mark (CTM). Regulation 40/94[38] goes some way towards establishing such a CTM. However, it does not replace the national trade marks, but co-exists with them on an optional basis. The conditions for registration, and other rules concerning the effects and use of the CTM are very similar to those set out in the trade mark directive. The CTM is valid for a period of 10 years, but is renewable.

---

37   This is the Paris Convention for the Protection of Industrial Property.
38   OJ 1994 L 11.

Copyright

Harmonisation in this field has occurred at both the EU and the non-EU level. As regards the latter, all the Member States are signatories of the Berne Convention for the Protection of Literary and Artistic Works on the one hand, and of the Universal Copyright Convention on the other hand. This has already served to approximate their copyright laws to a considerable extent, even before any Community initiative was taken in this regard. The first significant step on the road towards an integrated harmonisation policy in this regard was the Green Paper on Copyright[39] presented by the Commission on 14 June 1988. This document set out a number of issues which should be given priority in such harmonising legislation. This was followed by a 1991 Commission communication[40] in which the Commission highlights roughly the same priority areas, adding more flesh to the bones. They are listed below under eight subheadings, which will also include details of the relevant Community legislation hitherto adopted.

(i) Adopting a global approach

Here, the object was for Community action to feed into global attempts at finding solutions for global problems. This had, in fact, already been a de facto part of Community policy on harmonisation, since the majority of its Member States were parties to a number of international agreements on this issue. The first was the Berne Convention (above, p 284). This is an international agreement to which 97 nations are signatories, and which affords protection to works produced by citizens of any Berne Convention country. The second is the Universal Copyright Convention (UCC), which was concluded under the aegis of UNESCO, a specialist organ of the UN. It entered into effect in 1955. Under this Convention, signatories pledge themselves to uphold the reciprocity principle, in that they will give the same protection to foreign works complying with the Convention as they would give to their own. Third, the Community had already involved itself with other initiatives at the international level such as the Trade Related Property Rights negotiations, which formed part of the Uruguay Round.

(ii) Piracy of copyrighted material

The unauthorised reproduction, for profit, of copyrighted material has been a problem which has increased in seriousness as the means available for such reproduction have multiplied. Such practices have deprived the legitimate copyright holders of vast amounts of income, as well as seriously blunting the incentive to produce innovative work. Here too, it was possible for the EU

---

39   COM (88) 172.
40   COM (9) 584.

institutions to build on existing legislation, in this case, Regulation 3842/86 on the free movement of counterfeit goods. The latter was amended and extended by Regulation 3295/94 on Counterfeit and Pirated Goods.[41] The focus of the new Regulation appears to be audio-visual material since the printed word was already adequately protected by existing laws.

(iii) Home copying of audio-visual material

This is an even more intractable problem than piracy, because the latter is engaged in for financial gain. This must be done in the marketplace, however furtively, and the risk of detection whilst pirating material also serves as a useful deterrent. If, on the other hand, the practice is engaged in within the privacy of one's home, the risk of detection is infinitesimal, particularly where no attempt is being made to make commercial use of the material copied. Given that traditional prohibiting techniques are of little avail in this area, proposals have been made to spread the risk as widely and fairly as possible – eg by imposing a standard levy on blank audio and video cassettes. The nature of such an imposition is quite controversial, and several Member States are said to be opposed to this – hence the delay in adopting any legislation in this area.

(iv) Distribution rights, exhaustion and rental rights

The object here is to ensure that authors receive adequate remuneration for the works which are rented or used without being actually bought. This are was in need of particular attention because very often, renting or leasing leads to piracy. The major harmonising achievement in this field has been the adoption of Directive 92/100.[42] The Member States are required to make provision for the right to allow or prohibit the renting or lending of original versions and copies of their works. Those who are entitled to such exclusive rights are authors in relation to original and subsequent copies of his works, the performing artists for recordings made of his performances, the record, tape or CD producers in relation to these means of reproduction, and the film producers in relation to original and subsequent copies of their films. However, once a performing artist signs a contract with a film producer, he is deemed to have relinquished those rental rights, unless he can prove the contrary. The exclusive lending right conferred by copyright may be cancelled by the Member States for cultural reasons (Article 2). Some have objected to this, although there is no indication to date that the national authorities have allowed themselves to be tempted to abuse this escape clause.

41 OJ 1994 L 341.
42 OJ 1992 L 346.

(v) Computer programs

The exponential increase the amount and use of computer software has made it necessary for Community legislation in this field also. The main harmonising achievement in this field has been the adoption of Directive 91/250.[43] Under this instrument, the Member States are required to protect computer software along the same lines as the Berne Convention for the Protection of Literary and Artistic Works. This is a method which has met with a good deal of criticism, mainly because this has the effect of giving protection only to the idea expressed in the programme, leaving unprotected the principal underlying elements of a computer program. It is also somewhat unfortunate that the criteria for the eligibility for copyright protection are contained in the preamble to the Directive rather than in its main body, which considerably weakens the legal force of the these criteria – and therefore also of the Directive.[44]

Within the limited field of application of the Directive, however, the exclusive rights of the 'rightholder', as the Directive rather quaintly puts it, are quite extensive. They comprise not only the permanent or temporary reproduction of a computer program by any means and in any form, but also the reproduction of any translation, adaptation or arrangement of such programs, as well as any form of distribution to the public, including their rental (Article 4 of the Directive). These restrictions naturally do not apply to the lawful organisation of any such program (Article 5 of the Directive). Nor shall authorisation by the 'rightholder' be required where the reproduction of the program is necessary to achieve the interoperability of an independently created computer program with other programs, subject to certain conditions being met (Article 6 of the Directive).

(vi) Databases

In the present state of information technology, the realisation of a single market will not be complete without the establishment of a single market for information services. This in turn demands a set of rules which both protect databases and prevent their abuse. In 1992, the Commission presented a Draft Directive on the legal protection of databases.[45] This seeks the harmonisation of database copyright law, especially those rules which govern the originality test which must be satisfied, and a 15 year period of protection against the unfair extraction of information from databases. It also makes provision for the compulsory licensing of databases on equitable and non-discriminatory terms in certain conditions. As is the case with computer programs (above, p 286), the protection given is essentially that given to literary works.

43 OJ 1991 L 122.

44 Wehlau, A, 'Software Protection under European Community Law' (1993) Law, *Computers and Artificial Intelligence*, pp 7–8.

45 OJ 1992 L 156.

(vii) The part played by the EU in multilateral and bilateral relations

It is particularly important for the Community to engage in a dialogue with the global bodies in this field. Copyright protection for Community-based persons extends well beyond EU frontiers. Indeed, the knowledge that their copyright will be protected the world over will be an extra incentive to those producing works of art and intellectual value. This will require more particularly close liaison with such organisations as the World Trade Organisation, the World Intellectual Property Organisation (WIPO), which are dealing with the problems of international copyright. Copyright was in fact one of the areas discussed in the course of the GATT Uruguay Round.

(viii) Other EU initiatives

This leaves the widest possible scope for action in such areas which are likely to surface or become more important after the adoption of the Green Paper. One such issue is that of broadcasting, which is a constant state of development. Here again, the single market will not be complete without a single market in satellite and cable transmissions. This has all manner of implications for copyright protection, not least because of the ease with which broadcasts can be beamed into European countries from outside the EU. To this end, Directive 93/83 on the Co-ordination of Certain Rules concerning Copyright and Neighbouring Rights Applicable to Satellite Broadcasting and Cable Retransmission[46] was adopted. Central to the operation of this Directive are the various copyright collecting agencies in the Member States. Another area in which Community action is needed is design protection. Legislation has been proposed for the creation of a 'Community design' (on the same lines as the 'Community Trade Mark') which will protect industrial designs and models.

Work will also need to be done as regards the terms on which protection is given – for example the duration of such protection. Although the Member States are parties to various international agreements in this field, the latter leave the Member States free to apply longer periods. There is accordingly an unnecessary degree of diversity among the Member States in this field, which can create potential obstacles to the free movement of goods.[47] Thus it could also happen that a work within the public domain of one Member State could find itself protected by copyright in another.[48]

46 OJ 1993 L 248.

47 Cases C-92 and 326/92, *Collins v Imtrat Handelsgesellschaft GmbH* (1993) ECR I-5145.

48 Groves, P, *op cit*, p 157.

Patents

The need for harmonisation was quite acute for those who had made an invention and wanted to protect it. They were compelled to negotiate the required formalities in every country, and bear the attendant cost. The main initiatives in this field have taken the form of traditional multilateral agreements rather than Community legislation. Indeed, one of these conventions is not exclusive to the Community. Both Conventions are interlocking instruments.

The first of these is the Munich European Patent Convention, which was signed in 1973 and entered into effect in 1977. In addition to the Member States if the EU, it also counts such countries as Switzerland, Norway, Monaco and Liechtenstein amongst its signatories. The Convention has put into place a system for the issuing of patents, the first of which were issued in 1980. Applications must be made to the European Patent Office in Munich, which will issue the applicant inventor with a patent which will protect the invention, either in all the signatory states, or in those in which the applicant has requested protection. Whilst it cannot be denied that this has served to reduce considerably the formalities and costs involved, it must also be borne in mind that the practical implications of the Convention are in most cases purely national in character. This is because the rights conferred by the patent need to be enforced separately in each state in question. This means that the level of protection afforded continues to depend on the country in which the patent rights are being claimed. Because of the involvement of signatory states other than those of the EU, the ECJ does not in principle have any part to play in the application of the Convention. However, where a national court of an EU country refers a preliminary question on the interpretation of the Convention to the Community Court, the latter will give a ruling.

The European Patent has a duration of 20 years from the date of making the application. Each signatory state must give the European patent the same level of protection as that which is afforded by the national patent in that state. To be eligible for the European patent, an invention must meet three criteria: it must be capable of industrial application, it must be new, and it must involve an inventive step. A number of processes are, however, excluded from the scope of the European Patent, such as scientific theories and mathematical methods, as well as aesthetic creations and presentation of information.

The Community Patent Convention, on the other hand, has only the EU Member States as its signatories. It was signed in 1975, but has not yet been ratified by sufficient numbers to become fully effective. The reason for this has been the hostility shown to its contents by Denmark. Initially, Ireland also had certain reservations, but these have now been allayed. This is why, in 1988, the Council adopted an Agreement on Community Patents. As a result of an Intergovernmental Conference convened in Luxembourg in December 1989, the proposal was amended, and the Member States were given until the end of 1991 to ratify it. No Member State succeeded in meeting this time limit, and to date only a handful of states have ratified it.

The Convention introduces the notion of a Community Patent, producing uniform effects throughout the Community. It confers on the inventor a monopoly on the utilisation of the patented invention within the Community, subject to two provisos. One is the fact that he may not use this right in such a way as to partition the EU market along national lines. (Licences may, however, be restricted along territorial lines.) The other is the exhaustion of rights rule, under which the holder no longer may rely upon his exclusive right once he has placed the product in question on the market in any part of the Community.[49] The Community Patent may only be transferred, withdrawn or allowed to lapse throughout the Community. It makes provision for a system of Patent Courts in every Member State which will settle any litigation arising from patents. Appeal from the Patent Courts (or from the European Patent Office) would lie to a Common Appeal Court.

It is unlikely that the Convention will enter into effect without some kind of compromise solution. Groves[50] considers that some kind of 'two-speed' approach could be adopted, although Spain – which became a Community member in 1986 and at the time pledged itself to make a number of amendments to its law on patents, thus enabling it to ratify the Convention – is loathe to join any system which involves anything less than the participation of all the Member States. The author rather cynically concludes that this may have more to do with Spain's wish to have the Community Trade Marks Office located in Madrid than with any substantive quarrel with the Convention.[51]

Mention should also be made of the European Agency for the Evaluation of Medicinal Products (EAEMP). This makes provision for a single central evaluation and subsequent market authorisation for innovatory medicinal products, valid throughout the EU. The European Evaluation Agency is established in London, and should enable both veterinary products and those intended for human use to be commercially marketed more rapidly.[52]

49 Druesne, G, *op cit*, p 236.
50 *Op cit*, p 154.
51 *Ibid*.
52 Roney, A, *op cit*, p 162.

16 The Future

I Introduction

Regardless of the stage reached in its evolution, one of the most facile comments to make on the future of the Community is that 'it stands at a crossroads'. It is this constant expectation of mould-breaking developments which never quite materialise which go a long way towards explaining the uncertainty which grips many people – even those who are well versed in matters European – when contemplating the future of the EU. In the same way as successive Chancellors of the Exchequer have assured their electorate that an economic miracle is just around the corner, the European citizen is constantly being informed that the next significant event – be it direct elections to the European parliament, the Single European Act, the arrival of a new brace of Member States, or the prospect of economic and monetary union – constitutes the defining moment in the history of the EU. Disillusionment, cynicism and a loss of interest soon follow.

History, however, teaches us that incremental change, rather than dramatic turns of events, tends to be the norm in every area of human endeavour. This is particularly true of the EU. When observing, as was done in Chapter 1, the historical development of the Community, it is very difficult to identify events and developments which fundamentally changed it. Let us, for example, recall the ultimate fate of the SEA and the single market programme, which set up 31 December 1992 as the most important date in the history of the Community. The changes which were predicted in the media and amongst political commentators were quite staggering. Yet five years after the date in question, the Community does not look that much different from its appearance a decade ago. It was never very likely that some 300 directives, most of them concerning technical issues, were going to change the face of the Community as we knew it. Consequently, it is scarcely overstating the case to claim that 1992 was something of a damp squib.

It is in this light that the present author wishes to discuss the various prospects, proposals and blueprints which are currently being advanced as providing the answers to a number of difficult problems currently facing the EU. If they are realised, they will no doubt add a new dimension to the organisation, but are unlikely to define its ultimate shape and destiny. The main issues with which EU policy makers find themselves confronted are: the question of deepening integration; the issue of widening integration; the extension of membership; the prospect of a multi-speed Europe; the democratic deficit in Community decision-making, the balance of powers between the Community and its Member States, and the future of the EU institutions themselves. Each will be examined in turn.

II   Deepening integration

There can be no doubt that the effect of a number of recent fundamental instruments has been the deepening of economic integration. The process had already started with the SEA, and the requirement that the Member States' VAT rates be kept within certain bands. It was, however, particularly the TEU which has provided a major stimulus in this direction. The prospect of Economic and Monetary Union (EMU) has served to make the economic policies of the Member States a great deal more dependent on Community objectives and decisions than ever before. Other signs of deepening integration are the TEU initiatives on economic and social cohesion, industry and research and technological development.

With the deadline for EMU fast approaching, the question is already being asked as to whether this should be the last exercise in deepening economic integration for quite some time, or whether the momentum needs to be maintained in this direction by new initiatives. Those defending the former thesis argue that there is a limit to the amount of deepening integration which the public can accommodate; in addition, the principle of subsidiarity (above, p 96) means that Community policy-makers should now be even more careful than before when engaging in new areas of integration. Those advocating more integration point to the dangers of halting the momentum. Resorting to that over-used metaphor – which is now beginning to don the overtones of a cliché – they believe that once the European train has left the station, it must not be allowed to stop; to allow it to do so will involve the risks of complacency and, eventually, of Euro-sclerosis.

The present author has an ambivalent attitude towards this issue, in that his heart is with the former argument, but his head with the latter. He is of the opinion that, if EMU is realised in accordance with the relevant timetable, other aspects of economic integration will follow as a natural consequence. This is particularly true of interest rates policy. The relationship between monetary policy and interest rates is well documented, and once the Euro becomes the sole currency of the EU, there will be pressures to ensure that interest rates are set exclusively by the European Central Bank. This looks particularly likely because of the deflationary policies on which EMU is now being constructed, and which will be the hallmark of the ECB. Given that the impact of national interest rates on the Euro will be much lighter than they were in relation to domestic currencies, national policy-makers might fall for the temptation to cut interest rates and 'let the Euro take the strain'. Calls for uniform EU interest rates will become almost irresistible in these circumstances.

The head may admit the inevitability of deepening integration; the heart remains firmly opposed. There is a limit to the amount of integration which public opinion can accommodate. The point may well be reached some day when that limit is exceeded. This will be the more so as people realise that the fundamental problems afflicting Europe at the present time – unemployment, an increasing divide between rich and poor, environmental degradation – have not been solved by deepening the integration process. This is very likely to provoke a populist backlash not only against the process of economic integration, but against the very notion of European co-operation.

The problem of deepening integration will also continue to pose difficulties when it comes to considering the prospect of enlarging the Community. This will be returned to in greater depth at p 294, below.

III   Widening integration

The TEU not only made provision for the deepening of integration. By venturing into such areas as common foreign and security policy (Articles J–J.11), justice and home affairs (Articles K–K.9), cultural policy (Title IX EC Treaty), and public health (Title X EC Treaty), the EU has boldly gone where no Community instrument has gone before. Even though the provisions in question emphasise co-ordination and co-operation, rather than harmonisation, there can be little doubt that the object of the exercise is to build on any achievements which will be realised on the basis of these provisions in order to integrate these sectors more closely.

The object of inserting these policy areas into the working sphere of the Community was clearly to indicate that European integration need not be confined to the purely economic, but could also embrace other areas which were equally crucial to the operation of society. It is hoped that, as a result, public opinion will view the work of the Community with a more sympathetic eye than has sometimes appeared to be the case.

The main problem with this approach is that public opinion is just as likely to be alienated by attempts to centralise control over these areas in the hands of the EU institutions. Co-ordination and co-operation are normally viewed with a great deal more equanimity than downright harmonisation and centralisation. This, after all, was why the concept of subsidiarity occupies such a prominent place in the scheme of the TEU. It would therefore appear advisable to concentrate on adopting efficient and effective co-operation and co-ordination procedures in these areas, rather than see the TEU provisions on the subject as stepping stones towards harmonisation.

On the question whether more areas should be involved in the EU theatre of operations, the answer must be in the affirmative – subject to the reservations expressed in the previous paragraph. Areas such as the prevention, investigation and prosecution of crime, administrative procedures such as town and country planning, and areas of public policy such as housing and social welfare, would benefit considerably from co-operation and co-ordination, as the general thrust of such endeavours would be to level standards upwards. This is unlike the process of harmonisation, which has a tendency towards levelling downwards.[1]

IV Extending EU membership

One of the major challenges facing the Community in the years ahead will be the question of its enlargement. The first wave of new members is expected to consist of countries whose applications have been pending for some considerable time, to wit countries such as Malta, Cyprus and, possibly, Turkey. The second wave of new members will undoubtedly be those countries of Eastern Europe whose economies are considerably more advanced than those of other former Eastern Bloc countries, Hungary, Poland, the Czech Republic and Slovakia. Subsequent enlargements are not excluded, but remain at the time of writing a remote contingency.

There is little doubt that small nations such as Malta and Cyprus could be accommodated without undue difficulty. The membership of Turkey and the former Eastern Bloc countries, however, raises serious issues as to the future direction of the Community. This is all the more the case in the light of the momentum towards deepening the integration process, described earlier at p 292.

In Chapter 10, the mechanism laid down in the TEU for the achievement of a single currency is described. The economic convergence criteria in question will be difficult to achieve by the existing Member States, nearly all of whom are regarded as industrialised states having reasonable standards of living and of social protection. At the time of writing, not even Germany is fulfilling all the criteria in question. Exactly how the applicant countries will succeed in meeting these requirements without unacceptable social costs has yet to be explained by EU policy makers.

It could be argued at this point that there is a precedent for a former Eastern Bloc country to be integrated into the ever deepening integration process, to wit the former East Germany. However, two comments should be made at this point. First of all, it is a myth to believe that the former GDR has been fully integrated into the EU market. Secondly, such progress as has been made in this regard has only been made possible because of the massive subsidies poured into the *Neue Bundesländer* by the Bonn government. These are estimated to

---

1   See on this subject the excellent critique offered by Galtung, J, *The European Community – Superpower in the Making* (1973), Allen and Unwin.

have been of the order of DM 170,000 million per year as from 1991. Whether the EU taxpayer will be prepared to expend comparable amounts for the purpose of easing the integration of Poland into the EU is greatly to be doubted.

In spite of this, the extension of the EU to as many nations of this continent is a prospect that should be warmly welcomed. It is possible that the steep nature of the difficulties described in the previous paragraph will occasion a major rethink as to the future direction and profile of the Community. This in turn could lead to a more realistic approach towards economic and social integration. It could also hasten the advent of a multi-speed Europe, which is the next subject under discussion.

V   Towards a multi-speed Europe?

Even before the question of extending the Community to the former Eastern Bloc countries became an issue for serious consideration, doubts were being raised as to whether all the Member States could progress at the same speed. The possibility that, as a result, some areas of integration would be restricted to certain Member States was raised for the first time in the *Tindemans Report*.[2] It referred to a 'two-speed plan of economic integration' in which the integration of countries such as Italy, Ireland and the United Kingdom would proceed at a slower speed than that of the 'stronger' members.

At the time, no great enthusiasm for this idea was forthcoming, mainly for reasons of national prestige; it would have been difficult for the politicians of any Member State to have admitted to its citizens that they presided over a state which played in the second division of Europe. The seeds of this notion had been planted, however, and it continued to resurface as the process of integration deepened, and the more realistic policy makers began to face up to some of the uncomfortable issues broached in the previous section. It became a reality at the time of the adoption of the TEU – admittedly for reasons which were different from those raised by the Tindemans Report. The United Kingdom opted out of the Social Protocol, and both the UK and Denmark reserved the right not to participate in the final stage of EMU. Earlier, the UK had already refused to accede to the 1989 Social Charter, claiming it to be just one veneer away from Communism.

Those who oppose any extension of this notion argue that it could lead to the break-up of the Community. To operate a single market whilst a number of countries have opted out of some areas of EU economic policy-making would cause all manner of disruptions in the system and finally become unsustainable. Those advocating it claim that, on the contrary, it will only be some kind of

2   EC Bulletin, Supplement 1/76. See also Mitchell, JDB, 'The Tindemans Report – Retrospect and Prospect' (1976) CMLRev 455.

'variable geometry' in the EU that will keep the organisation together. To insist that all Member States participate in every aspect of integration will impose intolerable strains on the economic and social fabric of some of these countries, particularly the poorer ones. A multi-speed Europe is therefore the lesser of the two evils.

In view of the question marks raised earlier over the prospect of enlargement, it may come as no surprise to the reader to learn that the present author is an advocate of a Community whose members are allowed to progress at a pace in keeping with their economic capacity and social fabric. To do so might even accelerate the process of fundamentally rethinking and recasting the mould of European co-operation towards a looser and more confederal model.

VI Solving the 'democratic deficit'

One of the issues which has never ceased to preoccupy the commentators on Community law and politics is that of the 'democratic deficit'. This is generally taken as referring to the gap between the Community decision-making process and the democratic mechanisms and form which normally preside over this process – in the majority of cases in the shape of a directly elected legislature.

From the historical overview featured in Chapter 1 (above, p 11), it is clear that the gap presented by the democratic deficit is not so yawning now as it was when the Community first started to operate. This is mainly because of the evolution of the European Parliament. Whereas the input of the Parliament into the decision-making process was negligible at first, its role has become increasingly important as a result of a number of fundamental instruments such as the SEA and the TEU. The majority of the legislative procedures now require a major contribution on its part. In addition, it is now a directly-elected assembly instead of consisting of delegations from the national parliaments, as was the case until 1979.

In spite of this, the derived legislation of the Community continues to be elaborated through a decision-making process which is far from democratic. The two main legislative bodies remain the Council of Ministers and – in terms of initiating the process – the Commission. Neither of these bodies has any democratic mandate for enacting legislation. Yet, as is revealed in the section on direct effect (above, p 83), their enactments can be relied upon before the national courts, which must uphold the rights contained therein and even – by virtue of the principle of supremacy – take precedence over national laws. Accordingly, the remains a good deal to be done before the democratic deficit is overcome.

There are, in principle two ways in which this difficulty could be solved. The first approach would consist in conferring full legislative powers on the European Parliament. Any derived Community legislation would then in theory be based on the full-hearted consent of the European peoples. There are, however, two drawbacks to this solution. The first is the sheer long-term nature of this prospect. At the present rate of progress, it could take more than fifty years for this objective to be realised, and at this stage we should remember the famous statement by a certain Cambridge economist concerning an unfortunate but inevitable fate that awaits us all 'in the long run'. A great deal of undemocratic legislation will enter into effect until the dawning of that happy day, and diminish the respect for and prestige of the rule of law. Second, to what extent could the Parliament really 'represent' the European people? At present, the 'representation ratio' between MEPs and voters is 1:700,000 in some countries, as opposed to a ratio of 1:60,000 for most national parliaments. Does the notion of 'representativity' still have any meaning when confronted with such statistics?

The other solution consists in making all EU derived legislation subject to greater control by national parliaments, which can claim a democratic mandate for the exercising of their authority. Here, a wide range of possibilities present themselves. The most radical – and, some would argue, the most retrograde – step would be to make all Community legislation subject to prior approval by the national parliaments. This would virtually spell the end of direct effect as a legal mechanism, but would make EU legislation fully democratic. However, this is not the only option on offer. It would be possible to devise an 'opting out' system, whereby parliaments would be deemed to have accepted a Community regulation unless they notified the EU authorities of their decision not to be bound by it. Even this option presents several possibilities. The national parliaments could be allowed to do so only by a qualified majority, or could only do so by means of a properly reasoned decision which would subject to review by the ECJ. At the least radical end of this broad option, the Member States could adopt a system of enhanced Parliamentary scrutiny on the Danish model.[3]

VII Balance of powers between the Community and the Member States

The relationship between the Community and the national institutions is currently unique. It cannot be described as a confederal, intergovernmental or federal model. The question could be raised as to whether this state of affairs could and should remain the same on an indefinite basis.

The commentators who advocate or anticipate that this relationship remains the same are relatively rare. Generally, there is a feeling abroad that something

For more details of the Danish system, see Gulmann, C and Hagel-Sörensen, K, *EF-ret* (1993), Jurist og Økonom Forbundets Forlag, p 157 *et seq.*

will have to give, and that following that defining moment, the Community will either evolve towards a more federal model, or towards a more inter-governmental (or even confederal) model. The issue is all the more complicated because of two essentially contradictory forces at work at the heart of the Community decision-making process. On the one hand, it was noted earlier (above p 292) that the process of integration was likely to deepen over the coming years. On the other hand, the TEU has committed the Community towards the principle of subsidiarity. However many verbal and intellectual acrobatics are displayed in attempting to explain away this apparent contradiction, it is obvious that these two notions will collide at some point or other.

As matters stand at present, it is the considered opinion of the present writer that the direction ultimately taken will be an inter-governmental one rather than that of an increasingly close federation. The reasons for this are the pressures described under the earlier sections relating to the deepening of integration and enlargement. These pressures are likely to lead to a fundamental reappraisal of the direction of the Community and its relationship with the national authorities. As has been mentioned earlier, a looser model of co-operation both likely and desirable.

VIII Prospects for institutional reform

General

The Community stands and falls with its institutions, and the manner in which the latter operate is fundamental to its future. It is useful to take stock of the various criticisms which, with varying degrees of justification, have been levelled at these institutions, and draw the appropriate conclusions for the future. The future of the European Parliament has already been adequately discussed under the section on the 'democratic deficit'. This discussion will therefore be confined to the Council, Commission and the ECJ.

The Council

Various aspects of the modus operandi of the Council have been the butt of good deal of criticism. One is the secrecy of its proceedings, which is a unforgivable aspect of any legislature. The other is the fact that the Council consists of members whose main task lies at the national level. The principal legislature of the Community is a body which only spends a fraction of its time actually legislating for the Community.

At one time, it looked as though increasing involvement on the part of COREPER might go some way to remedying this defect, but this was thoroughly objected to by the Commission (above, p 29). The other solution might be to reserve membership of the Council to the various Ministers for

European Affairs (or their equivalents) in the Member States. This, in turn, would present the disadvantage of requiring a political 'general practitioner' to legislate on issues which sometimes require extensive expertise and experience in complex areas of knowledge.

Thirdly, is it not time that a permanent structure was found to organise the presidency of the Council? The six-monthly rotating presidency was all very well when the Community only consisted of six Member States, as each Member State was given the opportunity to chair the Council once every three years. At the current rate of expansion of the Community, it will not be long before this is reduced to once every ten years. This cannot be a healthy basis for guiding the direction of the chief legislature of the Community.

The Commission

The main criticism which is constantly being levelled at the Commission is that in many respects it is still operating as though it was the executive of a Community of six. At that time, it was a small body presiding over a Community whose Member States were similar in their economy, and administrative and legal systems. This picture has obviously changed along with the successive extensions of the Community. Another areas of controversy is the manner of its appointment.

There can be no doubt that the Commission is not the animal which it was 30 years ago. It has greatly increased in size, and now number about 15,000 officials of various descriptions. Yet the rules governing its functioning have changed very little, in spite of various attempt at reform. One of these was the 'Spierenburg Report' of 1979, which identified a number of fault lines, including the low level of motivation of its staff, the inflexible nature of its responses to changing circumstances, and the excessive sense of hierarchy which pervades the institution. Little was done to follow up these criticisms.

The Commission now consists of 20 members. Are there really sufficient areas of Community interest which can truly be said to warrant the attention of a Commissioner for his entire period of office? And are the right people being appointed? From the very vague specification as to the type of person required made in the Treaty, it is clear that the intention was to bring together people from as wide a range of backgrounds as possible. Instead, the majority of Commissioners have been politicians ('would-be' as well as 'has-been').

The manner of appointment of the Commission has changed a good deal since the days when it involved little more than an unseemly process of horse-trading amongst the governments of the Community. Yet it remains unsatisfactory that the governments can virtually place the European Parliament before a *fait accompli*, as is described above on p 21. The first try-out of the new system in 1994 can hardly be described as a thorough vindication of those who devised it.

Sooner or later, the Commissioners will need to be elected in some way or other. Either they could be elected by the European Parliament – who would be given a specific mandate to do so at the time of the European elections – or they should be directly elected by the voters of the EU. Only an electoral mandate will be adequate for a body which has the important task of proposing legislation.

The ECJ

The accusation that the Court has arrogated to itself a policy-making role, thus infringing the separation-of-powers principle and creating the danger of a *gouvernement des juges*, has been dealt with earlier (above, p 39). It has been pointed out that, if the Court has sometimes ventured into the area of policy-making, it has had to do so because the general and vague terms in which a great deal of Community legislation – both primary and derived – is framed often leave the ECJ with no choice but to resort to law-creation.

The ECJ has also come in for a good deal of criticism because of its allegedly 'political' nature. It has often been accused of attempting to force the pace in federalising the Community, whilst possessing no democratic mandate to do so. This particular criticism strikes me an being particularly unfair. In the course of the main body of this work, it has from time to time been pointed out that in fact the ECJ has often sided with the Member States' authorities when strictly speaking that should not have been the case (above, p 174).

There is, however, a valid critique to be made of the ECJ in this respect, which is its lack of consistency, and the fact that this lack of consistency is often politically motivated. The Court's decision in the *Van Duyn v Home Office*[4] is a good case in point. There is no way in which, even at that relatively early stage in its case law on the free movement of persons, the ECJ should have awarded the decision to the United Kingdom. The strictness with which the Court had already begun to interpret rules forming an exception to a general principle should normally have precluded such an outcome. (There is, however, a justified suspicion that this lack of consistency was inspired by more than a judicial lapse, and that political considerations which took account of the delicate state of British opinion during the run-up to the referendum confirming or rejecting Community membership took an upper hand (above, p 174).

There is every indication, however, that the Court will find it increasingly hard to produce such anomalous decisions. In the relatively early days of its case law on a particular topic, the odd inconsistency could be charitably ascribed to a lapse which was only natural whilst the Court was still 'finding its feet' on a particular issue. Such excuses become increasingly thin as the case law on particular topics becomes increasingly established. The Court may therefore

4   Case 41/74, *op cit*.

find that in the future, it will have little option but to act consistently if it wishes to safeguard its position as the supreme judicial authority on Community law.

Another valid criticism of the Court is that very often, it fails to give adequate guidance to the national courts when giving preliminary rulings under Article 177 of the Treaty. It has already been pointed out on a number of occasions (above, p 173) that the Court has often shied away from giving a conclusive answer which is related to the underlying action, thus leaving the national court to draw inferences rather than apply concrete rulings. It could be objected that the Court needs to keep its rulings on a general basis, because these are intended as milestones in the Court's established case law as much as they purport to solve the issue of EU law in the underlying dispute. In that case, why no split the ruling into two parts, the first giving the reply to the questions asked by the national court, the second extrapolating from this reply a general rule which is serve as a guide to the interpretation of Community law in the future? Surely it is in the interests of unity of interpretation that the national courts be given as little leeway and scope for discretion as possible?

IX   General conclusion

From the above analysis, a number of general conclusions can be drawn.

(i) The deepening of integration may have several question marks over it, but is almost inevitable given the momentum towards EMU. The widening of integration also has a certain momentum behind it, but it would be wise to refrain from harmonisation in these new areas.

(ii) This deepening and widening of integration could at some point collide with the problems of enlargement, the democratic deficit and the principle of subsidiarity. This could lead to a fundamental reappraisal of the direction of the direction of the Community and of the relationship between it and its Member States, which could then evolve towards a more inter-governmental, rather than federal, model.

(iii) Institutional reform is vital for the future prospects and health of the Community. The Council must become more efficient and less secretive. The Commission should be directly elected and streamlined. The Court should become more consistent and provide better guidelines to the national courts on judicial policy through the mechanism of Article 177 EC Treaty.

17 European Union Law: A Practical Guide

I Introduction

The object of this chapter is to provide the student of Community law with such practical information as will be of considerable assistance in the following respects:

- **Study advice and guidance.** This section contains practical information aimed at assisting the student in tackling the coursework set. To this end, it provides information on where to find Community law, and contains an explanation on the manner in which the instruments of Community law are normally cited and referred to;

- **Postgraduate advice.** Here, the object is to provide appropriate advice, by giving an insight into various opportunities available to the student of Community law as regards training opportunities and prospects of post-graduate education in this field;

- **Terminological assistance.** This section serves as an explanatory and linguistic glossary of the main terms of art used in connection with Community law.

II Finding and citing Community law

A Primary legislation

Official Community texts

The Publications Office of the Community (located in Luxembourg) publishes a comprehensive set of primary legislation, comprising not only the founding treaties, but also documents such as the various acts of accession and the agreements concluded with non-Member States. It is available in each official Community language (including Irish). It is available in all European Documentation Centres.

Her Majesty's stationery office

Britain's HMSO have also published a number of Treaty collections. They include the **ECSC Treaty** (Cmnd 7461) – remembering that the French text of the Treaty is the only authentic version – the **Euratom (EAEC) Treaty** and the **EEC Treaty** (Cmnd 7460), the **Treaty of Accession to the Communities of the**

United Kingdom, Denmark, Ireland and Norway[1] (Cmnd 7463), the **Single European Act** (Cmnd 9758) and the **Treaty on European Union** (Cmnd 9758).

Unofficial texts

There are a number of privately published collections of the Treaties, which in most cases are accompanied by a considerable volume of important derived legislation. The main ones are the **European Community Treaties** published by Sweet and Maxwell (loose-leaf edition – regularly updated), Blackstone's **EC Legislation** (edited by Nigel Foster), and the **Basic Community Laws** (Oxford University Press), edited by Bernard Rudden and Derrick Wyatt.

Attention should also be drawn to the annotated versions of the Treaty of Rome, which strictly speaking are not 'Treaty collections'.

B   Derived legislation and other Community instruments

Official texts

The main texts issued by the Community institutions themselves are the following:

The Official Journal. This is the most basic of all EU documents, and appears virtually on a daily basis. All issues are numbered consecutively, starting from 1.

Essentially, the Official Journal contains (a) all the adopted legislation whose publication is obligatory, (b) virtually all the adopted legislation whose publication is not obligatory, (c) proposed legislation, (d) policy documents and (e) important announcements.

The Official Journal (usually referred to in its abbreviated form, which is OJ) is divided into three sections: the L series, the C series and the S series. The L series is reserved for *adopted* legislation. Some items of legislation *must*, and some *may* be published in the OJ. Details of which legislation falls into either category are found in Article 191 of the Treaty. Although the Commission decisions on competition law are not featured in Article 191, they are also published in the L series. Many important Recommendations (eg the Recommendation on Childcare No 92/241) are also featured there.

The C section contains a very wide range of documents, which have little in common. In most cases, however, they are capable of influencing, directly or indirectly, Community legislation. It will accordingly contain the most important draft directives and regulations, opinions of the Economic and Social Committee, the 'common positions' of the Council, within the meaning of Articles 189b and 189c (above, p 54). Most Commission Opinions are also

---

1   Norway subsequently withdrew following the referendum on Community membership held in 1972.

included in this section (eg the 1993 Opinion on Equal Pay). In addition, it features announcements of various types – eg the notifications of EU civil service examinations. In relation to the European Parliament, it contains the Resolutions and Amendments, as well as the Questions put to, and Answers received from, the Commissioners and Council members.

The S series contains details of the various contracts awarded by public service organisations for work and supplies, pursuant to the EU directives on this issue. An appendix to the Official Journal contains regular reports on the debates taking place during the sessions of the European Parliament.

The Official Journal appears in all the official languages of the EU. When Britain and Ireland joined the Community in 1973, a special series, containing the most important legislative instruments to have been adopted prior to the accession of these two countries, was made available in English.

Directory of Community legislation in force. This directory is published twice per year, and comes in two volumes. Volume I contains a directory of legislation arranged by subject matter, each item of legislation being accompanied by its Official Journal reference. Volume 2 lists the legislation per reference number.

Other official Community documents. The Community institutions produce a vast array of documents which serve a variety of purposes. First, there are the *COM* documents. In most cases a legislative proposal by the Commission will first be published as a *COM* document – together with an explanatory memorandum – before being published in the C series of the Official Journal. Other documents to be published in the *COM* series are the various programme documents known as green and white papers, and various action programmes.

The Community also published a number of documents which provide an overall view of the activities of the Community. Three documents deserve particular attention in this respect:

(i) the **General Report on the Activities of the Communities**, published by the Commission in mid-February of the year following that to which the Report relates (although, as the present writer has found to his cost, its transmission to the various distribution centres can take some time!). Specialist annual reports are also available in a number of areas (eg competition law and agricultural policy).

(ii) the **Bulletin of the European Communities**, published by the Commission, which consists of a monthly account of developments on all fronts of Community activity, and of the various Supplements, which concentrate on individual topics.

(iii) the **Review of the Council's Work**, published by the Secretariat-General of the Council.

On the specific subject of competition law, the Commission has published a collection of regulations and notices called **Competition Law in the EEC** and in the ECSC (4th edn, 1991).

The European Parliament also issues a number of important documents. The reports of its Committees are reproduced in the **Session Documents.** The Debates are published in an appendix to the Official Journal, whereas the Questions and Answers and Resolutions and Amendments are featured in the C series of the Official Journal. The Parliament also publishes a regular List of Members, which features all the MEPs by reference to their political fraction, national party, Parliamentary committees and the delegations to which they belong. The Parliament also produces documents aimed at informing the general public of its activities. These are **The Week,** which covers the debates which take place during an EP session, and **The Briefing** which features the programme for the forthcoming session. At the most basic level, **EP News** gives information on the activities of, and developments in, the Parliament.

Finally, a most useful directory is the **SCAD bulletin.** This is issued on a weekly basis by the documentation service of the Commission, and covers a wide variety of Community instruments arranged under 28 subject headings. It is a trilingual bulletin (English, French and German).

Unofficial texts

Some of the private editions of the Community treaties also contain the most important instruments of derived Community legislation (above, p 65).

Summaries of Community derived legislation, and the domestic legislation implementing it, can be found in the **European Law Digest** (Sweet & Maxwell). Another useful compendium of this nature is **Butterworth's EC Brief,** in which the various instruments are arranged per subject heading. Not to be neglected either is the **European Access** series, which is published every two months, and contains, *inter alia,* a classified list of references to recently adopted legislation. Attention should also be drawn to the annotated texts found in **Halsbury's Statutes of England** (3rd edn), and the **Guide to EEC Legislation** published by the TMC Asser Institute of Amsterdam University, which comes together with a cumulative supplement.

C   Case reports

Official Community texts

The decisions of the European Court of Justice are published in the **European Court Reports** (known in their abbreviated form as **ECR**), which are available in all the official languages of the Community. The reports are most comprehensive, and include, in addition to the actual decision, a statement of the various arguments put forward by the parties, and the Opinion of the

Advocate-General (above, p 35). Each annual version contains a number of practical indices (by subject matter, by name of the parties, etc).

As from 1989, there have been three series: the first preceded by the letter C, which features the decisions of the actual Court; the second preceded by the letter T, which contains the decisions of the Court of First instance, and the third preceded by the letter P, which includes appeals from the Court of First Instance to the Court of Justice (above, p 35). Even though Britain and Ireland only joined the Community in 1973, a special series of the **ECR** covering the 1954–72 period is available in English.

Unfortunately, there is always considerable time lag between the date of the decision and its appearance in the **ECR**. The Court attempts to remedy this in part by publishing in word-processed form each decision as it is made. This is a far from satisfactory situation, and little appears to have been done by the Community institutions to remedy it. The reader wishing to consult the latest ECJ decisions can therefore more usefully be referred to such unofficial collections as the **Common Market Law Reports** (below).

Unofficial texts

The most comprehensive series of European law reports is undoubtedly the **Common Market Law Reports**. These not only publish Court of Justice decisions (both in English and in the language in which the proceedings were conducted) within weeks of their pronouncement – in sharp contrast to the **ECR** – but they also contain the most important Commission decisions on competition law, as well as foreign court decisions relating to Community law (in both the original language and their English translation).

The most extensive bulletin providing summaries of ECJ decisions as they are made is undoubtedly **European Court Monitor** (European Law Press Ltd). Unfortunately it only commenced publication in early 1996, so it will take time to establish itself. A selection of ECJ decisions is also published in the **Common Market Reports**, published by CCH. Summarised versions of a selection of ECJ decisions and national case law relating to Community law can also be found in **European Law Digest**. Both **The Times** and **The Guardian** regularly publish summaries of leading ECJ decisions.

There are also available a number of compendia of ECJ and national decisions on Community law. Brinkhorst and Schermers's **Judicial Remedies in the European Communities** (3rd edn, 1994) and Sperl and Usher's **Compendium on Case Law relating to the European Communities** (2nd edn, 1995) are excellent examples of this. In French, there is the excellent collection by Boulouis, J and Chevallier, R-M, **Grands Arrêts de la CJCE** (1991).

D   Statistical information

General

Contrary to popular belief, statistics are not the exclusive preserve of professional statisticians. Even such normally innumerate creatures as lawyers sometimes require statistical information in order to substantiate or refute arguments. Such statistical data are available from both official EU and from privately-published sources.

Official Community sources

The main source of statistical information on all aspects of Community policy is EUROSTAT, being an acronym for the Statistical Office of the European Communities. It produces an annual catalogue which appear in colour-coded series. These are called 'themes', which also form the subject matter of annual reports. Each series is itself divided into various types of publication, identified by the following capital letters: A (Yearbooks), B (short term trends), C (accounts, surveys and statistics) D (studies and analyses) E (methods) and F (rapid reports).

The statistical information produced by Eurostat is fully computerised, being available on disk, CD-ROM, or on-line. The main courses here are the following databases:

- CRONOS: contains statistics on economic trends, energy, industry, agriculture and fisheries, forestry, and external trade.

- COMEXT: contains trade statistics.

- REGIO: contains regional statistics.

- EUROCRON: contains statistics on national accounts, population and employment trends.

Eurostat publishes a number of indices and sources which enable the desired statistics to be traced without undue difficulty, even for the lay person: **Eurostat Index** (arranged per subject headings), **Basic Statistics of the Community** (includes data not only concerning the EU, but also regarding the EFTA states, the US and Japan), **Eurostatistics** (monthly issue giving up-to-date information on economic statistics) and **Europe in Figures** (general statistical overview of the Community).

Unofficial sources

Here, the most important sources are the monthly supplements (A and B) to the journal **European Economy**, and the **Results of the Business Survey of Managements in the Community**, a monthly publication containing statistics on business and consumer trends within the Community.

E   Databases

Official Community sources

In our information society, databases are increasingly becoming a powerful source of information, and this trend has obviously not circumvented the EU and its institutions. According to the **Sources of Information,** published by the European Commission, some 50 databases and five CD-ROMs were produced by either the Commission's various departments or other organisations. Some of these databases are made available to the public against payment of a subscription or flat-rate fee; others are available free of charge and accessible through ECHO (the European Commission Host Organisation) which is located in Luxembourg. ECHO also seeks to extend access to databases by means of training initiatives. In addition, ECHO issues two periodicals free of charge, to wit **ECHO News** and **I+T Magazine,** as well as a variety of brochures, guides and videos. The following are obtainable free of charge:

- **Introduction to electronic information services:** this is an A4 brochure containing a basic introduction to the part played by the various parties involved in the electronic information industry;

- **Echo Databases and Services:** this brochure introduces ECHO and explains its activities;

- **Brokersguide:** this is a printed version of all the brokers who are listed in the **I'm Guide** (below);

- **Echo Pocket Guide:** this is a summary of the Common Command Language (CCL), including directions on the main commands.

In addition, **Eurobases** (below) makes available the **I'm Guide. This** is an inventory of all databases, their hosts and producers, PTT contact points, networks and gateways and CD-ROM products, etc, available in the European Union. Three videos, **ECHO IN BRIEF, ECHO IN FULL,** and **TED** (presentation of the TED Database) are available at 15 ECUs, in English, French, Spanish, German and Italian. In addition, there is available an offline CCL training diskette at a cost of 15 ECUs.

NFO 92 contains the Commission's other two hosts centres are **EUROBASES** (which distributes the **ABEL, CELEX, SESAME, SCAD, OIL, INFO 92, ECLAS, RAPID** and **EUROCRON** bases) and **EUROSTAT.** Subscribers to **EUROBASES** receive a wide range of user documentation, to wit, reference manuals, thesauri, lists of descriptors and pocket guides.[2] A word of explanation for the most important of these systems is in order.

---

2   European Commission, *Source of Information* (1995) p A 105.

ABEL is a document delivery system for Community directives.

SESAME provides information on research and development in the energy sector.

RAPID is the database of the Spokesman's Department of the European Commission.

CELEX is the official Community law database, containing as it does the full text of all Community legislation and ECJ decisions. In addition, it features the texts of various legislative proposals, policy documents and European Parliament questions and answers, legislation relating to the Internal Market programme enacted under the Single European Act, as well as the legislation proposed under the Social Charter.

SCAD is a bibliographic database which contains references to EU documents rather than the text of these documents themselves. It indexes all relevant Community legislation, proposed legislation and other official publications.

TED (Tenders Electronic Daily) which contains the full text of all invitations to tender for public contracts as published in the S section of the Official Journal (above, p 305).[3]

Attention should also be drawn to CORDIS, which is the name given to a variety of databases covering EU support for scientific research and development, and to APC, which gives information on the precise stage reached by preparatory EU legislation (only available in French).

Unofficial sources

The most important on-line computerised source of information available in the commercial sector is the **LEXIS** system, which features ECJ reports, Commission competition cases, as well as giving access to the **CELEX** texts. It also includes national decisions relating to Community law.

Another major database is **JUSTIS** European References (Context Ltd, London), which is an enhanced CD-ROM version of **SCAD** (above), as well as containing material from the Spicers Centre for Europe database.

3   Wynne, B, *Brussels Bureaucracy? Official EC Information and How to Find It* (1994), University of North London Press, pp 34–35.

F   Citing Community law

As is the case with any law materials, there is an accepted way of citing them by way of reference.

Legislation

Regulations are cited by means of two number separated by a slash, the first figures being the consecutive number of the instrument, the second indicating the year in which it was adopted. Thus the Mergers Regulation is cited as Regulation 4064/89. Directives and Decisions are also cited by means of two such numbers, but for these instruments the first figure relates to the year of adoption and the second to the consecutive number. Thus the Equal Treatment Directive is cited as Directive 76/207; the Greenhouse Gas Emissions Decision is cited as Decision 93/389. (The more fastidious may add the letters 'EEC', 'Euratom' or 'ECSC' after a second slash, but many authors, including the present writer, omit this.)

Official Journal

Citations from the Official Journal should state (a) the abbreviation OJ, (b) the year in question, (c) the first letter of the series, and (c) the number in the series. Thus the Official Journal citation for the Mergers Regulation 4064/89, referred to above, is OJ 1989 L 395. The Official Journal citation for the Draft Directive on CO2 is OJ 1992 C 196.

COM documents

Here, the word COM appears first, followed by the year in which it was adopted in brackets, and its reference number. Thus the document featuring the famous 'Cockfield White Paper' on completing the internal market is cited as:

> COM(85)310.

Court of Justice decisions

The decision is cited by stating

(i)   The letter (C, T or P) indicating the type of action (above, p 307).

(ii) The case number. This normally consists of two figures separated by a slash, the second of which indicates the year in which the application was brought. Sometimes the citation will contain two or more such numbers; this occurs where these cases have been joined because they deal essentially with the same matter.

(iii) The names of the parties, including, where appropriate, the ex parte parties. This sometimes gives rise to confusion, since authors do not invariably adhere to the names of the parties in the exact manner in which they are referred to by the Court of Justice.

(iv) The year of the ECR in brackets, and the volume number (in Roman numerals).

(v) The page where the case report begins.

(vi) (Where appropriate) the page where the passage alluded to is featured.

Thus a typical case citation would be the following, for the famous *Francovich* case would be Cases C–6/90 & C–9/90, *Francovich and Bonifaci v Italian Republic* (1991) ECR I-5403 at 5422. (The more fastidious authors also add the Common Market Law Reports (CMLR) citation.)

III Career and training information

A   General

Community law has been studied at British and Irish universities for many years now – indeed, they now have become a compulsory part of the LLB. curriculum. Yet very few students ever make full professional use of this subject once they leave University. The opportunity to apply their knowledge and experience in this field may arise from time to time in the course of their careers, but only very rarely extends beyond such occasional use.

The reasons for this are many and varied. The finger of censure can be pointed in part at the Universities themselves, which seldom if ever go to the trouble of obtaining information on this subject from the various bodies involved. In addition, liaison between law schools and careers offices at most universities is capable of a good deal of improvement. The Community institutions cannot escape censure either, and only very rarely make the effort to make the relevant information available where it matters.

B   Postgraduate education

In the UK

There are essentially three possibilities at this level: (i) LLM (MPhil) by research; (ii) LLM by instruction and research; (iii) PhD.

(i) LLM (MPhil) by research.

There are no fixed programmes for this degree. Its subject matter depends on the subject of the dissertation (normally between 50,000 and 60,000 words) as agreed between the candidate and the supervisor. As all Law School/Departments now have specialists in Community law, there should be an opportunity to do this degree with virtually every University offering the LLB degree – particularly as law schools/departments are nowadays quite keen to attract LLM/MPhil students.

(ii) LLM by instruction and research

These are degrees which are subject to a distinct academic programme, and normally involve the taking of a number of examinations as well as the presentation of a dissertation. The duration varies, but is invariably no less than one year. The contents of these programmes vary, but normally include the major subject-areas of Community law. In some cases, the emphasis is quite heavily on business law (particularly competition law).

Such LLM programmes are currently available at many institutions of higher education. Those interested should consult the appropriate Higher Education handbooks.

Abroad

There are also a number of postgraduate programmes available abroad. Quite a few of them are taught in English, at least in part. Particular mention should be made of the following programmes:

- College of Europe, Bruges (Belgium)
- European University Institute (Florence, Italy)
- The Bologna (Italy) Centre of the John Hopkins University
- Vrije Universiteit Brussel (VUB (Dutch-speaking university)) and the Université Libre de Bruxelles (French-speaking)
- TMC Asser Institute, University of Amsterdam, The Netherlands.

C   Training opportunities

General

What better way of learning about the Community institutions than by working for them – if only in the lowly capacity of a trainee? The EU institutions make available a number of *stages*[4] which enable young graduates to do just that. They not only provide an invaluable insight into the internal workings of these apparently remote institutions, but also make an extremely favourable impression when included in one's curriculum vitae!

Some of these *stages* are highly practical in design and execution, whereas others are oriented exclusively towards research. It should be stressed from the outset, however, that these are not preludes to a post, whether full-time, temporary or even freelance, with the institution concerned. Although unsurprisingly the ranks of EU civil servants include a not inconsiderable number of former *stagiaires*, their employment was obtained through the normal channels, to wit, by competitive examination or on the basis of qualifications

---

4   This is a term which translates into English with the greatest of difficulty. It lies seomwhere between a traineeship and an internship.

and experience. Although strictly speaking the Council of Europe is a totally separate institution from the EU, its traineeship scheme is explained below for the sake of completeness, and because some graduates (including the present author!) see it as complementary to the EU *stage*.

The Commission *stage*

The purpose of this in-service training with the Commission is:

- to give *stagiaires* a general idea of the objectives of, and problems arising from, European integration,

- to provide them with practical knowledge of the functioning of the institution's departments,

- to enable them to acquire some personal experience through the contacts made in the course of performing their duties;

- to allow them to apply and put into practice the knowledge which they will have acquired in the course of their studies or professional careers.[5]

Part of the training period may be devoted to the preparation of a postgraduate thesis or academic paper. Whether this is possible or not will depend very much on the division where the *stagiaire* works, and the particular requirements of the post at the time.

How does the Commission *stage* work?

The *stage* is a period of five months spent with the Commission, performing work which would normally be expected of a junior full-time member of staff. Obviously the nature and range of the duties involved vary considerably along with the division to which the *stagiaire* is attached. There are two training periods every year: from October to February, and from March to July. For each period, there are approximately 180–200 places available. The vast majority of *stagiaires* are based in Brussels, although there are a number who will work with the Commission divisions in Luxembourg, and even those who will find themselves attached to the Commission's offices in the capitals of Europe.[6]

Although graduates covering every discipline, from nuclear physics to biblical studies, are invited to apply, the majority of *stagiaires* are graduates in the law, economics, social sciences and languages. They are spread over all the policy areas of the Community.

5 Decision of the Commission dated 16/3/1976.

6 This fell particularly hard on a nameless British stagiaire of the 1978-79 group, who, having just completed his studies at the London School of Economics, arrived in Brussels for the introductory sessions, only to find himself attached to the Commission's London offices! Fortunately this matter was solved by mutual agreement, and he exchanged places with an Italian *stagiaire* whose training as a journalist enabled him to derive much benefit from his experience.

As has been mentioned before, the work performed by a *stagiaire* can vary enormously, which is why it is dangerous to make any sweeping statements on the subject. However, it is safe to state that the majority of *stagiaires* will find themselves performing any combination of the following tasks:

a) *Research.* The Commission has a massive output of consultative and preparatory documents, which are drawn up in its various departments. The background research relating to these papers is often a task devolving on the junior members of staff, or on the *stagiaires*.

b) *Preliminary case studies.* The Commission has to examine hundreds of case files, which relate to the consistency of domestic legislation with Community law, and individual cases (eg competition law applications and complaints). The *stagiaire* may be required to take an initial look at the file and draft a preliminary report.

c) *Correspondence.* As can be expected from such a large organisation, the Commission has a mass of daily correspondence which requires attention. Even the full-time lawyers working for the Commission will spend a good deal of their time drafting such correspondence in a legally watertight manner. Many *stagiaires* make themselves useful by producing the initial draft.

d) *Translation.* This will obviously be the main task of those *stagiaires* who work for the translation divisions. This is where lawyers with linguistic skills truly come into their own, as legal translators are much sought after within the Commission. (Please note, however, that a minimum of two EU languages will be required for such a position.)

However, as every *stagiaire* is deemed to know at least one European language, even those working for other divisions will quite often be required to perform translation work, if only for internal purposes.

Where to apply   The Training Office, Secretariat-General,
                    European Commission,
                    200 rue de la Loi/Wetstraat
                    B-1049 Brussels – Belgium.

Stages with other institutions

Schemes similar to that organised by the Commission are available with the Council of Ministers, the European Parliament, the Economic and Social Committee, and the Committee of the Regions. The numbers involved are much smaller than is the case with the Commission. They are organised on roughly the same basis as the Commission *stage*.

Robert Schuman Scholarships

These are periods of research which can be spent with, and are financed by, the European Parliament. They are awarded to post-graduate students who should in principle be citizens of the EU Member States. The annual intake is approximately 45. Scholarship holders are based at the premises of the Secretariat of the Parliament, which is located in Luxembourg. They work under the supervision of a senior official of the Directorate-General for Research. Normally they are expected to assist with research projects initiated by this office, and have all the Parliament's research facilities – including an excellent and extensive library – at their disposal for this purpose.

The profile of the average scholarship holder is roughly the same as that of the average *stagiaire* with the Commission. Law graduates are therefore highly credible applicants. Those who wish to stress their language qualifications and experience, however, should apply for a *stage* with the Parliament rather than a Robert Schuman scholarship. Obviously the work of the Parliament takes priority, but the staff of the Directorate-General for Research normally also provide assistance and/or advice to those scholarship holders who have research work of their own to complete which is relevant to the Parliament's work.

The scholarship is relatively short (three months at the most), although the amount payable per month is considerably higher than that of the Commission *stage*. Awards are made four times per year, and usually start in January, April, July and September of each year. Those who have already enjoyed the benefit of a stage with another Community institution are not eligible. This safeguard is a sensible one, and prevents the development of the 'professional trainee', a concept which would go against the very purpose of these schemes.

Enquiries should be addressed to:

> European Parliament
> Director General of Research
> (Robert Schuman Scholarships)
> Schuman Building
> L-2929 Luxembourg.

Stages with the Council of Europe

The Council of Europe is an organisation which is totally separate from the EU. However, its traineeship scheme is relevant here because it attracts applicants with the same type of academic profile as those applying for Commission *stages*. Judging by the number of those who have completed the Commission and the Council of Europe scheme, the two are very much considered to be complementary to each other.

The scheme involves a period of three months spent with the Council of Europe at its headquarters in Strasbourg. It is intended as an opportunity to form a general idea of the Council's work, activities and objectives and of the problems involved in European co-operation. The *stagiaire* is thus able to supplement and put into practice the knowledge acquired during his or her studies and/or professional experience.

The *stagiaires* will be attached to one of the Council's Directorates. Their main duties consist in research, the preparation of draft reports and studies for the meetings of experts, and the drafting of minutes. They may also be called upon to assist with current work – which (especially for English-language *stagiaires*) in most cases comes down to translation.

Enquiries should be addressed to:

The Council of Europe,
Establishment Division
PO Box 431 R6
F-67006 Strasbourg
France.

Multilingual Glossary

English	French	German	Italian	Spanish
Accession	Adhésion	Beitritt	Adesione	Adhesión
Acquis communautaire	Acquis communautaire	Acquis communautaire	Fase raggiunta dalla legislazione comunutaria	Acervo comunitario
Admissibility	Recevabilité	Zulässigkeit	Ammissibilità di una acción	Cualidad de
Advance fixing	Fixation préalable	Vorbestimmung	Fissazione anticipata	Exacción reguladoria
Agriculture	Agriculture	Landwirtschaft	Agricoltura	Agricultura
Aid	Aide	Beihilfe	Aiuto	Ayuda
Amendment	Modification	Änderung	Emendamento	Enmienda
Annulment	Annulation	Nichtigerklärung	Annullamento	Anulación
Anti-dumping duty	Droit anti-dumping	Antidumpingzoll	Dazio anti-dumping	Derecho anti-dumping
Appeal	Appel	Berufung/Klage	Ricorso	Recurso
Assembly	Assemblée	Versammlung	Assemblea	Parlamento
Association agreement	Accord d'association	Assoziierungsvertrag	Accordo di associazione	Acuerdo de asociación
Autonomous duty	Tarif de douane autonome	Autonomer Zollsatz	Dazio autonomo	Derecho autónomo
Average rate	Taux moyen	Durchschnittssatz	Tasso medio	tipo medio
Base price	Prix de base	Interventionspreis	Prezzo base	Precio de base
Block Exemption	Exemption en bloc	Gruppenfreistellung	Esenzione per categoria	Exención por categoría
Budget	Budget	Haushalt	Bilancio	Presupuesto

English	French	German	Italian	Spanish
Cabinet	Cabinet	Kabinett	Gabinetto	Gabinete
Capital Movement	Mouvement de capital	Kapitalverkehr	Movimento di capitali	Transferencia de capitales
Chamber	Chambre	Kammer	Sezione	Sala
Comfort letter	Lettre de classement	Informelles Schreiben	Lettera amministrativa di archivazione	Carta administrativa favorable
Commission	Commission	Kommission	Commissione	Comisión
Commissioner	Membre de la Commission	Mitglied der Kommission	Commissario	Comisario
Common Agricultural Policy	Politique agricole commune	Gemeinsame Agrarpolitik	Politica agricola comune	Política agrícola común
Common commercial policy	Politique commerciale commune	Gemeinsame Handelspolitik	Politica commerciale comune	Política commercial común
Common customs tariff	Tarif douanier commun	Gemeinsamer Zolltarif	Tariffa doganale comune	Arancel aduanero común
Common Market	Marché commun	Gemeinsamer Markt	Mercato comune	Mercado común
Common position	Position commune	Gemeinsamer Standpunkt	Posizione comune	Posición común
Common transport policy	Politique commune des transports	Gemeinsame Verkehrspolitik	Politica comune dei trasporti	Política común de transporte
Community	Communauté	Gemeinschaft	Comunità	Comunidad
Community law	Droit communautaire	Gemein -schaftsrecht	Diritto comunitario	Derecho comunitario

319

English	French	German	Italian	Spanish
Community transit	Transit communautaire	Durchfuhrfreiheit innerhalb der Gemeinschaft	Transito comunitario	Tránsito comunitario
Competition	Concurrence	Wettbewerb	Concorrenza	Competencia
Concentration	Concentration	Konzentration	Concentrazione	Concentración
Concerted practice	Pratique concertée	Parallelverhalten	Pratica concertata	Práctica concertada
Conjunctural policy	Politique conjoncturelle	Konjunktur-politik	Politica congiunturale	Política conjuntural
Consultative committee	Comité consultatif	Beratender Ausschuß	Comitato consultivo	Comité consultativo
Conventional duties	Droits conventionnels	Vertragsmäßiger Zollsatz	Dazi convenzionali	Derechos convencionales
Co-operation agreement	Accord de coopération	Zusammen-arbeits-abkommen	Accordo di cooperazione	Acuerdo de cooperación
Co-operation procedure	Procédure de coopération	Zusammen-arbeitsverfahren	Procedura di cooperazione	Procedimiento de cooperación
Council (of Ministers)	Conseil (des ministres)	(Minister)rat	Consiglio (dei ministri)	Consejo (de los ministros)
Council working group	Groupe de travail du Conseil	Ratsgruppe	Gruppo di lavoro del Consiglio	Grupo de trabajo del Consejo
Countervailing duty	Droit compensatoire	Ausgleichszoll	Dazio compensativo	Derecho compensador
Court of Auditors	Cour des comptes	Rechnungshof	Corte dei Conti	Tribunal de Cuentas
Court of First Instance	Tribunal de première instance	Gericht der ersten Instanz	Tribunale di primo grado	Tribunal de primera instancia

English	French	German	Italian	Spanish
Court of Justice	Cour de Justice	Gerichtshof	Corte di Giustizia	Tribunal de Justicia
Customs duty	Droit de douane	Zoll	Dazio doganale	Derecho de aduana
Customs territory	Territoire douanier	Zollgebiet	Territorio doganale	Territorio aduanera
Customs union	Union douanière	Zollunion	Unione doganale	Unión aduanera
Decision	Décision	Entscheidung	Decisione	Decisión
Derived legislation	Législation dérivée	Abgeleitete Gesetzgebung	Legislazione derivata	Legislación derivada
Derogation	Dérogation	Ausnahme	Deroga	Derogación
Destination principle	Principe de destination	Bestimmungslandsgrundsatz	Principio di destinazione	Principio de tributación en destino
Development	Développement	Entwicklung	Sviluppo	Desarollo
Direct action	Action directe	Unmittelbare Klage	Ricorso diretto	Acción directa
Direct applicability	Applicabilité directe	Unmittelbare anwendbarkeit	Applicabilità diretta	Applicabilidad directa
Direct effect	Effet direct	Unmittelbare wirkung	Effetto diretto	Efecto directo
Direct taxation	Contributions directes	Direkte Steuer	Imposizione diretta	Imposición directa
Director General	Directeur Général	General director	Direttore generale	Director general
Energy	Energie	Energie	Energia	Energía
Environment	Environnement	Umwelt	Ambiente	Ambiente

English	French	German	Italian	Spanish
European Community	Communauté européenne	Europäische Gemeinschaft	Comunità europea	Comunidad europea
European Coal and Steel Community	Communauté européenne du charbon et l'acier	Europäische Gemeinschaft für Kohle und Stahl	Comunità europea del Carbone e dell'Acciaio	Comunidad Europea del Carbón y del Acero
European Council	Conseil européen	Europäischer Rat	Consiglio europeo	Consejo europeo
European Monetary System	Système monétaire européen	Europäisches Währungs- system	Sistema monetario europeo	Sistema monetario europeo
Exchange Rate Mechanism	Mécanisme de change	Wechselkurs- mechanismus	Mecanismo cambio	Mecanismo cambio
Executive	Pouvoir exécutif	Ausführende Gewalt	Potere esecutivo	Poder ejecutivo
Exhaustion of Rights	Épuisement des droits	Erschöpfung eines Rechts	Esaurimento dei diritti	Agotamiento del derecho
External relations	Relations extérieures	Außen- beziehungen	Relazioni esterne	Relaciones exteriores
Federalism	Fédéralisme	Föderalismus	Federalismo	Federalismo
Financial Supervision	Contrôle financier	Finanzkontrolle	Controllo finanziario	Control financiero
Fiscal neutrality	Neutralité fiscale	Steuerliche Neutralität	Neutralità fiscale	Neutralidad impositiva
Fisheries	Pêches	Fischerei	Pesca	Pesca
Founding treaties	Traités fondateurs	Gründungs- verträge	Trattati istitutivi	Tratados fundamentales
Four freedoms	Quatre libertés	Grundfreiheiten	Quattro libertà	Cuatro libertades
Free movement of goods	Libre circulation des marchandises	Freier Warenverkehr	Libera circolazione dei beni	Libre circulación de los bienes

English	French	German	Italian	Spanish
Free movement of persons	Libre circulation des personnes	Freizügigkeit	Libera circolazione delle persone	Libre circulación de las personas
Free trade area	Zone de libre échange	Freihandels-zones	Zona di libero cambio	Area de libre comercio
Guide price	Prix d'orientation	Richtpreis	Prezzo indicativo	Precio de referencia
Harmonisation	Harmonisation	Angleichung	Armonizzazione	Armonisación
Head of Division	Chef de division	Abteilungs-führer	Capo divisione	Jefe de división
High Authority	Haute Autorité	Hohe Behörde	Alta autorità	Alta autoridad
Indirect taxation	Contributions indirectes	Indirekte Steuern	Imposizione indiretta	Imposición indirecta
Industrial property	Propriété industrielle	Gewerblicher Eigentum	Proprietà industriale	Propriedad industrial
Interest	intérêts	Zinsen	Interessi	Interès
Internal market	Marché intérieur	Binnenmarkt	Mercato interno	Mercado interior
Intervention agency	Organisme d'intervention	Interventions-stelle	Organismo di intervento	Agencia de intervención
Inward processing	Perfectionne-ment actif	Aktive Veredlung	Perfezion-amento attivo	Perfeccionaminto activo
Joint venture	Entreprise commune	Gemeinschafts-unternehmen	Impresa comune	Empresa conjunta
Legislature	Législateur	Gesetzgeber	Assemblea legislativa	Poder legislativo
Legitimate expectation	Prévision légitime	Vertrauens-schutz	Legittima aspettativa	Expectativa legitima
Liberalisation	Libéralisation	Freigabe	Liberalizzazione	Liberalización

English	French	German	Italian	Spanish
Market share	Part du marché	Marktanteil	Quota di mercato	Cuota de mercado
Measure	Mesure	Maßnahme	Misura	Medida
Measure	Mesure	Maßnahme	Misura	Medida
Measure having equivalent effect	Mesure d'effet équivalent	Maßnahme gleicher Wirkung	Misura d'effetto equivalente	Medida de efecto equivalente
Member State	Etat membre	Mitglied-staat	Stato membro	Estado miembro
Merger	Fusion	Fusion	Fusione	Fusión
Mixed agreement	Accord mixte	Gemischtes Abkommen	Accordo misto	Acuerdo mixto
Monetary compensatory amount	Montant compensatoire monétaire	Währungs-ausgleichs-betrag	Importo monetario compensativo	Montante compensatorio monetario
National (domestic) law	Droit national	Nationales Recht	Diritto nazionale	Derecho nacional
Negative clearance	Attestation négative	Negativattest	Dichiarazione negativa	Declaración negativa
Nomenclature	Nomenclature	Nomenklatur	Nomenclatura	Nomenclatura
Non-tariff barrier	Entrave non-tarifaire aux échanges	Nicht-tarifäres Handelshemmnis	Ostacolo non tarifario agli scambi	Obstáculo no arancelario
Notification	Signification	Anmeldung	Notifica	Notificación
Official	Fonctionnaire	Beamter	Funzionario	Funcionario
Official Journal	Journal officiel	Amtsblatt	Gazzetta ufficiale	Diario oficial
Oligopoly	Oligopole	Oligopol	Oligopolio	Oligopolio
Opinion (Article 189 of the Treaty)	Opinion	Stellungnahme	Parere	Dictamen

English	French	German	Italian	Spanish
Opinion submitted by Advocate-General)	Conclusions	Schlußanträge	Conclusioni	Conclusiones
Origin principle	Principe de l'origine	Ursprungslandsprinzip	Criterio dell'origine	Imposición en origen
Outward processing	Perfectionnement passif	Passive veredlung	Perfezionamento passivo	Perfeccionamento pasivo
Own' resources	Ressources propres	Eigene Mittel	Risorse proprie	Recursos propios
Parallel import	Importation parallèle	Parallel-einfuhr	Importazione parallele	Importación paralela
Plea of Illegality	Exception d'illégalité	Rechtswidrigkeitseinrede	Eccezione di illegalità	Exceptión de illegalidad
Plenary session	Séance plénière	Vollsitzung	Sessione plenaria	Sesión plenaria
Preliminary investigation	Instruction	Ermittlung	Istruttoria	Instrucción
Preliminary ruling	Décision préjudicielle	Vorabentscheidung	Decisione preliminare	Decisión prejudicial
Proportionality	Proportionnalité	Verhältnismäßigkeit	Proporzionalità	Proporcionalidad
Protective measure	Mesure de sauvegarde	Schutz-maßnahme	Misura prottetiva	Medida de protección
Public policy	Ordre public	Öffentliche Ordnung	Ordine pubblico	Orden publico
Qualified majority voting	Majorité qualifiée	Qualifizierte Mehrheit	Maggioranza qualificata	Mayoria cualificada
Quantitative restriction	Restriction quantitative	Mengenmäßige Beschränkung	Restrizione quantitativa	Restricción cuantitativa
Quota	Quota	Quote	Contingente	Contingente

English	French	German	Italian	Spanish
Rapporteur	Rapporteur	Bericht-erstatter	Relatore	Relator
Reasoned opinion	Opinion motivée	Begründete Stellungnahme	Parere motivato	Opinión motivada
Recommendation	Recomman-dation	Empfehlung	Raccomandazione	Recomendación
Referring court	Cour (tribunal)	Vorlegendes Gericht	Giudice a quo de renvoi	Juez de reenvío
Regional policy	Politique régionale	Regional-politik	Politica regionale	Política regional
Regulation	Règlement	Verordnung	Regolamento	Reglamento
Relevant market	Marché pertinent	Relevanter Markt	Mercato rilevante	Mercado relevante
Resolution	Résolution	Ent-schließung	Risoluzione	Resolución
Reverse discrimination	Discrimination à rebours	Umgekehrte Diskrimin-ierung	Discriminazione all' inverso	Discriminación inversa
Right of establishment	Droit d'établissement	Nieder-lassungsrecht	Diritto di stabilimento	Derecho de establecimiento
Rule of Law	Etat de droit	Rechtsstaat	Stato di diritto	Estado de derecho
Rule of origin	Règle d'origine	Ursprungs-regel	Norma sull'origine Norma di origine	Norma de origen
Ruling	Arrêt	Urteil	Decisione	Resolución
Selective distribution	Distribution sélective	Selektiver Vertrieb	Distribuzione selettiva	Distribución selectiva
Services	Services	Dienste	Servizi	Servicios
Simple majority voting	Simple vote à la majorité	Entscheidung mit einfacher Mehrheit	Votazione a maggioranza semplice	Votación por mayoría simple

English	French	German	Italian	Spanish
Target price	Prix indicatif	Zielpreis	Prezzo limiti	Precio indicativo
Tariff	Tarif	Tarif	Tariffo	Arancel
Tariff preference	Préférence tarifaire	Zollpräferenz	Preferenza tarifaria	Preferancia aranceleria
Third country	Pays tiers	Drittland	Paese terzo	País tercero
Threshold price	Prix de seuil	Schwellpreis	Prezzo d'entrata	Precio umbral
Transport	Transports	Verkehr	Trasporti	Transportes
Treaty	Traité	Vertrag	Trattato	Tratado
Turnover tax	Taxe sur chiffre d'affaires	Umsatzsteuer	Imposta sul cifra d'affari	Impuesto sobre los ingresos brutos
Type approval	Homologation de type	Typenzulassung	Omologazione tipo	Aprobación tipo
Undertaking	Entreprise	Unternehmen	Impresa	Empresa
Value-added tax	Taxe sur la valeur ajoutée	Mehrwertsteuer	Imposta sul valore aggiunto	Impuesto sobre el valor añadido

Hi there!!

Bibliography

Materials on Community law

These works intersperse a systematic presentation of items of legislation, extracts from case reports and excerpts from the available literature with the author's own comments.

Craig, P and de Burca, G, *EC Law – Text, Cases and Materials*, 1996, Oxford: Oxford University Press.

Pollard, V and Ross, M, *European Community Law: Text and Materials*, 1994, London: Butterworth.

Tillotson, J, *European Community Law – Text, Cases and Materials*, 1994, London, Cavendish Publishing.

Weatherill, S, *Cases & Materials on EC Law*, 3rd edn, 1996, London: Blackstone.

General textbooks

These works provide a systematic analysis of all the main topics of Community law.

Cerexhe, P, *Le droit européen*, 1990 (in French), Brussels: Nauwelawrts & Bruylant.

Charlesworth, A and Cullen, H, *European Community Law*, 1994, London: Pitman, London: Blackstone.

Constantinho, P and Dony, M, *Le droit communautaire*, 1994 (in French), Paris: Armand Colin.

Dagtoglou, P, *Europaiko koinitiko dikaio*, 1995 (in Greek), Athens: Ekdosei's Anastasiodi.

Druesne, G, *Droit matériel et politiques de la Communauté européenne*, 1991 (in French), Paris: PUF.

Gautron, J-C, *Droit européen*, 2nd edn, 1995, Paris: Mementos Dalloz.

Isaac, P, *Droit communautaire général*, 3rd edn, 1992 (in French), Paris: Masson.

Kent, P, *Law of the European Union*, 2nd edn, 1996, London: Pitman.

Lasok, D and Bridge, JW, *Law and Institutions of the European Union* (6th edn by Lasok, D), 1994, London: Butterworth.

Lauria, M, *Manuale di diritto delle Comunità Europee*, 1989 (in Italian), Milan: Edizioni Simone.

Molina del Pozo, M, *Manual de derecho de la Comunidad Europea*, 1993 (in Spanish), Barcelona: Ariel.

Mathijsen, PSRF, *A Guide to European Union Law*, 6th edn, 1995, London: Sweet and Maxwell.

Opperman, T, *Europarecht*, 1991 (in German), München: CH Beck Verlag.

Pisuisse, CS, and Teubner, AMM, *Elementair Europees Gemeenschapsrecht*, 1995 (in Dutch), Groningen: Walters-Noordhoff.

Schweitzer/Hummer, *Europarecht*, 1990 (in German), Baden-Baden: Nomos.

Shaw, J, *European Community Law* (1993), London: Blackstone.

Steiner, J, *Textbook on EEC Law*, 4th edn, 1995, London: Blackstone.

Weatherill, S and Beaumont, *EC Law*, 2nd edn, 1995, London: Penguin.

Wyatt, D and Dashwood, A, *European Community Law*, 4th edn, 1995, London: Sweet and Maxwell.

Institutional law

These are works dealing not only with the institutions in the strict sense of the term, but also with such topics as the direct effect and supremacy of Community law, and the various actions before the Court of Justice.

Arnull, A, *The General Principles of EEC Law and the Individual*, 1990, Leicester: Leicester University Press.

Boulouis, J, *Droit institutionnel des Communautés européennes*, 2nd edn, 1990 (in French), Paris: Montchrestien.

Collins, L, *European Community Law in the United Kingdom*, 3rd edn, 1992, London: Butterworths.

Ehlermann, C-D, *Die Europäische Gemeinschaft und das Recht*, 1987 (in German), München: CH Beck.

Hartley, TC, *The Foundations of European Community Law*, 2nd edn, 1994, Oxford: Oxford University Press.

Louis, JV, *The Community Legal Order*, 2nd edn, 1990, Luxembourg: European Perspectives.

Maresceau, M, *De Directe Werking in het Europees Gemeenschapsrecht*, 1978 (in Dutch), Deventer: Kluwer.

Moreau Desfarges, P, *Les Institutions Européennes*, 1994 (in French), Paris: PUF.

Schwarze, J, *European Administrative Law*, 1992, London: Sweet and Maxwell.

Schwarze, J, *Europäisches Verwaltungsrecht*, 2nd edn, 1992 (in German), Baden-Baden: Nomos.

Soldatos, P, *Le système institutionnel et politique des Communautés européennes*, 1989 (in French), Brussels: Bruylant.

Steiner J, *Enforcing Community Law*, 1994, London: Blackstone.

Wagner, E, *Die Rechtsetzung in den Europäischen Gemeinschaften*, 1984 (in German), München: CH Beck.

Free movement of goods

Blaise, J-B, *Droit européen des affaires*, 1991 (in French), Paris: PUF.

Easson, A, *Taxation in the European Community*, 1993, London: Sweet and Maxwell.

Falkenstein, M, *Der Freie Wahrenverkehr in der EG*, 1989 (in German), München: CH Beck.

Goldman, B, Lyon-Caen, A, and Vogel, L, *Droit commercial européen*, 1991 (in French), Paris: Dalloz.

Grisoli, F, *L'Europa del mercato comune*, 1990 (in Italian), Milan: Mondadori.

Lasok, D, *The Customs Law of the European Economic Community*, 2nd edn, 1990, Deventer: Kluwer.

Oliver, P, *The Free Movement of Goods in the EEC*, 3rd edn, 1992, London: European Law Centre.

Seidel, D, *Die Vollendung des Binnenmarkts der EG als Rechtsetzungsprozess*, 1989 (in German), Baden-Baden: Nomos.

Slot, PJ and Van der Woude, MH (eds), *Exploiting the Internal Market: Competition and Co-operation towards 1992*, 1988, Deventer: Kluwer.

Free movement of persons

Cerexhe, E, *Le droit européen. La libre circulation des personnes et des entreprises*, 1992 (in French), Brussels: Nauwelaerts.

Gleichmann, K, *Perspectives on European Company Law*, 1991, London: European Editor.

Lang, D, *Soziale Sicherheit und Freizügigkeit im EWGV*, 1986 (in German), München: CH Beck.

Lasok, D, *The Professions and Services in the EEC*, 1986, Deventer: Kluwer.

Wooldridge, F, *Company Law in the United Kingdom and the European Community*, 1991, London: Butterworth.

Competition law

Beringer, F, *Das Wettbewerbsrecht der EWG*, 1962 – loose-leaf edition and regularly updated, (in German), Baden-Baden: Nomos.

Druesne, G and Kremlis, G., *Le droit de la concurrence de la CEE*, 2nd edn, 1990 (in French), Paris, PUF.

Fishwick, F, *Making Sense of Competition Policy*, 1993, London: Kogan Page.

Korah, V, *An Introductory Guide to EC Competition Law and Practice*, 5th edn, 1994, London: Sweet and Maxwell.

Van Bael, I and Bellis, J, *Competition Law of the EEC*, 1987, Bicester: CCH Editions.

Vogel, L, *Droit de la concurrence et concentration économique*, 1988 (in French), Paris: Dalloz.

Whish, RP, *Competition Law*, 4th edn, 1994, London: Butterworths

External customs law

Draeger-Stiftung (ed), *Die EG in der Weltwirtschaft*, 1988 (in German), Baden-Baden: Nomos.

Froment-Meurice, H, *L'Europe de 1992. Espace et puissance. La dimension extérieure du marché intérieur*, 1989 (in French), Paris: PUF.

Fuchs, C, *Zollrechtliche Vorbereitung auf eine Teilnahme am EG-Binnenmarkt*, 1989 München: CH Beck.

Kelly, P and Onckelinx, I, *EEC Customs Law*, 2nd edn, 1996, London: Sweet and Maxwell.

Lasok, D, *The Customs Law of the European Economic Community*, 2nd edn, 1990, Deventer: Kluwer.

Vaulont, N, *The Customs Union of the EC*, 2nd edn, 1987, Luxembourg: European Perspectives.

Social policy

Lichtenberg, S (ed), *Sozialpolitik in der EG*, 1986 (in German), München: Verla Vahlen.

Nielsen, R and Szyszczak, E, *The Social Dimension of the European Communit* 1991, Copenhagen: Handelshojskolens Forlag.

Philip, C, *Droit social européen*, 1985 (in French), Paris: PUF.

Troclet, L-E, *Europees Sociaal Recht*, 1976 (in Dutch), Deventer: Kluwer.

Intellectual property

Cornish, WR, *Intellectual Property: Patents, Copyright, Trade Marks and Allie Rights*, 2nd edn, 1989, London: Kogan Page.

Cawthra, D, *Industrial Property Rights in the EEC*, 1986, London: Professiona Books.

Index

Access
  to employment, 269–70
  to justice, 134–35
  to training, 270
Acquis communautaire, 10
Acte clair, 131, 132
Acts
  Community, 61
  annulment of, 109–15
  interpretation rulings on, 133–34
  non-standard, 69
  rulings on validity of, 134
  standard, 65–69
Administrative barriers to trade, 190
Advocates-General, 34–35
Animals, restrictions on free movement of goods and, 151–52
Arbitration panels, 126–27
Arrangements between firms, 196–204
  horizontal, 198–98
  prohibition of, 197–98
  exemptions from, 200–04
  types of, 199–200
  vertical, 199
Audio-visual materials, home copying of, 285

Bankruptcy, 251
Berne Convention, 284, 286
Brandt, Willi, 16
Broadcasting, copyright in, 287
Budget of the European Union, 32–33, 56–60
  compulsory/non-compulsory expenditure in, 57
  development of, 56
  implementation of, 60
  principles of, 56–57
  procedure of, 57–59
  rejection of, 59

Capital market
  See Free movement of capital
Case reports, 306–07
Certainty principle, 75–76
Charlemagne, 11
Churchill, Winston, 11–12
Citation of European Union law, 311–12
Citizenship, European, 6, 163, 183
Cockfield White Paper, 16, 48
Co-decision procedure of European legislation, 53–55
Cohesion Fund, 253
Collective dominant position, 207–08
Collusion
  See Arrangements between firms
Commission of the EU, 11, 20–26, 43
  actions against Member States by, 106–08
  budget and, 56–60
  competition policy and, 191–92, 195, 199–203, 205–07, 211–18, 221–22, 224, 225
  composition and appointment of, 20–22
  decisions of, 68
  directives and, 67
  free movement of capital and, 187
  free movement of goods and, 140, 142–43, 147, 159, 160–61
  free movement of people and, 181, 183
  functions and powers of, 23–26
  legislative process and, 49, 50, 52–53, 54–55

opinions/recommendations of, 68
policy-making process and, 46, 48
reform of, 299–300
regulations and,
social policy and, 66
stages in, 243, 246, 247
Committee of Permanent
Representatives
(COREPER), 314–15
Committee of the Regions, 28–29, 50, 298
Common Agricultural
Policy (CAP), 41, 49
Common Customs Tariff (CCT), 229
ECJ case law on, 227–36
exemptions from, 231
nomenclature, 228–29
rules of origin and, 230–31
special products and, 232–33
valuation and, 229
Common origin principle, 233–36
Community law, 278
See also European Union law 2
Community Patent Convention, 288–89
Community Support
Frameworks (CSF), 256
Community Trade Mark (CTM), 283
Community Transit Document, 239
Companies
abuse of dominant position,
arrangements between, 204–10
freedom of establishment, 196–204
harmonisation of
company law, 176–82
mergers, 181–82
subsidiary, 211–13
195
Compensating products, 240
Competition policy, 191–225
abuse of dominant position, 204–10
arrangements
between firms, 196–204
characteristics of, 193–94
criticism of, 224–25
enforcement of, 214–18
exemptions from, 200–04,
220, 222–24

intellectual property
rights and, 279–81
mergers, 211–13
objectives of, 191–92
private sector and, 194–213
procedural rules, 214–18
public sector and, 218–24
state aid to industry, 221–24
Compulsory reference
to the ECJ, 131–33
Computed valuation, 235
Computer programs, copyright in, 286
Concentration
notifiable, 212–13
notion of, 211–12
Concerted practices, 197
Conciliation Committee, 54–55
Conciliation procedure of
European legislation, 51
Concurrent jurisdiction, 83
Consultation procedure of
European legislation, 51
Consumer protection, 145
Contracts, tying of, 210
Convergence criteria, 188–89
Co-operation procedure of
European legislation, 51–53
Co-operative joint ventures, 212
Copyright, 274, 277,
281, 284–87
Coudenhove-Kalergi, Count, 11
Council of Europe, 12, 317
Council of Ministers, 26–29, 43
budget and, 56–60
composition and
appointment of, 26–27
COREPER and, 28–29
free movement of capital and, 187
free movement of
people and, 165, 172, 183
functions and powers of, 49, 50, 51,
legislative process and, 52–53, 54–55
policy-making
process and, 46, 47, 48

Presidency of, 26
reform of, 298–99
regulations and, 66
voting procedure in, 27–28
Counterfeit goods, 238
Court of Auditors, 15, 42
composition and appointment of, 42
functions and powers of, 42
Court of First Instance (CFI), 18, 33, 34, 35
competition policy and, 208, 216–17
Courts and tribunals, 126–27
Currencies, restriction on movement of, 177, 185–86
Customs declaration form, 237
Customs duties, 138–41
abolition of, 139–41
collection of, 241–42
Common Customs Tariff, 227–36
fiscal discrimination and, 156–57
rules of origin and, 232–33
standstill provision on, 139
valuation for, 233–36
Customs law
Common Customs Tariff (CCT), 227–36
customs debt, 241–42
customs procedures, 237–41
Customs warehouses, 239

Dassonville formula, 143–44, 147
Databases, 286
copyright in, 309–10
on EU law, 14, 15
de Gaulle, Charles, 21
Decisions
EU, 67–68
direct effect of, 93
European Court of Justice, 70–71, 108, 135
Deductive valuation, 235
Dehaene, J, 21
Derived legislation, 65–69, 304–06
definition of, 65
non-standard acts, 69
standard acts, 65–69

Direct applicability principle, 8, 94–95
Direct effect principle, 8, 83–94
conditions for, 85–86
of decisions, 93
definition of, 84
of directives, 89–93
horizontal direct effect, 88, 90–91
of international agreements, 93–94
of regulations, 89
of treaty provisions, 86–88
vertical direct effect, 88
Directives, 47, 66–67
Direct effect of, 89–93
Discrimination
discriminatory pricing, 210
equality principle and, 74, 163, 166–67, 170–71, 178–79
fiscal, 152–57, 189
gender and, 261–72
Distribution rights, 285
Dominant position, 204–10
abuse of, 208–09
examples of, 209–10
collective, 207–08
notion of, 205–07
Dualism, 99

Economic and monetary union (EMU), 188–89, 292
Economic and social cohesion policies, 253–56
Economic and Social Committee (ESC), composition and appointment of, 40–41
functions of, 41
legislative process and, 49
Education, in EU law, 312–13
Educational qualifications, harmonisation of, 180–81
Einaudi, Luigi, 11
Employment access to, 269–70
conditions of, 166–68

gender-based
  discrimination in, 261–71
health and safety in, 249–50
labour relations, 251–52
meaning of term 'worker', 163–65
  part-time, 264–66
  public sector, 175–76
  of sporting professionals, 168–69
  termination of, 168
Energy, Trans-European
  Networks in, 254, 256–59
Entry, right of, 165–66
Equal pay, 261–68
Equal treatment, 269–71
Equality principle, 74, 163, 166–67, 170–71, 178–79
Establishment, freedom of, 176–82
European Agency for the Evaluation of Medicinal Products (EAEMP), 289
European Agricultural Guidance and Guarantee Fund (EAGGF), 43, 223, 254
European Atomic Energy Community (Euratom), 2, 13, 45, 63, 64, 229
European Central Bank, 32, 292
European citizenship, 6, 163, 183
European Coal and Steel Community (ECSC), 2, 7, 13, 45, 62, 64, 74, 229
European Convention on Human Rights, 1, 3, 77–79, 84
European Council, 8, 15, 29, 252
European Court of Justice (ECJ), 6, 9, 18, 33–39
  case reports, 306–07
  competition policy and, 193, 194–95, 196–200, 205–11, 219, 223–24, 225
  composition and appointment of, 34–35
  customs law and, 230, 231, 232–33
  decisions of, 70–71, 108
  enforcement of, 135
  direct actions in, 105–23
  direct effect and, 84–94
  exclusive jurisdiction of, 82–83
  free movement of capital and, 185–86, 188
  free movement of goods and, 138–61
  free movement of people and, 164–65, 167–69, 170, 172–75
  functions and powers of, 34, 39
  gender-based discrimination and, 261–72
  general principles of law and, 73, 74, 75, 77, 78, 79
  intellectual property rights and, 273–81
  interpretation techniques used by, 38–39
  national laws and, 129–30
  preliminary rulings of, 39
  President of, 133–34
  procedure in, 36
  reference to, 36–38
  reform of, 125–34, 300–01
European Defence Community (EDC), 13
European Development Fund, 15, 254
European Economic Community (EEC), 2, 14–17
  See also European Union
European Exchange Rate Mechanism, 16
European Financial Instrument for the Environment, 254
European Investment Bank, 43
European Investment Fund, 254
European Monetary Co-operation Fund, 254
European Parliament, 6, 15–16, 30–33, 43–44
  budget and, 56–60
  composition and appointment of, 30–31
  functions and powers of, 31–33

legislative process and, 49, 50, 51, 52–53, 54–55
other EU institutions and, 21, 22
European Patent Convention, 288
European Political Co-operation (EPC), 7–8
European Regional Development Fund (ERDF), 223, 253, 254
European Social Charter, 244, 248–49
European Social Fund (ESF), 43, 247, 254
European Union
balance of power between Member States and, 297–98
decision-making process in, 45–60
budget, 32–33, 56–60
legislative process, 24, 31–32, 49–55
policy-making, 45–49
deepening of, 292–93
democratic deficit in, 296–97
division of powers between EU and Member States, 81–83
economic foundations of, 4–5
expansion of, 294–95
external customs tariff (CCT), 227–36
free movement of capital in, 185–89
free movement of goods in, 137–61
free movement of people in, 163–84
future of, 291–301
general foundations of, 2–3
institutions of, 19–44
reform of, 298–301
internal market programme, 148, 157–58
law of
See European Union law
legal foundations of, 8–11
'multi-speed', 295–96
political foundations of, 5–8
widening of, 293–94
European Union law, 18
citation of, 311–12
civil law nature of, 9–10, 18
competition policy, 191–225
concurrent jurisdiction, 83
customs law, 227–42

definition of, 1–2
direct applicability of, 8, 94–95
direct effect of, 8, 83–94
education and training in, 312–17
exclusive jurisdiction, 82–83
free movement of capital and, 185–89
free movement of goods and, 138–41, 274–78
free movement of people and, 163–84
gender-based discrimination and, 261–72
glossary of foreign-language terms, 318–27
historical foundations of, 11–17
intellectual property rights, 273–89
interpretation of, 38–39
legal foundations of, 8–11
legislative process, 24, 31–32, 49–55
national law and, 81–103
parallel jurisdiction, 83
practical guide to, 303–17
remedies in
direct actions, 105–23
indirect actions, 125–35
social policy, 243–59
sources of, 61–80
court decisions, 70–71
derived legislation, 65–69, 304–06
general principles of law, 73–79
international law, 71–73
primary legislation, 62–64, 303–04
subsidiarity principle, 6, 96–98
supremacy of, 8–9, 95–96
European Works Council (EWC), 251–52
Exchange rates
customs valuation and, 236
European Exchange Rate Mechanism, 16
Exclusive jurisdiction, 82–83
Exhaustion of rights rule, 279–81
Exporting, 241
customs debt on, 242

External transit procedure, 239
Extra-territorial principle, 193
Families of workers, rights of, 167–68
Fault
    commission of, 121–22
    damage and, 122–23
Federalism, 7
Financial Instrument for
    Cohesion, 258
Firms
    See Companies
Fiscal discrimination, 152–57, 189
Footballers, employment of, 168–69
Fouchet plan, 7–8
Free movement of capital,
    economic and monetary
    union and, 185–89
    movement of capital, 188–89
    movement of payments, 186–88
Free movement of goods, 185–86
    customs duties and, 137–61
    customs law and, 138–41
    fiscal discrimination
        against, 238
    intellectual property
        rights and, 152–57, 189
    internal market programme
        and, 157–58
    quantitative restrictions
        on, 141–52
    technical barriers to, 158–61, 189–90
Free movement of people,
    exceptions to, 163–84
    workers, 172–76
Freedom of establishment, 176–82
    definition of, 176
    exceptions to, 177–78
    scope of, 176–77
Functionalism, 7
Fundamental human rights, 77–79
Gaulle, Charles de, 14, 15
Gender, discrimination based on, 261–72

General Agreement on Tariffs
    and Trade (GATT), 228
    Gentlemen's agreements, 197
Geographical market, dominant
    position in, 206–07
Goods market
    See Free movement of goods
Health and safety at work,
    European social policy and, 249–50
Heath, Edward, 15
Horizontal agreements, 198–98
Horizontal direct effect, 88, 90–91
Identity cards, expiry of, 173
Illegality, plea of, 118–19
Import
    customs debt on, 242
    duties on
        See Customs duties
    temporary, 240
Indirect effect principle, 91–92
Industrial policies, competition
    policy and, 221–24
Information technology, 159–60
Insolvency, 251
Intellectual property rights,
    competition policy and, 273–89
    copyright, 279–81
        274, 277, 281, 284–87
    free movement of
        goods and, 274–78
    harmonising legislation on, 281–89
    patents, 274, 276, 278, 288–89
    trade marks, 274, 276, 278, 280–81, 282–83
Internal transit, 241
International agreements, direct
    effect of, 93–94
International Convention on the
    Harmonised Commodity
    Description and Coding
    System, 227–28
International law, 71–73, 99

ternational trade
  See Free movement of goods
terpretation rulings, 133–34
terpretation techniques, 38–39
ward processing, 239–40

int ventures, 212
dge-Rapporteur, 37
dges, in European Court of Justice, 34, 35
dicial remedies
  See Remedies in EU law

abour market
abour relations, 251–52
  See also Free movement of people
  working conditions, 249–50
anguages of the EU, 18, 61–62
egal barriers to trade, 190
egal certainty principle, 75–76
egislation
  See Derived legislation; Primary legislation
egitimate expectation principle, 76
iability
  actions in, 119–23
  tort liability, 119–21
ocus standi, 110–12, 116–17, 120
ondon Report, 8
uxembourg Agreement, 14, 27–28

Maastricht Treaty
  See Treaty on European Union (Maastricht Treaty)
Macmillan, Harold, 14
Market power
  See Concentration; Dominant position
Market sharing agreements, 200
Marshall, George, 12
Member States
  actions against, 105–09
  balance of power between EU and, 297–98

competition policy and, 194–95, 217–18
direct effect of directives and, 92–93
indirect actions and, 125–35
legal systems of
  See National laws
public sector in
  See Public sector
Merger Treaty, 14, 21
Mergers and acquisitions, 211–13
Misuse of powers, 115
Monism, 99
Monopoly power
  See Dominant position
Morality, restrictions on free movement of goods and, 149–51
Munich European Patent Convention, 288
Mutual recognition principle, 158

National laws
  competition law, 194–95, 218
  ECJ and, 129–30
  EU law and, 81–103
  direct applicability principle and, 8, 94–95
  direct effect principle and, 8, 83–94
  division of powers between EU and Member States, 81–83
  incorporation of EU law into, 1–2
  problems of, 98–102
  subsidiarity principle, 6, 96–98
  supremacy of EU law, 8–9, 95–96
New Community Instrument for Borrowing and Lending, 254
Non-discrimination (equality) principle, 74, 163, 166–67, 170–71, 178–79
Non-preferential rules of origin, 232–33
Non-retroactive legislation, 75–76
North Atlantic Treaty Organisation (NATO), 12

Oil crises, 16
Oligopoly
  See Dominant position
Opinions, 68–69
Optional reference to the ECJ, 130–31
Organisation for Economic Co-operation and Development (OECD), 12
Organisation for European Economic Co-operation (OEEC), 12
Origin
  common origin principle, 278
  rules of, 232–33
Outward processing, 240–41

Pan-Europe Movement, 11
Parallel jurisdiction, 83
Part-time employment, 264–66
Passports, expiry of, 173
Patents, 274, 288–89
Pay (salaries), equality of, 261–68
Payments, movement of, 185–86
Pension schemes, gender-based discrimination in, 262–63, 265, 272
Performance obligations, 200, 210
Piracy
  of copyright material, 284–85
  of goods, 238
Plants, restrictions on free movement of goods and, 151–52
Pleven plan, 13
Pompidou, Georges, 15
Predatory pricing, 209
Preferential rules of origin, 233
Prices
  competition policy and, 192, 199, 209–10
  price-fixing, 144–45, 199
Primary legislation, 62–64, 303–04
  definition of, 62–63
  scope of, 63–64
  treaties and, 62, 64
Procedural rights, infringement of, 79, 115

Processing
  inward, 239–4
  outward, 240–4
  under customs control, 240
Product market, dominant position in, 20
Professional qualifications, harmonisation of, 180–8
Property, intellectual property rights, 273–8
Proportionality principle, 7
Public health, restrictions on free movement of goods and, 151–5
Public morality, restrictions on free movement of goods and, 149–5
Public policy
  restrictions on free movement of goods and, 151
  restrictions on free movement of people and, 172–75
Public sector
  competition policy and, 218–24
  employment in, 175–76
Public security, restrictions on freedom of establishment and, 177–78
Public security, restrictions on free movement of people and, 175

Qualifications, harmonisation of, 180–81
Quantitative restrictions on trade, abolition of, 141–52
  exceptions to, 142–48
  measures with equivalent effect, 149–52
Reasonable means test valuation, 235
Recommendations, 68–69
Recordings, 285
Redundancies, 251
Reference to the ECJ, appeals against, 125–34
  compulsory, 128–29
  optional, 130–31

Regional policies
  competition policy and, 222, 223–24
  European social policy and, 253–56
Regulations, 65–66, 112
  direct effect of, 89
Remedies in EU law
  actions against Member States, 105–09
  actions for annulment, 109–15
  actions for failure to act, 116–17
  actions in liability, 119–23
  direct actions, 105–23
  indirect actions, 125–35
  plea of illegality, 118–19
Rental rights, 285
Repackaged goods, 276–77
Residence, right of, 165–66
Restriction orders, 172–73
Retroactive legislation, 75–76, 266–67
Rights
  entry and residence, 165–66
  European Social Charter, 244, 248–49
  fundamental human rights, 77–79
  intellectual property rights, 273–89
  procedural rights, 79
  vested rights, 75–76
Robert Schuman scholarships, 316
Rome Treaty
  See Treaty establishing the European Community (Treaty of Rome)
Rules of origin, 232–33

Saarbrücken Agreement, 184
Salaries, equality of, 261–68
Santer, J, 21
Schengen Agreement, 184
Schuman, Robert, 13
Secondary establishment, 176
Sectoral aid, competition policy and, 223, 224
Services, freedom to provide, 176–82
Single Administrative Document (SAD), 237

Single European Act 1986 (SEA), 5, 8, 16–17, 67
  free movement of capital and, 187
  fundamental human rights in, 77
  institutions of the EU and, 30, 34
  internal market programme and, 148, 157–58
  legislative process and, 51, 55
  policy-making process and, 47
  social policy and, 243–44, 253
  subsidiarity principle in, 97
Social disadvantage, 167
Social policy, 243–59
  European Social Charter, 244, 248–49
  evolution of, 243–45
  institutional and legislative framework, 247–48
  labour relations, 251–52
  regional policy and, 253–56
  Trans-European Networks, 254, 256–59
  treaty framework, 243–46, 252, 253–54, 257–58
  working conditions, 249–50
Social security
  free movement of workers and, 169–72
  gender-based discrimination in, 262, 271–72
Solidarity principle, 74
Spaak, Paul-Henri, 13
Spierenburg Report, 15
Sporting professionals, employment of, 168–69
Stages, 313–17
Standard exchange arrangements, 241
Standards, technical, 159, 160–61, 189–90
Standing (locus standi), 110–12, 116–17, 120
State aid to industry, 221–24
State sector
  See Public sector
Statistical information, 308

Subsidiarity principle, 6, 96–98
Suspensive arrangements, 238–41
Takeovers and mergers, 211–13
Tariffs
  See Customs duties
Taxation
  comparability of, 154–55
  customs duties, 138–41
  fiscal discrimination, 152–57, 189
Technical barriers to trade, 158–61, 189–90
Telecommunications, 159–60
  Trans-European Networks in, 254, 256–59
Teleological interpretation technique, 38–39
Temporal market, dominant position in, 207
Temporary importation, 240
'Three Wise Men' Report, 15
Tied contracts, 210
Time limits, in actions for annulment, 113
Tindemans Report, 15
Title to sue (*locus standi*), 110–12, 120
Tort liability, 116–17, 120, 119–21
Trade
  See Free movement of goods
Trade associations, 197
Trade marks, 274, 276, 278, 280–81, 282–83
Training
  access to, in EU law, 270
  313–17
Trans-European Networks, 254, 256–59
Transaction values, 234–35
Transfer of undertakings, 251
Transit procedure, 239, 241
Translation difficulties, 18, 61–62
Transport, Trans-European Networks in, 254, 256–59
Treaties, international law and, 71–73

Treaty establishing the European Community (Treaty of Rome), 2, 13
  budget and, Commission as guardian of, 56–57, 59, 60
  competition policy and, 23–24, 204–05, 207–25
  customs law and, 193–200, 203, 227–29, 231
  direct applicability and, 94, 95
  direct effect and, 86–88, 89
  economic foundations of European Union in, 4–5
  free movement of capital and, 185–88
  free movement of goods and, 138–46, 148–57
  free movement of people and, 163, 166–73, 183–84
  freedom of establishment in, 176–82
  gender-based discrimination and, 261–62
  general principles of EU law and, 73–74
  institutional structure of the EU and, 20, 21, 22, 23, 25, 26, 27, 28, 30, 32, 33, 34, 35, 36, 40–41, 42, 43
  intellectual property rights and, 273–79
  international treaties and, 72, 73
  judicial remedies and, 105–10, 112–21, 125–26, 128, 130–34, 135
  legal foundations of the European Union in, 8, 10, 11, 64, 65–68
  legislation and, 24, 49, 50, 51, 52, 55
  legislative process, 45–48
  policy-making process and, 63–64
  scope of, 243–46, 252, 253–54, 257–58
  social policy and, subsidiarity principle in, 97–98

Treaty on European Union (Maastricht Treaty), 2, 17
Amsterdam Treaty amendments to, 3, 6, 17, 22, 31, 41, 44, 52, 53, 55, 78, 97, 184, 245, 252, 271
budget and, 56, 60
economic foundations of European Union in, 4–5
free movement of capital and, 186, 187–88
free movement of people and, 183
fundamental human rights in, 77–78
future of the EU and, 292–95
gender-based discrimination and, 271
general foundations of European Union in, 2–3
general principles of EU law and, 77
institutional structure of the EU and, 29, 30, 32, 41, 42
judicial remedies and, 108
legal foundations of European Union in, 10
legislative process and, 50, 51–52, 53, 55
political foundations of European Union in, 5–8
social policy and, 244–45, 253
subsidiarity principle in, 97
Tribunals, 126–27

Ultra vires, 114

Undertakings
notion of, 195
See also Companies; Public sector
Unemployment, 245
Universal Copyright Convention, 284

Valuation for customs duties, 233–36
exchange rate rules, 236
procedural rules on, 236
substantive rules on, 234–35
valuation for other purposes and, 236
Value declaration form, 236
Vertical agreements, 199
Vertical direct effect, 88
Vested rights, 75–76
Video recordings, 285

Wages (salaries), equality of, 261–68
Wilson, Harold, 13
Women, discrimination against, 261–72
Workers
families of, 167–68
free movement of, 163–76
gender-based discrimination against, 261–71
labour relations, 251–52
meaning of term 'worker', 163–65
part-time, 264–66
public sector, 175–76
rights of, 165–68
social security and, 169–72
sporting professionals, 168–69
working conditions, 249–50